AF270080

MODERN CHINESE THEOLOGIES

MODERN CHINESE THEOLOGIES

Volume 1

Heritage and Prospect

Chloë Starr *editor*

Fortress Press
Minneapolis

MODERN CHINESE THEOLOGIES
Volume 1: Heritage and Prospect

Cover design: Kristin Miller
Cover image: Rev. Wang Chunren 王纯仁 : traditional ink painting with Hebrews 2:9

Print ISBN: 978-1-5064-8796-0
eBook ISBN: 978-1-5064-8797-7

CONTENTS

CONTENTS

ACKNOWLEDGMENTS

Many thanks to all of the scholars and students from China, Hong Kong, Taiwan, North America, Europe, and Australia who have attended the three Chinese Theology conferences online and in person between 2020 and 2022. The papers that have not made it into the volumes for a variety of reasons, including sensitivity of publication for authors, greatly enriched our discussions and understanding of the field. I am very grateful to the Council of East Asian Studies at Yale for funding the three conferences and for research funds that have enabled the translation of select chapters.

Carey Newman at Fortress Press has been an enthusiastic supporter of the project since the outset and I am glad to record our appreciation for his editorial oversight.

PREFACE

Chloë Starr

This is the first volume in a series of three exploring modern Chinese theology. This volume covers church theologians of mainland China whose writing and thinking engages (and disengages) a predominantly Western church heritage, and who were, for the most part, associated with "mainstream" missionary-established denominations. In the post-1949 era, the volume covers theologians and theological movements associated with the state-authorized church bodies in the People's Republic: the Chinese Catholic Patriotic Association and the (Protestant) Three-Self Patriotic Movement (TSPM). The second volume of the set, "Independent and Indigenous," presents a collection of essays on independent church theologians. In the early twentieth-century this comprises house-church and charismatic voices, including such household names as Watchman Nee and Wang Mingdao, while in the People's Republic attention turns to resurgent denominations operating outside of the state registration system. The third volume in the set, "Academic and Diasporic" theologies, expands the scope of China and our understanding of Chinese theology. It addresses scholarship by university academics within mainland China and the writings of Chinese-speaking theologians of other domains.

The rich terroir of Chinese theology has rarely exported its fruit. The English-speaking world has long been neglectful of theologies in languages it did not speak, and of peoples from whom it has generally imported material, not intellectual, goods. Earlier generations dismissed the possibility of worthwhile, world-changing writings coming out of China, while comprehension difficulties have daunted the recently curious. The sixteen essays of this volume represent a new generation of critical voices: of academics from the mainland, Hong Kong, and outside of China who have, for the most part, made the study of Chinese Christianity their life's work. As the academic study of Chinese theology expands beyond its recent heartland of Hong Kong and flourishes in mainland China and North America, and connections can readily be made across territories, this major compendium offers a timely yield.

The architecture of the set of volumes is as much a pragmatic statement as it is a theological one. The boundary, for example, between historic missionary denominations and independent or newer churches prior to 1949 is far from fixed, and many of the theologians discussed in Volumes I and II were raised or trained in one branch of the church before starting afresh in another. Theologians and writers across the divisions were aware of and read each other's work; some of them worked together on common national committees or for church or apologetic publications. The same political and social questions often animated their theological grappling, albeit with different outcomes. The "mainstream" of well-established denominational churches was, moreover, not the broad stream in China, since independent and house-church congregations far surpass numerically those of missionary-established or (post-1949) state-authorized churches, despite official figures to the contrary. The three volumes together allow us to draw together key themes in theological debates among natural conversation partners and to illustrate the commonalities and collective visions that stem from a shared social or spiritual habitus, while pointing to the fissures that traverse the ideological and geographical borderlines of Chinese theology.

These are selected essays by experts, not a comprehensive survey of the different types and topics of Chinese theology. Different anthologies have different goals, and their frameworks differ accordingly, but most aim to present coherently gathered examples of the "best" writing in a subject, giving readers a survey or snapshot of the field. Boundaries for inclusion can be thematic, chronological, regional, or some combination of the three, as they are here. Getting texts to speak to each other is key. If an edited volume is too narrowly conceived, intertextual references and echoes will abound, but there is an art to allowing more disparate pieces to spark against each other. Of his essay collection in *The Blackwell Companion to Postmodern Theology*, Graham Ward writes that it is "more a buffet supper in a British pub," with free circulation between the bar and the fireplace, than a sit-down meal.[1] This book is, to continue the metaphor, Chinese banquet in style: each dish on the table is piquant and satisfying, and together they make a sumptuous, communal meal—but the dishes may be passed around

---

1 Graham Ward, ed., *The Blackwell Companion to Modern Theology* (Oxford: Blackwell, 2001), xxv.

nearby tables, and others could have been substituted to produce a different balance of flavors.

Volume I

This volume traces the dominant currents and figures of Chinese theology who were working in the public sphere throughout the twentieth century and into the twenty-first. These individuals, for the most part, belong to what Daniel Bays termed the "Sino-Foreign Protestant Establishment,"[2] leaders, often trained in Western curricula or church schools, who were linked to the foreign mission world in China as well as to elite, urban circles. As prominent thinkers and writers, many of the individuals discussed were involved in theological education, whether in a university or seminary setting, or engaged in Christian publishing. Critical questions that galvanize the early twentieth-century church—Who are we, as Chinese Christians? How can our Christian faith serve the nation? What form should an indigenous church take?—recur in later decades, with different accents, as the relationship of church and state evolves and denominational churches loosen their ties with "imperialist" mother-churches.

The volume is broadly chronological, with each part forming a thematic unity. Part I, on Republican-era theologies, begins with an essay on Zhao Zichen (T. C. Chao), whose thought and writing has been, over the last century, at the heart of debate on what it means to speak of a "Chinese Theology." As the numerous references to Zhao in other chapters testify, the breadth and acuity of his thinking laid the foundation for many others' work. Chen Yongtao argues that Zhao should primarily be seen as a theologian of China, rather than a Neo-Barthian or Anglican thinker, and offers a reading of Zhao's *Life of Jesus* as a sinicized theology. The volatile years of reform, revolution, and the fledgling republic form the backdrop to the essays in Part I. This was a time when the focus among intellectual elites was on reason, science, human dignity, and—especially—national self-determination. Various essays, such as Jesse Sun's study of the theologically-conservative writer and editor Zhang Yijing, point to the tensions for Chinese Christians in negotiating their beliefs around a hardening national stance on foreign cooperation. Anti-imperialism fueled the anti-Christian movements of

---

2 Daniel H. Bays, *A New History of Christianity in China* (Oxford: Wiley-Blackwell, 2012), 92–120.

the 1920s and caused many, including Zhang, to rethink their ecclesiology and views on the necessity of an indigenous, self-standing church.

The majority of mainstream theologians in China in the early twentieth century embraced a Social Gospel vision of the kingdom of heaven and strove toward its construction on earth. As Liu Boyun's essay on Chinese hymnals indicates, even seemingly neutral translations of Western hymns could be vehicles for spreading the message of Christian socialism or indigenization. Yet, there could also be surprising allegiances and associations. Meng Jin's essay on Jia Yuming reveals the Quaker ties and spiritual heritage of the theologian and president of the (Presbyterian) North China Theological Seminary that might, to some, sit strangely alongside his fundamentalist theology. Quaker beliefs, and a core focus on experiential theology allowed Jia to transcend national church divisions and work with pro-communist leaders in the newly-formed TSPM.

If the nature of Jesus's character that had so appealed to non-Christian revolutionaries as well as believers in the first decades of the century had briefly aligned Christians and Communists, bitter divides that arose in the late 1920s and early 1930s were overcome only in the war years—starting in 1937, when the Japanese invasion threatened the existence of the country—as Nationalists and Communists, liberals and evangelicals, found common cause. Theological debate on the ethics of war and the nature of Christian participation remained highly contested, however. The experience of war sent believers on vastly different trajectories, as they forged new theologies born out of the pain of wartime devastation and seeming abandonment. In Part II, Qu Li traces Wu Yaozong's journey from Christian pacifism to the embrace of revolution and to his writings on the use of violence, while time in a Japanese-run prison and new appreciation of the reality of evil propelled Zhao Zichen away from liberal strands of theology to more evangelical, revelation-centered beliefs. Meanwhile, Roman Catholic clerics Yu Bin and Vincent Lebbe's controversial theology of resistance put them at odds with Vatican thought, and placed a Japanese price on their heads. Beginning with the justification for church support of a defensive war, Stephanie Wong's essay skillfully details the nuanced way in which Lebbe and Yu work with canon law and the situation on the ground as they embody a response that is both faithful to the church and loyal to their compatriots.

Threaded through this volume and the next two are questions that derive from deeper currents of Chinese culture and so affect all theologies to some degree. These include a this-worldly, immanent perspective rooted in a Confucian worldview that emerges, inter alia, in a concern with political theology.

It surfaces in frequent comparative work, both inter-religious and in dialogue with China's ancient classics and philosophical traditions. It appears in meta-commentary on the nature of Chinese theology, and one notable aspect to this is theology as textual practice, in a variety of genres. In Volume I, four chapters (4, 8, 14, and 16) consider textuality directly, in studies of magazine or journal collections (or radio broadcast transcripts) as both locus for, and means of shaping, theology. Zhou Yun's study on the wartime women's journal *Nü duo* offers an explicitly gendered perspective, as it considers a format that allows different views on the experience and meaning of war to reach the public gaze.

Part III raises the complex legacy of mission history in China and the relationship between denominational church belonging and theological development. Tim Yung's study of the Anglican-Episcopal Province of China shows both the complexities for a denomination in transmitting its own particular creeds and practices, and the difficulties of the reshaping process as those beliefs are transformed through enculturation and local theological reflection. The essays in this section highlight the global nature of the Chinese church as part of its theological history. At the beginning of the Protestant mission to China in the early nineteenth century, the few foreign missionaries cooperated closely, producing Bible translations and introductory church texts that were widely circulated, and rarely caused controversy for other Christian groups. By the end of the nineteenth century in the mission heyday, thousands of missionaries and scores of denominations were introducing a plethora of texts and teachings, and carving out their own geographic (and theological) jurisdictions. This volume focuses not on these inherited theologies but on the Chinese theological writings that respond to this legacy as well as to current circumstances. Early twentieth-century theologies are, in part, backlash against missionary misunderstandings and misrepresentations of Chinese culture—as detailed in Yung's essay—as well as a response to a growing disillusionment with Western political maneuvers following World War I. A recognition of the need for China to create its own theology suffuses the thinking of the period: a theology that would be different, taking its cue from Chinese understandings of the scope of theology and what it meant to be Christian.

If the late nineteenth century had seen a centrifugal tendency in the mission field, the early twentieth saw a period of amalgamation and synod-building. Mainstream churches like the Presbyterians, Methodists, and Anglicans all began creating national bodies, and Americans, Canadians, and Europeans cooperated across previous divisions. As denominations set up universities and denominational training facilities in China, and began to implement long hoped-for policies toward a self-supporting, self-governing local church, the balance of power began to shift. The national missionary conferences of the late Qing were English-medium and missionary-dominated. By 1922 when the National Christian Council was established, Chinese delegates were voted into leadership positions and spoke out prominently in setting the vision for the organization. The transition within denominations—which was not always smooth or amicable—is described in various essays, including Christie Chow's study of Seventh-day Adventists and medical mission. Here Chow explores both transitions, such as Chinese staff writers taking over the production of copy for denominational publications by the 1920s, and the theological continuities, which stretched even beyond the 1950s, of Adventist premillennial eschatological beliefs and their embodiment in a theology of health. The rethink of foundational denominational texts in a new setting was a concomitant feature of the growth of Chinese theology. Chris Payk's essay explores how John Wesley's treatise on prevenient grace was taken up by Methodists in China and used as an explanation for the existence of good works among the Chinese prior to the advent of Christianity, and especially for the divine light brought through God's grace working in Confucianism.

The final essay of Part III could equally appear in Part IV (and, as the subject of the study has now left the Three-Self church for independent realms, indeed, in Volume II), underscoring how much circulation there is between different church bodies and schools of thought. The career of Wang Aiming, who studied for his doctorate in Basel and rose to be vice president of Nanjing Union Seminary, the leading (official) Protestant seminary in China, offers an example of the resurgence of denominational ideas at the core of an avowedly post-denominational church. As Yim Tak Leung's essay documents, Wang drew extensively on the Reformation heritage in his development of Theological Reconstruction within the TSPM, using Luther and Calvin to give a rationale for Ding Guangxun's movement and shore up Ding's de-emphasis of justification by faith. This did not, as hoped, allow the Chinese church to bypass bad missionary theology, return directly to the Reformation heritage, and engage with the world church as an equal member devoid of the shadow of state supervision, but does chime with the great surge of Calvinist theologies in (unauthorized) Reformed churches across China.

The revival of the Chinese church in the era of Reform and Opening Up (1978–) was one of the great stories of the world church in the last century, even if its astonishing growth figures have not yet justified the extravagant predictions about the Christianization of China. Theological development in the authorized state churches has, however, been much more muted. The 1980s was a decade of recovery, of reopening seminaries and reinstituting theological training, of catching up with developments elsewhere in the world after the closed years of the Cultural Revolution. Priests worked hard to gather congregations and reinvigorate church life, and there was little spare time for writing; even in the seminaries, producing textbooks and training materials was the most urgent task. The church also had to overcome a generational gap in leadership, since no one was trained from the early 1960s to the early '80s. From the early 1990s, there has been great growth in church belonging, in ministerial vocations, and an expansion in seminary education that saw parallel upturns in theological writing. This period also enjoyed a remarkable expansion in university study of Christianity in different fields—history, literature, philosophy; as well as in rare religious studies departments—mostly at the graduate level. (This movement and the ensuing development of "Sino-Christian" and "academic" theologies is examined in Volume III). Since the 1990s, however, the picture has been more mixed, as government directives have stymied development, and more recently, censorship and self-censorship have gathered force in the wake of the Sinicization campaign under the Xi government. This has contrasted with the vibrant development of theologies emerging from unregistered churches, where work is frequently not submitted to censors and either published abroad, online, or self-published through unofficial channels. Since 2016, unregistered churches have also faced greater difficulties, with enforced closures and court procedures against certain pastors, which has evidently affected theological life and production.

Part IV begins in the closed era of Maoist China, when only sound could penetrate the country, with an essay by Joseph Tse-Hei Lee that explores the Christian radio broadcasts of the Far Eastern Broadcasting Company and the cache of letters that listeners exchanged with the broadcast HQ in Hong Kong. As Lee argues, radio shows offered a platform, albeit illicit, to gather communities of listeners around regular doctrinal and theological content, and fostered the development self-theologizing local communities. The Great Cultural Proletarian Revolution represents the most extreme period of communist ideology, which is still, slowly and painfully, being processed in literature and arts today. There is very little published theological reflection on the period, for reasons of political sensitivity. Zhong Zhifeng's essay on the early TSPM leader Wu Yaozong and his successor Ding Guangxun takes a surprisingly rare look in

English at the relationship between Christian thought and Communism more generally in China. The essay considers the different moves Wu and Ding make in their projects to reconcile Christianity and communism or Marxist materialism from the 1940s through to the 1980s. As leaders of Chinese Protestantism, their theological thought—whether on church reform and aligning with socialism or the universal domain of Christ and God's love for all in China—set the direction for church mission, church management, and church-state relations in the second half of the twentieth century.

A small number of TSPM theologians have produced work that has excited readers beyond state church circles. Wang Weifan is one such scholar, and his "theology of unceasing generation" has sparked book-length studies in China. Chloë Starr's essay places Wang in conversation with the Ming dynasty scholar Li Zhizao as each writes on the documenting of Jingjiao (Church of the East) history in China. As Starr argues, Wang produces a new conception of theology, a theological methodology that utilizes the Chinese Christian past to read non-Christian classical Chinese texts as a source for Christian theology in China, and so produces an alternative, non-Western theological history for China. The final two essays of the volume also foreground methodological questions. Michel Chambon's study examining the theology of ministry of Roman Catholic nuns in contemporary China stems from observation and interviews. It traces the historical, political, and social configurations of women's orders in China, as it explores their differences from other provinces and the diocesan, collective, gendered, and diaconal nature of nuns' ministry. Shanghai has for centuries been the epicenter of Roman Catholic theology and thought in China, and the final essay of the volume considers how a new church journal, *Divine Love*, has sought to create a space for high-level popular engagement with questions of Roman Catholic theology, particularly regarding inculturation, spirituality, and the global church. As Benoît Vermander argues, the creation of a Catholic culture in terms of values, inner life, and the use of reason, is foremost in editors' minds, but this is a culture that deliberately steers clear of contentious social or political questions.

Part I
Republican-Era Indigenizing

Chapter 1

YEARNING FOR CHINA

Zhao Zichen as a Chinese Theologian

Chen Yongtao, *Nanjing Union Theological Seminary*

Introduction

Zhao Zichen (T. C. Chao 1888–1979) was one of the most prominent and respected Christian theologians of his generation.[1] Zhao was a scholar, mystic, poet, and hymnodist; an educator and a patriot. He was also an esteemed figure in the ecumenical movement and was elected as one of six presidents at the founding conference of the World Christian Council in 1948. Zhao was converted and baptized while a student at Dongwu (Soochow) University, and remained for many years a member of the Methodist Episcopal Church. In 1941, however, aged fifty-three, he transferred into the Chinese Anglican Church. Zhao was confirmed in the Chung Hua Sheng Kung Hui in Hong Kong by Bishop R. O. Hall (1895–1975), and following his confirmation, was ordained on the same day both deacon (*huili* 會吏) and priest (*huizhang* 會長).

Research on Zhao Zichen has been accumulating steadily since the late 1960s, with a profusion of articles and books in recent years. Scholars have often divided Zhao's theology into different periods, with most bifurcating it into early and late periods. It has been all too easy for researchers to label Zhao's early theology "liberal." One scholar has even claimed that Zhao's theology is not indigenous, because it is merely grounded in Western liberal theology and not

---

1 Philip L. Wickeri refers to Zhao as "arguably China's most important modern theologian." See Wickeri, *Reconstructing Christianity in China: K. H. Ting and the Chinese Church* (Maryknoll: Orbis Books, 2007), 6. David M. Paton even affirmed that Zhao would be the foundation of a forthcoming Chinese theology. Because of Zhao's knowledge of Chinese tradition, he was regarded by Paton as a pioneer in undergirding the quest for Chinese theology. See Paton, David M., *R. O. Hall: The Life and Times of Bishop Ronald Hall of Hong Kong*, published by the Diocese of Hong Kong, Macao and the Hong Kong Diocesan Association, 1985, 47.

in indigenous thought patterns.[2] Meanwhile almost all researchers attribute his later theological reorientation to his prison experience and the influence of Karl Barth's neo-orthodox thought. This paper argues that although Barth's impact on Zhao is clear, it is inexpedient to say that the later Zhao's theology was reoriented toward Barth and neo-Orthodoxy. Similarly, although Zhao converted to Anglicanism, and the Anglican tradition had a significant impact on Zhao's later theological formation, it is inappropriate to label the later Zhao an "Anglican" theologian. No matter how greatly he was influenced by Western theological schools or Christian traditions, Zhao was, in essence, a Chinese theologian for his time.

This article offers an exploration of Zhao's theologizing as a Chinese theologian and tries tentatively to show how Zhao's theology as a whole, in both early and later periods, formed his reinterpretation of Christianity in his own Chinese context. The essay begins with two background sections, detailing the historical situation and the development of Zhao's contextual theology, before turning to its core argument. A case study of Zhao's *Life of Jesus* demonstrates the sinicization central to Zhao's theological project, while the final section of the essay considers the nature of the Anglican influence on Zhao. Despite considerable differences between his early theology and that of his later period, Zhao's theology in totality is Chinese in nature. He was a Chinese theologian; his yearning was for, and with, China.

1. Zhao's Era and Appeal for a Chinese Interpretation of Christianity

Zhao's theology is the product of his faith seeking interpretation, or reinterpretation, in his own cultural, social, and political contexts, and his thinking is deeply imprinted with his time and culture. A series of reform movements beginning in the late nineteenth century, including the Hundred Days Reform (*bairi weixin* 百日維新, 1898), the Boxer Uprising (*Yihetuan yundong* 義和團運動, 1900), and the May Fourth Movement (1919), revealed the new thinking of participants and the awakening of a national consciousness. Concomitant with this awakening, the first decades of the twentieth century saw the rise of nationalism among Chinese intellectuals. With nationalism came the New Culture–May

---

2 See Samuel Ling, *Xianqu yu guoke: zaisi Jidujiao xinwenhua yundong* 先驅與過客： 再思基督教新文化運動 [*Pioneers and Passers-by: Rethinking the Christian New Culture Movement*], Scarborough: Christian Communications (Canada), 1996, 126.

Fourth Movement that eventually resulted in an anti-Christian movement that lasted for more than a decade, and which greatly influenced Zhao's theological thinking. The May Fourth Movement promoted a revolution in Chinese cultural thought, guided by Mr. Democracy and Mr. Science. Its main characteristics were, according to theologian Liu Tingfang, a colleague and a friend of Zhao: highlighting reason and opposing religion; an emphasis on new science and a critical attitude; doing critical and analytical research in the Chinese classics; and emphasizing human value and human advancement.[3]

Nationalist sentiment led a number of Chinese intellectuals to attack Christianity in a completely intolerant manner at the height of the movement. In addition to being accused of being irrational, unscientific, and backward, one major accusation against Christianity offered by May-Fourth intellectuals was its relation to Western colonialism. Christianity was seen as closely related to Western imperialism and criticized as being responsible for China's recent historical humiliation.

The Anti-Christian Movement greatly influenced the direction of the Protestant Christian churches in China and the theological thinking of native Chinese Christian leaders and theologians. During the decades that followed, many prominent figures among Chinese Protestant Christians strove to create an indigenous or contextual Chinese theology. With a strong sentimental attachment to his time, Zhao, as a Chinese Christian, felt obliged to give his theological response to the criticisms of Christianity put forward by contemporary non-Christian intellectuals. In response to the charge of the irrationality and superstition of Christianity, Zhao ventured to demonstrate Christianity's rational side and attempted to establish a Chinese Christianity that could be measured by the criteria of science and rationality alone. In response to the charge that Christianity was the running dog of Western imperialism, Zhao tried to Sinicize Christianity, in an effort to somehow de-Westernize it. Both the modernization and the Sinicization of Christianity were the means of Zhao's theological contextualization, as I will detail in the next section.

---

3 Liu Tingfang 劉廷芳 (Timothy T. Lew), "Xinwenhua yundong zhong Jidujiao xuanjiaoshi de zeren" 新文化運動中基督教宣教士的責任 [The Responsibility of Christian Missionaries in the New Cultural Movement], 1921, cited in Zhang Xiping and Zhuo Xinping (eds.), *Bense zhi tan—ershi shiji zhongguo Jidujiao wenhua xueshu lunji* 本色之談—二十世紀中國基督教文化學術論集 [*An Exploration of Indigenization in Chinese Christianity: A Compilation of Scholarship on Twentieth-Century Chinese Christianity*], (Beijing: China Radio and Television Publisher, 1999), 133–34.

Zhao's theological efforts were aimed at making Christianity in China a Chinese Christianity. Confronted with the challenges of the time and the decline of the nation, many Chinese Christian intellectuals came to a new understanding of Christian faith based on a "scientific attitude and spirit." As Philip West has pointed out, "Religious experience was justified by converts in scientific terms. Being scientific became linked with being patriotic."[4] Caught up in this tide of Chinese Renaissance,[5] Zhao recognized that he could not avoid rationalizing his religious experience,[6] and consequently, in his early thought, he emphasized reason almost exclusively over revelation. In conformity with the spirit of his time, Zhao attempted to build up a scientific and rational Chinese Christianity that would be compatible with both the demands of the time and with the spirit of Chinese humanism represented by Confucianism.

In the face of political and social disturbances, Zhao, like many others, found a divided self, an inner struggle in the hearts of Chinese. He averred that in the midst of the national crisis, three evils prevailed in China, namely, "poverty, ignorance, and wrong thinking, which are at the root of all sin today." These "could prevent people from realizing urgent spiritual needs over and above material needs," while the combination of the three could "do almost any destructive thing."[7] The situation highlighted the great need of religious life for the nation. Herein too was the reason why the edification of personality and spiritual cultivation were so important in Zhao's early theological thinking: Zhao felt that the basis for building up China lay in establishing the hearts of the people, which could only be done through Christianity.

Zhao saw more clearly over time that the May Fourth Movement destroyed much, but built up little. There was thus a kind of spiritual vacuum in the Chinese

---

4 Philip West, *Yenching [Yanjing] University and Sino-Western Relations, 1916–1952* (Cambridge: Harvard University Press, 1976), 7.

5 The Chinese Renaissance is a label some have used for the May Fourth New Culture Movement (五四新文化運動), regarded by many Chinese intellectuals as a national and cultural awakening. See Hu Shih, *The Chinese Renaissance* (1933), reprinted in 1963 in New York; Chow Tse-tsung, *The May Fourth Movement: Intellectual Revolution in Modern China* (Cambridge: Harvard University Press, 1960), 338–47.

6 Zhao, "Wo de zongjiao jingyan" 我的宗教經驗 [My Religious Experience], 1923, in *The Collected Works of T. C. Chao* (趙紫宸文集), vol. 3, Beijing: The Commercial Press, 2007, 141, 143, 146.

7 Zhao, "Present-Day Religious Thought and Life in China" (1926), in *The Collected English Writings of T. C. Chao*, vol. 5, 198–99; "Jinri Zhongguo de zongjiao sixiang yu shenghuo" 今日中國的宗教思想和生活 [China's Religious Thought and Life Today, 1926], in *The Collected Works of T. C. Chao*, vol. 3, 2007, 185.

mind, which could be alleviated by Christianity.[8] Zhao was also aware, however, that Western Christianity could not meet the needs of Chinese intellectuals of his time. He understood that Western theologies had little relevance to his Chinese context, and it was precisely this kind of keen insight that made Zhao's theology such a distinctive response to the requirements of his time. Zhao's theological interest focused on how to make Christianity able to meet the needs of a rapidly changing Chinese society, and so he attempted to construct a Chinese theology that closely integrated Christian Theo-centrism and Confucian humanism. Under the influence of the anti-Christian movement, Christianity had been criticized by many of Zhao's non-Christian intellectual contemporaries as conservative, backward, superstitious, irrational, anti-scientific, and subservient to Western political and cultural forces. Confronting such a context as a Chinese Christian and sincere patriot, Zhao actively tried to build up a theology relevant to his context while striving to maintain the particularity of Christianity. He recognized that Western understanding(s) and interpretation(s) of Christianity could not be directly transplanted into China. Chinese Christians needed their own way to understand and interpret Christianity in order to make Christianity in China into authentic Chinese Christianity.

Zhao believed that the basis of national salvation lay in personality edification and in spiritual reconstruction. He brought his awareness of the relationship of Christianity with China's national crisis into his theologizing. In the mid-1930s, the Nationalist government launched the New Life Movement, the aim of which was to synthesize Chinese traditional culture with Western culture in order to revitalize China, and many aspects of the movement sought to improve personal morality, hygiene, and well-being. In Zhao's yearning for national salvation,[9] the regeneration of personality was crucial, and, for Zhao, the ideal model for personality[10] was Jesus: Jesus's universal love, service, and self-sacrifice. In his early period, Zhao emphasized the personality and

---

8 Winfried Glüer, *Zhao Zichen de shenxue sixiang* 趙紫宸的神學思想 [*T. C. Chao's Theological Thought*], (Shanghai: TSPM&CCC, 1999), 73.

9 As Alexander Chow points out, Zhao was very supportive of the May Fourth Movement for national salvation. He believed that Christianity should be the basis of the social reconstruction of China and that Christianity could only be relevant to his contemporary Chinese context in dialogue with Chinese culture and intelligible to the scientific mind of the May Fourth generation; see Alexander Chow, *Theosis, Sino-Christian Theology and the Second Chinese Enlightenment: Heaven and Humanity in Unity* (Basingstoke/New York: Palgrave Macmillan, 2013), 66–67.

10 Ed. note: or "character," as *renge* 人格 is translated elsewhere in the volume.

religious experience of Jesus Christ almost exclusively. Having faced the haunting experiences and humiliation of his people during the Sino-Japanese War, however, Zhao gradually came to recognize that humans could neither "enlarge the knowledge of the good" nor attain goodness unaided. They were unable to change their personalities themselves, and unable to save themselves through their own efforts.[11]

The eight years of Japanese invasion brought tragedy to China and Chinese Christians. In these stressful years, one of the first objectives of Protestants was to minister to those suffering from the Japanese attacks.[12] When the Japanese invaded, the life of the nation and of the churches was once again thrown into turmoil: missionaries had to be evacuated, Christian institutions had to be relocated, and believers suffered greatly.[13] The suffering of the Sino-Japanese War, and especially the experience of being imprisoned for six months by the Japanese army, led to Zhao finally giving up his early theological position and reinterpretation of Christianity.[14]

Zhao still believed that the natural world, and even different human cultures, could to some extent reveal God. Yet he also knew that such universal revelation could not help people to know God well, and so he began to emphasize the centrality of God's special revelation in Jesus Christ. He said of the Incarnated One, "Jesus Christ is the special revelation of God, and he is God's most important revelation."[15] Zhao, tirelessly working to create a contextual Chinese theology,[16] began to create a Chinese theology with a new approach, a change of direction

---

11 Zhao, *Jidujiao jinjie* 基督教進解 [A Further Interpretation of Christianity, 1947], in *The Collected Works of T. C. Chao*, vol. 2 (Beijing: The Commercial Press, 2004), 140.

12 C. Stanley Smith, "Theological Education in China," in *The International Review of Mission*, vol. 34, no. 4, 1945, 385–86.

13 Jonathan Chao (ed.), *The China Mission Handbook: A Portrait of China and Its Church* (Hong Kong: Chinese Church Research Centre, 1989), 23.

14 Zhao, "Xinshidai de Jidujiao xinyang" 新時代的基督教信仰 [Christian Faith for A New Time, 1940], in ed. Y. T. Wu, *Jidujiao yu xin Zhongguo* [*Christianity and the New China*), Shanghai: Youth Association Press, 6–7; *Sheng Baoluo zhuan* 聖保羅傳 [*Life of St. Paul*, 1947), in *The Collected Works of T. C. Chao*, vol. 2, 197; *Xiyu ji* 繫獄記 [*My Experience of Imprisonment*] 1948, 460–61.

15 Zhao, "趙紫宸博士演講録" [Lectures Given by Dr. T. C. Chao], 1941, in *The Collected Works of T. C. Chao*, vol. 4, 2010, 302.

16 Even in prison, he did not give up his dream to construct an indigenous Chinese church. Zhao, *Xiyu ji* [*My Experience of Imprisonment*, 1948], in *The Collected Works of T. C. Chao*, vol. 2, 487.

that cannot be separated from the suffering of his disaster-ridden native land. In the face of his people's struggle, Zhao slowly but gradually reoriented his theologizing.

World War II, especially the Sino-Japanese War, shattered Zhao's belief in human nature and his optimism in the human capacity to improve the world. He subsequently spent much time and effort reflecting upon the church's mission and its significance. During the Sino-Japanese War and the following civil war, his writings reflect his concern for the social problems that China was confronting.[17] During the first half of the twentieth century, Zhao devoted himself to the Chinese Protestant church and to constructing a contextual Chinese theology. For decades, his contribution was to both the Chinese church and the church ecumenical. He insisted that Christianity must be relevant to Chinese culture and to Chinese social-political reality.[18] One of his major concerns, especially in his early period, was that the church should be purified institutionally from its denominationalism and doctrinally from its unscientific views. His ideal remained to create a relevant, contextualized Chinese theology, in agreement with the spirit of his time, beneficial not only for the Chinese church, but also for the Chinese nation.[19] The latter, for Zhao, was of even greater importance.

---

17 Bob Whyte, *Unfinished Encounter: China and Christianity*, London: Collins, 1988, 183. See also Zhao, "Women de shizijia jiushi women de xiwang" 我們的十字架就是我們的希望 [Our Cross Is Our Hope, 1932], in *Truth and Life*, vol. 6, no. 5; "Jidujiao yu Zhongguo de xinli jianshe 基督教與中國的心理建設" [Christianity and Chinese Mental Construction, 1932], in *Truth and Life*, vol. 6, no. 8; "Zhongguo minzu yu Jidujiao" 中國民族與基督教 [Chinese Nation and Christianity, 1935), in *Truth and Life*, vol. 9, nos. 5–6; "Message of the Cross for China" (1936), in *The Chinese Recorder*, no. 67; "Christianity and the National Crisis" (1937), in *The Chinese Recorder*, no. 68; "Christian Faith in China's Struggle for Freedom" (1940), in *The Chinese Recorder*, no. 71; "Weiji yu zhuanji" 危機與轉機 [Crisis and Opportunities, 1948], in *Truth and Life*, vol. 14, no. 1.

18 Lam Wing-hung (Lin Ronghong 林榮洪), *Qugao hegua: Zhao Zichen de shengping ji shenxue* 曲高和寡 趙紫宸的生平及神學 *Too High to Be Popular: T. C. Chao's Life and Theology*, Hong Kong: China Alliance Press, 1994, 307–24; Glüer, *Zhao Zichen de shenxue sixiang*, 1999, 11; Samuel H. Zhao, "A Chinese Church and Theology: A Discussion," in *East Asian Journal of Theology*, 2:1, 1984, 84.

19 Lam concludes that Zhao's theology is a theology of relevance. Lam 1994, 307. Glüer also notes the truly Chinese character of Zhao's writings. He indicates that Zhao was deeply influenced by Chinese thought and struggled for most of his life to make the Christian church in China a *Chinese* church. Winfried Glüer, "The Legacy of T. C. Chao," *International Bulletin of Missionary Research*, vol. 6:4, 1982, 165.

2. Zhao's Theologizing as a Chinese Theologian

Zhao's theological thinking is conditioned by his own time and his own culture: it is both deeply rooted in Chinese cultural soil and attentive to China's rapid social change. Culture and social change are together constitutive of experience, as one theological source of Zhao's theologizing. His theologizing is thus contextual; and he is an authentic Chinese theologian, as biographer Winfried Glüer notes.[20]

Besides employing the Bible and Christian tradition as theological sources, Zhao was very concerned in his theologizing with experience as the third source. For him, the Chinese existential and spiritual experience was no less significant in constructing a Chinese theology. In his early thinking, experience even took priority among the theological sources. Although in his later period priority was given to the Bible as the revelation of God, experience (including cultural context and social change) continues to be an important source in his theologizing. Zhao's emphasis on experience for the Chinese understanding of religion has been persistently important throughout his thinking.

In his early and later periods, Zhao's theologizing was Christ-centered. He consistently affirmed that Christianity is Christ; without Christ there is no Christianity at all. One of the significant characteristics of Chinese culture is that it is character-centered. People form the center of history and society, and so Zhao put Christology at the core of his whole theological structure. His doctrines of God, the Holy Spirit, the church, salvation, eschatology, and anthropology, all extended from, and were conditioned by, his Christology. In his yearning for China, Zhao firmly believed that Christ was the only way to save China.

The personality of Jesus Christ was greatly appreciated by both Christian and non-Christian intellectuals of Zhao's time, in keeping with the common appeal among contemporary Chinese intellectuals of "saving the nation through personality" (*renge jiuguo* 人格救國).[21] There was a sense among intellectuals that the Chinese people needed a new kind of soul, and that a Jesus-like personality, which could aid the Chinese in nurturing the new rational and scientific soul, could save China from its current problems. In line with this perception,

---

20 Glüer, *Zhao Zichen de shenxue sixiang*, 1999, 7.

21 The idea "to save the nation through personality" was first proposed by Yu Rizhang (余日章), who was then the general secretary of the YMCA in China. Zhao expressed his appreciation for this idea and dedicated his second book *Yesu de rensheng zhexue* to Yu Rizhang. Zhao, *Yesu de rensheng zhexue* 耶穌的人生哲學 [*Jesus's Philosophy of Life*, 1926], in *The Collected Works of T. C. Chao*, vol. 1, 2003, 186.

Zhao's early theology was inevitably both Christ-centered and personality-centered. The early Zhao indeed made personality-building the primary task for China's salvation.[22] For this reason, too, he understood that the primary mission of Christianity is to let humans be human. This was the fundamental concern in all his theological thinking. According to Zhao, an indigenous Chinese Christianity must not suppress human beings.[23]

This may explain why Zhao's theology always concentrates on two foci: God and humanity, or Christ and China. In his effort to build up a Chinese theology, however, Zhao did not, of course, drink exclusively from his own Chinese well—namely, from Chinese culture alone. He also drank from Western well(s) in order to give his theological response to the problems he was facing in his context. It is true that he was extensively influenced by the Western philosophies and theologies of his day;[24] but he remained a Chinese theologian filled with the spirit of modern Christianity, Chinese culture, and national consciousness.

As a Chinese theologian, Zhao knew well that his theological mission was to construct a Chinese theology, not to implant any Western theology. As Glüer rightly says, Zhao's approach to Western philosophy and theology was quite pragmatic. From Western sources, Zhao "selects advisable and practicable elements and uses them as stones and bricks to build up his own theological system."[25] All Western sources could serve the purpose of his theological contextualization. For this reason, it might be better to refer to Zhao's theology as a Chinese theology rather than to label it with any particular Western terms, such as liberal theology (his early period), or neo-Orthodox theology (his later period).

In reality, Zhao was continually striving during the period from 1920 to 1950 to create a contextual theology which would be relevant to the historical, social, and cultural context of China. The characteristics of Zhao's early theologizing

---

22 Zhao, "Shengjing zai jinshi wenhua zhong de diwei" 聖經在近世文化中的地位 [The Place of the Bible in Modern Culture], in *The Collected Works of T. C. Chao*, vol. 3, 74.

23 Zhao, "Religious Situation in China" (1930), in *The Collected English Writings of T. C. Chao*, vol. 5, 293.

24 It is obvious that while Zhao created his Chinese theology, he was greatly influenced by various Western philosophies and theologies that flourished in his time. However, Zhao was not a follower of any Western school particularly, either philosophical or theological. Zhao's approach to Western philosophical and theological sources is a selective taking. On this, see Zhao, *Jidujiao zhexue*, in *The Collected Works of T. C. Chao*, vol. 1, 9, 49. For more details, see Chen Yongtao, *The Chinese Christology of T. C. Chao* (Leiden: Brill, 2016), 56–70.

25 Glüer, *Zhao Zichen de shenxue sixiang*, 77.

might be labeled missional theology or mission-focused theology.[26] His major concern at the time was how Christianity could be communicated efficiently to his Chinese compatriots. Zhao appealed with passion and compassion for the Christianization of Chinese society and the Chinese people, and related this to his dream of national salvation. In the preface to his first book, he wrote "My crucial question is, as a Chinese Christian, what kind of religious insights I can speak and what kind of great *Dao* (Gospel) I can spread to my compatriots both inside and outside of the church."[27] Succeeding in this task was a crucial question for Zhao and required an indigenous Chinese theology achieved through the sinicization of Christianity.

In his article "The Indigenous Church" (1924), Zhao wrote: "We are forced to answer the question whether or not the tree of Christian religion transplanted from the West and still artificially protected under artificial heat and moisture, will continue to live and grow."[28] The answer to this question must, for him, include the call for an indigenous or contextual Chinese theology. However, Zhao's striving for the relevance of Christianity to Chinese society was only one side of the coin. The other side was that a Chinese theology must be built on the universal Christian truths revealed in Jesus Christ. Among these universal truths, for the early Zhao, were the fatherhood of God, the brotherhood of humanity, the divinity and humanity of Christ, the power of the Holy Spirit, an earth-oriented Kingdom of God, a universal spiritual communion of believers, and so forth.[29] Through his "liberal" interpretation of Christianity in the early period, Zhao found the contact point between Christianity and his Chinese tradition. For him, a Chinese theology must preserve and unify all truths in both Christianity and Chinese civilization. With this as a motivation, Zhao attempted to reinterpret Christianity in his own context. Even though his

---

26 Zhao regarded himself as a missionary. In his early period, he cared more about the Christianization of China; in his later period, he was still concerned with the issue of how he could communicate Christianity to Chinese people and make Christianity understandable and acceptable to them.

27 Zhao, *Jidujiao zhexue*, 7.

28 Zhao, "The Indigenous Church" (1925), in *The Collected English Writings of T. C. Chao*, vol. 5, 2009, 178; "Bense jiaohui de shangque" 本色教會的商榷 [A Discussion on the Chinese Indigenous Church, 1924], in *The Collected Works of T. C. Chao*, vol. 4, 291.

29 Zhao, "The Indigenous Church" (1925), in *The Collected English Writings of T. C. Chao*, vol. 5, 2009, 177; "Bense jiaohui de shangque," 290; "Jinri Zhongguo de zongjiao sixiang yu shenghuo" 今日中國的宗教思想與生活 [China's Religious Thought and Life Today, 1926], in *The Collected Works of T. C. Chao*, vol. 3, 193.

theological stance changed in the later period, his effort to construct a Chinese theology remained.[30]

In his theologizing, Zhao enthusiastically integrated religion and ethics. According to him, religion can lead people to a resolute and determined reaction to the cosmos and life, through adventurous action and by striving ahead toward a mysterious union with God. Union with God is, in Zhao's opinion, the ultimate aim of religion[31] and something that differentiated Zhao from Chinese humanists. Because of his clear awareness of the weakness of secular humanism or pure humanism, Zhao always set God as the foundation of religion while maintaining the human being as one of the foci of his theology.[32] Without God, there is no real power for the individual or national regeneration; without humanity, Christianity has no relevance to China's construction.

Zhao understood that Christianity in China carried a burden from its past. Because of the relationship between Christianity's entrance into China and Western imperialism, there was a popular saying in Zhao's time: One more Christian, one fewer Chinese. For a patriotic Chinese, becoming a Christian was thus a problem. In response to this saying, like other contemporary Chinese Christians, Zhao had to ask himself, "Can we Chinese become Christians without being Westernized? How can we Chinese have our identity as 'Chinese Christians'?" These were serious questions to which Chinese Christians at that time—and even nowadays—had to find answers. For answering the questions, both Christ and China were the inevitable two points of focus in his effort for theological contextualization.

As a Chinese Christian and a child of his time, Zhao tried to seek this new identity as a Chinese Christian. For him, a Chinese Christian must be both a true Christian and a true Chinese citizen at the same time. In order to reduce the tension between the two, Zhao put forward the concept of "Christian nationalism," which was both a nationalism and an internationalism.[33] By this formulation, he intended to reconcile Christianity to rising nationalism. He felt that

---

30 Zhao, "Christian Witness in China: Where is the Church a Minority in a Non-Christian Environment" (1948), in *The Collected English Writings of T. C. Chao*, vol. 5, 525.

31 Zhao, "Xin jiu" 新酒 [New Wine, 1929], in *The Collected Works of T. C. Chao*, vol. 3, 418.

32 As early as 1929, Zhao pointed out that the contact between the Chinese inherent view of human life and Western science would inevitably result in humanism. He saw the creeping and silent influence of this humanism on Chinese Christianity, and the danger of this secular humanism only resulting in a foundationless life. "Xin jiu," 418–19.

33 Zhao, "Zhongguoren de jiaohui yishi" 中國人的教會意識 [The Church Consciousness of the Chinese, 1926], in *The Collected Works of T. C. Chao*, vol. 3, 227.

Christian nationalism could succeed in finding a common point between Christ and China.[34] Zhao was both a true disciple of Jesus Christ and an authentic patriot; Christ and China were thus inseparable in his thinking. For this reason, it was natural for him to seek a synthesis of the individual gospel with the social gospel. Keeping both Christ and China in his theologizing, Zhao was destined to reinterpret Christianity in both theocentric and anthropocentric terms. By doing so, he tried to make the Christian faith relevant to his Chinese nation.[35]

As a Chinese Christian, furthermore, Zhao saw the necessity of a double loyalty to both Christ and China; he recognized clearly that a Chinese Christian had to be a sincere Christian and a sincere Chinese at the same time.[36] With this double loyalty in mind, Zhao was convinced that when the number of Christians in China was constantly increased, Christianity would and could have a great role in the social reconstruction of China.[37] The actualization of the Christianized society was Zhao's great dream in his early writings. He had contended that Christ was the central appeal to China and China needed Jesus Christ in her reconstruction.[38] Although he later abandoned his dream of China's Christianization, and his interpretation of Jesus Christ changed, Zhao always tried to communicate Christ and gospel to the Chinese people, underlining Christ's relevance to modern China while retaining the essence of Christianity.

Under the influence of the New Culture Movement and the May Fourth Movement, Chinese traditional culture had been re-evaluated and even repudiated; Western democracy and science were widely accepted by Chinese

---

34 Zhao, "The Chinese Church Realizes Itself" (1927), in *The Collected English Writings of T. C. Chao*, vol. 5, 216–17.

35 Zhao once said, "I am not such a person who lives in a vacuum, and my Christian faith is not a faith that can be solely possessed by myself. I am a member of the Chinese nation, and my faith must have its relation to the Chinese nation." Zhao, "Xinshidai de Jidujiao xinyang" 新時代的基督教信仰 [Christian Faith for A New Time] in *Jidujiao yu xin Zhongguo* [*Christianity and New China*], ed. Y. T. Wu (Shanghai: Youth Association Press, 1940), 3.

36 According to Zhao, educated Chinese Christians "are reverent in their attitude toward the Bible, loyal to their Savior Jesus Christ, and earnest in their desire to serve God by serving China and by assisting in the reconstruction of the Chinese social order." Zhao, "The Strength and the Weakness of the Church in China" (1922), *The Collected English Writings of T. C. Chao*, vol. 5, 107–08.

37 Zhao, "Can Christianity Be the Basis of Social Reconstruction in China?" *The Collected English Writings of T. C. Chao*, vol. 5, 99–105.

38 Zhao said, "As Christ is the appeal of Christianity to all throughout the world, so is he the central appeal to China, and as Christ appeals through his loyal disciples to all men, so he uses us in his appeal to the Chinese mind." Zhao, "The Appeal of Christianity to the Chinese Mind," 67–68.

intellectuals as the solutions to national crisis. Some extremists even advocated an entire Westernization of China and scientism for national reconstruction. In confrontation with the cultural crisis, some scholars attempted to defend Chinese culture as an effective source for reconstructing China. A number of Christian intellectuals, such as Zhao, were among them. As a Chinese theologian of his time, Zhao inevitably had to deal with the relationship between Christianity and Chinese culture. There were different stances to traditional Chinese culture among the non-Christian May-Fourth intellectuals.[39] For Zhao's Christian contemporaries, accepting Chinese traditional culture was the precondition for Christian indigenization. A mutual necessity existed between Christianity and Chinese culture. Christian faith required Chinese culture for a better interpretation, while Chinese culture needed Christianity for enlightenment. For such Christians, constructing an indigenous theology was inseparably linked to the double loyalty: both to Chinese culture, which defined their identity as Chinese, and to Christianity, which defined their identity as Christians.

In his treatment of Christian faith and traditional Chinese culture, Zhao molded himself on two aspects of the spirit of Jesus, namely the "revolutionary spirit" and the "historical spirit."[40] His position on Chinese culture can be placed into the category of "fulfilling, not destroying."[41] Zhao attempted to seek a balance between Christianity and Chinese culture, in order to make Christianity relevant to the Chinese mind while retaining its essence. He contended that "Confucianism may find Christianity as its own source of life, and Christianity may see in Confucianism an agent of its own truth."[42] Though Zhao's attitude to traditional Chinese culture somewhat changed in different periods,[43] he

---

39 There are four different orientations to Chinese culture. For details, see Chen Yongtao, *The Chinese Christology of T. C. Chao* (Leiden: Brill, 2016), 75, footnote 225.

40 Zhao affirms that, with these two spirits, Jesus both criticized and preserved tradition at the same time. In Zhao's treatment of traditional Chinese culture and Christian tradition, he himself also had both a "revolutionary spirit" and a "historical spirit," critiquing and preserving tradition at the same time. Zhao, "The Indigenous Church" (1925), in *The Collected English Writings of T. C. Chao*, vol. 5, 178.

41 See Lam Wing-hung, *Fengchao zhong fenqi de Zhongguo jiaohui* 風潮中奮起的中國教會 [*Chinese Theology in Construction*], Hong Kong: Tien Dao Publishing House Ltd, 1980, 109–15; "Patterns of Chinese Theology," in *Occasional Bulletin of Missionary Research*, 4:1, 1980, 22.

42 Zhao, "Christianity and Confucianism" (1927), in *The Collected English Writings of T. C. Chao*, vol. 5, 253.

43 Hui Hoiming, "A Study of T. C. Zhao's Christology in the Social Context of China 1920 to 1949." PhD dissertation, University of Birmingham, 2008, electronic version, 186–87.

never gave up the stance in which he tried his best to integrate Christianity and Chinese culture. In this sense, his later theology remains a theology of indigenization, aimed at contextualization. However, he now understood that traditional Chinese culture was a human-centered culture, a sort of secular humanism, lacking the idea of a transcendent God, and lacking also a "sense of sin."[44] He was convinced that Christianity must fulfill the deficiency of traditional Chinese culture. For the sake of theological contextualization, Zhao insisted that Christianity must be "both theocentric and anthropocentric."[45] He also believed that Christianity could complete and perfect Chinese ethics.[46] Zhao clearly realized both the strength and weakness of the Chinese culture and advocated that the former must be preserved and the latter must be replaced or completed by Christianity. Several times he criticized Confucianism for emphasizing only human inner transcendence but overlooking absolute transcendence, seeing humankind but not God as the highest.[47]

Zhao insisted that the revival of Christianity in China relied on whether or not it could inject new blood and new life into Chinese culture. Although he recognized the great ethical strength in Confucianism, he admitted without hesitation that Confucianism was utterly inadequate to meet the deep spiritual need of the Chinese. Christianity alone could meet this need, and in this way Christianity could make its own contribution to Chinese culture.

According to David J. Hesselgrave, the missionary, as a subject of a particular culture, needs to communicate to the subjects of another culture the gospel message which is wrapped in its cultural particularity. In order to make the communication effective, two steps must be taken: first decontextualizing the gospel in terms of one's own understanding by a thorough study of the scriptural text, and then studying the respondent culture in order to contextualize the message in its particular terms—namely, re-contextualization.[48] The two things that

---

44 Zhao, "Christianity and Confucianism" (1927), in *The Collected English Writings of T. C. Chao*, 2009, 254.

45 Zhao, *Jidujiao zhexue*, 74; "Xin jiu," 421.

46 See Zhao, *Jidujiao jinjie*, 100.

47 See Zhao, *Cong Zhongguo wenhua shuodao Jidujiao* 從中國文化說到基督教 [Speaking of Christianity from the Perspective of Chinese Culture], in *The Collected Works of T. C. Chao*, vol. 2, 408–09; *Jidujiao lunli* 基督教倫理 [Christian Ethics, 1948], *The Collected Works of T. C. Chao*, vol. 2, 497; *Shenxue sijiang*, 526.

48 Hesselgrave summarizes: "De-contextualization is needed in order to arrive at the supracultural message which is conveyed in culturally meaningful forms. The cultural wrappings must be folded back in order to get the gift of truth—the Western wrappings of the missionary's

Zhao strived for, as noted above, were: the Christianization (基督化) of China, which was the goal of his efforts, and the Sinicization (中國化) of Christianity,[49] which was the method or means. In Zhao's usage, "sinicize" has almost the same meaning as contextualization. With Sinicization, Zhao dreamt of and yearned for building up a new China; with indigenization, Zhao appealed for an authentic Chinese Christianity. Zhao's efforts to bring about the contextualization of Christianity cannot be regarded simply as a matter of cultural accommodation. A Chinese theology for which Zhao struggled for decades must both express Chinese patriotic and religious aspirations and show people a reasonable way to individual as well as social salvation. Zhao's effort in building up a Chinese theology, relevant to the Chinese mind, while maintaining its uniqueness, is clearly discernable.

Zhao's work of contextualization was thus closely related to his context, in which his theological thinking could not be separated from his awareness of the human situation.[50] The major concern in his theological thinking was how to let humanity be truly human within the salvation from God in Jesus Christ. For Zhao, human being is human becoming, and human actualization can be finally realized through the grace of God in Jesus Christ. As a Chinese theologian of his time, Zhao attempted to draw implications from theology for this struggle of humanization. In this sense, salvation was humanization, which was the central orientation of both his early and his later thinking. In his early period, the validity of theology was based less on its doctrinal orthodoxy than its contribution to the human quest for a better quality of life and social justice. Zhao attempted to develop a Christ-centered humanism based on his view of Christianity and Chinese culture, which sets both God and humanity as two foci of his theology. In

---

culture (where the missionary is a Westerner) and also the wrappings of biblical culture itself. When one comes to the Scriptures, he must be especially cautious, for in the Bible God himself chose the language and forms by which the truth came to be unfolded." "As for contextualization it is needed to make the message meaningful, relevant, persuasive, and effective within the respondent culture." Hesselgrave, David J., *Communicating Christ Cross-Culturally: An Introduction to Missionary Communication* (Grand Rapids: Zondervan Publishing House, 1978), 86.

49 Zhao, "Jidujiao zai Zhongguo de weilai" 基督教在中國的未來 [The Future of Christianity in China, 1926], in *The Collected Works of T. C. Chao*, vol. 3, 235–36.

50 Zhao saw, for example, that both political and economic forces could turn people into machines, transform them into tools. According to Zhao, therefore, being alienated was an authentic human situation. Zhao, *Jidujiao zhexue*, 157–58; see also *Yesu de rensheng zhexue*, 196, 204.

his later theology, the orientation of humanization remained, but he recognized that only God's grace could let this radical humanization be actualized.[51]

3. Zhao's Chinese Interpretation of Jesus in *Yesu zhuan*

In response to the appeal of his time, Zhao firmly believed that only Christianity could save the "broken old China" by the way of Christianization (that is, *Jiduhua*, Christ-ization but not *Jidujiaohua* Christianit-ization). To reach this goal, he was convinced of the necessity of indigenization (or sinicization) of Christianity as a means. Indigenization, or sinicization here, contains two different meanings. One is that Christian faith must be interpreted through the lens of traditional Chinese culture, especially that of Confucian humanism. The other is that Christianity must be explored within the changing social context of the time. Because of the anti-Christian tide and the intellectual ethos of his time, which appealed to China's modernization by advocating the spirit of democracy, science and rationality, Zhao conceived, and attempted to construct, a Chinese theology through a process of rationalizing religious experience. His early Christological focus therefore concentrates almost exclusively on the historical Jesus, especially the humanity and personality of Jesus. For his purpose of creating a relevant Chinese theology while seeking the particularity of Christianity, however, Zhao tried to maintain both the divinity and humanity of Jesus in a Chinese way.

Zhao's *Yesu zhuan* (耶穌傳 *Life of Jesus*) reflects his effort to indigenize or contextualize Christianity in China. *Yesu zhuan* is one of Zhao's early representative writings and reflects his Chinese interpretation of Jesus; it is full of imagination, if not historical authenticity. When he wrote the book, Zhao had a clear intention to make his sinicized and rationalized interpretation of Jesus relevant to his time and his culture, in order that this Jesus could be appreciated and accepted as the Savior by his compatriots. This section offers a brief discussion of early Zhao's interpretation of Jesus, as exemplified by his *Yesu zhuan*.

Zhao was acutely aware that the national crisis was relevant to Chinese Christians. In his article "Christianity and the National Crisis," Zhao contends

---

51 The content of this section has appeared in part in my book chapter on T. C. Chao, see "T. C. Chao (1888–1979)," in *Twentieth Century Anglican Theologians*, edited by Stephen Burns, Bryan Cones, and James Tengatenga (Hoboken/West Sussex: John Wiley & Sons Ltd, 2021), 25–28.

that: "For Christians . . . religion is not merely a matter of relationship between the individual and his God, but also a matter of ethical concern and social consequence. To them, the national crisis of China is the greatest challenge to and the severest test of, their faith, [sic] they have ever known."[52] He was obviously not indifferent to the crises of China, both national and cultural, and his early theology is characterized by both his response to the national crisis and his wrestling with the relationship between Christianity and Chinese culture for the purpose of contextualization of Christianity. These may also have been motivations for Zhao to write his *Yesu zhuan*. In this book, Zhao surely "does more than just counter prevalent criticisms of Christianity" but "provides a model for a constructive cultural engagement,"[53] as Starr indicates. With this in mind, Zhao provides in it "the mode of seeing, the way a Chinese lens is used to calibrate the gospel."[54]

In the introductory chapter of *Yesu zhuan*, Zhao points to four reasons to explain why he had to write the book. First, he recognizes that though there are already many biographies of Jesus in the world, so far no Chinese has written a biography of Jesus that ingeniously and uniquely gets rid of the mortar of the Westernized Jesus biographies, written in terms of the experiences of Western Christians. Second, he is clearly aware that among Chinese people and especially the Chinese disciples of Jesus, few really know Jesus. What Chinese Christians believe is a Western interpretation of Jesus. Chinese needed not only to obtain knowledge about Jesus, but also to follow what Jesus did and learn from Jesus how to be a human. Third, Zhao wished to help the Chinese youth, especially Christian youth, to read the Bible, and to imitate Jesus. Fourth, he wrote because of his personal admiration of Jesus. Zhao thus hoped that Jesus could be understood more appropriately through a book written by a Chinese author wearing the glasses of indigenization.[55]

All of these reasons motivated Zhao to give a Chinese interpretation of Jesus and paint an image of Jesus relevant to his time and context. He believed firmly that this Jesus would be appreciated and accepted by contemporary intellectuals. In Zhao's portrait, Jesus is a great patriot, the greatest teacher in the world,

---

52 Zhao, "Christianity and the National Crisis" (1937), in *The Collected English Writings of T. C. Chao*, vol. 5, 2009, 399.

53 Chloë Starr, *Chinese Theology: Text and Context* (New Haven: Yale University Press, 2016), 97.

54 Starr, *Chinese Theology*, 98.

55 Zhao, *Yesu zhuan* [*Life of Jesus*, 1935], in *The Collected Works of T. C. Chao*, vol. 1, 455–56.

a best friend, and a filial son. As a patriot, Jesus strove to save his compatriots and his nation from being oppressed and trampled by the Roman empire. Since childhood, Jesus had realized with his full God-consciousness that he, as Son of God, had a mission to save the Israelite people.[56] Jesus prepared himself for this mission, and "had a close relation to God, his Heavenly Father, in meditation."[57] He often recalled the national heroes of Israelite history, who saved Israel from the invasion and oppression of foreign forces. According to Zhao, the whole life of Jesus was for his nation and his compatriots. Similar to those patriots who devoted themselves to saving China in Chinese history, Jesus sought national justice, at the expense of his life. For Zhao, Jesus was an authentic patriot but not a narrow nationalist. He is both a nationalist and an internationalist; he loved his nation and also loved the whole of humankind.

Ten years earlier, in his first book *Jidujiao zhexue* (*Christian Philosophy*, written in 1925), Zhao had drawn a similar image of Jesus. He wrote with admiration in that book that "as a son, Jesus is to be filial; as a friend, Jesus is to be sincere and loyal; as a teacher, Jesus is to be a great example; as a religious person, Jesus is to be pious and to serve God; and as a citizen, Jesus is to do his best to develop the spirit and culture of his nation as much as possible."[58] In *Yesu zhuan*, Zhao painted the image of Jesus in the same hue. Through this Chinese interpretation of Jesus, Zhao attempted to respond to the call of his time and create a Chinese understanding of Christianity relevant to his time and culture.

In support of his aim of contextualization, Zhao invested many Confucian virtues in the image of Jesus in *Yesu zhuan*. In this sense, he does seem to describe Jesus as "Sage of sages," as Xu Ximian concludes.[59] For Zhao, Jesus was not a man who rejected or protested against tradition; rather he inherited and renewed it. Even Jesus's baptism in the Jordan was, in Zhao's eyes, for the purpose of following conventional rites. Furthermore, Zhao repeatedly explored Jesus's actions of filial piety. Filial piety is a core value in Confucian tradition, and Zhao underscored Jesus's filial piety from two perspectives. As the elder son in his family, Jesus obeyed his human parents and was responsible for supporting

---

56 Zhao, *Yesu zhuan*, 484.

57 Zhao, *Yesu zhuan*, 485.

58 Zhao, *Jidujiao zhexue*, 121.

59 In his article "Sage of Sages: T. C. Chao's Christology in *Yesu Zhuan*" in *Studies in World Christianity*, 23.2 (2017), Xu reaches this conclusion after his analysis that under the influence of Western liberal theology and with the effort to indigenize Christianity in China, Zhao actually portrays a Jesus who is the most prominent sage, the sage of sages.

his mother and his brothers and sisters after his human father, Joseph, died. Although Jesus was strongly conscious of the need to save his country and compatriots, he did not ignore his family responsibilities or the value of filial piety. It was only after his brothers and sisters grew up and could maintain the family life that Jesus left home to initiate the movement of the Heavenly Kingdom.[60] This corresponds with the stages of the pursuit of the Confucian *junzi* (ideal human, superior person): to cultivate oneself, to manage the family, to rule the country, and to forge world peace.

Zhao also, however, interpreted Jesus's obedience to God, the Heavenly Father, as the greatest filial piety. To highlight this filial piety, Zhao underlined how Jesus was a devotional person who enjoyed a close relationship with God through his uninterrupted prayers. Because of his filial piety toward God, Jesus followed God's will and attempted to change human hearts through God's love. Because his compatriots did not understand what he did for them, Jesus recognized ultimately that he had "to sacrifice his life in order to waken the Israelite people."[61] Zhao also interpreted Jesus's suffering and Crucifixion from the perspective of Confucian virtue, identifying Jesus's suffering and Passion as an action of filial piety, as Glüer points out.[62] For Zhao, not only was Jesus in his life completely directed by the will of God,[63] but his death also expressed his filial piety.

It may be worth noting that, according to Zhao, Jesus had not been aware of the meaning of his death until he realized that the movement of the Heavenly Kingdom in Galilee had failed. From this point on, Jesus sensed the necessity of his death to awaken the Israelite people to save their country. Doubtless, here Zhao related Jesus's death to the sacrificial spirit of the patriots in traditional Chinese culture, as Xu Ximian suggests.[64] It is evident too that Zhao's *Life of Jesus* keeps firmly in mind the national crisis: as Glüer remarks, Zhao actually parallels Jesus's death with the spirit of patriotic martyrdom in traditional Chinese culture.[65] Jesus's death is thus not vicariously atoning, but illuminating.[66] Zhao further highlights how the death of Jesus was an action by which humans

---

60 Zhao, *Yesu zhuan*, 492.

61 Zhao, *Yesu zhuan*, 565.

62 Glüer, *Zhao Zichen de shenxue sixiang*, 152.

63 Zhao, *Yesu zhuan*, 570, 585.

64 See Xu Ximian, "Sage of Sages," 170.

65 Glüer, *Zhao Zichen de shenxue sixiang*, 211.

66 Lam Winghung, *Qugao heguan*, 198.

could be inspired to be fully human.[67] By indicating this, Zhao tried to differentiate Jesus's death from those historical figures with lofty ideals, so as to maintain the particularity of the event of Jesus's death.

Samuel Ling has criticized Zhao's theology as merely grounded in Western liberal theology "rather than in indigenous thought patterns."[68] Here I agree with Xu Ximian's critical response to Ling. As Xu says, although Zhao's *Yesu zhuan* may have some characteristics of liberal theology in form, it is, in essence, a composition of its time. Zhao's Christological thinking in the biography is intimately related to his contemporary historical context. As Xu comments, Ling overlooks the point that for Zhao "Western liberal theology is an instrument by which to build a bridge between Christianity and Chinese culture."[69] Xu points out that Zhao's rendering of Jesus in *Yesu zhuan* does not "side with Chalcedonian Christology" but "is characterized by liberal theology."[70] As a Chinese theologian, however, Zhao does not abandon the Bible and Christian tradition as theological sources while adding in experience as a third theological source for a Chinese theology, or ignore the particularity of Christianity. Even in his early period, he manages to maintain, at least in form, the Chalcedonian formula of Christology: namely the two natures of Christ, albeit in a Chinese way. Under the framework of Chinese humanism, Zhao could employ the Confucian concept of heaven and humanity in unity to underscore the significance of Jesus as a mere Galilean man with a perfect humanity, while still maintaining his divinity at the same time. In this Chinese context, it was natural for Zhao to believe that true humanity is true divinity, because God and humanity share the same divinity, as the concept of Heaven and humanity in unity indicates.[71]

Finally, a few words on Zhao's Chinese interpretation of the miracles that Jesus performed in *Yesu zhuan*. According to Japanese church historian Yamamoto Sumiko, Zhao's rational explanation of the miraculous events in *Yesu zhuan* "may well be classified in terms of its theological bent as a form of modern liberalism, but on the other hand, his rendition of what happened must also be understood as a feature of Chinese thought which espoused the principles of

---

67 Zhao, *Yesu zhuan*, 609–10.

68 Samuel Ling, *The Other May Fourth Movement: The Chinese "Christian Renaissance," 1919–1937*, PhD dissertation, Temple University, Philadelphia, 1981, 111–12. Cited in Xu Ximian, "Sage of Sages: T. C. Chao's Christology in *Yesu Zhuan*," 172.

69 Xu Ximian, "Sage of Sages," 172–73.

70 Xu Ximian, "Sage of Sages," 172.

71 See Chen, *The Chinese Christology of T. C. Chao*, 116–20.

science and rationalism from the time of the New Culture movement."[72] What Yamamoto says clearly reflects Zhao's intentions to modernize and to sinicize Christianity so that it may be relevant to the modern Chinese mind. In *Yesu zhuan* as in his other writings, Zhao continuously endeavored to depict a "Chinese" Jesus who could be recognized and accepted by the Chinese people of his time.

4. The Later Zhao: A Barthian or an Anglican Theologian?

In his first book, *Jidujiao zhexue* (1926), Zhao firmly claimed, "whether we Chinese are to be Christians or not, we must neither be controlled by the churches, especially Western churches, nor by any people involved in the Anti-Christian Movement. Only when we take facts as facts, can we have a thorough understanding of Christianity."[73] Zhao built his own theological edifice for his own purpose of contextualization, selectively using different [Western] philosophical and theological materials.[74] As Tang Xiaofeng points out, Zhao "found in Western theologies those factors which were consistent with and helpful for his own theological expression . . . but for Zhao those Western theologies were only borrowed, to serve his construction of a Chinese theology."[75]

Many researchers have contended that the later Zhao reoriented his theology to Barth's theology and to neo-orthodoxy, yet this assertion is problematic. Although the later Zhao obviously was influenced by Barth and his theological reorientation during the 1930s, and his view of God and revelation in particular was inspired by Barth and neo-orthodoxy, it is still not appropriate to say that Zhao's later theology is Barthian or neo-orthodox. He is not a Barthian. When Zhao published a small book on Karl Barth in 1939, in which he expresses his appreciation of Barth's theology, he clearly claims that he is not a Barthian. As I have discussed above, Zhao's later theology remains contextual; in his yearning for China, he has little intention to reorient to any mere Western theology or Western Christian tradition.

---

72 Yamamoto Sumiko, *History of Protestantism in China: The Indigenization of Christianity* (Tokyo: Toho Gakkai/Institute of Eastern Culture, 2000), 257.

73 Zhao, *Jidujiao zhexue*, 125.

74 See Glüer, *Zhao Zichen de shenxue sixiang*, 76–77.

75 Tang Xiaofeng, *Zhao Zichen shenxue sixiang yanjiu* 趙紫宸神學思想研究 [*A Study of T. C. Chao's Theological Thought*], (Beijing: Zongjiao wenhua chubanshe, 2006), 276–77.

Similarly, it may be problematic to label the later Zhao an Anglican theologian.[76] From the perspective of institutional religious belonging, of course, Zhao converted to Anglicanism and became an Anglican priest. In this sense, he is an Anglican theologian. Theologically speaking, however, the later Zhao had little interest in spreading Anglican tradition or Anglican theology in China. His priority was to make Christianity Chinese, but not to make it into any denominational identity, including Anglican. In 1941, when Zhao became an Anglican and Anglican priest, he wrote ten poems to commemorate his ordination ceremony. One of them includes the four lines: "Since long ago, I had an intention to be ordained/ for fourteen years I have kept this wish.// All my life is a holy sacrament, /church office has its rights and should be fully respected.// I bowed my head to receive confirmation, / by ordination I have wholly inherited the apostolic tradition,/ having troubled many good friends to get together in the small chapel,/ to help and lead me to worship God in the front of the altar.//"[77] These lines indicate Zhao's self-understanding on entering the Anglican tradition. The influence of the Anglican tradition on the later Zhao's theology, which concentrates on questions of incarnation and salvation, cannot be undermined.[78] But, the question raised here is: was the later Zhao theologically an Anglican? The answer is most probably negative. According to David Paton," . . . R.O. Hall knew that T.C. Chao was seeking a profounder and more deeply Chinese understanding of the Christian faith than was currently available, and was proceeding in the Anglican Catholic tradition some way into this mystery."[79] What Paton observed seems incisive, and it therefore may be more appropriate for us to say that the later Zhao was a Chinese theologian greatly influenced by the Anglican tradition but not an "Anglican" theologian.

What is certain is that the later Zhao drew toward Anglican tradition. According to this tradition, the authority or the norm of faith is based on Scripture, tradition, and reason.[80] The Bible is the central norm of faith, by which the

---

76 In my book chapter "T. C. Chao (1888–1979)," 28–30, I have analyzed this idea.

77 蓄意由來久，/持心十四年，/生涯咸聖禮，/教職自尊權。//堅振低眉受，/純真託體全，/重勞嘉友集，/導引拜壇前."

78 See Peter Tze Ming Ng, *Chinese Christianity: An Interplay Between Global and Local Perspectives*, (Leiden: Brill, 2012), Chapter 8. Ng was one of the first to consider the relation of Zhao's thinking to Anglican tradition.

79 David Paton M., *R. O. Hall: The Life and Times of Bishop Ronald Hall of Hong Kong*, (Hong Kong: The Diocese of Hong Kong, Macao and the Hong Kong Diocesan Association, 1985), 103.

80 See Paul Avis, *The Anglican Understanding of the Church: An Introduction*, (London: Society for Promoting Christian Knowledge, 2000), 50–59. In his early period, Zhao regarded

other norms of faith, such as creeds, tradition, and beliefs are judged. The Bible is the norm of theology and Christian ethics. However, reason also occupies a very important place in the life of faith. Faith is beyond reason, yet faith is also in line with reason. The mystery of faith and rationality are not contradictory.[81] The later Zhao's understanding of the relationship between faith and reason is undoubtedly in agreement with that of Anglicanism. The early Zhao gave particular significance to human religious experience, where both the Bible and the Christian tradition are under the judgment of human experience and rationality. In his later theology, however, we may see the threefold authority of the Anglican tradition.[82] In Zhao's later theology we can also observe the four cardinal elements of the Lambeth Quadrilateral: namely, the Bible, the creeds (Apostles' and Nicene), sacraments (Eucharist and Baptism), and episcopacy.[83] His highlighting the doctrine of incarnation, his emphasis on the significance of the church, and his respect for the episcopacy all reveal the influence of the Anglican tradition on Zhao's later theological thinking.

From his book *Shenxue sijiang* (神學四講 *Four Lectures on Theology*, 1948), we can see Zhao's understanding of the sequential order of the importance of the Bible, Christian tradition, and reason in his discussion of theological themes and methods. Zhao maintains that the theme of theology is God's revelation and reason its tool. Reason without revelation is ineffective, and real power comes from revelation. What reason can accomplish is an interpretation of God's revelation, in order that we may better understand our faith.[84] God's revelation in Jesus Christ is "recorded in the Bible, demonstrated in the history of the church, and experienced by the saints."[85] As the Word of God, the Bible is the testimony

---

religious experience as the source and norm of theology; although he no longer regarded human experience as the foundation of theology, he did not deny the role of experience in the process of theologizing. Cf. McGrath on theology interpreting experience: what theology should do is narrate experience, interpret experience, and then transcend and transform experience. See Alister McGrath, *The Renewal of Anglicanism*, (London: Society for Promoting Christian Knowledge, 1993), 86–98.

81 See Stephen Sykes and John Booty, ed. *The Study of Anglicanism*, (London/Philadelphia: SPCK/Fortress Press, 1988), 79–117. See also McGrath, *The Renewal of Anglicanism*, 74–78.

82 See Avis, *The Anglican Understanding of the Church*, 50–55; see also McGrath, *The Renewal of Anglicanism*, 86–89.

83 See Avis, *The Anglican Understanding of the Church*, 57.

84 Zhao, *Shenxue sijiang*, 519.

85 Zhao, *Jidujiao lunli*, 500.

of God's incarnation.[86] In an article written in 1950, Zhao emphasized the importance of God's revelation and human reason. He argued in the essay that the point of departure for a true theologian is the revelation of God, which must be accepted and obeyed by theologians in trust. However, they should also neither underestimate reason nor despise scholarship. God's revelation is explained and interpreted with the help of their intelligence.[87]

For Zhao, however, doing theology in the Chinese context must also take seriously the historical, cultural, and socio-political situation. We are not in a vacuum, as he put it, when speaking of Christian thinking and theology. We have our own background and our own environment; we exist within the social realities of China. Our theological interpretation must take cognizance of these realities; yet we also need to explain the nature of Christianity in such as a way as to meet the needs of Chinese society.[88] This kind of reasoning defines Zhao as a truly Chinese theologian. His later soteriology also indicates both theological contextualization and the influence of Anglican tradition. When Zhao expressed his uneasiness with traditional Western interpretations of atonement, he pointed to his own theories of redemption (or atonement; *chengzhilun* 成志論, literally "a theory of completing God's own will") and "union or identification theory" (*tongyilun* 同一論). Both of these theories were the fruit of his theological contextualization. In Zhao's understanding of justification and sanctification we see a paradox: both the influence of Anglican tradition, and his differentiation from other Anglican theologians.[89]

Zhao's letter to Bishop T. A. Scott (his diocesan bishop) of Good Friday, 1949, also indicates that Zhao was more of a contextual than an Anglican theologian. In the letter, Zhao expressed his wish to resign from the priesthood and begged his bishop to suspend his permission to function as a clergyman in the Church. Later, Zhao even considered the step of leaving the Chung Hua Sheng Kung Hui completely.[90] The precipitating factor for the letter was his request to

---

86 Zhao, "Cong Zhongguo wenhua shuodao Jidujiao," 402.

87 Zhao, "The Possible Development of the Dogmatic Theology of the Chinese Christianity in the Next Forty Years" (1950), in *The Collected Works of T. C. Chao*, vol. 4, 184.

88 Zhao, *Shenxue sijiang*, 520.

89 On Zhao's soteriology and the impact of the Anglican tradition, see Chen Yongtao, "T. C. Chao and the Sheng Kung Hui: With Particular Emphasis on Theology, as Exemplified by His Later Soteriology," in *Christian Encounters with Chinese Culture: Essays on Anglican and Episcopal History in China*, ed. Philip L. Wickeri (Hong Kong: Hong Kong University Press, 2015), chapter 9.

90 He writes, "I beg you to suspend your permission to me to function as a clergyman in the Church. Ultimately, it may become necessary for me to leave the Chung Hua Sheng Kung

administer a Holy Communion service for all Christians at the Yenching University Christian Fellowship. An English missionary at the university objected because this was not permitted in the Anglican rubric; so presumably did Bishop Scott. Zhao saw this as a conflict between loyalty to the Church that he loved and "loyalty to the truth that Christ grants us to see."[91] The truth he saw was that which was relevant to his own Chinese context.

The issue of intercommunion led Zhao to think more broadly about all church constructs inherited from the missionary movement. He was being pressed by Christian students at Yenching University who saw the church as increasingly irrelevant to their lives, and so began to think again about the reasons behind his own ordination.[92] As Philip Wickeri indicates, Zhao was not experiencing a crisis of faith but a rejection of the narrow denominationalism represented by the Chung Hua Sheng Kung Hui. He saw Anglican opposition to intercommunion with the wider Christian fellowship as absurd and irrelevant, but this was also indicative of something more fundamental. Zhao was an expansive thinker who could not be bound by denominationalism. In writing the letter, he presented the challenge of contextual theology to missionary Christianity.[93]

Zhao did not write on particularly Anglican themes. It may be true that a change of tone in his theological writings can be detected after his ordination, but this change has mostly to do with his reflections on his own experience in prison, his appreciation of Karl Barth, and most significantly, his critical reflections on the Chinese church and the urgent challenges of the Chinese context. Anglicanism was not at the forefront of his thinking. His theology was undeniably dedicated to contextual thinking, and he had little intention of simply copying Western theology or following any particular Western Christian tradition, including the Anglican one. Zhao was thus not an "Anglican" theologian in this

---

Hui, completely. I hate to think of such a step, but when it becomes inevitable, I shall not hesitate to take the step at all. I am thinking that when I take that step, I shall not ask for membership in any other Church but shall remain Churchless to the end of my days. Every broken member of the Body of Church, i.e., every so-called Church is built upon indefensible presuppositions which I cannot accept. If, in accordance with the teachings of St. Augustine and others, a person cannot see salvation outside the Church, I shall remain outside, for now there is not the Church anywhere existing."

91 Later letters suggest that he continued to celebrate the Anglican Eucharist at the Yenching University Fellowship and other interdenominational settings, with or without Bishop Scott's permission.

92 Zhao expressed this in a letter. See Philip L. Wickeri, "Was T. C. Chao an 'Anglican' theologian?" 2016, unpublished essay, Hong Kong.

93 Wickeri, "Was T. C. Chao an 'Anglican' theologian?"

sense, as Wickeri argues. The fact that the later Zhao may have been attracted to Anglican churchmanship and might have seen Anglicanism as a path or a tool useful for the indigenization of the church in China, does not make him a truly Anglican theologian.

Wickeri offers further comment on the affiliation: long before he became a priest in 1941, Zhao's thought embodied the best of what we might call a distinctively Anglican theology. He emphasized the connection between creation and redemption in his theology of culture. He saw God in nature and in Chinese culture and he expressed this in his poetry and hymns. He had a sacramental sense of the world, although he wrote very little about the sacraments per se. Like other Chinese theologians, he wanted the church to be Chinese, and he was certainly drawn to the churchmanship of the Chung Hua Sheng Kung Hui. Anglicans might be tempted to claim him as one of their own, but Anglican theology has rarely lived up to its own insights and sensibility. We need to remember that Zhao, the greatest Chinese theologian of the twentieth century, was broadly ecumenical, thoroughly contextual, and deeply engaged in the issues of society. There is no evidence that he sought to identify himself as an Anglican thinker. Indeed, he was at home in different cultures and ways of theological thinking, and as a Chinese Christian, beyond the theological traditions that had been inherited from Europe.[94]

Conclusion

As the above analysis shows, Zhao's clear goal and long-term aim was to make Christianity Chinese. His theology had its genesis in his yearning for China and for the Chinese people. In the cultural and social context in which he lived and theologized, Zhao believed that religion and ethics were inseparable, a concern that makes his theological thinking inevitably and absolutely contextual.

In his effort to construct a Chinese theology, Zhao consistently sought after a Chinese Christian identity. He was always deeply aware that he was at the same time a Christian and Chinese. Zhao remained passionately patriotic and dedicated his life to building up a Chinese theology that was relevant to China and able to provide a way of saving China As he pursued this concern, the early Zhao was inclined to a theistic-humanistic understanding of Christianity, formally somewhat similar to Western liberal theologies, in order to interpret

---

94 Wickeri, "Was T. C. Chao an 'Anglican' theologian?"

Christianity in the spirit of the time. His goal of contextualization, should, however, make us hesitate to label the early Zhao a liberal theologian, or to pin the label of a particular denomination or theological school on the later Zhao.

Zhao's contextualizing thought has been elucidated here through analysis of *Yesu zhuan* in the early period and by his later contextualized theologizing. In Zhao's later period, as the result of his theological reorientation, God's special revelation in Jesus Christ became the major source of his theological thought. Even at that stage, however, the idea of the moral transformation of humanity acquired a central place in his soteriological thought, because of the strongly contextualized nature of the Christian faith that grounded Zhao's thought throughout his academic life. Barth and neo-orthodoxy evidently shed their light on him, yet to say later Zhao was a Barthian theologian or to say that he reoriented his theology to neo-orthodoxy is problematic. Notwithstanding the fact that Zhao's later theology is influenced by Barth and neo-orthodoxy, and recognizes Jesus's authentic divinity and humanity, an emphasis on Jesus's perfect personality, love, and religious experience continues to sustain his writings.

Zhao's original Methodist background and theological orientation caused him little difficulty in becoming an Anglican and an Anglican priest. The impact of the Anglican tradition on his later thinking, especially on his Christology and soteriology, cannot be ignored. However, it is inappropriate to label the later Zhao an "Anglican" theologian. His intention and his theological effort was concentrated on constructing a Chinese theology for China, and avoiding copying any Western theological model or given Christian tradition. We may say with confidence that his primary concern was to be a Chinese theologian, not a Chinese Anglican theologian. Zhao was the most creative, productive, and thoughtful Chinese theologian of the first half of the twentieth century. His theology belongs to the rich heritage of the Chinese Protestant church, and at the same time belongs to the heritage of the church ecumenical.

Chapter 2

THE TURN OF AN APOLOGIST

*Zhang Yijing on the Foreign Association
of Christianity in China*

Jesse Sun, *Duke University*

Introduction

Zhang Yijing (張亦鏡, b. Zhang Wenkai 張文開　1871–1931) was arguably the leading Christian apologist in early twentieth-century China. Born to an illiterate peasant family in Guangxi, Zhang had to drop out of school at a young age.[1] However, a passion for learning led to his conversion to Christianity and a career at the *Zhenguang zazhi* 真光雜誌 (*The True Light Review*).[2] From 1905 to 1930, Zhang labored for *Zhenguang*, first as a journalist, then as the chief editor and columnist. He produced a cornucopia of articles and editorials, making his pen name "Yijing" a trademark for Christian apologetics during the turbulent decades of the early twentieth century.[3] Under Zhang's leadership, *The True Light Review* won national fame within the Christian communities, selling as many as 4500 copies per issue in 1925.[4]

Zhang and his journal, despite their fame, were not the only producers of Christian apologetics in the early twentieth century. By then, broader changes in print culture had been ushered in, with Chinese Christians prominent in the

---

1　For more biographical details, see Zha Shijie, "Zhang Wenkai," in *Zhongguo jidujiao renwu xiaozhuan* 中國基督教人物小傳 (Taibei: China Evangelical Seminary Press, 1983), 79–90.

2　*Zhenguang* was founded by the American Southern Baptist missionary Roberts E. Chambers in Guangzhou in 1902. The publication later changed its name from *Zhenguang bao* 真光報 (*True Light Monthly*) to *Zhenguang zazhi* 真光雜誌 (*True Light Review*) in 1917.

3　Zhang is usually remembered by his pen name (*hao*) rather than his birth name "Wenkai."

4　Wang Zhixin, "Jidujiao xinwen shiye 基督教新聞事業" in *Zhonghua jidujiaohui nianjian no. 8* (Shanghai: Zhonghua quanguo jidujiao xiejinhui, 1925), 138.

development of the periodical press, through which they eagerly publicized their arguments for communal solidarity and social responsibility.[5] One such competitor was "the Peking Apologetic Group" (*Beijing zhengdao tuan*, 北京證道團) organized in early 1920 by a group of Chinese and foreign Christians in Beijing, the epicenter of May Fourth radicalism.[6] For the Apologetic Group, which included famous liberal-leaning Christian intellectuals like Zhao Zichen (T. C. Chao, 1888–1979), Wu Yaozong (Y. T. Wu, 1893–1979), and Xu Baoqian (P. C. Hsu, 1892–1944), the heightened demands of the time called for an indigenized Christian message, to respond to the cultural and social craving for modernization. Indigenized apologetics became a central agenda for its official journal, *Shengming* 生命 (*Life Monthly*).

In comparison, Zhang Yijing, with his theologically conservative stance, was more ready to highlight the uniqueness of Christianity in distinction to its "heathen" surroundings.[7] Converted by Chinese evangelists of the Guangdong-based Southern Baptist mission, Zhang's theological position reflected that of his denomination, which was among the conservative groups that refused to join the National Christian Council (NCC) when it was organized in 1922 along modernist lines. Meanwhile, unlike independent church leaders such as Wang Mingdao who restricted his *Lingshi jikan* 靈食季刊 (*Spiritual Food Quarterly*) to spiritual and moral topics, Zhang never shied away from commenting on public events and debates.

Zhang's apologetic works encompassed three broad periods. From roughly 1917 to 1920, the first span witnessed a national controversy over whether China should establish Confucianism as its state religion. Engaged in this public discussion, Zhang wrote many articles against having a Confucian established

---

5 On the importance of this print culture to the church and theological building at the time, see Chloë Starr, *Chinese Theology: Text and Context* (New Haven: Yale University Press, 2016), 60–69.

6 On Christian faculty at Yenching University and their interaction with the Life Fellowship movement, see Peter Chen-main Wang, "Were Christian Members of the Yenching Faculty Unique? An Examination of the Life Fellowship Movement, 1919–1931," *The Journal of American-East Asian Relations* 14, no. 1–2 (2007): 103–30.

7 Zhang was clearly committed to the Southern Baptist tradition, which he saw as the foundation of Western civilization to which many in China aspired. On the interaction of Zhang's multiple identities—denominational and others—and their implication for his thought, see Jue Wang, *Zhang Yijing (1871–1931) and the Search for a Chinese Christian Identity* (Carlisle, UK: Langham Publishing, 2021).

clause, while also paying attention to Christianity's relation to other traditional Chinese cultural and religious practices.[8]

Then came the anti-Christian movement in the 1920s. During the movement's early stage, from 1922 to the first half of 1925, Zhang demonstrated his apologetic fervor by writing to counter the various charges from anti-Christian groups.[9] Zhang's critique during this second period was unrelenting. For example, Zhang critiqued the anti-Christian league's manifesto section by section, mocking the charge that the Chinese Christian church was the vanguard of capitalist interests in China. Zhang's polemics were uncompromising, while most of them in this period focused not on the issue of nationalism but on Christianity's relationship with capitalism and science.

This focus changed in the third period of Zhang's apologetic works, which became increasingly politicized following the May Thirtieth Incident in Shanghai in 1925. As the incident rapidly galvanized the entire nation, whether Christianity was scientifically warranted or socially useful was no longer the focal point. Ideological conformity to anti-imperialist nationalism became the new rallying cry. Zhang's apologetics also adopted a firm anti-imperialist position with the same uncompromising stance as before.[10]

While existing studies tend to focus on Zhang's engagement with specific issues—such as Chinese religions and educational rights—this paper examines the dramatic change in Zhang's thinking due to the May Thirtieth Incident.[11] Despite differing priorities over the first two periods, these consistently

---

8 For a collection of articles Zhang wrote on the debate of having the Confucian religion, see Zhang Yijing, *Daguang po'an ji* 大光破暗集 (Guangzhou: Meihua jinhui yinshuju, 1923). For a collection of his treatises on the topic of Chinese folk religion, see Zhang Wenkai, *Zhenguang congkan* 真光叢刊 (Shanghai: Zhonghua jinxinhui shuju, 1928).

9 Most of his polemics in this early stage of the anti-Christian movement can be found in Zhang Yijing, ed., *Piping fei jidujiao yanlun huikan quanbian* 批評非基督教言論匯刊全編 (Shanghai: Meihua jinhui shuju, 1927). For a selection of Zhang's polemic responses in a recent publication, see Tang Xiaofeng and Wang Shuai, ed., *Minguo shiqi feijidujiao yundong zhongyao wenxian huibian* 民國時期非基督教運動重要文獻彙編 (Beijing: Shehui Kexue Wenxian, 2015).

10 In the historical Chinese context, patriotism and nationalism are often used interchangeably without marked difference.

11 For example, Fan Daming, "Shenpan yu xuanze: xunsuo jidujiao yu Zhongguo wenhua de guanxi 審判與選擇：尋索基督教與中國文化的關係. *Shijie zongjiao yanjiu* 147, no. 3 (2014), 130–42; Fan Daming, "Zongjiao jiaoyu yu guoquan: Zhang Yijing yu jindai zhongguo shouhui jiaoyuquan yundong," 宗教、教育與國權：張亦鏡與近代中國收回教育權運動 *Zhanjiang shifan xueyuan xuebao* 34, no. 1 (2013), 101–07.

demonstrate Zhang's apologetic efforts in defending Christianity against external attack. However, the outburst of nationalism in 1925 proved to be a turning point, as Zhang came to critique Christianity's Western associations. By 1927, Zhang had developed an argument on Christian patriotism that emphasized the indigenization of Christianity, to defend against charges of imperialism and to retrieve China's national rights. Such a conviction turned out to resemble that of his liberal counterparts, whom Zhang had previously criticized.

Cautioning against Indigenization: Zhang Before the May Thirtieth Incident

On July 31, 1924, in a talk in English at the National Council of Churches, Zhao Zichen spoke on the necessity of building a Chinese indigenized church. The speech later appeared in print in the official journal of the YMCA in China, *Qingnian jinbu* (青年進步 *Association Progress*).[12] Responding to this article, Zhang elucidated his principles regarding indigenization.[13] While sympathetic to Zhao's stance, Zhang nonetheless thought Zhao overly critical of Western missionaries and excessively concerned about Chinese culture as a mark of the indigenized church. Disagreeing with Zhao that Western missionaries created barriers for Chinese churches to become independent, Zhang pointed to his Southern Baptist pastors in Guangzhou who were pushing their Chinese colleagues to be independent. The Baptist foreign missionaries were, he noted, content with domestic donations, and they refrained from intervening in the church's government. Since the church government lay in the congregation, Zhang claimed that the missionaries did not possess much more power than any full church member.[14]

Furthermore, Zhang showed that the missionaries were conscious of delegating ministries and tasks to the Chinese church leaders. In at least two instances in his own experience, missionaries learned that native agency would bring better efficiency.[15] After transferring authority over personnel decisions to Chinese

---

12 Zhao Zichen, "Bense jiaohui de shangque," 本色教會的商榷 *Qingnian jinbu* 76, (1924): 8–15. For Zhao's view on Christianity and Chinese culture, see Zexi Sun, "Deliverance Through Culture or Of Culture? T. C. Chao on Christianity and Chinese Culture." *International Bulletin of Mission Research.* 2019. 43(4): 335–44.

13 Zhang Yijing, "Zhao Zichen xiansheng de 'bense jiaohui de shangque' he wode ganxiang," 趙紫宸先生的 '本色教會的商榷' 和我的感想" *Zhenguang* 23, no. 11 (1924): 17–32.

14 Zhang, "Zhao Zichen xiansheng," 24.

15 Zhang, "Zhao Zichen xiansheng," 24–28.

evangelists, Baptist missionary P. H. Anderson jokingly referred to this issue in a conversation with Zhang. Anderson admitted to their own poor choice of personnel—a tendency that often resulted in fiascos in front of Chinese coworkers. "Now that you are in charge of personnel, we get to laugh at you," the missionary said, "so please do not repeat our mistakes."[16] With missionaries like Anderson and Robert E. Chambers (Zhan Luobi 湛羅弼, 1870–1932), who founded *Zhenguang* and later entrusted it to Zhang, Zhang confidently saw himself as the true leader of their local Christian ministry. Rather than blaming the missionaries, therefore, Zhang exhorted Chinese Christians to fulfill their own responsibilities for church growth and independence. The pragmatist Zhang argued that the first step toward an indigenized church lay in Chinese members achieving financial independence rather than making Western missionaries sensitive to the essence of Chinese culture, as suggested by Zhao.[17]

For Zhang, as long as a church fulfilled what essentially amounted to the three-self principle (self-support, self-government, self-propagation), it was already an indigenized church.[18] Zhang warned his readers that if indigenization became the sole measure, Christians would risk Sinicizing Christianity instead of Christianizing China, since practices like gambling, having concubines, smoking opium, and idol worship were all part of Chinese culture. If Christians incorporated these into church practice, the church might, of course, be better attended and less hated. Zhang insisted that things consistent with the Bible and the apostolic tradition had always caused irritation and friction, whether in the West or China.[19] Even the brighter side of traditional culture—such as filial rituals after the death of one's parents—had become too superficial for their intended purpose. For example, Zhang observed how people insisted on holding a cane as part of the mourning ritual without knowing that, according to the Confucian classics, the cane was meant to help a filial son rise after a rigorous three-day fast.[20] In this case, appearing with a cane eclipsed the true essence of fasting itself.

---

16 Zhang, "Zhao Zichen xiansheng," 29.

17 Zhang, "Zhao Zichen xiansheng," 32.

18 Zhang Yijing, "Yu Weiqing xiansheng lun bense jiaohui," 與唯情先生論本色教會 *Zhenguang* 25, no. 7–8 (1926): 53–58. This is a reprint of an earlier essay.

19 Zhang, "Yu Weiqing xiansheng," 53–55.

20 See *Liji*, Tan Gong I: "Hence, when a superior man is engaged in mourning for his parents, no water or other liquid enters his mouth for three days, and with the aid of his staff he is still able to rise." Translation adopted from James Legge, 1893, "Liji," accessed October 14, 2017, http://www.cnculture.net/ebook/jing/sishu/lunyu_en/17.html.

In this way, Zhang asserted that what many people had conceived of as a culturally indigenized church (*bense jiaohui* 本色教會) was actually a superficially indigenized church (*mose jiaohui* 末色教會) that prioritized form over substance.[21] He even admired the resoluteness of those scholars who advocated wholesale Westernization, which Zhang differentiated from Christianization. Either way, he viewed the drive for indigenization as potentially catering to Chinese Christians' cultural vices and denoting a lack of seriousness in their pursuit of Christianization.[22]

At this early stage in Zhang's writing, the issue of Christianity as imperialist cultural aggression received only indirect mention. Patriotism and nationalism scarcely appeared, if at all. Concluding a report on the harassment of churches and Christian schools during "anti-Christian week," for example, Zhang offered a one-line retort: "If Mr. Liao Zhongkai truly believed his speech to the students that Christianity was but imperialist cultural aggression, he had better first rescue his own son and daughter out of the Christian schools to which he sent them."[23] Another case he gave was that of a Pui Ching Middle School student in Guangzhou—one of the earliest Christian schools funded by Chinese Christians—baptized during the "anti-Christian week." The students sneered at the imperialist charge thrown at them, Zhang reported, since many of their fellow students or family members had overseas experience and knew what the separation of church and state meant. Furthermore, their schools and churches were run by Chinese Christians without any "foreign lords" to whom they could be "slaves." As a result, the students dismissed the anti-Christian rhetoric and the imperialist charge as—in Zhang's characteristic sharpness—"mindless barking."[24]

However, Zhang's position on the Chinese church and its foreign associations would change very soon. Less than six months from the writing of the report above came the May Thirtieth Incident, where on May 30, 1925, a British inspector ordered his constables to fire into a demonstration, leaving at least twelve protestors dead and dozens wounded. The incident quickly sent shockwaves across China and stirred up an unprecedented level of nationalist sentiment.

---

21 Zhang, "Yu Weiqing xiansheng," 56.

22 Zhang, "Yu Weiqing xiansheng," 57–58.

23 In 1924 the anti-Christian league mobilized mass demonstrations at Christmas and distributed handbills advocating anti-imperialism. There were many reported cases of forced entry into churches and Christian schools. Zhang Yijing, "Rushi wowen zhi 'fei jidujiao zhou' de fan jidujiao yundong," 如是我聞之 "非基督教週" 的反基督教運動 *Zhenguang* 24, no. 1 (1925): 89–94.

24 Zhang, "Rushi wowen," 94.

Intellectual debates no longer occupied the center of the national arena. Instead, political mobilization took the center stage, demanding ideological conformity.[25] As a result, Zhang found himself writing on topics of patriotism that he had not cared much about before, often with surprisingly acerbic words. Gone was the confidence in Sino-Foreign cooperation and the caution over cultural indigenization. The charge of imperialism could no longer be treated as a joke but as a sin in need of immediate purgation. Judging from Zhang's later polemics, the best way to cleanse the sin was to jump into the torrents of national vengeance.

Christian Patriotism: Zhang's Radicalization after the May Thirtieth Incident

In the July 1926 issue of *Zhenguang*, Zhang publicized his new views regarding imperialist aggression over three successive editorials.[26] These three essays conveyed what he had found inconvenient to say the previous year. Unforeseen perhaps even by Zhang himself, the editorials, with their broadly patriotic tone, triggered a series of responses that involved two additional authors and Zhang's further articulation on the topic. This debate in *Zhenguang* proved to be a good window into Zhang's radicalization that eventually contributed to a changed view on the indigenization of the Chinese church.

The first essay, entitled "The Fury of All Christ-Lovers," vented Zhang's anger against "the country that sends out preachers of Christ" (i.e., Britain) yet still committed the atrocities during and following the May Thirtieth Incident. It was a great dishonor, Zhang lamented, to the name of Christ as well as to all Christians. Therefore, Christians should attack such "life-destroying imperialist evil" with "a million times more fervor" than non-Christians.[27] All who wish to preach Christ in China, especially foreign missionaries, should denounce imperialism and its loyal subjects, to open the door of evangelism in China.

The second essay refuted any Christian ethics that would forgive the foreign aggression of the May Thirtieth Incident. Christ's command to "love your

---

25 Jessie Gregory Lutz, *Chinese Politics and Christian Missions: The Anti-Christian Movements of 1920–28* (Notre Dame: Cross Cultural Publications, 1988), chapter 3.

26 Zhang Yijing, "Aijidu zhe zhi nu;" "Aijidu zhe suo buneng ai zhi choudi yu xiaoer qi choue ci choudi zhi fangfa;" "Xunqiu Zhongguoren zhi zui" 愛基督者之怒; 愛基督者所不能愛之仇敵與消弭其恨惡此仇敵之方法; 尋求中國人之罪 *Zhenguang* 25, no. 4–6 (1926), 233–36. These short essays are called *suigan lu* (隨感錄 essays of reflection) and are equivalent to editorials.

27 Zhang, "Aijidu zhe zhinu," 233.

enemy," Zhang asserts, applies only to private and personal enemies, not on a public or national scale. The fact that such aggression came from the same country that sent many missionaries to China was especially abhorrent to Zhang. How could the British themselves not practice Christian values such as peace, love, justice, and fairness? Along with their reluctance to admit the crime and the attempts to blame the Chinese people, Zhang saw them as practicing "absolute cold-bloodedness and shamelessness and irrationality."[28]

The third essay, the longest of all, bemoaned the tragedy of the Shakee (Shaji) Massacre on June 23, 1925, in which British and French gunfire claimed two hundred casualties. After describing the bloody scene and citing condemnatory verses from the imprecatory psalms, Zhang turned to the missionaries who had failed to stand by the Chinese people. Regarding those sympathetic to the Western governments or who dismissed the incident as a Communist conspiracy, Zhang found himself unable to hold the old apologetic line—that the missionaries were not vanguards of imperialist aggression. Instead, Zhang contended that the church and missionaries must not hinder patriotic movements. Otherwise, Christians would be "wearing the same pants as the imperialists."[29]

When questioned, Zhang's nationalistic tone became even more passionate. Three months after the July issue, an essay came out with the explicit purpose of "Discussing patriotism with Mr. Yijing."[30] In this essay, Lu Boai—a pseudonym that meant "universal love"—tried to explain why patriotism should not merit as much attention and affirmation from Chinese Christians. He pointed first to the parochial and finite nature of loving one's country. Just as one progresses through the love of parents, the love of home, the love of hometown, and the love of one's ethnic group successively when growing up, so should Christians, Lu argued, transcend the love of nation to the love of all people in the world. Did not John 3:16 say, Lu so challenged, "For God so loved the world?"[31]

Lu's second issue over patriotism was concerned with political propaganda. He cautioned people not to be deceived by the warlords, skilled in using patriotism to muster support and cover their incessant fighting against each other. How come Christians remained silent in the face of domestic warlords who killed a hundred times more people than the comparatively small number of

---

28 Zhang, "Aijidu zhe suo buneng ai zhi choudi," 233–34.

29 Zhang, "Xunqiu zhongguoren zhi zui," 235–36.

30 Lu Boai and Zhang Yijing, "Yu Yijing xiansheng tantan aiguo," 與亦鏡先生談談愛國 *Zhenguang* vol. 25, no. 9–10, (1926): 31–42.

31 Lu and Zhang, "Yu Yijing xiansheng tantan aiguo," 31–32.

casualties caused by foreigners? Rather than blaming others, should it not be the Chinese people's responsibility to restore domestic order and earn respect from other countries?[32] This was a line of reasoning reminiscent of Zhang's earlier comments on church independence.

In response, Zhang recognized the progressive nature of a person's love as outlined. However, he also pointed out that one should not abandon "the lesser loves," even after attaining the next level. Furthermore, it was simply inappropriate, Zhang reasoned, to tell the Chinese to "love the world" while the country that ought to know and practice the same did otherwise and oppressed China. Finally, to seal his point, Zhang raised a curious argument that lacked his usual lucidity: Since the world is God's country (*guo* 國), he interprets "God so loved the world" (*Shangdi ai shiren* 上帝愛世人) as just another way of saying God loves his country (*Shangdi de aiguo* 上帝的愛國). Thus, we should also do likewise and be patriotic.[33]

Zhang's passionate polemics—some more baffling than others—continued. For instance, he insisted that the casualties caused by warlords were entirely among enlisted soldiers. Therefore, the domestic case was qualitatively different from that of "a country with Christianity as its state religion yet which shoots down non-combatants of another country who are just being patriotic."[34] More-over, while northerners might complain about the tyranny of their warlords, Zhang somehow acquitted Guangdong of the same problem.[35] He then developed an argument about divinely sanctioned "vengeance" (*fuchou* or *shenyuan* 復仇, 申冤) by the aggrieved: should the Chinese people inflict punishment on the perpetrators of the recent calamities, "the God of vengeance" would undoubt-edly bless their vengeance and bring it to a rapid fulfillment. In fact, Chinese Christians were particularly charged with such responsibility to restore justice. Just as in David's prayer to God, Zhang argued, God expects us not to meet aggressive neighbors with obeisance but active resistance. Referencing cases from Chinese history, Zhang encouraged his compatriots to follow Goujian's prece-dent in enduring hardship to plan retaliation (*woxin changdan* 臥薪嘗膽). In contrast, Zhang likened Lu to those oppressive officials (*kuli* 酷吏) who cooked up corrupt charges.[36]

32　Lu and Zhang, "Yu Yijing xiansheng tantan aiguo," 34.

33　Lu and Zhang, "Yu Yijing xiansheng tantan aiguo," 36.

34　Lu and Zhang, "Yu Yijing xiansheng tantan aiguo," 37.

35　Lu and Zhang, "Yu Yijing xiansheng tantan aiguo," 38.

36　Lu and Zhang, "Yu Yijing xiansheng tantan aiguo," 39–40.

Interestingly, Zhang chose not to rest his argument on an explicitly nationalistic line. Instead, he framed his fervor in terms of Christian faith and attributed his protest to the Christian identity of the aggressor country. Should the aggressor adhere to any other religion, Zhang exclaimed, it was of no particular concern to him, no matter how ferociously that nation treated China.[37] For Zhang, imperialism caused a severe decline in attendance and reputation to the Chinese church. Therefore, Chinese Christians ought to "guard the way" (*weidao* 衛道) with "arms" (*zhi gan'ge* 執干戈) against the true enemy of Christ's Word, which Zhang now saw as an imperialism that had been increasing the death toll and giving ammunition to domestic anti-Christian forces. Zhang mourned that if the "motherland" of the missionaries were to join the anti-Christian forces in China, it would be an ironic disaster "a million times worse" than the Boxer rebellion.[38]

Zhang's argument on vengeance, unsurprisingly, spurred further debate. In January 1927, Tongre (another pseudonym) published "Patriotism for Christians" in *Zhenguang*. While he recognized the grievance of the Chinese people in recent atrocities, he was nonetheless concerned that patriotism based on vengeance, not distinguished from other radical voices at the time, would lead to endless reprisals. Instead, Tongre argued that Christian patriotism ought to transcend that of non-Christians, who always sought hegemony over other countries. For Christians, however, the basis for patriotism should be the love of justice and hatred of evil. Foreign soldiers who killed Chinese civilians should be brought to justice by the law, as love would dictate. However, it would no longer be loving when Christians demanded to kill as many foreigners as Chinese victims for revenge.[39]

Furthermore, Tongre warned readers not to be blinded by vengeance. Just as the evil of the Boxers in killing foreigners should not be blamed on the rest of the Chinese population, the evil of the British soldiers in killing Chinese civilians should not tar the missionaries. Therefore, rather than expelling all foreigners as certain people proposed, Tongre claimed that the Chinese ought to be confident enough to take up the responsibility to protect their own nation.[40]

---

37 Zhang, "Yu Yijing xiansheng tantan aiguo," 40. In this regard Zhang was consistent. He did not mention Japan in his articles, though the violence of those Japanese factory owners against their Chinese employees was the actual spark that paved the way to the May Thirtieth Incident.

38 Zhang Yijing, "Diguo zhuyi zhi youhai yu jiaohui ruci," 帝國主義者之有害於教會如此 *Zhenguang* 25, no. 12 (1926): 94–95.

39 Tongre and Yijing Zhang, "Jidutu aiguo wenti," *Zhenguang* 26, no. 1 (1927): 6–16.

40 Tongre and Zhang, "Jidutu aiguo wenti," 7–8.

Against this familiar line of reasoning that he once adopted for church independence, Zhang chose a different path of indigenous initiative this time. Nowadays, Zhang insisted, patriotism was the only way (*weiyi liangfa* 唯一良法) for evangelism. If Christians were to join the patriotic movement, anti-Christian groups would surely wake up from their misunderstanding of Christianity—so it seemed to Zhang—and the gate of evangelism would be wide open. But, should Chinese Christians distinguish patriotism from the gospel as Tongre proposed and prioritize the latter, Zhang was concerned this would discourage patriotism and run the risk of validating the anti-Christian charge that Christianity was an imperialist tool for the destruction of China.[41]

To Zhang, it was the missionaries who needed to sift imperialism out of their patriotism, not the Chinese Christians. Reiterating the Christian basis for "patriotic vengeance" (*baofushi de aiguo* 報復式的愛國), Zhang affirmed that it was a righteous cause for Chinese Christians to join the army and fight the aggressor country—with Christianity as its state religion—in a life-or-death struggle. To die for such a cause would not be out of patriotism but to represent Christ's chastisement to a country that bore the name of an "advanced Christian country" (*jidujiao de xianjinguo* 基督教的先進國) and failed to love its neighbors as it should.[42] Regarding the missionaries, Zhang exhorted them to renounce any political benefits that accrued to them as a result of the unequal treaties their countries had signed.[43]

This discussion on imperialism culminated in two articles in *Zhenguang*, "Trends in Church Thinking Today" and "Christianity and Imperialism."[44] These two articles solidified Zhang's drastically different views from pre–May Thirtieth days. The central issue was the relationship between Christianity and imperialism: while rejecting their association in terms of biblical teachings, Zhang admitted the historical entanglement between the two. Consequently, to purge imperialist elements from Chinese Christianity, he set out a list of issues—many adopted from anti-Christian attacks—for the church to address.[45] First, any treaty clause offering privileges to missionaries ought to be abolished.

---

41 Zhang, "Jidutu aiguo wenti," 9.

42 Zhang, "Jidutu aiguo wenti," 11–12.

43 Zhang, "Jidutu aiguo wenti," 14.

44 Zhang Yijing, "Jinri jiaohui sichao zhi qushi," 今日教會思潮之趨勢 *Zhenguang* 26, no. 7–9, (1927): 91–100; Zhang Yijing, "Jidujiao yu diguo zhuyi," *Zhenguang* 26, no. 4 (1927): 22–28.

45 For a detailed discussion on the treaty system and educational rights, see Lutz, *Chinese Politics and Christian Missions*, chapter 5.

Zhang explained that the Chinese people were comparatively more open in the Republic than during the Qing dynasty, and local governments rarely enforced the clauses anyway due to rising nationalism. So instead, the missionaries should seek protection from the Chinese government as a way to show respect. This gesture would also spare their Chinese co-religionists shame in front of Chinese nationals.[46]

Like many critics in the late 1920s, Zhang bemoaned the treaty system as a sign of political expediency too often exploited by foreigners, which inevitably tarnished Christians' reputation in China. Now Zhang urged the missionaries to follow through with their principle of the separation of church and state, abandon the treaty benefits they had accrued, and reform the political situation to save the church in China from another disaster like the Boxer Rebellion. In fact, Zhang concluded, the missionaries were morally and religiously obliged to do so, as it would free the Chinese church from anti-imperialist harassment—an overly optimistic assessment, perhaps.[47]

Second, in contrast to his earlier understanding of indigenization, Zhang sought to purge Westernization from the Chinese church. Music, governance, finance, levels of respect, and choice of words all needed to be reformed and Sinicized. For example, the Bible and hymns should use terms and expressions drawing on Chinese literary traditions.[48] The Chinese church needed to shed its foreign cloak to avoid tripping up the Chinese people with an "imperialist look," which might dampen respect and the efficiency of evangelism.[49] Zhang's new position now closely resembled the indigenization principles of Zhao Zichen, which Zhang once criticized as not gospel-centric.

In addition to financial and administrative independence, Zhang advocated an active and unconditional transfer of mission churches, schools, and hospitals from the foreign missionary establishment to local Chinese Christians. The Chinese congregation must strive to purchase the institutions and should use all possible means to separate itself from the missionary establishment.[50] For Zhang, the Western association of Chinese Christianity was now a liability rather than an asset.

---

46 Zhang, "Jidujiao yu diguo zhuyi," 24–25.
47 Zhang, "Jinri jiaohui sichao zhi qushi," 96–97.
48 Zhang, "Jinri jiaohui sichao zhi qushi," 94.
49 Zhang, "Jidujiao yu diguo zhuyi," 25–26.
50 Zhang, "Jinri jiaohui sichao zhi qushi," 94.

In contrast to his previous confidence in them, Zhang now seriously criticized the influence of Western missionaries. Zhang saw them as violating Jesus's commandment by receiving financial support not from local congregations but their missionary societies.[51] Not only that, but missionaries had taught Chinese Christians to do the same. Zhang deplored the fact that the missions, by giving wages to Chinese Christians, made Chinese look like employees of foreigners. "No wonder the anti-Christian groups accuse us of being slaves and lackeys of foreigners."[52] The reason for the Chinese church's lack of independence was clearly "the Word-breaking sin of Western pastors."[53]

Third, Zhang reviewed the thorny charge of cultural aggression, often tied to the issue of educational rights. Before the May Thirtieth Incident, Zhang criticized the inconsistency of anti-Christian groups who accepted many other components of Western culture, such as philosophy and science. Back then, Zhang had argued that their particular issue with Christianity, permitted only in private schools, was unjustified. Now, however, Zhang affirmed that there were indeed legitimate reasons behind the charge of cultural aggression. The mission schools, for example, prioritized English over Chinese components in the curriculum, which had impaired students' ability in Chinese.[54]

In addition to the curriculum, the mission schools tended to observe foreign holidays and ignore Chinese ones, and they often forbade Chinese students to participate in patriotic movements. Furthermore, agreeing with many non-Christian nationalists, Zhang saw the worse offense of mission schools being their independence from the Chinese ministry of education. While the foreign presence might have once been considered a necessary corrective to native cultural evils, it was now seen as encroaching on China's educational rights.[55] For many critics in the revolutionary parties, such encroachment meant sabotaging the unity of the country. In the end, regarding the charge that Christianity served as a tool for imperialist aggression, Zhang argued that "half of it is a misunderstanding, half of it is the church's own invitation to mischief."[56] Zhang believed, therefore, that the only way to rid the church of all anti-Christian charges was to

---

51 Zhang cites Matthew 10: 9–10 here: "Take no gold, or silver, or copper in your belts, no bag for your journey, or two tunics, or sandals, or a staff, for laborers deserve their food."

52 Zhang, "Jinri jiaohui sichao zhi qushi," 92–93.

53 Zhang, "Jinri jiaohui sichao zhi qushi," 93.

54 Zhang, "Jidujiao yu diguo zhuyi," 26–27.

55 Zhang, "Jidujiao yu diguo zhuyi," 27.

56 Zhang, "Jidujiao yu diguo zhuyi," 28.

join the majority of the Chinese people in opposing imperialism and the unequal treaties.

Conclusion

The star of Christian apologetics in early twentieth-century China, Zhang Yijing represented a significant Christian input to public discourse. During the Confucian controversy and the early stages of the anti-Christian movement, he and his journal gave a conservative and rigorous defense of Christianity in China. His apologetics were confident of Sino-Foreign cooperation, cautioned against indigenization, and dismissed charges of imperialism.

However, the intellectual debates and inquiries of the New Culture Movement quickly gave way to ideological construction and a political mobilization that came to dominate the era of the Nationalist Revolution in the late 1920s, with the defining event being the May Thirtieth Incident. "Leninist nationalism displaced Social Darwinist nationalism,"[57] as one commentator has written. The cause of China's plight was no longer to be found within—as corrupted morality and values that the New Culture movement strove to correct. Instead, in Leninist theory, it was the external evil of the capitalists who were representatives of the larger aggressive forces of imperialism. When fighting imperialism and its political and economic minions came to represent the surest path to national salvation, the nationalist agenda, shaped by the revolutionary parties, began to overwhelm other identities and concerns.[58] Like many, Zhang found himself no longer addressing anti-Christian charges regarding capitalism and scientism. Instead, he had to confront charges of imperialism as political as they were personal—Zhang was infuriated that a "Christian country" like Britain had committed humiliating atrocities against his nation.

---

57 Lutz, *Chinese Politics and Christian Missions*, 57.

58 For the active role of the Chinese Communist Party and the Comintern in orchestrating much of the rhetoric during the anti-Christian movement and harvesting from the popular mobilization, see Ka-che Yip, *Religion, Nationalism, and Chinese Students: The Anti-Christian Movement of 1922–1927* (Bellingham, WA: Western Washington University, 1980), 25–27, 45–48 and Tao Feiya, "Gongchan guoji daibiao yu Zhongguo fei jidujiao yundong," 共產國際代表與中國非基督教運動 *Jindai shi yanjiu* no. 5 (2003): 114–36. See also John Fitzgerald, *Awakening China: Politics, Culture, and Class in the Nationalist Revolution* (Stanford, CA: Stanford University Press, 1996) and Rebecca Nedostup, *Superstitious Regimes: Religion and the Politics of Chinese Modernity* (Cambridge: Harvard University Press, 2009).

To cleanse the name of Christianity and reform the Chinese church, Zhang insisted on a patriotic agenda advanced in Christian terms. This new position marked a dramatic change from refuting anti-Christian charges to rectifying the church in light of these charges. For the later Zhang, Christianity needed both his earlier apologetics as well as a patriotic Sinicization to make itself acceptable to the Chinese nation now under foreign attack. Essentially, Zhang came to an indigenizing discourse surprisingly similar to liberal Chinese Christian intellectuals like Zhao Zichen, whose efforts to indigenize Christianity across multiple levels—aesthetics, theology, sociopolitical priorities—also peaked in the wake of the May Thirtieth Incident. Zhang's case suggests that the influence of nationalism, rather than existing theological positions, might better explain the radicalization of the late 1920s, where Christian intellectuals from both ends of the theological spectrum converged.

Chapter 3

JIA YUMING'S EXPERIENTIAL SPIRITUALITY[1]

Meng Jin, *Edinburgh University*

This paper examines Jia Yuming's (1880–1964) engagement with Western theological resources. It investigates Jia Yuming's theological background, with particular attention paid to his involvement in Quaker circles in China. By looking at Jia's spirituality in light of the Wesleyan Holiness Movement and Quakerism, the syncretic nature of his spirituality and the dynamics of his theologizing become clear. Inner spiritual experience, together with the Bible, form the foundation of his faith and provide the background for Jia's eclectic spirituality.

Jia's Theological Background

Jia Yuming was born in Shandong province in 1880 to a Christian family of two generations.[2] Wang Delong has suggested that it was impossible for Jia's family to be Protestant converts and deduced that Jia's ancestors might have been members of some local secret Catholic group. Jesuits and Franciscans were still secretly active in Shandong after the prohibition of Catholicism.[3] Due to the lack of records for the period, Jia's Christian family background remains unclear, yet it is reasonable to believe that Jia had not received any formal or systematic Protestant theological education until he went to missionary schools, and likely that his Christian family background predisposed them to send him to a missionary-established school. In his youth, Jia attended the Wenhua Middle School founded

---

1 The opportunity to undertake this study has been generously funded by the China Scholarship Council.

2 Jia Yuming 賈玉銘, "Yiwei mushi de jianzheng" 一位牧師的見證 [A pastor's testimony], *Lingsheng*, no. 2 (1937), 46–51.

3 There were 5020 converts in Shandong by 1842. Williamson, H. R. *British Baptists in China, 1845–1952*, (London: Carey Kingsgate Press, 1957), 7. See Wang Delong 王德龍, *Yi "Xin" Fei "Yong"–Jia Yuming shengping ji sixiang yanjiu* 以"信"廢"用"—賈玉銘生平及思想研究 [Abolishing "Function" with "Faith": On Jia Yuming's Life and Thought] (Beijing: China Social Science Press, 2017), 25.

by the South Presbyterian missionary Robert McCheyne Mateer (1853–1921). After graduation, he continued his study at Tengchow College, established by Robert's elder brother Calvin Wilson Mateer (1836–1908). These two schools had a similar curricular structure, and the core curriculum of Tengchow College included not only basic training in Christian theology but also Confucian classics, history, philosophy, and literature.[4] During his days at Tengchow, Jia first gained his Bachelor of Arts and then continued his study in theology. Although Jia received a traditional Chinese education, he was diligent in studying English[5] and had at one point planned to go to America to study theology.[6] Proficiency in English enabled him to access Western theological works with ease. After graduation, Jia was ordained as a Presbyterian pastor and served the Xinzhoufu Presbyterian church in Shandong for twelve years, from 1904.

Jia's early school years at the Presbyterian Tengchow College were the foundation for his later appreciation of mystical experience. The experiential approach of the Tengchow education and stress on students' spiritual growth profoundly shaped Jia's personal devotional life. On top of intellectual pursuits, individual spiritual development played a vital part of students' lives. Apart from attending classes, in the morning students prayed, sang hymns, and read the Bible with teachers; they also had evening prayer. On Sundays, all students had to attend church services in the morning and Sunday school in the afternoon where they studied the Scriptures. Moreover, Calvin Wilson Mateer and his wife Julia Brown Mateer valued helping students understand and deepen their faith through daily experiences. Mrs. Mateer enjoyed spending time with students, helping them solve personal problems and giving them advice—and in terms of spiritual growth, she believed that learning from daily experiences was more effective than class. Jia claimed to have some mystical experiences during his school years. The spiritual environment of Tengchow College enabled him to form a strong appreciation for individual devotional time, which he later acknowledged he had benefited from greatly.

---

4 Wang Yuande 王元德 and Liu Yufeng 劉玉峰, eds., *Wenhuiguan zhi* 文會館志 [The Chronicles of Tengchow College] (Wei Xian: Guan Wen Xue Xiao, 1913). 52–53. See Kwok Wai-luen, "The Christ-Human and Jia Yuming's Doctrine of Sanctification: A Case Study in the Confucianisation of Chinese Fundamentalist Christianity," *Studies in World Christianity* 20, no. 2 (2014): 145–65.

5 Tse, Ambrose L. Y. (Xie Longyi 謝龍邑), *Jiduren: Jia Yuming de Lingming Shenxue* 基督人：賈玉銘的靈命神學 [Christ-Human: Jia Yuming's Spiritual Theology] (Taipei: China Evangelical Seminary, 2008), 46.

6 Jia "Yiwei mushi," 46–51.

The connotation of "mystical experience" here can be understood as the "inner and hidden realization of spirituality through a transforming consciousness of God's immediate presence."[7] Mysticism is usually conceived in two paradoxical ways—the language of negation (*via negativa*), and the positive language of presence (*via positiva*). The former goes beyond expressions such as words; the latter usually makes use of various forms of illustration.[8] Jia's experience reflects the paradox of both negative and positive paths. Jia mentioned that he spent a great deal of time praying when studying in Tengchow college.[9] In particular, his experience of an ineffable encounter with God in silence embodied the negative side of mystical experience:

> I remember when I was in college, even though my schoolwork was extremely heavy, I would sit in front of the Lord silently in a private room alone. Sometimes I felt my heart was full of joy and my mind was active, sometimes my tears would flow down my face instantaneously, albeit in silence, my heart and mind were in union with Christ. Prayer is not merely about asking for help from the Lord, but more about opening widely your heart towards the Lord, connecting with Him spiritually.[10]

Moreover, Jia gave emphasis to the extraordinary power of prayer as well.

> Once when I was very ill, I went into a room alone and locked the door. I started praying and made up my mind that I would not leave that room unless I got well. I prayed for two hours and my disease was cured. Thus, my faith was strengthened since then. I learned from that experience of faith that when I prayed for something, surely my request would be answered by the Lord, as long as I asked in faith without any doubt in my heart. It worked every time.[11]

---

7 Bernard McGinn, "Mystical Consciousness: A Modest Proposal," *Spiritus: A Journal of Christian Spirituality* 8, no. 1 (2008), 44.

8 Carole Dale Spencer, *Holiness: the Soul of Quakerism: an Historical Analysis of the Theology of Holiness in Quaker Tradition* (Milton Keynes: Paternoster, 2007), 30.

9 Jia Yuming, "Daogao de zhenji" [The Truth of Prayer]. *Lingguang Bao* 1, no. 5 (1950). See in Wang, *Yi "xin" fei "yong,"* 36.

10 "Daogao de zhenji," 36.

11 Jia, "Yiwei mushi," 46.

Miraculous events happened to Jia more than once. Jia had a serious heart attack right before he started his theological studies, and doctors thought that he could only survive for another two years at most. However, Jia prayed and believed that his disease could be cured. The day after, as he expected, Jia recovered completely and went to school. Jia notes that his then-fiancée Zhu Dexin prayed also for him, concluding "it is obvious that prayers for others are powerful too!"[12] Jia's descriptions of his early devotional life indicate that such extraordinary experiences were pivotal to his spiritual growth and, together with the Bible, became the foundation of his faith. Intriguingly, this tendency fits well with the Quaker spirituality he would later encounter.

Jia built close connections with Quakers when he worked in Nanjing. He became a professor at the Bible Teachers' Training School for Women (*Jinling nuzi shenxueyuan* 金陵女子神學院) in Nanjing, which was the fruit of the ecumenical movement of the twentieth century in China.[13] The school was founded by various denominations, including Quakers. The Quaker group that was active in the Nanjing area was mainly the Holiness Quakers, who embraced the prevailing Holiness Movement teachings in America. Holiness Quakerism at the turn of the twentieth century manifest some new features that distinguished it from the original form of Quaker spirituality in the seventeenth century. Through the influence of traveling ministers such as Joseph John Gurney (1788–1847), Quakers had been exposed to literature outside their canon, and some gradually formed close connections with other Protestant denominations within the Holiness Movement. The Holiness Movement spirituality appealed to Quakers mainly due to its zealous longing for holy living and perfectionism. As Carol Spencer has pointed out, Quakers found parallels in the Holiness Movement, with women playing crucial roles in both traditions.[14]

A strong Wesleyan inclination was thus evident in this generation of Quakers. They adopted the idea of the "second blessing" and considered sanctification a second work of grace, separate from justification. The traditional Quaker house gathering became the Friends church meeting; preaching, altar calls, emotional congregational singing and public testimonies replaced plain silent worship.

---

12 Jia, "Yiwei mushi," 47.

13 Kwok Wai-luen, *Fan Dui He Yi!?: Jia Yuming, Jiyao zhuyi yu heyi yundong de jiujie* 《反對合一！？：賈玉銘、基要主義與中國教會合一運動的糾結》 [Advocating Separatism? Chia Yu Ming, Fundamentalists, and their Difficulties in the Chinese Church Union Movement] (Hong Kong: Tien Dao Publishing House, 2002), 64.

14 Spencer, *Holiness*, 163, 162.

Moreover, in many Holiness Quaker meetings, Wesleyan theology and the works of the National Holiness Association even outweighed the early Quaker works of George Fox (1624–91) and Robert Barclay (1648–90),[15] while they also downplayed some key notions held by Quakers in the seventeenth century, such as Inward Light.[16]

From 1860 to 1895, nearly two-thirds of Quakers in America gradually accepted Wesleyan Holiness teachings and departed from their Quietist tradition of spirituality.[17] The Holiness wing among Quakers later became the Evangelical Friends Church in the twentieth century. Driven by evangelic enthusiasm, the earliest Quaker mission in Nanjing began in 1890,[18] initiated by nurse Esther Butler from a Holiness branch of Quakers in America—the Ohio Yearly Meeting. In 1892, a Quaker church was set up in Nanjing,[19] and by 1907, the church had a Chinese pastor—Gao Shizhu (d. 1929). Gao was the first Chinese Quaker leader in China and became one of the founders of the Lingguang Publishing House (*Lingguang baoshe*).[20]

The Lingguang Publishing House, which had a distinctive Quaker heritage, featured in both Jia's writing ministry and his personal spiritual life. Jia was elected chair of the publisher's committee, playing an important role there. Lingguang Publishing House originated from a series of special revival meetings in 1919, where Jia preached tirelessly for two weeks.[21] The attendees were mainly ministers of various denominations from the Christian Council of Nanjing (*Nanjing Jidujiao Xiejinhui*).[22] There were prayer meetings held at Gao's home

---

15 Carole Dale Spencer, "Quakers in Theological Context," in eds. Stephen W. Angell and Ben Pink Dandelion, *The Oxford Handbook of Quaker Studies* (Oxford: Oxford University Press, 2013). https://www-oxfordhandbooks-com.ezproxy.is.ed.ac.uk/view/10.1093/oxfordhb/9780199608676.001.0001/oxfordhb-9780199608676-e-009

16 Spencer, "Quakers in Theological Context."

17 Spencer, *Holiness*, 163.

18 The earliest Quaker mission in China began in the 1870s, established by Irish Friends Robert and Mary Jane Davidson in Chongqing, whom were sent by the Friends Foreign Missionary Association (FFMA).

19 John Ormerod Greenwood. *Quaker Encounters*, Vol. 3, (York: William Sessions, 1978), 135.

20 Li Ji'an, Jia Yuming, Jiao Weizhen, "Dao Gao Shizhu mushi" 悼高師竹牧師 [A eulogy for Minister Gao Shizhu], *Lingguang bao* 靈光報 8, no. 3, 52–55.

21 "Benxiao Jiwen" 本校紀文 [School Report]. *Shenxue zhi* 神學志 [Theology Records] 5, no. 2 (1919). See in Wang, *Yi "Xin" Fei "Yong,"* 56.

22 The council was based at No. 1 Hanjia Alley (the Xinde building today) in Nanjing. At the beginning, it was a prayer group initiated by ministers from various denominations, including the Presbyterian Church in the United States of America, Methodist Episcopal Church, Christian Church (Disciples of Christ), the Episcopal Church, American Advent Mission

and gatherings at the Quaker church every evening.[23] The press was finally established in 1920.[24] Its original location was Gao's house at Luosi Bay in Nanjing, near the Bible Teachers' Training School for Women. Jia was frequently asked to arrange and organize school events at the Quaker church due to his close connections with Gao and the publishing house. Many of Jia's important works were published through the press, such as *Xin bian huo* （新辯惑 New Apologetics] and *Shendao xue* (神道學 Study of Divinity] in 1925, as well as *Wushi'er lingcheng jiangti* (五十二靈程講題 Fifty-five Notes on Spiritual Journey] and *Xuandao fa* (宣導法 Homiletics) in 1930. Jia and Gao's articles were often published in the Lingguang newspaper (*Lingguang bao*), the main publication of the Lingguang Publishing House.

Frequent cooperation and interaction deepened Jia's friendship with the Nanjing Quaker circle. Gao Shizu even became Jia's spiritual mentor. In Jia's eulogy for Gao, Jia expressed his high respect for Gao and his spiritual power, knowledge, and experience, before acknowledging Gao's deep impact on him: "Our fellowship in the Lord lasted for eighteen years. My life and work benefited greatly from your faithful teaching and timely prayer. . . . Our time on earth is so short and precious, how can I follow your steps and continue your ministry, until the day when I finish the race in this world?"[25] Jia's involvement with Quaker circles indicates that friendship and spiritual commonalities mattered more than strict denominational affiliation to him. Quakers did not have a clear boundary with other Protestant denominations, and trans-denominational cooperation was quite common at the time. For example, Jia's friend Li Ji'an (1894–1969), with whom Jia formed a friendship at those small meetings at Gao's place, and a graduate of the Presbyterian seminary, later became the second Chinese Quaker leader after Gao's death. Jia believed "there were neither denominations, nor newness and oldness either. The only thing that matters is whether there is

---

Society, and the Society of Friends. It was formally established in 1920, with John Leighton Stuart as its first president. The mission of the council was to promote the idea of "Christian family," to carry out social services, attract new members, and help churches to develop in China. See "Christianity in Nanjing," Nanjing Local Chronicles, The office of Nanjing Local Chronicles Committee, June 29, 2009, https://web.archive.org/web/20110811221104/http://njdfz.nje.cn/HTMLNEWS/1111/2009629220743.htm

23 "Benxiao Jiwen" in Wang, *Yi "Xin" Fei "Yong,"* 56.

24 Wang, *Yi "Xin" Fei "Yong,"* 56.

25 Li, "Dao Gao Shizhu mushi" 52–55.

life [in a church] and whether [a church] is spiritual."[26] In general, in the early-twentieth-century holiness teachings were appreciated across any perceived denominational boundaries.

Adopting holiness spirituality and cooperating with other Protestant denominations did not erase the distinctive Quaker characteristics of the Lingguang publishing house or of Jia's Quaker spiritual heritage. The name *Lingguang* (spiritual light) reveals its Quaker source, with the notion of Inner Light essential to Quakerism since the seventeenth century. For early Friends, the divine Light of Christ universally exists in the conscience of all humanity. They held that through the Light of Christ, everyone, no matter whether a person has heard the gospel or not, has already been reached by God. Early Quakers thought highly of the Bible. They also believed that revelation was not restricted to Scripture but could happen inwardly thanks to the Light within. The Light of Christ, once a person obeys it, would expose one's sins and enable one to live in holiness. This unique Christology was controversial among their contemporaries. It overturned Calvinist doctrines such as that of total depravity, predestination, and limited atonement.[27] As a result, early Friends were accused of denying the doctrine of the Trinity, focusing solely on the in-dwelling Christ as the Inner Light and neglecting the historical Jesus, even though they did not deny the incarnated Jesus in human history. Holiness Quakers in America in the twentieth century tried to emphasize the absolute authority of Scripture and downplayed the notion of the Light within or the Inward Light of Christ. But the Lingguang press was named after the defining early Quaker idea of spiritual light. This distinguished them somewhat from their American Holiness Quaker roots, through adoption of this point of early Quaker spirituality. The principles of the Lingguang newspaper also exhibited their stress on individual experiences in Christ:

We welcome the sharing of individual experiences in Christ instead of conversion stories. The ideal content is the genuine experience of walking in Christ, which is able to build up servants under the guidance of the Spirit.[28]

---

26 Jia Yuming, *Wanquan jiufa* 完全救法 [Full Salvation] (Hangzhou: Zhejiang Sheng Jidujiao Xiehui, 1949), 40.

27 Spencer, "Quakers in Theological Context."

28 "Tougaozhe qingzhuyi" 投稿者請注意 [Attention contributors]. *Lingguang bao*, no. 5 (1923). See in Wang, *Yi "Xin" Fei "Yong*,"57.

As Jia was the chair of the publisher's committee, the mission that the publisher conveyed to some extent also reflected Jia's vision. Jia and the publisher both preserved the experiential characteristics of Quakerism by stressing personal spiritual experience as a primary basis of authority in Christian life alongside the Bible. Scripture and inner experience, mutually intertwined, served as the foundation of faith.

Apart from his writing ministries, Jia also devoted himself diligently to building up theological education in China. In 1936, Jia, together with his colleagues Liao Enrong and Bi Yongqin, left the Bible Teachers' Training School for Women and established the China Christian School of Spirituality (中國基督教靈修學院) in Nanjing. However, in 1937, due to the Japanese occupation of Nanjing, they had to close the school. Jia left Nanjing and moved to Chengdu in Sichuan Province, but his commitment to spiritual education remained unshakable despite the turbulent environment. In 1939, with the support of many churches in the Chengdu area, Jia reestablished the school at *Lingyan* Mountain (today's Dujiangyan).[29] In 1940, the school moved to Chongqing. In 1945, when the Sino-Japanese war came to an end, Jia decided to go back to Nanjing and restore the School of Spirituality. In 1947, a believer, Ms. Zheng, generously donated two houses as the school buildings.[30] Jia also established a church there. The name that Jia chose for the church reflected again his favor of the Quaker notion—Lingguang church (Lingguang tang), or Spiritual Light Church.

Apart from theological education, Jia was also concerned with the prevailing influence around the world of modernist theology. In 1948, Jia was invited to attend the first delegates conference of the International Council of Christian Churches (ICCC) in Amsterdam. The conference was led by the American Presbyterian minister Carl McIntire (1906–2002), and the main purpose of the conference was to confront and criticize the modernist theological position. McIntire believed that there were two theological camps, the modernist and the fundamentalist, and differentiated them by the former's ultimate goal of building a single world church, against the latter's vision of a personal and visible return of Christ.[31] Fundamentalists held to the full truthfulness of the Bible and founded councils of Christian churches all around the world to oppose modernists.[32]

---

29 Tse, *Jiduren*, 57.

30 In 1949, the school was relocated to Shanghai. It remained open until 1956.

31 Carl McIntire, "History of the ICCC," *History of the ICCC* (blog), n.d., https://www.iccc.org.sg.

32 *Ibid.*

Jia was even elected as vice president at the conference. His deep involvement showed his agreement with the ICCC's theological principles.

However, in the 1950s, Jia's interactions with modernists experienced a shift, one that had much to do with Jia's involvement with TSPM. The foundational theological divergence between modernism and fundamentalism did not seem to bother him very much anymore. Jia's theologizing remained consistent, with the motif of life continuing to be the focal point in his thinking. Yet, Jia's view of spirituality manifested a more and more experiential inclination, a shift that was reflected in his attitude toward the two camps. Jia tried to cut off his association with the ICCC completely and later expressed his regret for attending the conference: "I was not vigilant enough and not aware that I was being used. I blame myself for my lack of knowledge of American ways," he wrote.[33] Although Jia did not express explicitly a new toleration of modernist theology, his attitude toward modernist theologians became more moderate. He cooperated with them during the early days of the Three-Self Movement and followed the leadership of Wu Yaozong (1895–1979), a prominent modernist. In 1956, Jia gave a speech titled "the future of the church in new China" at the second TSPM committee (extended) conference in Beijing.

> I, as a useless 78-year-old man, feel very honoured to attend this meeting. I have gained much inspiration and help at this conference, especially from listening to Mr. Wu Yaozong's report on the Three-self Patriotic Movement, which pointed out a good and bright future prospect for our church in new China.[34]

Instead of addressing differences in the foundations of faith, Jia emphasized the common ground of ethical living that he shared with modernists, the experiential

---

33 Jia Yuming, "Tuijin jidujiao sanzi gexin yundong qieduan yu meiguo zhuyi de yiqie guanxi" 推進基督教三自革新運動切斷與美國的一切關係 [Promoting the Christian Three-Self Reform Movement, severing all relationships with Americanism], *Jiefang ribao (Shanghai)*, 1951. See in Tse, *Jiduren*, 62. NB this was during a period of extensive criticism (and self-criticism) of church members and others.

34 Jia Yuming, "Jiaohui zai xinZhongguo guangming de qiantu," 教會在新中國光明的前途 [The bright future of the church in new China], *Tianfeng* No. 502 (1956) repr. in *Zhongguo sanzi aiguo yundong wenxuan* 1950–1992 中國三自愛國運動文選 1950-92 [Selected works of the Three-Self Patriotic Movement in China 1950–1992], ed. Luo Guanzong 羅冠宗 (Shanghai: National Committee of the Three-self Patriotic Movement of the Protestant Churches in China, 1993), 85.

aspect of Christian faith. In his speech, Jia addressed three points: firstly, "our faith should be experiential, and we should try to embody our faith in practice."

> Our faith is neither a theory, doctrine, and creed, nor something objective, hypothetical and inherited. Rather, it is practical, experiential, embodied in our behaviour in life. If we act out faith in our practice, then we have experiential knowledge.[35]

Living out the faith weighs far more for Jia than theoretical knowledge of doctrine, in a continuation of his earlier focus on practical holiness. As he indicated in *Full Salvation*, the ultimate goal of Christian spirituality was to realize the perfect state where "Christ is in me and I am in Christ,"[36] whereby Jesus's life has been embodied in my life and my life has been turned into Jesus's life.[37] Here the self has been transformed into a Christized-self (*Jiduhua de wo* 基督化的我), which is a Christ-human (*Jidu ren* 基督人).

Secondly, "we should have an abundant life as well as try to keep enriching our life." Jia's stress on life in his theologizing was pronounced in his speeches as well.

> Christianity is life, spiritual life. What Jesus has given us is his life, his incarnate life. It is an abundant life that Jesus has given us. Jesus said, "I came that they may have life and have it abundantly" (John 10:10). Therefore, our foremost task in building the church of new China consists in the offering of life. The offering of life first requires the generating of life, just as Paul said, "For though you have countless guides in Christ, you do not have many fathers. For I became your father in Christ Jesus through the gospel" (1 Corinthians 4:15). Furthermore, "My little children, for whom I am again in the anguish of childbirth until Christ is formed in you!" (Galatians 4:19). Second, nourishing that life also matters. Paul said, "I fed you with milk, not solid food" (1 Corinthians 3:2). The "milk" is not something imported, rather, it is life that flows out of a mother, just like Jesus came to this world, living among us, which reveals the Father. Hence, we should have a spiritualised as well as abundant life. "To live is

---

35 Jia Yuming, "Jiaohui zai xin Zhongguo guangming de qiantu."
36 Jia, *Wanquan jiufa*, 85.
37 Jia, *Wanquan jiufa*, 85.

Christ" (Philippians 1:21), is the way to bear testimony for God among people.[38]

This is in accordance with his thinking in the 1930s. Spiritual life and deep spiritual experience should be the cornerstone for true ministry.

> A true minister ... must be a Christ-human who has abundant spiritual life. What they preach includes not only doctrines, but also the power of life that outflows from their spiritual living. They would demonstrate vividly the experience along their spiritual journey to people. If preachers do not have a godly spirituality, do not have deep and rich spiritual experience, and are only able to preach with their mouths instead of being a good example, they cannot be true ministers. A true minister does spiritual work. People without spiritual experience cannot do spiritual work. True evangelizing is preaching life. People without a spiritual life cannot preach life.[39]

Jia believed that the core of Christianity was obtaining the abundant life that Jesus gave us. It is important to be aware that it is Jesus who is the only source of spiritual life—so gaining spiritual life from Jesus is the foundation for building the church of new China. Since the foundation lies in Christ Jesus and the gospel, believers cannot find it elsewhere; the truth that can nourish the life of the church does not come from outside. As Jia noted, believers' abundant spiritual life should flow from within; the future of Christianity in China lies in demonstrating the image of Christ in individual lives. To Jia, the development of the experiential aspect of faith is the most important aspect to church growth. This inclination resonates well with Confucian moral ethics in the Chinese cultural context, as the value of the unity of knowledge and action (*zhixing heyi* 知行合一) was broadly accepted by Chinese people. Laying stress on abundant life and the practical dimensions of faith in particular makes Jia's spirituality more context-sensitive and therefore allows more room for theologizing independently from the missionary heritage.

In his early writings, Jia's expectation that spirituality should be subjective and independent from missionary impact was already pronounced:

---

38 Jia, "Jiaohui."

39 Jia Yuming, *Wushier lingcheng jiangti* (Hong Kong: Chenxing, 1986), 5.

There is another testimony that I must mention. I was jealous when I saw other people studying abroad, so I prayed that God would give me an opportunity too. Later someone was willing to fund me to study in a seminary in the United States until my graduation. However, the night before my departure, with everything regarding going abroad, including the boat ticket, prepared, I prayed, thinking I must know the Lord's will on this matter clearly, whether or not that He is willing to let me go. I prayed sincerely for a long time yet didn't hear the Lord's voice. So I prayed intensely. I was anxious. Why hasn't the Lord answered me! It was not until after midnight that a voice came to me. The Lord said, "I am not willing to put stones on young people's shoulders." Once I heard this, I knew immediately that the Lord did not want me to study abroad, so I obeyed the Lord. I resigned from everything the next day and decided not to study at the seminary in the United States. Thankfully, I can still teach theology in Nanjing. I have written so many letters and books on religions and essential doctrines of spirituality. None of those are imported from the West.[40]

From his testimony, Jia especially favored a spirituality that developed from private experience and was free from what he now considered the fetters of Western theological traditions or denominational limits. His faith relied heavily on direct revelations that happened inwardly. Again, his words demonstrate a tendency in accord with the Lingguang Publishing house position that individual inner experience was fundamental to building up faith. Jia formed close connections with Western missionary circles, and some Western theological currents of his day can be easily discerned in his thinking. But he also purposefully distinguished his theology from the missionary legacy. This can be seen in his advice to the Three-Self Movement in the 1950s, where his third point suggested that "we should discover the truth and try to be cautious in our approach."

In the past, most of the doctrines that our churches received were introduced by imperialistic missionaries. Their perspectives were biased and carried some poisonous and deceptive elements. Therefore, we should liberate the truth. . . . The Bible contains plentiful treasures, which we must dig up; it also holds endless mysteries of life, which we must experience

---

40 Jia, "Yiwei," 46–51.

and grasp. The Bible we have at the moment was translated through a cooperation full of misunderstanding between foreigners who did not know Chinese and Chinese who did not understand the original biblical text. Thus, it was unavoidable that the translation is incorrect, and therefore, it is necessary to re-translate the Bible. I suggest that we re-translate the Bible.[41]

At this stage, Jia's evaluation of missionary teachings was fairly negative and suggested a reading of the Bible that was independent from Western missionary influence and relevant to Chinese believers' own lives. Jia's position in the 1950s contrasts with his inheritance of Western theological traditions in his early days. His *Study of Divinity*, published in 1925, was mainly translated from Augustus Hopkins Strong's *Systematic Theology* (1836–1921). That is to say, Jia's attitude toward Western theological traditions went through a shift. Probably due to the change of political environment, Jia tended to theologize in a more experiential way.

Even though he longed to discover the truth of the Bible independently, Jia's theologizing to a large extent was a process of synthesizing and refashioning the prevailing Holiness Movement theology of his day. Yet Jia's stress on direct inner spiritual revelation and the experiential dimension of faith made it easier for his spirituality to adapt to the new socio-political atmosphere. Jia's loose engagement with different theological traditions as well as his lifelong dedication to the motif of life showed that his interest did not lie in dogmatic theologizing. Rather, he saw his focus as encouraging and developing instructions on Christian spiritual self-transformation that were relevant to the context of China.

Jia Yuming's View of Sanctification

Practical holiness features prominently in Jia's view of spirituality. Jia points out the human spiritual dilemma after regeneration, where regenerated believers usually find themselves at a spiritual impasse caused by the coexistence of two different streams of life: one from the first Adam, the other from Jesus Christ, the second Adam.[42] Jia described regeneration as where "God through the work of the Holy Spirit bestows the new life of Jesus on the human heart. It is the

---

41 Jia, "Jiaohui."
42 Jia, *Wanquan jiufa*, 32.

beginning of the Christian's new life and separate from sanctification."[43] After regeneration, the law of sin impedes the process of spiritual growth: as Jia explains, the law of sin is in nature an abnormal state of the natural law of the human being and functions as the engine of sin.[44] The life derived from Christ can reveal the original state of humans that exhibits the image of God, whereas the one governed by the law of sin tends to veil the truth of spiritual life. Believers are being pulled by two opposing forces and are in a constant battle with their old sinful nature. In this regard, Jia emphasized the importance of the agency of believers in sanctification.

> Believers' advancement in sanctification does not rely on their own passive suppression of the old self. It is facilitated by their proactive cultivation. . . . A person's mind and spirit are transformed unexpectedly in the process of this cultivation.[45]

Jia believed, in accord with the pursuit of a higher Christian life, that there were three phases of Christian life: the justified life, sanctified life, and victorious life.[46] Accordingly, in terms of sanctification, there is positional sanctification (*diwei chengsheng* 地位成聖), daily life sanctification (*shenghuo chengsheng* 生活成聖) and full sanctification (*wanquan chengsheng* 完全成聖).[47] Believers can only enter the first stage of positional sanctification by relying on the blood of Christ. "Believers themselves cannot be sanctified by their own deeds, it is all because of being identified with Christ. In other words, it is all because of a person's relationship with Christ."[48] He also held that believers ought to proceed to embody this legal sanctification in their own experience. In other words, daily life sanctification should follow positional sanctification. Believers should manifest the character of Christ and exhibit holiness in their everyday practice. Specifically, the key step to realizing holy living is the act of consecration (*xian* 獻), which means that believers should fully deny their selfish desires and surrender themselves to the Lord and let the Lord govern every aspect of their lives. They should

---

43 Jia Yuming, *Shen dao xue* [Study of Divinity] (Taibei: Ganlan shiye jijin, 1996–97), 167.

44 Jia, *Wanquan jiufa*, 70.

45 Jia, *Wanquan jiufa*, 70–71.

46 Jia, *Wanquan jiufa*, 106.

47 Jia, *Wanquan jiufa*, 216, 254.

48 Jia, *Wanquan jiufa*, 250.

live a life of consecration and no longer live for themselves but for the Lord. In this way, their lives would exhibit holiness.[49]

Jia's teaching about ultimate or full sanctification showed his adoption of perfectionism. This is the stage of eradication of sin, where believers are transformed into a completely perfect image of Christ, namely, a Christ-human. Jia called a person manifesting the truth of human spiritual life a genuine or authentic human (*zhen ren*, 真人 true person), and pointed out that the *zhen ren* was Jesus Christ.[50] In other words, the ultimate goal of sanctification for believers is to eradicate their sinful nature in this life, in Jia's term, "to obliterate the sinful body" (*mie zui shen* 滅罪身).

> That humans sin is due to the law of sin; the trigger of the law of sin is the sinful body, which also can be called the old self or self. . . . Since we are already identified with the Lord's death and crucified on the cross with the Lord, "so that the body of sin might be destroyed" (Romans 6:6), this means that the action of self has disappeared.[51]

Believers should be able to overcome sin and present humanity's original perfect state of holiness.[52] The term "sinful body" (*zui shen* 罪身) here should not be understood as the carnal part of humanity: in Jia's writing, it refers to the whole person, including the spirit, soul and body. Specifically, Jia called the sinful body the "old person" (*jiu ren* 舊人), which equaled the self.[53] Therefore, demolishing the sinful body as the last stage of the process of sanctification means completely destroying the old sinful self as well as the law of sin.[54] Jia also described this phase of sanctification as the salvation of the body (*ti de jiu* 體的救), which means the transformation of the whole person: spirit, soul, and body.[55] Jia is radical in that for him living as a Christ-human, or the state of entire sanctification, is attainable in this life.[56]

---

49 Jia, *Wanquan jiufa*, 252–53.

50 Jia, *Wanquan jiufa*, 20.

51 Jia, *Wanquan jiufa*, 71.

52 Jia, *Wanquan jiufa*, 76.

53 Jia, *Wanquan jiufa,* 71.

54 Jia, *Wanquan jiufa*, 71.

55 Jia, *Wanquan jiufa*, 116–17.

56 Jia's optimistic vision is fundamentally different, however, from the modernists' perfectionist stance, like the ideas of Wu Leichuan (1870–1944) on building the Kingdom of God in this world. For Jia, the foundation of ethical living is the life of Christ. The mystical inner

For Jia, sanctification is a developmental process that comprises three stages as well as a crisis that marks the beginning of a higher stage of holiness. Jia emphasized the work of the Spirit when expounding on the instantaneous aspect of sanctification.

> It is instantaneous when a person is saved; it is also instantaneous for a believer to become the Lord's through consecration; it is still instantaneous to die within the Lord's death. It is an instantaneous death rather than a gradual one. . . . It all depends on the work of Holy Spirit.[57]

For Jia, sanctification as a crisis is crucial not only because it is a defining moment that initiates the adjustment of a person's spiritual dislocation but also because it is a miraculous experience of the Holy Spirit itself. Jia's emphasis on the beginning of each sanctifying stage shows his interest in dramatic and subjective experiences, something also reflected in his many testimonies on his mystical experiences.

Synthesizing Contemporary Theological Trends

Jia's Perfectionist position can be found in the Methodist tradition. His Wesleyan influence is shown explicitly in his *Fifty-two lectures on the Spiritual Journey* (1930), where Jia stresses that justification and sanctification are both crucial. Justification concerns one's nominal position in front of God; God considers us innocent and adopts us as legitimate children. Sanctification is about the reality or realization of that legal status in one's experience.

> As Mr. Wesley has said, "Genuine Christians must not sin. First, they do not commit habitual sins; secondly, they do not commit deliberate sins; thirdly, they do not commit sins that are caused by the weakness of

---

revelation that individuals receive directly from God is critical in their spiritual growth and self-transformation. Modernists like Wu did not accept the supernatural aspect of Christianity or the idea of fallen human nature in need of Christ's restoring power. For example, Wu believed that through imitating the moral model of Mozi, whose personality was as loving and righteous as Jesus, people can transform their minds and reform society. See Wu Leichuan, *Mozhai yu Yesu* 墨翟與耶穌 [Mozi and Jesus], Chin Kenpa (曾慶豹 Zeng Qingbao) ed. (Xinbei: Ganlan, 2015), xiii–lxvi. Jia's trajectory of perfectionism must be distinguished from a modernist interpretation.

57 Jia, *Wanquan jiufa*, 254–55.

the flesh. It is clearly stated in the Bible that: 'Those who have been born of God do not sin, because God's seed abides in them; they cannot sin, because they have been born of God.' (1 John 3:9)" Moreover, genuine Christians are not only justified but also sanctified gradually. This sanctified state is attainable in this life." I have never seen a true Christian who has the life of Christ but does not make any progress day by day in the salvation brought about by Christ until the holy and perfect state.[58]

Even though Wesley believed that humans are totally corrupt, and that corruption affects every aspect of human nature, he holds to the idea of "optimistic grace," that it is possible that the perfect loving relationship with God which humans lost at the Fall would be fully restored. Wesley, moreover, related love to law. He believed that the satisfaction of the "royal law of love" taught by Jesus Christ in the New Testament in the Sermon on the Mount also fulfills the moral obligations of the Ten Commandments: that is to say, he linked the fulfilment of the law more to believers' sanctification than justification. For Wesley, it is crucial that Christ's atoning work on the cross means that His life becomes ours at our new birth and therefore entire sanctification is attainable.[59] The atonement has an experiential aspect, and this dimension is pivotal to Wesley's theologizing and his perfectionist position. Similarly, for Jia, the subjective/experiential side of atonement rather than its objective/legal side interests him more. Both Wesley and Jia interpret atonement from an anthropological and experiential perspective; thus, the subject of sanctification becomes the center of both Wesley and Jia's thinking. For Wesley, Christianity is all about having "the mind of Christ."[60] True Christianity manifests itself in believers' practical holiness. Sanctification is embodied in loving actions. Salvation is ethical and practical:

[It is] not barely, according to the vulgar notion, deliverance from hell, or going to heaven; but a present deliverance from sin, a restoration of the soul to its primitive health, its original purity; a recovery of the divine

---

58 Jia Yuming, *Wushier lingcheng jiangti*, 59–60.

59 Melvin Easterday Dieter, "The Wesleyan Perspective," in *Five Views on Sanctification* (Grand Rapids, Michigan: Zondervan Publishing House, 1987), 24–27.

60 John Wesley, Sermon, "The Almost Christian" in *The Works of John Wesley*, ed. Thomas Jackson, 14 vols. (London: Wesley Conference Office, 1872), 5:21–22. See in Dieter, "The Wesleyan Perspective," 27.

nature; the renewal of our souls after the image of God, in righteousness and true holiness, in justice, mercy, and truth.[61]

For Jia, the end of sanctification is to reach the spiritual state of Christ-human. Jia's interest in individual spiritual self-transformation, adoption of perfectionism as well as the focus of sanctification in his theologizing are all in line with the ethical inclination of Wesleyan spirituality.

In addition to the Methodist tradition, the broad holiness movement such as the Keswick convention, which had its roots in Wesleyan theology, was influential in Jia's day. Jia's three-stage view of sanctification, appreciation of the dramatic spiritual experience of the Holy Spirit, emphasis on instantaneity of sanctification, and adoption of perfectionism were all promoted among the holiness movement more broadly.

Jia's encounter with Quakerism was another factor in his appreciation of mystical spiritual experience. As shown above, Jia had a chance to immerse himself in Quaker spirituality through his frequent personal contact with Quaker circles. Jia's experience of repentance on a river bank when he was twenty resembled George Fox's, and both bore remarkable emotional and mystical elements. Jia recounted how, while praying at a river bank at midnight, he became aware of all of his sins and repented for each one in front of the Lord. Then he felt joy in his heart, "like a man who has put down his heavy burdens. I felt my heart was purified."[62] Both Fox and Jia highlighted the significance of direct inward revelation. As Barclay emphasized, "the testimony of the Spirit is that alone by which the true knowledge of God hath been, is and can be only revealed" while inward revelation was "absolutely necessary for the building up of true faith."[63] In his discussion on the unity of faith, practice, and knowledge, Jia defined true knowledge as knowledge with experience, which would build up one's faith and guide one's actions, in line with the stress on the experimental aspect of knowledge.[64]

Jia shared with Quakers common ground in the conviction of entire sanctification. According to Barclay, the perfect state was attainable in this lifetime and believers could be kept from transgressing God's law and fulfill God's

---

61 Wesley, "A Father Appeal to Men of Reason and Religion," 8: 47.

62 Jia "Yiwei," 46–51.

63 Robert Barclay, *Apology for the True Christian Divinity: Being an Explanation and Vindication of the People Called Quakers.* (Birmingham: Friends Book Store, 1880), 28.

64 Jia, *Wanquan jiufa*, 262.

commandments by the work of Spirit through revealing the law of the Spirit of life.[65] Quakers were optimistic about human nature precisely because of their conviction of the Inner Light. They believed that sin could be completely removed and the newborn person would be guided by the Spirit and given the strength to overcome sins. Yet for early Quakers, there were no ideas such as "second blessing" and different stages of sanctification, even though their understanding of spiritual growth was also developmental. The only watershed was the moment of new birth.[66] In this respect, it was very likely that it was from the Keswick convention that Jia adopted the idea of three decisive phases in sanctification, although the convention never espoused perfectionism.[67]

Given his close connections with Quakers and the Quaker terms and concepts that he adopted in his writing, it is reasonable to connect Jia's mystical tendency with Quaker spirituality. The notion of Inner Light is mentioned frequently in Jia's writing, although it differs from the Quaker version in that he did not adopt universalism. For Jia, one receives the true light (*zhen guang*) only when regeneration happens, which serves as the sign of new spiritual life. Both Jia and Quakers pointed to the transforming power of the spiritual light (*ling guang*), as well as its impact on the human mind:

A person whose soul is spiritualized is someone whose reason has been baptized by the Spirit and become spiritualized. Their reason must have been largely transformed and have spiritual knowledge and intuition. This

---

65 Barclay, *Apology for the True Christian Divinity*, 231, 229

66 Bebbington, *Evangelicalism in Modern Britain*, 156.

67 For the Keswick movement, practical holiness required cooperation between proactive human effort and the counteracting power of the Holy Spirit, and should be a lifelong pursuit. The process of separating believers from sin was understood as sanctification; according to Keswick teaching on this subject, the process of sanctification is progressive in the sense that it includes different stages: positional, experimental, and ultimate sanctification, of which positional sanctification was fundamental. This was wrought by Christ's atoning work on the cross for all true believers. Believers are sanctified in three senses: the condemnation of sin is removed; they are justified in the sight of God; and they are regenerated and delivered from the lordship of sin. Experimental sanctification is a process of believers being transformed gradually by the Spirit on the foundation of the cross into the likeness of Christ and displaying more and more the character of Christ in daily life. Ultimate sanctification, which equals glorification, means the nature of sin is eradicated and believers are transformed into the image of Christ—something not attainable in this life that can only be achieved in the life to come. Jia differs from Keswick adherents in that he espoused perfectionism.

is all due to the fact that the spiritual light has shined within the soul and enlightened the mind.[68]

The revealing power from within was always prominent in Jia and Quaker testimonies. Given its Quaker background, it was obvious why the Lingguang press favored testimonies of believers' spiritual experiences as their major publishing content. As a regular participant of Quaker meetings and close friend of Gao, Jia's passion in sharing his direct experiences of Christ may also be traced back to Quaker influence.

Conclusion

This chapter has investigated Jia Yuming's life experience as well as theological background to clarify his engagement with Western theology and especially spirituality. It demonstrates the profound but neglected impact of Quakerism on Jia's theological thought, alongside the broader holiness movement. For Jia, beside the Bible, direct inner revelation is fundamental and indispensable to spiritual growth and self-transformation. Jia valued the experiential aspect of faith more than dogmatic theology, an inclination that became more pronounced in the later stages of his life. Looking at Jia's spirituality from a Quaker perspective offers insight toward understanding his syncretic way of theologizing and eclectic attitude toward modernists during the Three-Self Movement. Quaker mystical spirituality, especially its profound dependence on direct inner revelation, encouraged Jia to depart from the mainstream missionary legacy and develop a spirituality in line with the Three-Self pursuit, that was able to evolve in the new Chinese context. Quaker faith is, according to Jon R. Kershner, "at least theoretically, a noncreedal religious expression that prioritizes the experience of the adherent as essential to an efficacious faith."[69] A low view of doctrine, church, and outward profession of faith makes Quaker spirituality more flexible and sensitive to the sociocultural context where it evolves. As a result, Quaker spirituality is amorphous in nature, which allows it to absorb and manifest more easily and freely religious convictions, as well as sociocultural elements, in a particular context. Jia's deep immersion in Quaker circles influenced his way of theologizing in a more significant way than we might expect if we focus upon select theological

---

68 *Jia, Wanquan jiufa,* 75.

69 Jon R. Kershner, *Quakers and Mysticism: Comparative and Syncretic Approach to Spirituality* (Cham: Springer International Publishing, 2019), 1.

texts. Simply seen from Jia's works, one might consider him only a systematic theologian who focused on the theme of life. However, Jia's personal interactions with various theological traditions and his reactions to sociopolitical changes of his day complicate his theologizing; the Jia Yuming of *The Study of Divinity* is not the theologian of his later years. The spirituality of Jia provides a point of continuity and explanation for his willingness to adapt to his context in a way that does not fit comfortably with his earlier theology and associations at the ICCC. It is through his spirituality, and the influences that formed it, that we can understand Jia and his ideal for a Chinese church for China.

Chapter 4

A THEOLOGY OF CHINESE HYMNAL TRANSLATIONS IN THE 1920s AND '30s

Liu Boyun, *Beijing Language and Culture University*

This article analyzes the translation of English hymnody by the Chinese Protestant Church in the 1920s and '30s, exploring the texts, methodology, and theology involved in in the process. Liu Tingfang (劉廷芳, Timothy Ting-fang Lew) and Yang Yinliu (楊蔭瀏, Ernest Y. L. Yang) are two of the most prominent translators, among those from several denominations who contributed to the project. The numerous Chinese translations, original works, and research articles published in such collections as *Amethyst* or *Hymns and Sacred Music* reveal both translators' and composers' endeavors to indigenize Christianity as well as a notable inclination toward Christian socialism. The hymn translation project, indeed, sometimes appears less concerned with a faithful representation of the original texts than with translators' theological stance or the ethos of the era. In 1934, for example, when Liu Tingfang, Chairman of the Compiling Committee for a Chinese Hymnal for Six Denominations translated "For the Beauty of the Earth," he rendered the words "linking sense to sound and sight" as "sound and sight are transformed from emptiness to Reality."[1] The original text conveys that when the congregation sings praises to God, the sound and words of sacred music and the vision of the divine will give the congregation a deeper understanding of God. Liu's translation, or rather paraphrase, is quite different from the source text and includes words borrowed from Chinese Buddhism, such as "emptiness" (空 *kong*) and "realness" (真 *zhen*). But the message is orthodox and clear: namely, that praise and a vision of God become genuine and meaningful in devoted worship.

---

1 Lew Ting-fang, trans., "For the Beauty of the Earth," 大地風光歌, *Zijing* (紫晶, *Amethyst*), Vol. 6, No. 2, (June 1934), 270.

Praise is perceived as a channel between the human and the divine. That same hymn in Chinese can itself be seen as such a channel. The translators were not only linking the source text to the target text but also linking Christian doctrines and practices to a highly heterogeneous culture, which was endeavoring to renew and assert itself after decades of colonial influence and was open to revolutionary ideas such as nationalism and socialism. When Christian hymn translators in the 1920s and '30s were deciding on which hymns to translate and how to translate them, these were the issues that concerned them, as they put special emphasis on their identity as Chinese Christians. This article introduces their translation (or paraphrase) of hymns, and discusses how their theology, in response to the times, shaped the translations.

1. An Overview of Hymn Translation into Chinese

Christian hymns were first introduced to China in the seventh century, as the Xi'an Stele erected by the Church of the East (Jingjiao 景教) indicates, "at the seven hours there is ritual praise, greatly helping the living and the dead."[2] In such services, hymns would be sung in Syriac, the liturgical language of the Church of the East. There is not yet much evidence of hymns in Chinese circulating in the Tang Dynasty, apart from such occasional examples as "A Hymn of the Brilliant Teaching of Daqin to the Three Majesties for Obtaining Salvation" (大秦景教三威蒙度讚).[3] As later Catholic missions during the Ming and Qing Dynasties introduced their rituals to China, they impressed the imperial court with Western instruments and successfully converted some high-ranking officials as well as eunuchs in the Forbidden City to Catholicism.[4] Hymn translations and adaptations from this period have been preserved and include Matteo Ricci's *Xiqin quyin* (西琴曲意, Composition with Western Instruments), Joseph-Marie Amiot's *Shengyue jingpu* (聖樂經譜, Musique Sacrée) as well as Wu Li

---

2 Translation of this line in the Xi'an Stele text is from Moule, A.C., *Christians in China before the Year 1550* (London: Society for Promoting Christian Knowledge, 1930), 38.

3 "*Daqin Jingjiao sanwei mengdu zan*," See Dennis T.W. Ng, "The Sinicization of Sacred Music: A Study of T. C. Chao," in *Sinicizing Christianity*, ed. Yangwen Zheng (Leiden: Brill), 261–89, 263–64.

4 See, for example, Michela Fontana, *Matteo Ricci: A Jesuit in the Ming Court*, trans. Paul Metcalfe (Lanham, Maryland: Rowman & Littlefield Publishers, Inc., 2011), 143, and David Francis Urrows, "The Pipe Organ of the Baroque Era in China," in *China and the West: Music, Representation, and Reception*, eds. Hon-Lun Yang and Michael Saffle (Ann Arbor: University of Michigan Press, 2017), 21–48.

(吳歷)'s *Tianyue zhengyinpu* (天樂正音譜, Score of Heavenly Music). The Jesuit missionaries did not limit themselves to liturgical hymns: with the help of local believers, they also "combined Christian themes with popular tunes and encouraged women and children especially to sing along." However, unlike in Christian mission fields in Africa and the Americas, these indigenization efforts for the common people did not seem to be very effective and the songs have not been preserved.[5]

Protestantism reached China in 1807. The first Protestant missionary, Robert Morrison, produced the first Chinese hymnal, *Yangxin shenshi* (養心神詩, Hymns for Nurturing the Spirit), and this title was retained for hymnals translated and compiled by later missionaries such as Walter Henry Medhurst, James Legge, or William Young. It was not until the twentieth century, however, that major hymn translation and composition efforts were undertaken by Chinese Christians.

In the 1920s and 1930s, faculty and students of the School of Theology at Yenching University began to translate hymns from English to Chinese. Liu Tingfang, Dean of the School of Theology, founded the journals *Life Monthly* (生命) and *Truth Weekly* (真理周刊) along with his close associates, together known as the "Life Fellowship" (生命社). Members of this group included Wu Leichuan (L. C. Wu 吳雷川), Zhao Zichen, and Xu Baojian (Hsu Pao Chien 徐寶謙), all of whom served at Yenching University and played a significant role in indigenizing Christianity in China.[6] In 1926, the two journals merged into *Truth and Life* (真理與生命). In 1934, Liu Tingfang created *Hymns and Sacred Music* (聖歌與聖樂) as a supplement to *Truth and Life* with his friend Yang Yinliu, a Christian musicologist. Liu Tingfang gives an account of this in his article "Words from Experience," (過來人言) in the very first issue of *Hymns and Sacred Music* in 1934. Liu had been paying attention to the compiling of hymns for over a decade, ever since the North China Kung Li Hui (Congregational Church) had invited him to join their compiling committee for a common hymnal and he had continued working on hymns throughout. The purpose of the supplement that he established with Yang Yinliu, *Hymns and Sacred Music*,

---

5 Liam Matthew Brockey, *Journey to the East: the Jesuit Mission to China, 1579–1724* (Cambridge, MA: Belknap Press, 2008), 412–13.

6 Alexander Chow, *Chinese Public Theology: Generational Shifts and Confucian Imagination in Chinese Christianity* (Oxford: Oxford University Press, 2018), 39.

was to select, translate, and set hymns to music, and offer reflections on translation process and methodology.[7]

Earlier in 1930, Liu had started another journal, *Amethyst* (紫晶), with Yang. Liu served as the editor-in-chief, with Yang as the assistant to the editor-in-chief. Apart from their own hymn translations, they also started to publish in the journal a corpus of hymns translated or paraphrased by other faculty and students at Yenching University, including Li Rongfang (李榮芳), Xu Dishan (許地山), and Bingxin (冰心, pen name of Wu Hsieh Wan-yin 吳謝婉瑩). The latter two were well-known writers, who brought their literary flair to the project. The scope of the project was further developed in 1935 with advertisements in *Amethyst* for new translations and compositions of hymns, from which the editors would select the best for publication.

Meanwhile, from 1931 to 1936, a landmark compilation task was undertaken for a common Chinese hymnal across six denominations,[8] resulting in the publication of *Hymns of Universal Praise* (普天頌讚) in 1936 by the S.D.C.K. (廣學會, Society for the Diffusion of Christian and General Knowledge among the Chinese). Most of the 512 hymns in the volume were translations of English hymns written in the nineteenth century, but this was the first time that the work of hymn compilation, in both translation and composition, was done primarily by Chinese Christians.

Many of the hymns published in *Hymns and Sacred Music* and *Amethyst* found their way into the 1936 first edition of *Hymns of Universal Praise*, but this was not the end of the endeavor. Even in the last issue of *Amethyst* in 1937, a call still appeared for hymns in Chinese, including "new translations of well-received hymns in the Church, with more natural expressions in Chinese and closer to the original," as well as "translations from Western hymns that have not been translated before."[9] Unfortunately, the project was disrupted by the Japanese invasion, and there would not be another major publication of a church hymnal until the *New Hymnal* (新編讚美詩) of 1983.

---

7 Liu Tingfang, "Guolairen yan" (Words from a Veteran), Liu Tingfang and Yang Yinliu, eds. *Shengge yu shengyue*, No. 1, in *Zhenli yu shengming* 真理與生命, Vol. 8, No. 1, (March 1934), 31–35, 32.

8 Namely, Church of Christ in China (中華基督教會全國總會), Chung Hwa Sheng Kung Hwei (Zhonghua Sheng Gong Hui 中華聖公會, Anglican-Episcopal Province of China), Methodist Episcopal Church, North (美以美會), North China Kung Li Hui (華北公理會), East China Baptist Convention (華東浸禮會), and Methodist Episcopal Church, South (監理會).

9 "Hymn," *Zijing*, Vol. 12, No. 1, (May 1937), 93.

2. Hymn Translation as a Method of Indigenization

Indigenization has been from the very beginning a prime concern of the Christian Church in China and a shared concern of both foreign missionaries and Chinese believers. Seventy years after the first Protestant missionary arrived, the first General Conference of Protestant Missionaries in China in 1877 gave special emphasis to indigenization, as indicated in the record of their proceedings.[10] Among the issues discussed, hymn translation was mentioned frequently. A list of missionary publications showed twenty-six hymn books "in general language" (Mandarin) and thirty-seven in dialects.[11] Although the hymns were said to "compare favorably with the best in other lands," they were not well received by Chinese believers, as one author readily admits: "it has been found hard to teach the Chinese to sing them."[12] Even Rev. Chauncey Goodrich, one of the most important figures in Chinese bible translation and co-editor with Dr. Henry Blodgett of the *Chinese Hymnal* of 1877, acknowledged that "we have often made serious failures, especially in Mandarin Colloquial hymns."[13] He would again call for a high-quality hymnal in Chinese at the 1890 General Conference.[14]

Indigenization became a more urgent issue in the wake of the Boxer Rebellion of 1900, during which foreign missionaries and Chinese Christians became targets of persecution. Afterwards the consensus was strengthened that it was imperative that Christianity spoke in Chinese for the Chinese. In the two decades following the Boxer Rebellion, Christianity in China enjoyed what is frequently termed a "Golden Age." During this time, the local churches grew increasingly independent from foreign missions and initiated ecumenical cooperation, breaking down the barriers of denominationalism that had been the unfortunate byproduct of foreign missions.[15]

---

10 M. T. Yates, R. Nelson and E. R. Barrett eds., *General Conference of the Protestant Missionaries of China, held at Shanghai, May 10–24, 1877* (Shanghai: Presbyterian Mission Press, 1878). See especially "Self-Support of the Native Church," 283–293; "The Native Pastorate," 299–315; "Should the Native Churches in China be United Ecclesiastically and Independent of Foreign Churches and Societies," 422–38.

11 Rev. S. L. Baldwin, "Christian Literature, what has been done and what is needed," *General Conference of the Protestant Missionaries of China*, 206.

12 Baldwin, "Christian Literature," 208.

13 "Discussion," in *General Conference*, 429.

14 Chauncey Goodrich, "Service of Song in China," in *Records of the General Conference of the Protestant Missionaries of China held at Shanghai, May 7–20, 1890* (Shanghai: Presbyterian Mission Press, 1890), 395–401.

15 Liu Yi, "From Christian Alien to Chinese Citizen: The National Identity of Chinese Christians in the Twentieth Century," *Studies in World Christianity* 16.2 (2010): 145–68, 147.

In a speech entitled "The Responsibility of Christian Missionaries in the New Culture Movement," delivered in 1921 at the China Continuation Committee (中華續行委辦會), Liu Tingfang openly lamented the lack of a decent Chinese hymnal, given that translations from English hymns were inadequate and could not reproduce the religious expressions and sentiments as accurately and profoundly as the originals. Liu believed that the New Culture Movement, which promoted a wider use of vernacular Chinese, would be helpful for the Chinese Church in creating a vernacular hymnal that truly touched hearts and could be readily used.[16]

In January 1922, Liu published an article in English entitled "Making the Christian Church in China Indigenous" in *The Chinese Recorder*, the main interdenominational mission journal. He began by giving several reasons for the necessity of indigenization and proposed some possible solutions for the Chinese Church to achieve "self-support, self-propagation and self-government."[17] As for rituals and the forms of worship, Liu emphasized that Chinese Christians would inevitably adopt a different approach to the Western one, especially with hymns, since "hymns in Chinese, even in the best translations, do not give them [i.e., bilingual Chinese Christians] the spiritual value they found in the English version and which they still long for."[18] He went on to say that although there were skilled translators, Christians should not be content with translated hymns alone but aspire to produce "religious poetry directly in the Pai Hua" (vernacular Mandarin Chinese). This was one of Liu's guidelines in translating, paraphrasing, or composing hymns: they should be presented in artfully crafted vernacular Chinese verse, instead of classical Chinese, which would be inaccessible for the majority of Chinese believers.

For Liu Tingfang, translation was not an end in itself, but the final text needed to be sufficiently accommodating for a Chinese audience and embody traditional

---

16 Liu Tingfang, "Xinwenhua yundong zhong jidujiao xuanjiaoshi de zeren" 新文化運動中基督教宣教師的責任 [Responsibility of the Christian Missionaries in the Renaissance Movement], in Tang Xiaofeng 唐曉峯, Wang Shuai 王帥, ed., *Minguo shiqi feijidujiao yundong zhongyao ziliao huibian* 民國時期非基督教運動重要資料彙編, [A Selection of Important Publications in the Anti-Christian Movement in the Republican Period], (Beijing: Social Sciences Academic Press, 2015), 153–81. Note that he refers to the New Culture Movement as the "Renaissance Movement," seeing commonalities with the Renaissance Movement in Europe.

17 T. T. Liu, "Making the Christian Church in China Indigenous," *The Chinese Recorder*, Vol. LIII (Shanghai: Presbyterian Press, 1922), 297–312, 311.

18 Liu, "Making the Christian Church," 305.

Chinese values. Liu would often paraphrase a line or even create a new stanza in a hymn to make it sound more natural to a Chinese ear. Accuracy, which is greatly emphasized in traditional translation approaches, might be sacrificed to express the gist of a hymn in a manner both literary and devotional. Yang Yinliu, his friend and collaborator, took a similar view. Yang recognized and praised the expertise of the members of the Compiling Committee for a Chinese Hymnal for Six Denominations in terms of their different skills: "some are very familiar with the historical background of the hymns . . . some have a deep understanding of theology, some are well-versed in Chinese poetry, and others are masters of modern literature."[19] For Yang, in order to translate or compose hymns for the Chinese Church, contributors should have a sound theology, as well as a superb style, and express religious ideas and emotions elegantly in the hymns. Xu Dishan, who had studied Sanskrit extensively and later taught at Yenching University, had criticized Chinese Buddhist sutras for their frequent practice of retaining and even forging Sanskrit vocabulary, making the texts incomprehensible to Chinese audiences.[20] In contrast, all of his own contributions to Chinese hymnody were vernacular compositions. Zhang Yijing, editor-in-chief of *Zhen guang* (真光 *True Light*), also held that in addition to conveying the meaning of the original, a good hymn translation should have high literary value in Chinese—otherwise it would be a laughingstock to non-believers.[21]

It is worth noting that none of Yang, Liu, Xu, or Zhang ever emphasized mastery of the source language. For them, acquaintance with English was a prerequisite to translation but merited no special mention, especially when engaged in an indigenization project. In creating truly Chinese hymns for Chinese believers, literary faithfulness to the source text was apparently a secondary consideration. In fact, when we look at their translated texts, even those familiar with the hymns in both English and Chinese may find it difficult to recognize immediately the Chinese version as an adaptation of the English original because of the license in translation. The hymn translators themselves are very aware and frank about their approach, admitting that what they present may not be a literal

---

19 Yang Yinliu, "Shengge Tantao zhi Chubu," 聖歌探討之初步 [Preliminary Discussions on Hymns], *Shengge yu Shengyue*, No. 1, in *Zhenli yu Shengming*, Vol. 8, No. 1, (March 1934), 33–35, 34.

20 Xu Dishan, "What Kind of Religion Do We Want?" 我們要什麼樣的宗教? *Life Monthly* (Shengming Yuekan, 生命月刊), Vol 3. No. 9 (May 1923), 1–4.

21 Zhang Yijing, "Jinri jiaohui sichao zhi qushi" 今日教會思潮之趨勢 [Ideas for the Church Today], *The China Church Year Book* (中華基督教會年鑒), 1924(9), 22–23.

translation. This is clearly indicated in their published hymns. If the work is a reproduction or close to a reproduction of the original, the term "translated by" (譯) is included next to their names. If the hymn is to a large extent a paraphrase or retelling, then it is "narrated by" (述); a new composition is "written by" (著). Sometimes the demarcation between the first two is not so clear, since even in the "translated" versions, the translator may take liberties and insert verses not found in the English original. In the following paragraphs, I will give some examples and offer an analysis.

In Liu Tingfang's translation of "For the Beauty of the Earth," we can see that in the fourth stanza, "For the joy of human love" is rendered "benediction from our ancestors" (祖宗遺澤). The idea that one's ancestor can bless one from the afterlife is very Confucian and would probably not have been sanctioned were the translation project operated by missionaries, because of the "questionable" theology in elevating pagan ancestors of Chinese believers to some sort of biblical patriarch status. Yet this is precisely the theology of Liu, who is baptizing Chinese culture into Christianity to the point of honoring Chinese cultural heritage in a hymn, as if it had always been part of the Christian narrative.

He then goes one step further. In the fifth stanza of the 1864 hymn, the lines "For each perfect Gift of Thine/ To our race so freely given," are replaced by "The Chinese race is favored by God/ With grace abundant for five thousand years."[22] In his translation, Liu uses the word "di" (帝) for God, which is an epithet for the supreme deity that appears in the six Confucian classics. Although the translation of "God" as Di or Shangdi had been controversial since the time of Matteo Ricci, Liu does not hesitate to equate the Confucian-Daoist notion of a supreme heavenly ruler to the Christian God. This notion of God's universal manifestation of Godself including (if not especially) in Chinese culture and of God's special care for the Chinese people is a prominent feature in Liu's hymn translations, as well as his selection of hymns translated/written in Chinese by others.

Another hymn, "Fling out the Banner," has been freely reworked by Liu, as indicated by the designation "paraphrased." The 1848 English original expresses a missionary spirit in lines such as "heathen lands/ Shall see from far the glorious sight," while these have disappeared altogether in the Chinese version, which declares instead "millions look up at the majestic truth."[23] Liu avoids phrases

---

22 Lew Ting-fang (Liu Tingfang) "For the Beauty of the Earth," 270. (中華民族神所眷，五千年來受惠深，地上香花天上蕊，人尊美德帝垂恩。)

23 Liu Tingfang, paraphrased, "Fling out the Banner," (得勝歌), *Zijing* (紫晶, *Amethyst*), Vol. 6, No. 2, (June 1934), 278.

such as "heathen lands," since he believes that they are inappropriate for Chinese believers; it would not be very uplifting for them to realize that, in the missionaries' eyes, they are still living in a "heathen land." To retain the expression amounts to a painful reminder that Christianity remains a foreign religion and that Chinese could be alienated from their own people in their own land, simply by being Christian.

The same kind of approach to indigenization is shared by Shen Zigao (沈子高), a fellow member of the Compiling Committee for a Chinese Hymnal for Six Denominations and an Anglican Bishop. Shen published his paraphrase of Cecil Frances Alexander's "Jesus Calls Us o'er the Tumult" in *Amethyst*. He adopts the same type of domestication approach as Liu, using the Chinese literary expression "to subdue the demons" (降魔) in place of the original wording "from each idol that would keep us."[24] When Buddhism came to China, the Buddhist missionaries fashioned stories of the Buddha and his followers conquering local deities, which they called demons, turning them into Dharma protectors (護法). By employing the same phrase, Shen has produced a Christian version of the triumph of the True Way, one that Chinese people can readily recognize, understand, and accept: that is, subduing demons by renouncing worldly desires. In the final line of the verse, Jesus issues a command, "Christian, love me more." In the Chinese translation, Shen added the clause "and love your compatriots."[25] This is one of the traditional Confucian virtues, a radical rephrasing of "love your neighbor."

As is evident, when hymn translators rendered hymns from English to Chinese, they might use expressions borrowed from Buddhism or from classical Chinese literature. There are many such examples: again in Shen Zigao's paraphrase of "Jesus Calls Us o'er the Tumult," for example, he rewords the "wild, restless sea" as the "sea of suffering" (苦海),[26] a term traditionally used by Buddhists to express the concept of *dukkha* (pain, suffering). In Liu Tingfang's and Yang Yinliu's translation of Samuel Johnson's "Life of Ages, Richly Poured," the common word "pilgrim" is replaced by a typical Buddhist term "good men and devoted women" (善男信女, Sanskrit *kulaputra* and *kuladuhitri*). The phrase "wild war music" in "O Brother Man, Fold to Thy Heart Thy Brother" is rendered "sad war

---

24 The verse reads: Jesus calls us from the worship/of the vain world's golden store/from each idol that would keep us/saying, "Christian, love me more."

25 Shen Zigao, paraphrased, "Jesus Calls Us o'er the Tumult," (耶穌呼召歌), *Zijing* (紫晶, *Amethyst*), Vol. 6, No. 2, (June 1934), 279.

26 Shen, paraphrased, "Jesus Calls Us," 279.

tunes from a reed whistle" (戰樂悲笳). The reed whistle was an instrument frequently played in military camps in ancient China and evokes border skirmishes in early dynasties. We can even find direct quotation of a well-known phrase in the *Songshu* (宋書), "riding on strong wind from afar," (乘長風) in the Chinese version of "Fling out the Banner."[27] These hymns present an array of imagery found in Chinese classical literature.

Although the translators have intentionally "sinicized" hymns composed originally in English, this does not mean that they are endorsing a nationalistic or ethnocentric agenda, or hold a parochial rather than ecumenical vision. Instead, rather like their predecessors from the Church of the East in the Tang Dynasty,[28] they borrow freely from other spiritual traditions without necessarily compromising Christian doctrine. Besides, in the 1936 *Hymns of Universal Praise*, Liu and his colleagues have also selected and translated hymns from various countries such as Japan, Germany, Russia, and Ireland, to make the hymnal truly "universal."

3. The Anti-Christian Movement, Christian Socialism, and Hymn Translation

The indigenization endeavor achieved significant success in the first two decades of the twentieth century, which inspired and facilitated the process of Chinese hymnal compilation. At the first National Christian Conference (the Morrison Centenary Conference) in 1907, there was no Chinese delegation and no Chinese speakers. Only a few Chinese pastors were granted a "look-in and a listen-in." By the third Conference of 1922, however, thirty-eight out of the sixty-four council members were Chinese, including Cheng Jingyi (誠靜怡), the chairman himself.[29] Everything looked promising for the Christian Church in China.

---

27 Liu Ting-fang, paraphrased, "Fling out the Banner," (得勝歌), 278.

28 In fact, Liu and Yang have adopted the term "wondrous body in three persons" (三一妙身), 妙身 being originally a Chinese Buddhist description for the Buddha and Bodhisattva) used by the Church of the East in China for "trinity." See Liu Ting-fang and Yang Yinliu, trans., "Holy Holy Holy Lord God Almighty," (聖哉三一歌), *Zijing*, Vol. 4, No. 1, (January 1932), 78–79, later included in *Hymns of Universal Praise* (普天頌讚) (Shanghai: Christian Literature Society, 1936), No. 1.

29 See Frank Rawlinson, "The Chinese Christian Speaks for Himself," *Congregationalist*, 1923, Vol. 108(35), 289; and Fletcher Brockman, "The National Christian Conference in China," *International Review of Mission*, 1922, Vol. 11(4), 502–14.

However, the year 1922 also saw a surging Anti-Christian movement, which did not end until 1927 when the nation was plunged into civil war. The Anti-Christian movement began as a protest against the World Student Christian Federation (WSCF), scheduled to convene at Tsinghua University in April, 1922. One of the triggers for the Anti-Christian movement was the bilingual publication of *The Christian Occupation of China* (中華歸主) earlier that year by the "Special Committee on Survey and Occupation" of the China Continuation Committee. The poorly titled volume immediately provoked the suspicion that the goal of Christian missions was espionage for future military invasion. Christians in China were viewed by many as the "running dogs" of foreign powers and as traitors to their own country. Some radical leftists in Shanghai, using the language of Marxism,[30] published a "Manifesto of the Anti-Christian Student Federation," calling Christianity and the Christian church "devils" who support the property-holding classes and "loot and oppress" the proletariat.[31]

The Communist Party of China (CPC) was especially vocal in the Anti-Christian movement. In an article published in the CPC official newspaper *Xiangdao Zhoubao* (嚮導週報, *The Guide Weekly*), Grigori Naumovich Voitinsky, the Comintern representative, accused Christianity of being a tool of Western imperialists for oppressing the Chinese people, both economically and politically.[32] In 1925, the nation was appalled by the May Thirtieth Massacre in Shanghai's International Settlement. Chinese protesters attending a peaceful demonstration were calling for better working conditions and wages in the factories and mills, as well as a release of previously arrested workers and students, when the British Shanghai Municipal Police opened fire, killing nine and wounding many others. The Shanghai Executive Branch of the Guomindang soon published a declaration denouncing the atrocity, declaring that British Police brought "shame

---

30 Daniel Bays points out that although the campus branches of the Anti-Christian Student Federation were assisted by organizations with connections to the Chinese Communist Party, such as Socialist Youth League and The Young China Association, there was no national-level campaign, and that the actions of anti-Christian and anti-religion associations were largely uncoordinated. See Daniel H. Bays, *A New History of Christianity in China* (Chichester, West Sussex: John Wiley & Sons, 2012), 109.

31 For a more lengthy quotation of the Manifesto in English, see Tatsuro Yamamoto and Sumiko Yamamoto, "The Anti-Christian Movement in China, 1922–1927," *The Far Eastern Quarterly*, Vol. 12, No. 2 (Feb., 1953), 133–47, 144.

32 Wei Qin, "Diguozhuyi yu fanjidujiao yundong" 帝國主義與反基督教運動 [Imperialism and the Anti-Christian Movement], *Xiangdao Zhoubao* (嚮導週報, The Guide Weekly), 1925(98), 818–19. Wei Qin (魏琴) is the pen name of Grigori Naumovich Voitinsky.

on the Anglo-Saxons, who call themselves Christians and who value freedom and independence."[33] In the same vein, the CPC-led All-China Federation of Trade Unions demanded a condemnation session against Christianity on Christmas Day 1925, as part of a world revolution against imperialists.[34] The Communist Youth League of China labeled Chinese Christians forerunners of imperialists, who have nothing else on their mind except the "Christian occupation of China."[35]

Chinese Christians were not unfamiliar with such charges. While the Communist Party represented a more militant idea of atheist socialism, many leading figures in the Church in China were themselves not opposed to Socialism. Instead, they found common cause in Friedrich Engels's famous statement, "The history of early Christianity has notable points in common with the modern working-class movement. Like the latter, Christianity was originally a movement of oppressed people."[36]

Zhang Yijing, in a response to anti-Christian propaganda from the Communist Party, insisted that the Church, as a promoter of freedom and equality, has been always on the side of the workers against corrupt government and capitalists, and was therefore not a foe but a friend of the CPC.[37] In the aftermath of the May Thirtieth Massacre, the National Christian Council of China wrote a formal letter to the Shanghai Municipal Council demanding a fair investigation into the killing of innocent Chinese people.[38] The National Christian Council

33 "Zhongguo Guomindang Shanghai zhixinbu xuanyan Yi" (中國國民黨上海執行部宣言 （一） [Declaration of the Shanghai Executive Branch of the KMT, part 1] *Dongfang Zazhi* (東方雜誌, *The Eastern Miscellany*), Vol. 22, Special Supplement (July, 1925), 5. The declaration was made during the "First United Front" of the Guomindang and the CPC. Members of the Shanghai Executive Branch included Mao Zedong, Qu Qiubai and other prominent figures of the CPC.

34 "Fanjidujiao Xiaoxi" 反基督教消息 [News about the Anti-Christian Movement], *Gongren zhi lu* (工人之路, Way of the Workers), 1925(182), 3.

35 Zhong Wen, "Zhunbei fanjidujiao yundong zhou de gongzuo" 準備反基督教運動周的工作 [Get Ready for the Week of Anti-Christian Movement)], Zhongguo Qingnian Zhoukan 中國青年週刊 [The China Youth Weekly] 1927(6), 454–73. Zhong Wen (仲雯) is the pen name of Liu Changqun (劉昌群), one of the leading figures of the CYLC.

36 Friedrich Engels, "Contribution to the History of Primitive Christianity," in Karl Marx and Friedrich Engels, *On Religion* (New York: Schocken Books, 1964), 316–47, 316.

37 Zhang Yijing, "Piping Feijidujiao Xuesheng Tongmeng xuanyan," (批評非基督教學生同盟宣言, A Criticism of the Declaration of the Anti-Christian Student Alliance), *Minguo shiqi feijidujiao yundong zhongyao ziliao huibian*, 188–93.

38 David Z. T. Yui (余日章) and Edwin C. Lobenstine, "Zhonghua quanguo jidujiao xiejinhui zhi gongbuju han" (中華全國基督教協進會致工部局函, A Letter to Shanghai Municipal Council from the NCCC), *Dongfang Zazhi*, 19–20.

was established in 1922 by Yu Rizhang (David Z. T. Yui 余日章), Liu Ting-fang, and others to replace the China Continuation Committee, in an effort to promote self-governance of the Chinese Church. By publishing such statements, Chinese Christians were sending out a message that they aligned themselves with workers—against imperialists and capitalists.

This was not an expedient but a genuine stance, given the support for Christian Socialism within Chinese Christianity in the Republican Era. Christian Socialism was proposed in the UK in the mid-nineteenth century by F. D. Maurice, and promoted by such eminent figures in the Anglican Church as Charles Kingsley.[39] It was still very active in the UK and the US in the first decades of the twentieth century, at the time of the anti-Christian movement.[40] China had entered the Industrial Age at the end of the nineteenth century, and for China to become a modern and prosperous nation was a shared aspiration during the Republican era. An ever-growing working class, that started to encounter poor working conditions and low wages like their counterparts in the UK and the US, drew the attention of Chinese Christians and foreign missionaries. As a direct response to accusations from the anti-Christian movement that Christianity was aiding imperialists and capitalists, the third National Christian Conference in 1922 called for the setting up of standards for industrial labor, including stipulations on the employment of children, reduced working hours, and the installation of safety devices. Liu Tingfang was one of the signatories to this proposal.[41] Similar moves were being made by the YMCA and the YWCA in China, which saw evil in the industrial system as an obstacle to establishing the Kingdom of God on earth.[42] An editorial article in the *Chinese Recorder*

---

39 For the nineteenth-century leading figures and campaigns of the movement, see Jeremy Morris, *F. D. Maurice and the Crisis of Christian Authority* (Oxford: Oxford University Press, 2005); Colwyn E. Vulliamy, *Charles Kinsley and Christian Socialism*, second reprint (Westminster: the Fabian Society, 1935); C. Masterman, *John Malcolm Ludlow: The Builder of Christian Socialism* (Cambridge: Cambridge University Press, 1963); and Mauritz Kaufmann, *Christian Socialism* (London: Kegan Paul, 1888).

40 For Christian socialism in the US around that time, see John Spargo, "Christian Socialism in America," *American Journal of Sociology*, Vol. 15, No. 1 (Jul., 1909), 16–20; and Robert T. Handy, "Christian Socialism in America, 1900–1920," *Church History*, Vol. 21, No. 1 (Mar., 1952), 39–54.

41 "Some Other Important Resolutions," *The Chinese Recorder*, Vol. LIII No. 6 (1922) 432–34.

42 Zung Wei Tsung, "The Chinese Church and the New Industrial System," *The Chinese Recorder*, Vol. LIII No. 3 (March 1922) 186–90. For an overview of the YWCA's endeavor to improve the labor conditions for women during the Republican Era, see Zhao Xiaoyang

praised the Industrial Christian Fellowship for its admirable work in resolving to protect employees and its disapproval of luxury production.[43] One foreign missionary, in a naively idealistic manner, even claimed "the most advanced form of communism" was during the time of Jesus, and that now was a great opportunity for the Chinese to establish a "real Christian Commonwealth" on earth.[44]

One prominent thinker at the time was Harry F. Ward, a leading figure of Christian Socialism and the chief drafter of the 1908–1912 Social Creed, which was proposed by the Methodist Episcopal Church in the US, and later widely accepted by many other denominations. This creed became a symbol for the Church's social service in ameliorating the ills of the Industrial Age. It demanded "higher wages, one day a week to rest, and the adoption of protective legislation aimed at women and children as well as workers in general."[45] All of these measures were adopted by the third National Christian Conference. In 1925, Liu invited Ward to give lectures in China, an event celebrated by faculty and students at Yenching University.[46] One of his lectures was boldly entitled "What

---

(趙曉阳), "Jidujiaohui yu laogong wenti: yi Shanghai Nüqingnianhui nügong yexiao wei zhongxin," 基督教會與勞工問題： 以上海基督教女青年會女工夜校為中心 [The Christian Church and Labor Issues: Centered on the YWCA Night Schools for Women Laborers] in Tao Feiya (陶飛亞), ed., *Xingbie yu Lishi: Jindai Zhongguo Funü yu Jidujiao* 性別與歷史： 中國婦女與基督教 [Gender and History: Modern Chinese Women and Christianity) (Shanghai: Shanghai People's Press, 2006), 183–209. For that of men, see Zhao Xiaoyang, "Fuyin yu shehui de qihe: yi Zhongguo jidujiao qingnianhui yu laogong wenti weili" 福音與社會的契合： 以中國基督教青年會與勞工問題為例 [The Bridging of Gospel and Society: a Case Study of the YMCA and Labor Issues], *Minguo Yanjiu* (民國研究, Studies on Republican China), 2009(1), 38–50 and Jun Xing, *Baptized in the Fire of Revolution: the American Social Gospel and the YMCA in China, 1919–1937* (Bethlehem: Lehigh University Press, 1996).

43 "Editorial: The Christian Spirit Wakes Progress," *The Chinese Recorder*, 557–62.

44 F. E. A. Shepherd, "The Appeal of the Modern Mind to China," *The Chinese Recorder*, 465–71.

45 Doug Rossinow, "The Radicalization of the Social Gospel: Harry F. Ward and the Search for a New Social Order. 1898–1936," *Religion and American Culture: A Journal of Interpretation*, vol. 15, No. 1 (Winter 2005), 63–106, 69.

46 Ward was introduced in Chinese newspapers, and some of his works were translated into Chinese. See, e.g., Jian Youwen, "The Personal Struggles of Dr. Ward" 華德教授奮鬥小史 *Chenbao Fukan* (晨報副刊, *Supplement to the Morning News*), 1925 (56), 2–4; Harry F. Ward, "The Place of Religion in Social Reconstruction" (社會改造中的宗教地位), trans. Jian Youwen, *Chenbao Fukan* 1925 (87), 1–7. Jian Youwen (簡又文) was Liu's colleague at the School of Theology, Yenching University. He was deeply sympathetic to Soviet Communism, and used a penname Dahualieshi (大華烈士), a transliteration of the Russian word товарищ, comrade.

May Be Expected from Communism" (although this was canceled, since a college chancellor did not wish his students to be radicalized by Communist ideas.) In his numerous talks, Ward constantly "challenged the country's intellectuals to avoid the mistakes of their Western counterparts and stay in touch with the workers."[47]

Under the influence of Ward, Liu Tingfang and others wholeheartedly embraced Christian Socialism. Liu promoted the cause, declaring, "in recent decades, many Christian scholars and faithful ministers have devoted themselves to studying the Bible, and realized that Christ is more than just a personal savior, and that salvation is not just about the otherworld." Rather, Christ was especially concerned with the well-being of working people in their life on earth. This is why many Christian scholars and ministers had written books and given talks on Christian Socialism. Moreover, "the Church, after inquiries into the social reality as well as careful reading of the Bible, has gradually come to accept Christian Socialist doctrines."[48]

Naturally, misgivings about a booming Industrial Age and a thriving Christian Socialism had a significant impact on the translation project of hymns into Chinese, as three hymns translated by Liu Tingfang and Yang Yinliu in Vol. 8, No. 1 of *Amethyst*, 1935, show clearly. The first one is "My Master was a Worker," rendered "Song of a Worker Comrade" (勞動同志歌) in Chinese.[49] The English original was written by William George Tarrant, a Unitarian clergyman. His emphasis on the humanity of Jesus, which is the core of Unitarian theology, finds its counterpart in Liu's Christian Socialism. Jesus, rather than an entirely divine and detached figure, has joined the workers, thus sanctifying the act of labor and the fraternity of humanity. By praising the virtue of labor and through dedication to their work, believers, suggests Tarrant, are doing the Lord's work and will thus receive his blessings.

The second hymn is "Jesus, Thou Divine Companion." In the Chinese version, Liu Tingfang and Yang Yinliu have intentionally employed terms such as "comrade" for the original "companion," and "working class" for "workers," to add a more Socialist flavor. "You have taught us toil is good" is upgraded to "all labor is

---

47 David Nelson Duke, *In the Trenches with Jesus and Marx: Harry F. Ward and the Struggle for Social Justice* (Tuscaloosa, Alabama: The University of Alabama Press, 2003), 216.

48 Liu Tingfang, "Editorial for the National Christian Conference," *Shengming Zhoukan* [Life Weekly], Vol. 2, No. 3, 1921, 1–4.

49 Liu Tingfang, trans., "My Master was a Worker" 勞動同志歌, *Zijing*, Vol. 8, No. 1, (1935), 83.

sacred," while the more devotional expression "ev'ry task, however humble/ Fills the soul with grace anew" is transformed into "however ordinary the work is, it makes the worker free."[50] It sounds as if work, sanctified by Jesus, now has salvific value. This freedom is not directly given from above but achieved through the labor produced by the ever-expanding community of workers in an Industrial Age.

A third example is "When through the Whirl of Wheels," originally written by Geoffrey Studdert Kennedy, a Christian Socialist and army chaplain during World War I. He wrote this hymn especially for the Industrial Christian Fellowship.[51] In it, Studdert Kennedy praises labor in the Industrial Age as splendid and glorious, so that by patient toil, the workers are ushering in the Second Coming of Christ. This hymn matches Liu's Christian Socialist ideas perfectly, presumably why he decided to translate this piece and to render the title even more universal: "The Worker's Song."[52] Liu's translation is quite faithful, although he adds "in factories all over the globe" to "the furnace fires aflaring" to present a worldwide picture of industrialization. Now the line sounds more inclusive, and Chinese workers would undoubtedly see themselves in it. What is more, the image is now global instead of regional, befitting the international spirit that Liu sees in Christian Socialism.

The importance of labor is evident in all three hymns. In others, it is yet more explicit that the Kingdom of God will come into this world through good work. In the original version of "O brother Man, Fold to Thy Heart," the "holy work" of Jesus lies precisely in "doing good," so that "the wide earth seems our father's temple." This fits in well with Liu and Yang's inclination toward the Social Gospel, where the translation becomes an even more assertive: "the wide earth will be turned into the Father's temple"[53]—not as a mere resemblance, but as an imminent reality. Similarly, in "Little Drops of Water," the original lines "little deeds of kindness/ little words of love/ make out earth an Eden/ like the heav'ns above" is rendered more radically as "little deeds of kindness/ little words of love/ can

---

50 Liu Tingfang and Yang Yinliu, trans., "Jesus, Thou Divine Companion" 神聖同志歌, *Zijing*, Vol. 8, No. 1, (1935), 84. The translation is reprinted in *Zijing*, Vol. 8, No. 2 (1935), 280.

51 For a more detailed background of Kennedy's composition of the hymn, see Raymond F. Glover, *The Hymnal 1982 Companion: Essays on Church Music*, Vol. 1. (New York: The Church Hymnal Corporation, 1990), 498.

52 Liu Tingfang, trans. "When Through the Whirl of Wheels" 勞工歌, *Zijing*, Vol. 8, No. 1, (1935), 85.

53 Liu Tingfang and Yang Yinliu, trans., "O Brother Man, Fold to Thy Heart," (愛人歌), *Zijing*, Vol. 6, No. 2, (1934), 280.

improve the world/ and make it the home of the Heavenly Father."[54] Instead of an idyllic scene, the hymn promises a literal Heaven on earth made possible by social improvement. In the same vein, "Fling out the Banner" connects the words "our only hope, the Crucified" to "our hope is ahead of us: the glorious Kingdom of Heaven established in this world."[55]

This kind of "religious Utopia"[56] reflects Liu's conviction—in line with many other theologians of the era—that Christ had come into the world to set up himself as the perfect example of a worker, that organized labor promoted fellowship among workers, and that the goal of Christian mission was to reconstruct society to bring justice and equality for all, thus establishing the Kingdom of God on earth. In the face of anti-Christian sentiment, hymn translation served as a counter measure, where translators could prove that Christians were not "running dogs of imperialists and capitalists" but members of the proletariat, toiling along with the rest of the working class and striving for the improvement of the society for all. Class differences and clashes are acknowledged, but instead of the proletariat overthrowing the capitalist in a violent revolution, Christian Socialists called for brotherly love through gradual social reform and reconstruction.

All of these hymn translations by Liu Tingfang and his colleagues expressing Christian Socialist ideas were published in the 1936 hymnal *Hymns of Universal Praise*. Most of them were later rejected by the editors of the 1983 hymnal.[57] By that time, Christian Socialism had passed its heyday in Europe and the US— and this alternative, early twentieth-century version of socialism would almost certainly be regarded as heterodox in a country that now upholds "Scientific Socialism."

---

54 Liu Tingfang and Yang Yinliu, trans., "Little Drops of Water," (小小水滴歌), *Zijing*, Vol. 8, No. 1, (1935), 87.

55 Liu Tingfang, paraphrased, "Fling out the Banner," 278.

56 Wu Chang Shing (吳昶興), *Christian Education in China: A Case of Timothy Tingfang Liu (1891–1947)*: 基督教教育在中國：劉廷芳宗教教育理念在中國的實踐, (Hong Kong: Chinese Baptist Press (International) Limited, 2005), 236.

57 "My Master was a Worker," "Jesus, Thou Divine Companion," "When Through the Whirl of Wheels," and "Fling out the Banner" are deleted from the 1983 edition. Two hymns, "O Brother Man, Fold to Thy Heart" and "Little Drops of Water," do not touch on labor issues and talks of improving the society, and are kept. See Union Hymnal Committee, ed., *Hymns of Universal Praise*, No. 226, 253–62, 465; Hymnal Committee, ed., *New Hymnal* (新編讚美詩) (Shanghai: National TSPM and CCC, 1983), No. 357, 360.

Conclusion

Rev. Chauncey Goodrich, one of the preeminent Bible translators into the Chinese language, once envisioned a first-rate hymnal book for the Chinese people where "Hymns and tunes heaven-mated, and with a rhythmic movement and melody having in them a pulse of life, and adapted to strike the different heart chords will be sung and loved in China."[58] Though he did not live to see the translation projects of Liu Tingfang and his colleagues or the publication of *Hymns of Universal Praise*, Goodrich's words may serve as an appropriate description for hymns in Chinese in the 1920s and '30s. Those hymns, translated, paraphrased, or even freely re-versified, reflected the hymnodists' concern to make the Christian hymns truly Chinese, and truly relevant for the times. Their indigenization efforts and commitment to Christian Socialism helped to create a positive image for Christianity in China and may still serve as an inspiration today.

---

58 Chauncey Goodrich, "Service of Song in China," 399.

Part II

Wartime Theologizing

Chapter 5

SEARCHING FOR THE TRUE MEANING OF RECONCILIATION

Understanding Wu Yaozong's Pacifism and Zhao Zichen's Prison Experience

Qu Li 璩理, *Hong Kong Baptist University*[1]

In his early years, Wu Yaozong (Y. T. Wu), one of the twentieth-century leaders of the Chinese Christian church, was a believer in Christian pacifism and a member of the Fellowship of Reconciliation (*Wei ai she* 唯愛社[2]). After the Mukden and the January 28 incidents in the 1930s,[3] Wu began to distance himself from pacifism and ultimately stepped down from his position as president of the Fellowship of Reconciliation in 1937. After the breakout of the Pacific War in 1941, theologian Zhao Zichen (T. C. Chao) was imprisoned by the Japanese military for 193 days and subsequently wrote *My Experience in Prison*, a record of, and theological reflection on, his life in prison, for which Wu wrote a preface. This chapter examines the theological background to Wu and Zhao's thinking on reconciliation in a time of great change and the implications of their thought for Sino-Japanese relations today.

---

1 Translated from Chinese by Bin Xia.

2 Ed. note: the Chinese name of the Fellowship, *Wei ai she*, means society of "love alone" or "solely through love."

3 Ed. note: the Mukden Incident of September 18, 1931, an explosion by railway tracks near Mukden (present-day Shenyang) probably contrived by Japanese troops, led to the Japanese invasion and occupation of Manchuria and the puppet government of Manchukuo; the January 28 Incident (or Shanghai War of 1932) was a five-week war between Japanese and Chinese forces that left thousands dead, provoked by skirmishes between ultra-nationalist Japanese monks and Chinese protestors in the Shanghai International Settlement.

Wu Yaozong's Shift of Opinion on Pacificism

In August 1914, one month after the outbreak of World War I, Henry Hodgkin, a British Quaker, and Friedrich Siegmund-Schultze, a German Lutheran, two Christians from belligerent nations and different denominations who were attending a Christian pacifist conference in Germany, came to a resolution to unite in Christ and refuse to make enemies of each other. The Fellowship of Reconciliation (FoR) was established in Cambridge, England, the following year. The first principle of the 1914 Basis of the FoR was:

> That love as revealed and interpreted in the life and death of Jesus Christ, involves more than we have yet seen, that is the only power by which evil can be overcome and the only sufficient basis of human society.[4]

The key biblical foundation for the Fellowship was from the Sermon on the Mount, Matthew 5:43–44: "You have heard that it was said, 'You shall love your neighbor and hate your enemy.' But I say to you, Love your enemies and pray for those who persecute you." Rev. Henry Hodgkin, one of the founders of the FoR, had been a missionary to Sichuan, China, and introduced the idea of pacifism to China during a return visit in 1920.

In 1917, Wu Yaozong read the three chapters of the Sermon on the Mount at a YMCA bible study. Deeply moved, he decided to believe in Jesus. Wu retained a vivid recollection of this experience, writing in "My Personal Religious Experience" in 1923:

> My heart was freed! My joy was full! I could not help but wave my hands and dance with my feet. I could not read any more! At this moment, a strong impression came into my mind—it was Jesus. How powerful his word is! Truly he is a person who has found the secret of life, the meaning of the universe, and the solution to all of my problems. What more could I say? I could only prostrate myself and submit to him.[5]

---

4 "The FoR (Fellowship of Reconciliation) Basis," retrieved November 22, 2017, from https://web.archive.org/web/20070720154446/http://www.for.org.uk/about/basis.

5 Wu Yaozong, "Wo geren de zongjiao jingyan" 我個人的宗教經驗 [My personal religious experience], in *Wu Yaozong quanji (Di yi juan)* [吳耀宗全集（第一卷）[*The Collected Works of Y. T. Wu, Vol. 1*], (Hong Kong: The Chinese University of Hong Kong Press, 2015), 94.

In 1918 Wu Yaozong was baptized and became a Christian, and in 1920 he left a hard-earned and well-paid position working for the Customs and joined the Beijing YMCA. Wu's family was not rich; to leave a stable job because of religious faith was a difficult decision for Wu and his family, and was naturally strongly opposed by his family. Wu's choice would have been unfathomable had it not come from noble ideals or faith. At the time, Wu's visionary ideals could be summarized in the slogan, "Character saves the nation (人格救國)." This held that the inspiring power of the noble personality of Jesus could reform the national character of the Chinese people, and China could be thoroughly transformed as a nation. In terms of a distinction between goals and means, to save the nation was evidently the goal, and Christian faith and character reform were the means. As Ka-lun Leung has suggested, this kind of clear confession of the social gospel "bears strong overtones of pragmatism and utilitarianism."[6]

Wu believed the pacifist thought of the Fellowship of Reconciliation, based in the Sermon on the Mount, was highly compatible with his ideals of "saving the nation through character," and so joined the FoR in October 1921 and began to prepare for the launch of a local chapter of it in China. In 1922, *Wei ai she*, the Chinese chapter of the FoR was launched in Beijing, together with a periodical, *Wei ai* (*The China Fellowship of Reconciliation Bulletin and Newsletter*). From 1924 to 1927, while the Anti-Christian Movement was in full swing in China, Wu was studying in New York at Union Theological Seminary and Columbia University, and maintained links with the local chapter of the FoR. In 1929, Wu became the president of the *Wei ai she* and a major promoter of pacifism in China. In the first issue of *Wei ai* in 1931, Wu Yaozong summarized the principles of the Chinese chapter of the FoR as follows:

1. We are dedicated to ensuring that "the spirit of love" fills individual lives, eliminating the spirit of selfishness and fearfulness which causes quarrels, revenge, falsehood, and hatred.
2. Since false perceptions of life are rooted in all sorts of existing social institutions and systems, we cannot just reform existing institutions and systems but also need to create new institutions and new systems to implement "the spirit of love."

---

6 Ka-lun Leung, *Wu Yaozong: san lun* 吳耀宗三論, [Y. T. Wu's Understanding of Christianity and Its Relation to Chinese Communism], (Hong Kong: Alliance Bible Seminary, 1996), 12.

3. We should never take part in war, because we believe that wars can never solve problems. We condemn all violence that stems from the spirit of hatred and revenge.[7]

It is not hard for pacifism to attract believers and followers in peacetime. However, pacifism is more vulnerable to severe challenge in wartime, when it is frequently regarded as outworn dogmatism or foolish, empty talk. This world believes in a violent society! In retrospect, we can see how in Wu Yaozong's thought and practice the second principle above overwhelmed the third and eventually overcame the first, too.

The national crisis came to a head after the Mukden Incident in 1931, and pacifism in China faced a similar sort of test to when it was first introduced in Europe during World War I. Living in the tension between personal faith and collective crisis, Wu at first advocated for the former, but not long after the Mukden incident, he published "A letter to young patriots," in which he proposed four actions for the youth movement to work on: "First, no cooperation with the Japanese. Secondly, increase propaganda work among the masses. Thirdly, foster public opinion and apply appropriate means to hold the government accountable. Fourth, nurture a life of fellowship to find the right direction for personal life and for the nation."[8] All of these accord with the aims of pacifism, since pacifism is not about passively accepting reality but actively seeking change through the way of peace. As Wu asserted in 1930,

Pacifism is to love actively, to fight actively against evil forces, to fight actively for democracy. . . . Guns and swords are for killing, to eliminate and sacrifice the "bad people" in society. Pacifists believe that human nature has been shaped by environmental forces; there is no absolute good or evil. A pacifist uses the power of love to change the heart and the environment, and if necessary, will sacrifice themselves, not others. To love is life; those who use guns and swords have not understood love. Guns and swords lead humanity only to death and extinction. They may succeed for a while, but can never fully resolve the problems of human beings.[9]

____

7 Wu Yaozong, "Proposed beliefs and ideas of '*wei ai she*,'" *Wei ai* No. 1, 1932: 16–17.

8 Wu Yaozong, "A letter to young patriots," *Wu Yaozong quanji (di er juan)* 吳耀宗全集（第二卷）[The Complete Works of Y. T. Wu (Vol. 2)] (Hong Kong: The Chinese University of Hong Kong Press, 2015), 3.

9 Wu Yaozong, "The debate on pacifism," *Wu Yaozong quanji (di yi juan)*, 398–99.

However, as the war continued to expand and intensify, Wu became less and less confident of his pacifist position. When the January 28 Incident broke out in 1932, Wu Yaozong's house in Hongkou came under attack from Japanese artillery, and he had to take shelter with his family in the Baxian Qiao YMCA in the French Concession. Wu and his wife, Yang Sulan, went to the front line and took part in the campaign to boost morale, "Shanghai civilians for frontline troops." Although at the time Wu Yaozong still adhered intellectually to pacifism, emotionally, he approved of the use of violence against Japanese troops.

In the course of the past month, my feelings have not been so different from those of a non-pacifist. On the morning of the 29th, when I heard that Zhabei has not been occupied by the Japanese army and the 19th Route Army had resisted valiantly, I was overjoyed. The anger that I have been feeling in my chest for four months was finally released a little. From then on, like everyone else, I could not wait to read the latest news in the daily papers, and whenever there was news of victory for Chinese troops and defeat of the Japanese army, I would be so excited that daily life lost all propriety. I felt anger about the killings of innocent fellow citizens by the Japanese, but as for the hundreds and thousands of deaths of Japanese soldiers, I considered them deserved and felt no sympathy. I only hoped that China would continue to resist and fight to the end. Victory was of course best, but even if we were defeated for a time, I believed that we would have the final victory.[10]

In 1933, after the Japanese occupied the three Northeastern provinces, Wu Yaozong believed that the situation left no other choice but resistance. During this period he was in touch with Li Gongpu, Zou Taofen, and other patriots. Wu's thinking and feelings were changing, and he started gradually to embrace communism. In an article entitled "Pacifism and Social Transformation" in 1934, Wu compared pacifism and communism from three aspects, writing that: first, communism only upholds collective value, and individual value is subject to sacrifice for the sake of collective value, while pacifism supports individual value in all circumstances. Secondly, communism would eliminate "antisocial" individuals, while pacifism believes that transgressors have the capacity to reform.

---

10 Wu Yaozong, "The Shanghai Incident and the ideas of pacifism," *Wei ai*, No. 4 (1932), 2. See Derong Shen, "Wu Yaozong yu wei ai zhuyi" [吳耀宗與唯愛主義 Wu Yaozong and pacifism], *Tian Feng*, Issue 9 (1989).

Thirdly, communism is not selective about means in achieving its goals: if the cause is just, violence and killing are deemed necessary and legitimate. Pacifism meanwhile considers both ends and means. If goals are attained through violence, extra effort should be taken to restrain the consequences of the means.[11] Wu's pacifist position had, however, been shaken and considerably weakened. Violence is not an ideal means, but if violence can better achieve the aims, should it be used? As Ng Lee Ming holds: "If violence can deliver the results we desire, if it can achieve the transformation of society, we can adopt violence as a means to the end."[12] So far, the lofty nature of the aims has prevailed over the legitimacy of the means.

In 1935, Wu Yaozong joined successively the National Salvation Society (*Jiuguo hui*, 救國會) organized by Soong Ching-ling, the Society of National Crisis Education (*Guonan jiaoyu she*, 國難教育社) founded by Tao Xingzhi, and other patriotic organizations for national salvation. In December 1936, Wu was invited to speak in the United States and stayed for five months. He now felt that pacifism could not save China and in February 1937 wrote a letter of resignation from the presidency of the Chinese chapter of the Fellowship of Reconciliation, marking his departure from pacifism. The Marco Polo Bridge (or Lugou Bridge) Incident and the breakout of the Second Sino-Japanese War in July 1937 led Wu to further distance himself from his original mindset, and the rupture with the past was as disruptive and callous as "the autumn wind sweeping away the withered leaves," to the point where, in 1948, he denounced pacifism as "fantasy."[13] In 1950, Wu even stated, in rhetoric typical of political textbooks in Mainland China, "I know that pacifism is merely a kind of propaganda used by imperialists to anaesthetize oppressed and invaded peoples."[14]

In 1945 after the Second Sino-Japanese war came to an end, the national crisis abated but civil war resumed. For Chinese people, the Second Sino-Japanese War

---

11 Wu Yaozong, "Pacifism and social transformation," in *Social Gospel* (Shanghai: YMCA Press, 1934), 105–07; see Ambrose L. Y. Tse, *Wei qu qiu quan? Wu Yaozong de shengping yu jiuguo qinghuai* 委曲求全？吳耀宗的生平與救國情懷 [Tolerance for the Sake of Survival? Christianity, China's Reconstruction and Y. T. Wu], (Hong Kong: Logos Ministries Ltd., 1995), 80–81.

12 Ng Lee Ming, *Jidujiao yu Zhongguo shehui bianqian* [基督教與中國社會變遷 Christianity and social change in China], (Hong Kong: Chinese Christian Literature Council Limited, 1981), 109.

13 Wu Yaozong, "Christian thought in the last thirty years," in *Heian yu guangming* 黑暗與光明 [Darkness and light], (Shanghai: YMCA Press, 1949), 197.

14 Wu Yaozong, "How the Communist Party has educated me," in *Tian Feng*, No. 271 (1951), 6.

and the Chinese Civil War were wars of two completely different natures. At the beginning, Wu Yaozong believed that the reality was that neither Nationalists nor the Communists could each defeat the other, and therefore placed his hope on a third power beyond these two, hoping for a reconciliation between the two parties so that China could travel the road to real democracy.[15] In that historic moment, there was space for Wu Yaozong to reinstate the banner of pacifism and call for the end of civil war between the Communists and the Nationalists. But he had abandoned pacifism completely as a belief and turned to embrace the violent revolution advocated by the Communists. As the situation of the Guomindang Party deteriorated rapidly, Wu's thinking was moving closer to the Left. On the eve of the establishment of the Peoples' Republic, Wu wrote,

> When we object to the revolutionary means of revolution that others use to transform society, but fail to provide a better solution ourselves, we are actually advocating maintaining the status quo; that is to say, we are advocating the various types of visible and invisible violence that already exist in contemporary society and continue to cause suffering among the people. We may preach absolute love, but we are not living out absolute love. We are not even living out reciprocal love, since reciprocal love is fair and reasonable, and does not prevent the pursuit of ultimate goals through provisional means.[16]

If we allow for the use of violence to save the nation during the Second Sino-Japanese War, then could transforming an "unequal and unfair social system" be a sufficient reason for the use of violence during the Chinese Civil War? Who decides if a social system is fair or not? How unfair must it be before the system should be overturned by violence? When should the use of violence stop? Who is privileged to use violence? Against what range of targets can it be used? If these questions cannot be answered clearly, is "maintaining the status quo" necessarily more dangerous than using violence?

---

15 See Fuk-tsang Ying, "'Love the country' and 'love the church:' Wu Yaozong's understanding of the relationship between church and state before and after the founding of the People's Republic of China," in *Da shidai de zongjiao xinyang: Wu Yaozong yu ershi shiji Zhongguo jidujiao* 大時代的宗教信仰：吳耀宗與二十世紀中國基督教 [Abiding Faith for a Nation in Crisis: Y. T. Wu and Twentieth-Century Chinese Christianity] (Hong Kong: Christian Study Centre on Chinese Religion & Culture, 2011), 472–75.

16 Wu Yaozong, "Christianity under the People's Democratic Dictatorship (Part II)," *Tian Feng*, No. 177 (1949), 3.

The question is not whether it is right to use violence to stop violence, but why use violence? Is it used to protect the interests of a country and a nation under threat? Is it used to change an unfair social system? Or for justice, or even for "love"? We have seen how Wu's pacifist position shifted along with the changing social and historical situation, and gradually became more flexible. He started as a pacifist who had advocated saving the nation through strength of character, but his pacifism finally gave way to violent reform of the social system[17]—the roots remained his personal theological background.

Wu's conversion was inspired by the Sermon on the Mount, and the core of his belief lay in the Sermon on the Mount, but he had taken an axe to the theological content of its teaching. "The incarnation, the Virgin birth, resurrection, the Trinity, the Last Judgment, Jesus' second coming—these are ridiculous and bizarre, and are implausible doctrines. . . . I do not think my religious faith will change at all if I do not believe them."[18] But if Christians do not believe these things, what is left of their faith? Can what remains still be called Christian faith? A Sermon on the Mount stripped of divinity is reduced to a set of secular moral codes. Although according to secular moral principles, pacifism is a *good* set of moral codes because feelings change with circumstances when times and the world change, it is not difficult to find suitable reasons to abandon a pacifist standpoint.

In 1952, as Wu Yaozong recalled his former pacifist beliefs, he said, "Thirty years ago, I was an enthusiastic pacifist. I misunderstood Jesus's teaching, and took 'love your enemies' to mean loving without boundaries and non-resistance without principles, and I failed to recognize Jesus's patriotism, his hatred of evil, and his ruthless fight against the enemies of the people."[19] This is not just a misrepresentation of Jesus but also a misrepresentation of Wu's own past. As shown above, Wu's early pacificism was not a cowardly evasion; on the contrary, he had been fighting with love and peace in a most principled way. If it had truly been as unprincipled as he claimed at that point, then his initial upholding of pacifism over many years in extremely complex and difficult situations would have been somewhat ridiculous.

---

17 Yao Xiyi (Kevin Xiyi Yao) concludes that Wu Yaozong's shift of opinion on pacifism was "from radical pacifism to moderate pacifism, then to abandon pacifism." See Yao, "The Second Sino-Japanese War and pacifism," in *Zhonghua bense: jindai Zhongguo jiaohui shilun* [中華本色：近代中國教會史論 China's indigenization: essays on the history of Christianity in modern China], (Hong Kong: Alliance Bible Seminary, 2007), 206.

18 Wu Yaozong, "Christianity and materialism," *Darkness and Light*, 76.

19 Wu Yaozong, "On the building of a broader and stronger peace front," *People's Daily*, June 6, 1952, p. 3.

Zhao Zichen's Prison Experience

Zhao Zichen was five years older than Wu Yaozong and baptized ten years earlier. Zhao graduated from the missionary-founded Dongwu (Soochow) University in Suzhou in 1914 and continued his studies in the United States. In 1917, the year when Wu Yaozong felt the call and decided to believe, Zhao received his master's degree in sociology and his Bachelor of Divinity from Vanderbilt University, a Methodist university in Tennessee. By 1927, when Wu finished his theological education and returned from the United States, Zhao was already Dean of the School of Religion of Yenching University. In the history of Chinese theology, Wu's prestige cannot be compared with that of Zhao, yet Zhao's standpoint prior to the 1930s was very similar. Both held to a rationalist and humanist liberal theology, although Zhao's thinking and reasoning was a little more sophisticated and systematic.[20]

The Divinity School at Vanderbilt University put more stress on religious ethics than theology. It also emphasized discovering religious truth through a scientific spirit and interpreting basic Christian principles in the light of democracy.[21] These ideas profoundly shaped Zhao's early theological perspective. In 1920, he published "My Opinions on the Creed," in the apologetics journal *Life* (*Shengming* 生命) in response to the doubts his students raised regarding the Apostles' Creed. In the article Zhao affirmed the significance and value of the Apostles' Creed, but agreed that there were serious issues with the creed: "Firstly, there are some non-credal words in the Creed. Words like 'he suffered under Pontius Pilate, was crucified, died, and was buried' are about historical facts; they are not statements of faith.... Secondly, the Apostles' Creed contains some non-significant words like 'born of the virgin Mary' and 'the resurrection of the body.' How can these two be important doctrines?... Thirdly, the Apostles' Creed excludes many important doctrines. As I have noted, the Creed ought to express a cosmology and an outlook on life and society.... Fourthly, The Apostles' Creed is all about metaphysical theology, and says nothing on ethics and morality....

---

20 See Duan Qi, "A comparative study of Wu Yaozong and Zhao Zichen's responses to 'religion is not (is anti)-scientific,'" in *Da shidai de zongjiao xinyang*, 47–56.

21 See Ying Fuk-tsang, "Zhao Zichen's religious experience," e-version published by Christian Study Centre on Chinese Religion & Culture (http://www.csccrc.org/files/c%204.4%20 passage.pdf), p. 9. This section is omitted in the version published in *Zhao Zichen xiansheng jinian wenji* [赵紫宸先生纪念文集 Festschrift in memory of Mr. Zhao Zichen], (Beijing: China Religious Culture Publisher, 2005).

Fifthly, The Apostles' Creed completely leaves out Jesus' character, truly a significant omission."[22]

These were Zhao Zichen's deconstruction of the Creed; constructively, he drafted "a proposed creed:"

1. I believe in the ruler who created, manages and sustains all things (Gen. 1), the holy (Isaiah 6:3; 1 Peter 1:16), loving (1 John 4:8) heavenly father of humanity, who is also the standard for human morality (Mat. 5: 48).

2. I believe that through Jesus' sanctified birth (John 17: 19) and sacrificial love (Lk. 23: 33, 34), that is, his self-established character (Heb. 2: 9, 10, 17; 5: 8), he became God's only perfect son (John 3: 16), of one body with God, one glory, one age (John 1: 1, 14); sufficient to commend the moral character of God (John 14: 9) and the possibility of humanity (Heb. 2: 10, 11); he is teacher (Lk. 11: 1), friend (Jn. 15: 14, 15), elder brother (Heb. 2: 11) and saviour (Acts 4: 12; 1 Jn. 4: 14).

3. I believe in the Holy Spirit, that is, the spirit of God's Christ (Rom. 8: 8), who seeks us out (Luke 15), who wants us, through his love, to escape sin and evil (Mat. 1: 9, 21), to live in harmony with him (Rom. 5: 1. 5) . . .

4. I believe that all who share a heart and will with Christ, share in his life and death, his glory and humiliation, share in his labour (Phil. 3: 10–16) are all Christians, and that as Christ lives eternally, Christians will also have eternal life (1 John 5: 12).

5. I believe that through their spiritual friendship, Christians become a united church . . .

6. I believe that the Kingdom of Heaven is gradually realized in line with God's will (Mk. 4: 26, 28), that is, the realization of the good society of new humanity (2 Cor. 5: 17; Rev. 21: 1–2; Mat. 6: 10) . . .[23]

This is an outline of Zhao's belief in the 1920s, suffused with the science, reason, and morality of liberal theology. A Christology close to the heretical

---

22 Zhao Zichen, "My Opinion on the Creed," in *Zhao Zichen wen ji (Di san juan)* [赵紫宸文集（第三卷） The collected works of Zhao Zichen, Vol.3], (Beijing: The Commercial Press, 2007), 33–35.

23 Zhao Zichen, "My Opinion on the Creed," 38. Translation from Chloë Starr, "From Missionary Doctrine to Chinese Theology: Developing xin 信 in the Protestant Church and the Creeds of Zhao Zichen," in *From Trustworthiness to Secular Beliefs: Changing Concepts of Xin 信 from Traditional to Modern Chinese*, eds. Christian Meyer and Philip Clart (Leiden: Brill, 2022).

Adoptionism, a rejection of Jesus's divinity and his miracles, an emphasis on Jesus's character, and an approach to saving the nation and reforming society through the character transformation of Christians are all very close to Wu Yaozong's beliefs in the same period.

In the 1930s, while Wu Yaozong was drifting away from his pacifist position because of the escalation of the war, Zhao Zichen was emerging from what was for him the trap of liberal theology. His *Barth's Religious Thought* (巴德的宗教思想) written in 1928, was the first systematic introduction to Karl Barth's theology in Chinese. In 1932, Zhao had further exposure to the neo-orthodox theology while in Oxford, England. At the time he must have come across English theologians who were influenced by Barth and their works, since the English translations of Barth's *The Epistle to the Romans* and the first volume of his *Church Dogmatics* had not yet been published.[24]

Since Yenching University was an American Christian college, registered in the United States not Chongqing, it was able to continue its educational activities after the fall of Beiping (Beijing) and Tianjin (to the Japanese) in 1937. On December 8th, 1941, Japan launched a surprise attack on Pearl Harbor and the War in the Pacific broke out. Due to the enmity between Japan and the United States, Christian colleges and schools, hospitals, and other institutions across North China were shut down by the Japanese military. Yenching University faced a precarious situation: a few hours after the attack on Pearl Harbor, Japanese troops surrounded the campus. Eleven professors including Zhao Zichen, Zhang Dongsun, Lu Zhiwei, and Hong Weilian were arrested. Zhao would be imprisoned by Japanese soldiers until his release on June 18th, 1942 and spent in total 193 days in prison. *My Experience in Prison* (系獄記) is not technically a prison diary and was written down as a memoir after the end of the Second Sino-Japanese War in 1948. Researchers believe that the content of the book is

---

24 Concerning the time when Zhao Zichen started to be influenced by neo-orthodox theology, Wing-hung Lam suggests it was during Zhao's time at Oxford as a visiting scholar. See Wing-hung Lam, *Qu gao he gua: Zhao Zichen de shengping ji shenxue* 曲高和寡：趙紫宸的生平及神學 [Too highbrow to be popular: life and theology of T. C. Chao], (Hong Kong: China Graduate School of Theology, 1994), 214. Winfried Glüer argues that Barth's theological standing concerning grace alone only started to have a more profound impact on Zhao after 1937; until the end of 1938, Zhao Zichen's stance was liberal. See Winfried Glüer, *Zhao Zichen de shenxue sixiang* [趙紫宸的神學思想 Die Theologische Arbeit T. C. Chao], translated by Joe Dunn, (Hong Kong: Chinese Christian Literature Council Limited, 1998), 212, 230–31.

not only based on his experience in prison but also reflects his theological thinking in the late 1940s.[25]

The particular, tough experience of prison was an important religious experience in Zhao Zichen's life and helped bring a fundamental change in his theological thought. In the preface to *My Experience in Prison*, Wu Yaozong wrote,

> Brother Zichen was not defeated by sufferings; physical torture and mental torment rather caused him to stand more tenaciously and become a powerful witness to the truth of which he was deeply convinced. During his more than six months in prison, Zichen's faith has become more profound, transcendent, and purified. His genuine fellowship with God enabled him to receive more immediate and intimate revelations, like the prophets who were persecuted for righteousness's sake in ancient times. We give thanks for him, and we give thanks for the Christianity in China. Brother Zichen's witness, together with the witness of many other Christians in the War of Resistance, like that recorded in another book, *Baptism by Fire*, convince us of this: that Christianity has become rooted in China.[26]

On his imprisonment, Zhao went suddenly from comfortable faculty housing and freedom to the food and hygiene of a Japanese military prison, and his suffering can only be imagined. However, Zhao was not consumed by suffering, bitterness, or hatred. At the beginning, instead of complaining about the unfairness of his imprisonment and condemning the brutality of the prison officers like others who were newly jailed, Zhao repented deeply. He was not repenting for those who made him suffer but asking the world, including himself, to repent for the evil of war. "The world is soaked in evil, and I am part of the world, and specifically, part of China. I can only truly repent," he wrote.[27] Christmas Day fell less than three weeks after his imprisonment, and although distressed, he did not turn away from God or the sacrificial love of Jesus; he reflected on the origins of war and wrote a poem that set the tone for his reflection on human sin and God's salvation while in prison: "The world is tamed but the heart is not; greed and anger give rise to wars. On earth, brutes and demons

---

25 See Wing-hung Lam, *Qu gao he gua*, 261.

26 Wu Yaozong, "Preface," in *My Experience in Prison* (*Xiyu ji* 系獄記), see *Zhao Zichen wen ji (di er juan)*, 414.

27 Zhao Zichen, *My Experience in Prison*, 417.

are adored; in Heaven, sacrifice is prepared. You overcame sins and paid the price, took on flesh and gave up life. Alas, your suffering is great, at this thought my tears flow with abandon."[28]

The reason for the imprisonment of the Yenching professors may well be because John Leighton Stuart, the president of Yenching, visited the Nationalist Government in Chongqing many times before the outbreak of the War in the Pacific to promote "Sino-Japanese Cooperation." Yet none of the imprisoned Yenching faculty members engaged in any substantial anti-Japanese speech or action, and so all were later released, the last on the same day as Zhao. Interrogations were, however, inevitable in prison. When he was interrogated for the first time, Zhao merely expressed his regret and sorrow for the war and argued that he had never been involved in politics:

> Although I studied in the United States as a student, it has always been an important principle for me not to favor the United States in any way that might jeopardize my own country. My faith in Christ is a religious faith, not submission to a foreign regime. In terms of the Japanese occupation of Manchuria, I feel sorry for Japan, since because of what has happened, Sino-Japanese cooperation has become impossible. I feel even more perplexed by the Japanese advance on the interior of China—how can the two nations be friends after this? I have never been involved in politics and am dedicated to teaching and preaching the gospel. My love for my nation and my fellow citizens is not false, and my sympathy for the displacement of my fellow citizens is also real. As for my political opinions, I do not think I have the ability or knowledge to give a response to the Japanese. . . . If Japan withdraws its troops voluntarily and immediately, the Chinese people will not hold a grudge; there is room for negotiation in everything. Unfortunately, the Japanese troops have refused to withdraw; I fear that the future developments will be detrimental to both countries.[29]

Zhao sincerely hoped that the two countries, China and Japan, could be good neighbors and would not resort to war. In his deposition before his release, he mentioned that he went to Japan after the Great Kantō earthquake in 1923 as a

---

28 Zhao Zichen, *My Experience in Prison*, 420.
29 Zhao Zichen, *My Experience in Prison*, 422–23.

delegate sent by the Chinese church and took a large sum of funds to Yokohoma and Tokyo for relief work among the Christians affected by the disaster. At that time, he believed that China and Japan should coexist peacefully, but unfortunately "both sides got it wrong"[30] afterwards. When the Japanese military police gave him paper and pen and asked him to report his "feelings," Zhao used the metaphor of brothers to illustrate Sino-Japanese relations:

> Since ancient times, if lips perish, the teeth will be cold; why would brothers bitterly fight each other?

> For five years, the flames of war have been raging across the land; scholars from both countries sigh together.

> Can quarreling brothers resist invasion by outside enemies? They should know that usurping power breaks relationships.

> As a capped captive,[31] I worry about the whole country all day long. Even after pouring my heart out, I still have no peace of mind.[32]

When the Japanese soldiers asked about what was discussed in faculty meetings at Yenching, Zhao's answer was lighthearted: "Most Chinese scholars sit and pontificate, but only a few will stand up and do what they say; they hardly merit the attention of Japanese soldiers."[33] This was a sincere criticism of Chinese academia, but also served as an appropriate response to the Japanese soldiers: as a Christian, Zhao did not give false witness to deceive his neighbors.

When he was brought out from prison to court for the second time, Zhao Zichen took the chance to make some requests to the judge: to send a letter home asking his family to send a Bible to him in prison, to meet with his wife, and such. The judge acceded to his requests, and Zhao could write gladly:

> Yesterday I went to military court, the judge was rather amiable;

---

30 Zhao Zichen, *My Experience in Prison*, 487.

31 Trans. note: literally, a crown from the South (*nan guan*, 南冠), another word for captive. Zhao was planning to compile his poems from prison into a volume titled *Nan guan ji* (南冠集, Collected poems in captivity).

32 Zhao Zichen, *My Experience in Prison*, 428.

33 Zhao Zichen, *My Experience in Prison*, 423.

He permitted me to write letters home, to read the Bible,

Permitted me to meet with my poor wife, to share our distress and anger.[34]

However, none of his requests were fulfilled. These prison poems were written from memory after his release. Zhao could have left out these poems about unfulfilled promises, or written others to denounce the Japanese judge for not fulfilling the things that had been promised, but there are no such records in *My Experience in Prison*.

Zhao Zichen made no accusations against his enemies in his book, apart from documenting some excessive events, such as his own solitary confinement, an assault on Zhang Dongsun or the confiscation of Zhang's bedding for several days. He did record directly the more "civilized" actions of the Japanese, like giving therapeutic injections to prisoners who were troubled by lice and fleas, or sanitizing the cells. Zhao showed no jealousy toward those prisoners who had fewer responsibilities, who enjoyed a more favorable reception, or who were released earlier than him.[35] Zhao was imprisoned in December with another eleven Yenching professors, five of whom were released the following April and May. Zhao had no idea why they were released before him and merely commented, "The way Japanese do things has no evident rationality, and science and logic do not work either. I just pray, and give thanks to God for them and for myself. My heart has been purified and is clean. In a place where I have no money, no power, and nothing to rely on, I set my hope on God alone."[36] Zhao showed no repugnance toward those who were almost ubiquitously caricatured as *han-jian* (traitors) in later anti-Japanese literature and art, like Interpreter Zhao, even after Interpreter Zhao bragged in front of him that those Chinese who could speak Japanese were more "favored" than those who could speak English.[37]

In all of his writings recording half a year in prison, how could Zhao not complain to God or blame others, not exhibit self-righteousness or envy, or do anything shameful—and even pray for his enemies? Without great faith or love how could he have done this? Zhao's answer was "through Christ's love alone; his love can be fully trusted."[38] In another poem he wrote after being brought out

---

34 Zhao Zichen, *My Experience in Prison*, 455.

35 See Zhao Zichen, *My Experience in Prison*, 418–19.

36 Zhao Zichen, *My Experience in Prison*, 476.

37 See Zhao Zichen, *My Experience in Prison*, 425.

38 Zhao Zichen, *My Experience in Prison*, 476.

from prison to court for the second time, Zhao revealed the source of his faith and love:

> God has come in person, opening the eyes of the blind;
> heaven and earth are no longer as they were.
>
> The spirit of religion guides what I say, a life of love I live out every day.
>
> Sitting facing a barbarian gaoler from afar, I resolutely hold to the holy word with all my heart.
>
> The crown of thorns and wooden cross is with me always, a disciple inherits from the Master virtue and favor abundant.[39]

This is the forgiveness and reconciliation that Zhao Zichen demonstrated in his daily life in prison, through trusting and looking to God. Around the same time, he had a breakthrough in his theological thinking, a soteriology that he named *tong yi lun* (同一论) or "the union or identification theory."[40] During his imprisonment, Zhao Zichen remained unconvinced by traditional substitution theory. He thought the logic of substitution theory flawed, whereby a sinless Jesus replaces us sinners and dies, and from this we are no longer condemned by God.[41] Zhao went back to the Bible and reflected on Paul's teaching in Romans, which brought him to the conclusion that "It was not that he (Jesus) could die on our behalf, or receive punishment on our behalf, but that he opened a way in front of us that we can follow behind, until we enter eternal life. What he has done, we must do, and thus we will be united with him in death as well as in life.[42] At this point, "the union theory" was still in the shadow of the synergism that he had advocated in his 1926 book, *The Philosophy of Christianity* (基督教哲學), and evinced major differences with Barth's more Christocentric and more objective doctrine of reconciliation articulated in the fourth volume of his

---

39 Zhao Zichen, *My Experience in Prison*, 453.

40 Trans. note: on this terminology, c.f. Yongtao Chen, "T. C. Chao and Sheng Kung Hui," in *Christian Encounters with Chinese Culture: Essays on Anglican and Episcopal History in China*, edited by Philip L. Wickeri (Hong Kong: Hong Kong University Press, 2015), 179ff.

41 See Lin Hong-hsin 林鴻信, "A Salvation of Identification: Zhao Zichen's Chinese Indigenous Christology," in *Zhao Zichen xiansheng jinian wenji* [趙紫宸先生紀念文集 Festschrift in memory of Mr. Zhao Zichen], 83–85.

42 Zhao Zichen, *My Experience in Prison*, 448.

Church Dogmatics.[43] But the pre-existence, the transcendence, and the proactivity of Jesus Christ are sufficiently emphasized in Zhao's union theory, and he was already moving away from traditional liberal theology and drawing much closer to neo-orthodoxy. Another merit of Zhao's soteriology is that it eschewed the downside of Barth's objective soteriology, which necessarily leads in a mistaken universalist direction.[44] Zhao Zichen's proximity to neo-orthodoxy is also manifest in his reflection on the relationship between religion and moral ontology. "In the past I was convinced by religion based on scientific methodology and rationalism, but in reality I was practicing morality in the name of religion. Both became empty and failed to be truthful. Religion is not just living a moral life, but is the true liberty and freedom that people have when they accept Christ by faith and are reconciled with God. In this way, religion may become a reality and morality find its compass, and both will be complete."[45] Theology is the foundation for morality, not the other way around; theology cannot be regulated into a set of moral principles: which is a typical neo-orthodox (Barth) or even "old" orthodox (Luther, Calvin) understanding. As Wing-hung Lam put it, "The basic purport of Neo-orthodoxy is fully revealed in this."[46] After he was released from prison, and following several more years of arduous study and thinking, Zhao Zichen's theological thought was distilled into his *Life of St Paul* (聖保羅傳 1944) and *Four Lectures on Theology* (神學四講 1948), two exemplary works of Chinese neo-orthodox theology.

Reconciliation in Christ

During my time studying at the London School of Theology, I had a close classmate, Ruben Morris, who was from Israel. He served in the military and had the experience of killing on the battlefield. Morris said that it happened during a border patrol, when his unit of seven was ambushed. The chief of the unit was killed, and he killed two enemies in the counterattack. As he told me this

---

43   See Zhou Weichi, "Zhao Zichen's idea of salvation" in *Zhao Zichen xiansheng jinian wenji*, 142–44; Tang Xiaofeng, *Zhao Zichen shen xue si xiang yan jiu* [趙紫宸神學思想研究 Study of Zhao Zichen's Theological Thought] (Beijing: China Religious Culture Publisher, 2006), 136–37.

44   Does Barth's soteriology entail a conclusion of universalism? Barth only talks in vague terms during his lifetime, but scholars have not stopped debating this since his death, and there is an extensive literature on this topic.

45   Zhao Zichen, *My Experience in Prison*, 461.

46   Wing-hung Lam, *Qu gao he gua*, 233.

incident from years ago, he had a worried look on his face. I tried to comfort him by saying, "You were on a battlefield, so had to kill." He replied, "No, we went to the battlefield to fight, not to kill." It was a perfect illustration of the conflict between violence and pacifism. I am not an absolute pacifist and would sanction the use of violence under certain circumstances (including fighting back after attack, as a last resort when all peaceful means have been exhausted, under limited circumstances to stopping extremely inhumane actions, without adopting other inhumane or excessively violent means, not targeting non-military targets, ceasing when the offense ceases and justice is served, etc.). Because of the complexity of the real world, it is difficult to list exhaustively all conditions for the use of violence, but these conditions should all be strictly met before it is permissible to employ violence.

Wu Yaozong overcorrected when he gave up his pacifist position. When he realized that his standpoint was no longer tenable in the real world, he began to move from one extreme to the other and unconditionally to embrace violent means. He was not an opportunist but a person easily overwhelmed by circumstances. Whenever reality and his beliefs clashed, the former always won. Zhao Zichen was different from Wu, although he too could not always make his beliefs prevail. Zhao Zichen was never a pure pacifist and believed that China's position in the Anti-Japanese War could find support in Christianity,[47] while he had reservations about, and remained vigilant to, the use of violence in society.[48] Because of his position of differentiated, and limited, use of violence, Zhao Zichen both protected himself in prison and did no harm to his enemies. Zhao and Wu's differing positions on pacifism and violence were reflected in the different roles they played and modes of participation in the later Three-Self Patriotic Movement, an issue beyond the scope of this paper.

Living in an era of great change, both Wu and Zhao felt that "today is in the right, yesterday in the wrong," and they help us to see how different theologies shaped these two Christian leaders in different ways. Owing to its fundamental flaws, a humanist liberal theology failed in the real world to bring national reconciliation. True reconciliation can only come from a transcendent dimension, achieved through Jesus Christ in the world. The devastation to humanity of the war between China and Japan can hardly be overstated. However, after the end

---

47 See Zhao Zichen, "Christian faith in a new age," in *Jidujiao yu xin Zhongguo (xia bian)* 基督教與新中國（下編）[Christianity and New China (Part II)], (Shanghai: YMCA, 1940), 168.

48 See Glüer, *Zhao Zichen de shenxue sixiang*, 200–01.

of hostilities and once all post-war issues were settled (the most important ones being investigating war responsibility and collecting war reparations), will the wounds and hostility caused by the war remain forever? Based on the post-war history and current situation in China, the answer is yes: in the life-and-death violence of the Senkaku/ Diaoyu Islands disputes of 2012–13; in the verbal violence against Japan rife on the internet; in ubiquitous TV series about the Anti-Japanese War. If there is no transcendent being above and beyond humans, the offenders can justify themselves by distorting history, and the victims can fabricate history to continue fostering hatred. "Only when China forgives and Japan repents, will peace and justice be fully established in East Asia."[49] Without a fundamental reconciliation rooted in faith, the tragedy of history may yet repeat itself. People can always play the nationalist card; excuses for the unlimited use of violent means are never difficult to find. If God does not exist, everything is permitted; if there is no transcendent creator and sustainer of morality, all morality is relative.

---

49 Zhao Zichen, "Christian faith in a new age," 172.

Chapter 6

YU BIN AND VINCENT LEBBE'S THEOLOGY OF RESISTANCE

Catholic Participation in the Chinese War Effort Against Japan

Stephanie Wong, *Villanova University*

Throughout history Christians have wrestled with the question of how to pursue a just peace. When faced with an assault against one's people, is it appropriate for Christians to resist with arms? In the early modern period, many countries transformed from monarchies with established religious traditions into self-consciously secular nation-states, and thus Christians also had to reconsider the nature of the entity to be defended. If the Church were to support a defensive war effort, did the justification rest in protecting a Christian socio-ecclesial order, defending a secular sovereignty, promoting humanitarian ends out of Christian motivation, or some combination thereof?

During the Second Sino-Japanese War, several prominent leaders of the Catholic Church in China wrote on this subject, arguing that Catholics should join the fight against the invading Japanese Imperial Army. In particular, the bishop of Nanjing Paul Yu Bin 于斌 (1901–1978) and the priest and abbot Vincent Lebbe 雷鳴遠 (1887–1940) urged the Church not to adopt a pacifist approach in its desire for peace. First, though lamenting the horrors of violence, they argued that the Catholic community could and should join the resistance effort as a matter of justice. Second, rejecting any privatization of church affairs apart from socio-political ones, they drew on Christian history and the Chinese Catholic Bible to call the faithful to defend the Church and nation of China as an integrated whole.

Yu and Lebbe's theology of resistance is evident in open letters and public statements they issued during the war. Some of these writings were addressed to local Chinese Catholics. For instance, Bishop Yu Bin wrote "Be Prepared" (1937) and "Christian Patriotism" (1937) as pastoral letters to the Catholics of his vicariate. Other documents were intended for European audiences. Vincent Lebbe served as the ghostwriter for the Chinese bishops' "Joint Letter to the League of Nations" (1932)[1] and Yu Bin gave multiple speeches presenting the Chinese perspective on the war to European Catholics.[2] Finally, Lebbe's most extensive exposition of his case for why Chinese Catholics must keep fighting was issued to Catholics of the enemy nation. In his open letter "The Kingdom of God and its Justice: A Response to the Circular of Some Japanese Catholics Addressed by them to the Clergy and Faithful of China" (1938), Lebbe responds to a proposal from Japanese co-religionists, which he rejects as a premature settling for peace while injustices against the Chinese continued.[3] While foreign missionaries were typically more reserved, encouraging Catholics to express their patriotism in the Church's charitable works but remaining silent about arms,[4] Yu and Lebbe's essays consistently argue that Catholics should support the war effort by fighting.

Both of these clerics were themselves active in the war effort, and this made them much-wanted targets. The Japanese Imperial Army put out a $100,000

---

1 The Chinese Bishops, "Joint Letter to the League of Nations," in *The Voice of the Church in China*, 5–12.

2 Yu, *The Voice of the Church in China, 1931–1932, 1937–1938, With a Preface by Dom Pierre-Célestin Lou Ttseng-Tsiang*, edited by Marius Zanin, Auguste Haouisée, and Yu Pin (New York: Longmans, Green and Co, 1938); Yu, "Fructus Justitiae: Pax—Lettre de Son Excellence Mgr. Paul Yu Pin aux Catholiques d'Europe et d'Amérique," Speech given 24 June 1939 in Washington DC, printed by J. Duvelot in Gembloux, Belgium, in Fonds 7 July 1939, Fonds 1, A.47.1, 34, Archives Vincent Lebbe, Université catholique de Louvain, Louvain la Neuve, Belgium.

3 Lebbe, "Le Royaume de Dieu et sa justice : réponse à la circulaire de quelques Catholiques Japonais adressée par eux au Clergé et aux fidèles de Chine," (July 1939), in Fonds I, A.47.38b, 2.

4 For instance, see Marius Zanin (Apostolic Delegate to China), "Circular Letter to all the Ordinaries of China: 'Inter Arma Caritas,'" (31 October 1939), in *The Voice of the Church in China*, p. 23–26. An exception was Louis Janzen M.E.P. As the bishop of the frequently bombed wartime capital city of Chongqing, Jantzen wrote, "In the face of such scenes of horror, it is impossible to remain neutral, and I should consider it monstrous to be asked to keep my mouth shut," quoted in Jacques Leclercq, *Thunder in the Distance*, translated by George Lamb (New York: Sheed & Ward, 1958), 295.

reward for the capture of Yu[5] and $10,000 for the capture of Lebbe.[6] After all, their writings were no merely armchair reflection. Each was assisting the state and its military in concrete ways.

The bishop of Nanking, Yu Bin put his significant personal clout and international connections to work in raising support for the Chinese armed services. Domestically, he urged Church institutions to make their facilities available for troops in transit and care for refugees. After the Nationalist government relocated to Chongqing, he helped Lebbe to reestablish the Catholic paper *Yishibao* (which was initially founded in 1915 in Tianjin but had in the meantime fallen into financial and political scandal) in the wartime capital to print news for "free China."[7] Yu served as the head of the national labor corps and promoted fundraising campaigns to donate needed resources like airplanes and ambulances to the Chinese.[8] Yu was not the only Christian leader to undertake such efforts, but of the Catholics he was the most prominent. Internationally, he undertook a grueling speech campaign to raise funds to help the hundreds of thousands of Chinese refugees.

Meanwhile, the naturalized Chinese citizen and Catholic priest Vincent Lebbe served several roles on the front lines. He organized Catholic brothers, sisters, and other laity to serve as medics and stretcher-bearers; he served as an unarmed general in the Chinese Army over a Chinese Catholic guerilla unit; finally, he served directly under Generalissimo Chiang Kai-Shek as the leader of a propaganda and intelligence-gathering unit (the North China Battlefield Supervisory Corp 督導團)[9] tasked with rousing Catholic farmers to fight the Japanese in occupied parts of the North China plain.

While their activities were different—Yu fundraising in 'free China' and abroad in the West, and Lebbe accompanying the Chinese troops in the occupied

---

5 "A Mission for the Archbishop," *TIME Magazine* LXXVI.11 (September 12, 1960). According to Yu Delan of Xinde Faith Weekly, the bounty on Yu Bin's head was at some point raised to $200,000.

6 V. Lebbe to Adrien (Dom Bède) Lebbe, No. 153 (19 November 1938, Chongqing) in Goffart and Sohier, eds., *Lettres du Père Lebbe* (Tournai: Casterman, 1960), p. 303.

7 Andre Boland, "Notes de voyage en Chine" (February–May 1937), in Archives V. Lebbe, Fonds 1, A 46.1,8.

8 Yu Delan 于德蘭, "于斌主教抗戰時期對國家社會的貢獻" [Bishop Yu Bin's Contribution to State and Society during the War of Resistance Against Japan], *Xinde* 信德 [Faith Weekly] (11 September 2015), accessed 2 January 2021, https://www.xinde.org/show/32934.

9 The full title was "軍事委員會華北戰地督導民眾服務團" but Lebbe referred to it in shorthand just as "督導團."

North China—both believed that geopolitical justice was an integral part of the work of the Kingdom of God.

Historical and Intellectual Context

To understand Yu and Lebbe's perspective, it is important to note how their time was shaped by repeated conflicts born of foreign imperialism. Both were men of transnational experience who observed upheaval in both Europe and China. They felt the Church must carefully navigate a world in which the *ancien régimes* were passing away, and they embraced the modern zeitgeist that rejected empire in favor of the ideals of independent nationhood. It is not surprising, then, that they looked for cases of foreign oppression and national deliverance in history and Scripture to support a Christian ethic of defensive war.

The older of the two, Vincent Lebbe, was born a Belgian in 1877 and grew up in the cultural and ecclesial shadow of France. He first went to China as a Lazarist seminarian of the Congregation of the Mission 遣使會 headquartered in Paris, arriving in China in 1901 shortly after the Boxer Uprising. From the start, Lebbe was troubled by France's geopolitical imperialism and cultural hegemony in the Catholic mission. He was inspired by nationalist movements both in China (the Xinhai Revolution and founding of the Republic of China in 1912) and in Europe (where his native Belgium was occupied by Germany from 1914 to 1918). As he saw it, the Church must divest its sociopolitical witness of any association with foreign imperialism. Throughout the 1910s and '20s, Lebbe protested the power of France and advocated for the indigenization of the Chinese Church, convinced that structural change was the first step in any meaningful indigenization. In China and then during a period of ministry to Chinese students in Belgium and France, Lebbe campaigned for Chinese bishops and eventually saw the first six native bishops consecrated in Rome in 1926.

Despite opposition from fellow European missionaries, Lebbe then returned to China in 1927 to serve under Bishop Sun Dezhen 孫德楨 in the prefecture of Lixian 蠡縣. He became a naturalized Chinese citizen and founded two Chinese religious congregations in Anguo 安國 for whom he served as a sort of abbot: the Little Brothers of St. John the Baptist 耀漢小兄弟會 and the Little Sisters of St. Therese of the Holy Child 德來小姊妹會. In this last part of his life, military conflicts racked the Chinese countryside. First there was civil war between the Nationalist military, northern warlord generals, and local militias like the Red Spear Society. Then there was an initial round of conflict between rival Communist and Nationalist forces. Finally there was the Second Sino-Japanese War, during which the armies united, though uneasily, to fight the foreign invader. Lebbe died in 1940 as the Second United Front between Communists and Nationalists began to disintegrate, and Yu Bin preached at his funeral in the wartime capital of Chongqing.[10] Lebbe did not live to see either the bombings of Hiroshima and Nagasaki, nor the resolution of the Chinese Civil War.

In this context, Lebbe's nationalism must be understood as a response to foreign imperialism that seemed to loom on every side. Foreign powers like France, Japan, and Russia continually pressed for influence in China. If Lebbe favored a strong nation-state, it was because the China he knew and loved was a fragile one. He took a practical attitude toward domestic politics, concerned most of all with unity. For instance, Lebbe welcomed the founding of the Republic in 1912 and celebrated the unification of the country under the Nationalist flag in 1928. In the 1930s, he worked willingly with Communist military units during the Second United Front, believing that a strong and united China was essential for holding Japan at bay.[11]

Yu Bin was born in 1901 in what is now Heilongjiang province in the northeastern corner of China. He was baptized as a young teen by missionary priests and attended the Jesuit Aurora University in Shanghai. He then spent the 1920s in Europe, where he was ordained a priest, earned three doctorates in philosophy, theology, and politics, and then taught at the Pontifical Urbaniana University until 1933.[12] After arriving back in China, where Lebbe greeted his boat and welcomed him home, Yu became a professor of ethics at Furen Catholic University, the National Director of Catholic Action in China 中華全國公教進行會, and the secretary of the Holy See's apostolic delegation in Beijing.[13] He was appointed bishop of Nanking in 1936, shortly before the formal outbreak of war with Japan.

---

10 Jacques Leclercq, *Thunder in the Distance*, translated by George Lamb (New York: Sheed & Ward, 1958), 317.

11 Suess Rolf, *Temps Present* (19 May 1939), in Fonds I, A47.1, 37; V. Lebbe to M. Zanin, 13 February 1938; Raymond de Jaegher, "Notes-Souvenirs de Quelques conversations avec le Prior a Linhsien du 28 Fevrier au 9 Mars 1940," in Fonds I, A47.69, 4.

12 Tang Dunhe 楊敦和, Wang Xinghua 王興華, 于斌樞機畫傳 [Memorial Collection of Paul Cardinal Yu Pin's Photographs], (New Taipei City: Fu Jen Catholic University Press, 1998).

13 V. Lebbe to Adrien (Dom Bede) Lebbe, 19 January 1934, in Fonds 1 A 54.1, 2; De Jaegher to André Boland, 17 July 1936, in Fonds I A 45a.1, 24.

Yu Bin became a nationally and internationally prominent figure in the anti-Japanese resistance. In addition to his domestic roles, he was appointed by General Chiang Kai-Shek to travel abroad representing the Chinese Relief Committee for Disaster Victims. Having had positive life experiences in Europe, he was dismayed to see media of Western nations dither in their assessment of the situation in East Asia. He gave hundreds of speeches to overseas Chinese and Western audiences to counter Japanese claims upon Chinese territory, raise awareness of wrongs done in China, and to raise funds for war refugees and orphans. Yu's international experience and command of many languages—Chinese, Latin, English, French, Spanish, Portuguese, and German[14]—made him a valuable international asset for the Church and the state.

Yu Bin's sense of patriotism was informed by both European and Chinese nationalist heroes. One of these was the "supreme example of religion and patriotism: the immortal Cardinal Mercier."[15] Indeed, the Belgian cardinal Désiré Mercier had emerged during World War I as a hero of the Belgian Catholic resistance to German occupation. Mercier's writings stressed the sacred inviolability of national sovereignty and the virtues of Christian patriotism. Yu's other hero was the Chinese revolutionary Sun Yat-Sen, who "imbibed the spirit and the principles of our liberation" from other examples of other respected nations and also insisted these others "leave intact the honor of the Chinese nation and the integrity of her territory."[16] For Yu, the value of patriotic action had both Catholic and Chinese precedents.

At the same time, Yu and Lebbe's patriotism for China was not a trigger-happy one. While both felt the violence of armed defense was necessary, they were all too familiar with the sufferings of war and the trauma it brought upon combatants and civilians alike. After all, Yu was the bishop seated at the Nationalist government's first capital in Nanking, which was frequently bombed. When the government moved west and the Japanese Imperial Army infamously invaded the city with massacres and rapes, the local people suffered enormously. Throughout the war, Yu agonized over the "frightful massacres and terrible devastation" and consistently drew attention to its effect on the most vulnerable:

---

14 "Death of Cardinal Yu Pin," *Sunday Examiner* (25 August 1978), archived in "于斌樞機," Archives of the Diocese of Hong Kong, accessed 3 January 2021, https://archives.catholic. org.hk/In%20Memoriam/Chinese%20Cardinals/P-Yu.htm

15 Yu, "The War in the Far East," in *Voice of the Church in China*, 73.

16 Yu, "The War in the Far East," 49; Yu, "Joint Letter of the Bishops of China," in *Voice of the Church in China*, 9.

"after four months of war, how many are homeless, workless, orphaned, how many children deserted?"[17]

So too, Lebbe had a front-row seat to wartime suffering. For instance, in 1937 as he and the stretcher-bearers accompanied the Nationalist 12th Army retreating southwest to Zhongtiao Mountain, they were encircled by Japanese troops and resorted to evacuating wounded soldiers to villagers' homes and mountain caves, trying to avoid snagging their wounds on the briars along the goat trails.[18] Meanwhile the town of Anguo, where the Little Brothers' Monastery of the Beatitudes 真福院 was located, fell to the Japanese Imperial Army. Japanese troops locked the city gates and outside the gates bayonetted all those who had not taken refuge in the monastery; afterwards, the monks and surviving villagers struggled to dig graves fast enough to avoid dogs eating the bodies.[19] Lebbe's letters from the battlefields of the North China Plain express his "horror for war" and his hopes for a time when Catholics could commit themselves to more constructive campaigns: "Tomorrow, when we have set to building new China, we shall be in the front line, shoulder to shoulder with the working people and the peasants.[20] In other words, Yu and Lebbe wanted to fight the war in order to win it and end it.

Nonetheless, military involvement was not uncontroversial and had to be justified to Catholics at home and abroad.

First, there was an ecclesiastical question of whether Catholics, especially clergy, could serve in the Chinese Army. Of course, throughout the late Middle Ages, many Catholics and even saints had served the monarchs and militaries of Europe. However, this has long been a knotty issue in the thinking and practice of the Church. In the first millennium of the Latin Western Catholic tradition, there was a strict ban on clergy bearing arms. In the twelfth century, however, the Church's position began to shift under Pope Alexander III, whose papacy developed principles of Roman and natural law to acknowledge that every person possessed the right to repel violence with violence—allowing military orders like the Knights Templar—though also a responsibility to moderate the defense.[21]

---

17 Yu, "Appeal to the Catholics of Europe and America for the Relief of War Victims," (December 15, 1937), in *Voice of China*, 77–78.

18 Leclercq, *"Thunder in the Distance,"* 297.

19 Raymond de Jaegher 雷震遠 and Irene Corbally Kuhn, *The Enemy Within* (Garden City, NY: Doubleday, 1952), 82.

20 V. Lebbe, 1 July 1928, *En Chine, il y a du nouveau* (Liege: La Pensée Catholique, 1930), 81–82; Leclercq, *"Thunder in the Distance,"* 299.

21 Lawrence Duggan, *Armsbearing and the Clergy in the History and Canon Law of Western Christianity* (Boydell & Brewer, 2013), 102–44; see also Duggan, "Armsbearing and the

Over the following centuries, legislation for secular clergy and religious orders tended to discourage clergy from offensive use of arms yet allow bearing them so long as the priest or monk had the permission of bishop or superior for purposes of self-defense.[22]

The 1917 code of Canon Law in effect during the Second Sino-Japanese War preserved this nuance or even ambiguity. On the one hand, Canon 141 of the 1917 Code of Canon Law stated curtly that "clerics should not volunteer in secular armies, except with the permission of the local Ordinary, which they might do in order to be free of an earlier draft; nor should they become involved in civil wars or disturbances of the public order in any way (Article 1)"; it followed this up with a warning that "a minor cleric who freely gives his name to the army in violation of the prescription of § 1 falls by law from the clerical state (Article 2)."[23] On the other hand, in a section on what is appropriate and inappropriate to the clerical state, Canon 138 includes an enormous exemption: "They shall not carry arms, except when there is just cause for fearing."[24] For a variety of reasons, the applicability of these canons to the Chinese situation was unclear. The 1917 Code exhibited reserve about clerical involvement in the armies of a civil war, but it did not give guidance on an international war of defense against a foreign aggressor, as in the case with Japan. It also warned about involvement in "secular" armies, presumably to preserve the legitimacy of clerical involvement in the religious wars of Western Catholic history—but this raised questions about the status of the Sino-Japanese war; after all, Japan's declaration of war was framed in highly religious terms of divine emperorship and mandate, and the Chinese war effort of Chiang Kai-Shek was also promoted in Confucian and even Christian language of virtue and "New Life."[25] Finally, the Code could only awkwardly

---

Clergy and the Fourth Lateran Council," 63–77, in *The Fourth Lateran Council and the Development of Canon Law and the* Jus Commune, edited by Atria Larson and Andrea Massironi (Turnhout, Belgium: Brepolis Publishers, 2018).

22 Duggan, "Armsbearing in the Legislation of the Late Medieval Religious Orders," Paper Presented at International Medieval Congress, University of Leeds, July 3 2017.

23 Canon 141, *Codex Iuris Canonici* (1917), Intratext, accessed 14 July 2018, <http://www.intratext.com/X/LAT0813.HTM>

24 Canon 138, *Codex Iuris Canonici* (1917), Intratext, accessed 14 July 2018, <http://www.intratext.com/X/LAT0813.HTM>

25 Japan's declaration stressed the divine emperor's possession of the grace of heaven and the protection of ancestral spirits over the nation: "We, by the grace of Heaven, Emperor of Japan seated on the throne of a line unbroken for ages eternal, enjoin upon you, our loyal and grave subjects . . . the situation being as it is, our Empire for its existence and self-defense has no other recourse but to appeal to arms and to crush every obstacle in its path. Hallowed spirits

apply to circumstances that crossed geographic lines of episcopal authority, since the Holy See had not yet articulated any wider guidelines for chaplain service to military personnel nor established vicariates to the military distinct from geographical dioceses, as it would do in 1951.[26]

The status of Catholic participation in the Sino-Japanese war was thus murky: for example, Lebbe first organized Catholic medic and stretcher-bearer teams (*brancardiers*, 救護隊, 戰地服務團) for the battlefields in the winter of 1932–33 when the Japanese invaded the northern Chinese province of Jehol/Rehe.[27] Were these teams a part of the secular army or just accompanying it as Catholic aid workers? The Little Brothers had the approval of the local "Ordinary"—as they did from Bishop Wang Zengyi 王增義 of Anguo. Yet what happened if the troops' movements took them into a different bishop's jurisdiction? Lebbe strictly banned the Little Brothers from carrying guns as clergy, but they nonetheless served as officers over combatant units. Was it appropriate for Lebbe to serve as a military general?

Lebbe maintained to the end that he and the Little Brothers were in accordance with Church protocol, but the work raised concerns. Even when Lebbe began organizing the clearly healthcare-related stretcher-bearer teams, the Lazarist leadership of North China and European missionaries of other religious orders thought it inappropriate and wanted to censure him. After a long period of conflict with the Lazarist leadership and with interventions from the Holy See's delegate Celso Costantini and advice from Yu Pin, Lebbe finally requested release from the Lazarists.[28] At fifty-six years old, Lebbe left the Congregation of the Mission to become the superior of the Little Brothers. Later, when Lebbe was leading the Supervisory Corp in 1939, Lebbe wrote to reassure his biological brother, the Belgian Benedictine Dom Bède, that they never

---

of our imperial ancestors guarding us from above . . . ." Quoted in Kosuke Koyama, *Mount Fuji and Mount Sinai: A Critique of Idols* (Maryknoll: Orbis Books, 1985), 21.

26 On 25 April 1951, the Holy See's Instruction "Sollemne Semper" proposed the establishment of vicariates for the apostolate to military personnel separate from the norms governing geographical dioceses. The Holy See's management of these apostolates continued to undergo restructuring through the 1970s and 80s, when the Holy See created an office in Rome to manage Military Ordinariates around the world in a systematic way.

27 During the Battle of the Great Wall (長城抗戰), Lebbe recruited the Little Brothers of St. John, and later also the Little Sisters, to serve the wounded on the front lines with the 29th "Big Sword" Corps. V. Lebbe to Paul Staes, 28 June 1933, in Goffart and Sohier, eds., *Lettres*, No. 146, p. 283.

28 Raymond de Jaegher to L. Gosset, (5 October 1933), A 42a.1, 11; V. Lebbe to Adrian (Dom Bède) Lebbe, 19 January 1934, A.43.1,2.

armed themselves even for self-defense: "It seems, you told me, that a reporter represented me as also shooting and directing the military operations. . . . No, I know my canon law; whatever the danger, neither I nor the Brothers wear the smallest weapon; I dismissed a Brother for disobeying and carrying a gun (on a very dangerous journey)."[29] Lebbe was constantly defending the Chinese clergy's involvement in the war effort to European associates.

Second, there was a larger question of whether Catholics should concern themselves with the war effort at all. As *Xinde* (Faith) *Weekly* 信德報 reported in 1939, some European listeners heard Yu Bin's speeches on the war in the East and wondered, "How can Bishop Yu Pin talk about such issues? Since these kinds of questions seem to go beyond the responsibilities of the priesthood, what authority does he have to talk about such questions?"[30] In fact, some of the Chinese priests and Little Brothers of St. John the Baptist also worried whether involvement might mean leaving religious activities for secular and political ones. When Lebbe had initially founded the Little Brothers, their primary purpose was to serve the parishes and villages under the recently consecrated Chinese bishops. Thus the expansion of the Little Brothers' apostolate led to some tensions with the local clergy who were reluctant to lose exclusive use of the monk apostles, as well as a few of the Little Brothers themselves who felt their vocation was to stay in local parish work.[31] Lebbe defended the war-related work, explaining that he had founded the congregation, always considering their purpose to be "to offer the support of Catholicism, especially its spirit, to the work of the reconstruction of China." It was "therefore natural that the whole national crisis be considered for them as an aspect of work, and they consider their participation in the efforts of their compatriots to be a strict duty."[32] Most of the Little Brothers and Little Sisters did eagerly join the anti-Japanese resistance.

---

29 V. Lebbe to Adrien (Dom Bède) Lebbe, No. 156 (19 September 1939), published in Goffart and Sohier, eds., *Lettres*, p. 307.

30 "外國眼中的于斌主教 「一個歐洲記者」原著羅馬傳信大學中華學會譯," 信德報 (1 June–1 July 1939), included in 于斌樞機, Archives of the Catholic Diocese of Hong Kong, accessed 5 January 2021, https://archives.catholic.org.hk/In%20Memoriam/Chinese %20Cardinals/P-Yu.htm.

31 R. De Jaegher, "L'Esprit et l'évolution de la Congrégation de St. Jean-Baptiste," p. 3–4, Fonds I, A46.1,13.

32 Lebbe, "Catholiques dans la Guerre de Chine: Nos Cloitres dans la tempête," *Le Cite chrétienne* (5 December 1938), 75.

My point is that Catholic support for the Chinese war effort was understandable enough given the threats of foreign imperialism but also controversial within the Church such that the theological case for it needed to be made. After all, there was still the matter of the lay Catholic guerilla fighters themselves. Were Catholics justified in participating in the war, and in defense of what?

Yu and Lebbe's Theology of Resistance

In July 1937, Yu Bin issued a pastoral letter, "Be Ready," urging his vicariate to prepare for service in rear support and on the front lines: "We must set the example of obedience to the Government; we must rise as one man to accomplish the duties which the war imposes upon us; we must take arms, defend our country and, if necessary, die honorably for her!"[33]

Refusing to Settle for a Premature Peace

The first clarification that Yu and Lebbe make in their writings is that peace, although it is a great good and the desire of the Church, cannot be declared while injustices continue. In the Japanese government's presentation of the war to Western powers, the Chinese shared blame for the war. According to the Japanese Catholics' appeal, the Chinese Church should hasten to put aside differences and join a movement for peace.

In his open letter responding to the Japanese Catholics, Lebbe points out how the circular unevenly employs religious sentiments and political aims: the Chinese faithful are asked to reflect with "Christian gentleness" and "Christian pity" on the blood and tears that come with war, but the solution they are to accept is the militaristic "new order" of Japan.[34] He therefore rejects the premise that Chinese and Japanese Catholics might join in sorrow over both nations' losses while the destruction of the Chinese countryside continues:

> You are telling us about Japan's sufferings. . . . But believe that we know what suffering means, perhaps even better than Japanese citizens. Because we have not bombed your cities; our soldiers did not set fire to your villages, massacre your children and your old people by the tens

---

33 Yu, "Be Ready," in *Le Cite chrétienne.*, p. 42.

34 Lebbe, "Le Royaume de Dieu et sa justice : réponse à la circulaire de quelques Catholiques Japonais adressée par eux au Clergé et aux fidèles de Chine," 1.

of thousands, rape and torture to death your wives and little girls and mothers—in a word, change the countryside and the cities into a sea of fire and blood. . . . No, right? Japan has not seen any of this.[35]

No conversation about peace could begin so long as the Japanese imagine they come together from equal positions of sorrow.

Similarly, Yu Bin refused to be pressured into what he felt would be a false peace while the invasion continued. As he saw it, the Christian tradition took care to distinguish between righteousness and sinfulness, and that distinction should not be lost. In a speech written for the second anniversary of the outbreak of the war, he clarified that "Apart from righteousness, words of peace are but words of lies. . . . We will be full of mercy for all sinners who repent, but we cannot grant forgiveness so long as they remain in their sins."[36] In 1939, he noted that the Japanese Imperial Army had not ceased its attacks on Chinese sovereignty nor its violence upon Chinese civilians, much less begun to make the reparations necessary for repentance.

In their discussions of peace, Yu and Lebbe grant that true peace is the hope of Christians, yet they are unwilling to seek peace at any cost. When Lebbe considered Catholic scripture and tradition, he found them full of stories where the people of God had died rather than settle for an unjust peace:

> The history of the people of God rises against it. Read again the Holy Scriptures, the beautiful stories of David, Judith and the Maccabees; they are summed up in this famous saying of our Saints: "It is better for us to die than to lose our honor." The beautiful Chinese proverb echoes: "Better broken jade than an intact tile" (寧為玉碎 不為瓦全). After Christ, King of Peace, two thousand years of the history of the Christian peoples come to repeat the proud motto.[37]

In sum, for both Yu and Lebbe, peace could only be the fruit of something more foundational, namely justice.

---

35 Lebbe, "Le Royaume de Dieu et sa justice," 2.
36 Yu, "Fructus Justitiae: Pax," 2.
37 Lebbe, "Le Royaume de Dieu et sa justice," 2.

The Nobility of Fighting for Justice

In their case for justice as the "more precious and more absolutely necessary" virtue,[38] Lebbe drew especially frequently on passages from the Catholic deuterocanonical texts of the Old Testament. While some of these texts from Jewish history might seem obscure especially to Protestants, it is not surprising that Lebbe would have thought of them. Although Judith and 1–2 Maccabees are 'apocryphal' in Protestant traditions, they are canonical in the Catholic Old Testament. These stories were also featured in the ritual and social life of Republican Era Chinese Catholicism. The Maccabees are honored annually in the Catholic liturgical calendar.[39] So too, the stories were performed as plays such as the 1918 "Story of the Maccabees" 瑪加白阿傳, by Fei Jinbiao 費金標.[40] Through the liturgical calendar and such dramas, the Church familiarized the faithful with scriptural stories of martyrdom and sacrifice.

It is easy to see why Lebbe appreciated the book of Judith, as it could be applied as a fairly straightforward and favorable parallel to the Chinese Catholic guerilla and espionage work. In this story, a Jewish woman turns the tide of a war on the Israelites by infiltrating the enemy camp and assassinating their general. The narrative emphasizes the theme of a faithful representative of Israel (Judith's name means 'Jewish woman') acting to defend her religious community in the face of an overwhelming foreign force (identified as Nebuchadnezzar, who ruled over the Assyrians).[41]

In Lebbe's reading, the violence-seeking and land-hungry Assyrians are akin to the Empire of Japan. The Japanese Catholics had echoed their government's characterization of the war as a defensive one by calling attention to Japanese casualties in the conflict. In this, Lebbe sees at work the same self-serving logic of Nebuchadnezzar as he terrorized the land: "Read the Book of Judith, how the

---

38 Lebbe, "Le Royaume," 2.

39 The Catholic Old Testament generally follows the canon of the Greek Septuagint used at Jesus's time and therefore includes the books of Tobit, Judith, 1 Maccabees, 2 Maccabees, Wisdom of Solomon, Sirach, and Baruch, as well as longer versions of the Daniel and Esther than are included in Protestant Bibles.

40 John T. P. Lai, "Dramatizing the Bible in Chinese: The Making of Martyrdom in *The Story of the Maccabees*, 1918," *Journal of Biblical Reception* 5.1 (2015): 61–79.

41 It is generally recognized that the book of Judith is a rhetorical and fictional narrative, since Jewish readers would have known that Nebuchadnezzar was king of the Babylonians and not the Assyrians.

King of Assyria, having decided in his heart to 'subjugate all the earth,' declared in large council that he would send armies to 'defend himself'—the word is there—from all the people who would not accept this 'new order.'"[42] So too, the Japanese are dying because of their own government's aggression. Meanwhile, in the book of Judith and in the war with Japan, the Israelites/Chinese are simply victims, having never gone looking for a fight yet facing potential annihilation as a people.

For Lebbe's purposes in working out a Chinese Catholic ethic, Judith also holds useful contrast between factions within the Israelite mountain town of Bethulia. When the enemy general Holofernes lays siege to Bethulia, seizing control of the passageways and waterways to starve them into submission, the starving and thirsty Israelites become desperate. The leader Uzziah is prepared to surrender the town to Holofernes for the sake of survival. However, the widow Judith chastises Uzziah and the elders for their lack of faith in God. It is she who courageously and cleverly infiltrates the enemy camp and then, when she has gotten the Holofernes drunk, uses his sword to cut off his head. Lebbe was impressed with Judith's willingness to take personal risks for the protection of the Temple and the whole of Israel below the mountain pass: "for their lives depend upon us" (Judith 8:24). If Chinese Catholics are to choose between being doubting, self-protective Uzziahs or courageous and self-sacrificial Judiths, the biblical narrative seems to endorse the latter approach.

It is clear in all this that Lebbe closely associates the fight for justice with attendant virtues such as courage. To go to the front lines might well cost the individual everything. Of himself, he noted that "it is only through determination to win or die that the people of China will live more gloriously. . . . It is because I am willing to die for China that I have joined the Chinese Army."[43] However, he thought this resolve was justified by many Old Testament stories wherein an Israelite underdog went up against some stronger foreign force. In addition to the book of Judith, Lebbe also cites David courageously going up against the Philistine giant Goliath, and the "fine" bravery of the Maccabee freedom-fighters taking up arms to overthrow foreign Greek Seleucid rule.[44]

---

42 Lebbe, "Le Royaume de Dieu et sa justice," 3.

43 Lebbe, quoted in "Belgian Priest Fights for China," News Release No. 234. Hankow, Sept. 15, 1938, China Information Committee, Archives Vincent Lebbe, Fonds 1, A47.88, p. 1596.

44 Lebbe, "Choses vues par un missionnaire en Chine," *Lectures pour tous* (1 Octobre 1913): 705.

National Sovereignty as Belonging to the Justice of the Kingdom of God

While leading Catholics in China did not offer a full exposition of their thinking on church–state relations, they did emphasize that national identity and sovereignty was a matter of justice with which the Church should be concerned. As the former Premier of China, the Benedictine Dom Lu Zhengxiang 陸征祥 put it, the Japanese invasion of Chinese territory was "a violation of rights" in which "the Church could not remain quiescent."[45]

In his pastoral letters, Bishop Yu Bin urged Chinese Catholics not to view the country's welfare as something unrelated to the justice of God. He believed the nations of the world were "intended to co-exist as neighbors"[46] and that each had a right to seek and defend its own cohesion.

First of all, Yu insisted that China should be counted among the nations of the world. Interestingly, Yu did not ground this nationhood in ethnic conceptions of Chineseness. (Yu calls the Japanese a "neighboring people, a brother people, a people of the same race as ours, of the same race and of the same blood."[47]) Rather Yu saw the nation as a geopolitical and cultural community. Even before the establishment of the republic, China possessed "a unity of language, a unity of culture, unity of moral life, and unity of history."[48] With the founding of the Republic of China in 1912, this national character was given modern political form.

Second, he believed that every nation had a natural impulse and right to protect its own integrity. Yu quoted the Belgian Cardinal Mercier on patriotism: "Patriotism . . . is the universal and irresistible urge which carried with it the wills of the nation in a concerted effort to cohesion and resistance to the enemy forces that menace its unity and its independence."[49] This took on a religious character in that, for Mercier and Yu, international justice was a participation in God's justice.

Third, Yu and Lebbe argued that enacting justice would finally bring true peace. In a discussion of Augustine and Thomas Aquinas on just war theory, Yu explains that the Japanese attacks do not meet the classic justifications for

---

45 Lu Zhengxiang, "Preface," in *Voice of the Church in China*, xxii, xxiii.

46 Yu, "Be Ready," in *The Voice of the Church in China*, 41.

47 Yu, "The War in the East," 58.

48 Yu, "The War in the East," 54.

49 Yu, "The War in the East," 73–74.

a just war. For that reason, the Chinese Church is well within their rights to defend the nation. At the same time, insofar as the Chinese defense is just, then it is ultimately a tool for the restoration of peace. Yu writes: "Our soldiers and those who are helping in the defense of the country and of our national hearth, deserve to have applied to them the words of St. Thomas: 'Qui juste bella gerunt, pacem intendunt: those who make war justly are helping the cause of peace.'"[50] Also in the spirit of the Augustinian and Thomistic just war tradition, then, it is imperative that Chinese Catholics not adopt a retributive spirit but maintain a "recollected and prudent" spirit to eventually lead their attackers to the blessings of peace.[51]

Fourth, all these moral imperatives made it legitimate, in these leaders' eyes, to support the ruling government. In closing his letter "The Kingdom of God and its Justice," Lebbe paraphrases Romans 13 to emphasize the duty that Chinese Catholics owe not to their coreligionists in Japan but to their ruling authority Chiang Kai-Shek. Romans 13 has often been interpreted as a full-throated injunction to obey all public authorities. In the Catholic tradition, Thomas Aquinas tempered this somewhat with conditions: first, Christians only owe obedience to others when their authority is derived from God; this "ceases when that ceases." Second, "authority may fail to derive from God for two reasons: either because of the way in which authority has been obtained, or in consequence of the use which is made of it."[52] In particular, Aquinas specified that authority would be invalid from the outset if that power was acquired by illegitimate means such as "violence, or simony, or some other illegal method."[53] Authority must be legitimate in order to merit Christian obedience.

At any rate, for Lebbe the 'legitimate' authority in his time was clear. If the choice to be made was between foreign Japanese officials who had seized the land with violence or the Chinese Nationalist government with its efforts at constitutional rule, then clearly Chinese Catholics should render obedience to their own governing officials. He expresses his own sense of duty to Chiang Kai-Shek in lofty terms:

50　Yu, "Christian Patriotism" 90–91.

51　Yu, "Christian Patriotism" 90–91.

52　Thomas Aquinas, *Commentary on the Sentences of Peter Lombard,* Book 2, Dist. 44, Question 2.

53　Aquinas, *Commentary,* Book 2, Dist. 44, Question 2.

Our duty, especially our duty as Catholics, is to obey our Government. For the Holy Spirit has told us for two thousand years by the mouth of St. Paul: "Every man is bound to obey the legitimate authority because all legitimate power comes from God, so the one who resists him, resists God himself." Now our legitimate Government has mobilized the whole nation, and has assigned to it as a duty to continue the war until the total liberation of the territory, whatever the sacrifices to be made, and to endure the sufferings to endure, however long the war may prove to be. With all our heart, not only as citizens, but also, especially as Catholics, we obey our magnanimous leader, whose sentiments so Christian honor us before the whole world, the Generalissimo Chiang, knowing that by obeying him we obey God.

After this statement of obedience to Chiang, Lebbe like Yu goes on to connect Chinese Catholics' duties to the domestic authority with the realization of the Kingdom of God on earth:

In following him, we sacrifice everything, the sweetnesses of peace and all the rest, and our lives, so that by the victory against Evil, a little of the Rule of God and his righteousness will come to our land of China.[54]

In this closing passage, Lebbe concludes that fighting the war is a necessary part of bringing about the Reign of God to China. He insists the Catholics of China cannot abandon the war effort, since to do so would violate their scripture-supported duties.

A Modified Catholic Integralism

I highlight these passages to demonstrate that Yu and Lebbe's theology of resistance drew on very traditional lines of exegesis that had long supported Christendom-type societies even as they argued for modern nation-states and their independence.[55] They were transitional figures still animated by many

---

54 Lebbe, "Le Royaume de Dieu et sa justice," 3.

55 By using the term 'Christendom,' I am (1) referring to the historical arrangement of the social order, notably in Europe, in which ecclesial and governmental powers cooperated to establish or maintain a Christian society; and (2) alerting us to the constructed nature of the concept and especially its modification for the Chinese context.

ideals of the *ancien régime*, especially the integration of church and society, even as they threw in his lot with modern China.

Lebbe's hope was not to extend European Christendom in China, but rather for the creation and preservation of a Chinese iteration. Indeed, it was most often in moments when Lebbe was fighting for the national church in opposition to foreign interference that he appealed to the idea of "Christendom." For example, early in his ministry, Lebbe wrote to his brother that he hoped for "open Christendoms" in the plural (*les chrétientés ouvertes*")[56] though the French Religious Protectorate dominating Catholicism in China made it difficult. When in 1921 the French Lazarist leadership suppressed the patriotic efforts of Lebbe and the Chinese priests at Tianjin, Lebbe lamented that the Lazarists' dispersal of the Tianjin community threatened to "lead this beautiful Christendom to the edge of the abyss."[57] In the war-torn last decade and a half of his life, the fledgling new Chinese Christendom is what Lebbe believed God was preserving against all odds. [58]

Undoubtedly, Lebbe's concept of Christendom inherited much from the Western European example. His scriptural prooftexts for the resistance were predictable ones. After all, Old Testament examples of Jewish theocracy had undergirded the Catholic monarchies of Europe. When Lebbe began his seminary studies in Paris, he was surrounded by images of religious rule—for instance, the statues of the good kings of Judah that adorned the west façade of the Cathedral of Notre Dame de Paris. So too, Romans 13 was a key prooftext for the European theory of the divine right of kings. He cited the defender of France against England, the military saint Joan of Arc, as an example of what Chinese freedom-fighters might be for China in their own fight against foreign invaders.[59] For all his desire to create a Chinese church, Lebbe inherited many of his categories and models from his native Europe where the Church had traditionally held a place of power and influence.

---

56 Vincent Lebbe to Dom Bede, 12 Septembre 1910, in *Lettres du Pere Lebbe*, 88.

57 Lebbe to G. Vanneufville, Shaohing, January 9, 1021, in *Pour L'Eglise Chinoise 1. La visite apostolique des missions de Chine, 1919–1920*, Recueil des Archives Vincent Lebbe, Cahiers de la *Revue Theologique de Louvain*, 73.

58 After worrying that a passing army would destroy the community of Lixian, he notes with relief, "Christendom has been miraculously preserved." Lebbe, 4 June 1927, Gaojiazhuang, *En Chine, il y a du nouveau*, 35.

59 Lebbe, "Le Royaume de Dieu et sa justice," 2.

At the same time, however, Lebbe's goal was not to prop up European Christendom, but to create an alternate and improved version. China was to surpass the former strongholds of ecclesiastical and political power to reach new heights. "Long live God!" wrote Lebbe to his brother back in Belgium, "When he reigns over China, then China will be the first country in the world."[60] This would require significant modifications to the Christendom model. For instance, Lebbe's ambition did not entail that Catholicism should become the state religion of Republican China. In fact, he along with many other missionary and indigenous Catholics in China during the 1910s had lobbied hard for the non-establishment of religion during controversies over China's Provisional Constitution.[61] The Church in China, like the Church everywhere in the twentieth century, would have to accommodate itself to modernity and the likelihood that the state would not be a Christian one.

Yu was more persuaded by the discourses of freedom and independence that had animated Western nations as well as the Chinese revolution. For instance, he discusses approvingly how Sun Yat-sen adopted the American president Abraham Lincoln's hope that the nation might have "a new birth of freedom, and that government of the people, by the people, for the people, shall not perish from the earth."[62] He uses the language of monarchy less frequently than Lebbe to describe the role of the Church in society. Nowhere—at least not in the texts reviewed here—does he use the word "Christendom" to describe the Christian presence in China.

Nonetheless, Yu still promoted an integralist picture of church and state sharing in the life of society. He was impatient with European missionaries who posited any fundamental separation between church and state affairs. (For instance, many Chinese nationals were at times frustrated with the relative timidity of the Apostolic Delegate from Rome, Marius Zanin, who carefully avoided rallying the Church for secular causes. When Zanin issued his own directive to the ecclesiastical leadership of the Chinese Church in winter 1937—namely to pray for salvation from violence, work together to help the poor and distressed, and sacrificially give up fine delicacies, expensive drinks, and tobacco, while respecting

---

60 Lebbe, *En Chine, il y a du nouveau*, 24.

61 See Wong, Stephanie, "Ch. 4 Catholicism and Confucianism: Contested Modernities in Republican China" in "From Subjects to Citizens: Vincent Lebbe and the Chinese Catholic Church in Republican China," Ph.D. Dissertation, 2018, Georgetown University.

62 Yu, "The War in the East," 49.

local authorities and avoiding any disorder— this was not the message of engaged patriotism that Lebbe and the Chinese bishops had hoped for.[63]) Yu did urge the people to pray and to engage in works of charity, but he undertook such practical steps as directing the Catholic Action societies in the parishes and schools to organize military training for the laity.[64] For him, the military fight against Japan was not in fact a secular or purely political conflict, but indeed a socio-spiritual battle with the "modern militarism" of "this Japanese god Moloch."[65] Far from promoting a separation of ecclesiastical and political affairs, Yu described patriotism as a "religious precept" under which the faithful "as Christians and Catholics may rightly fulfil our obligations as citizens."[66] Yu called the Vicariate of Nanjing to do all it could to support Chiang Kai-Shek's war effort.

Conclusion

In conclusion, these Catholic leaders tried to meld a Catholic "integralist" vision of religion and society with the nationalism of the modern nation-state in order to defend violent resistance to Japan.

As it happens, their theological case did not anticipate longer trends in Catholic social teaching. As Lisa Cahill has pointed out, the Catholic magisterium in the latter part of the twentieth century has tended to marginalize the just war tradition in Catholic thought. In the wake of World War II and especially since Vatican II, papal teaching has emphasized that the church cannot accept violence. Pope Paul VI urged the United Nations, "No more war, war never again! Peace, it is peace which must guide the destinies of people and all of mankind."[67] In the wake of World War II and with the threat of nuclear annihilation, the popes in the second half of the twentieth century came to see violence as inherently immoral and self-defeating.[68] Late twentieth-century social teaching has

---

63 Marius Zanin, "Circular Letter to all the Ordinaries of China: 'Inter Arma Caritas,'" in *The Voice of the Church of China*, 30.

64 Yu, "Be Ready," 43.

65 Yu, "The War in the East," 63.

66 Yu, "Christian Patriotism," 84.

67 Paul VI, *Evangelium nuntiani*, 1975, Art. 37, http://w2.vatican.va/content/paul-vi/en/apost_exhortations/documents/hf_p-vi_exh_19751208_evangelii-nuntiandi.html.

68 Lisa Cahill, "The Future of (Catholic) Just War Theory: Marginal," *Expositions* 12.1 (2018): 20–32.

been critical of "the utility of widespread violence," even "at the service of defending or restoring an order of justice."[69]

No doubt, Yu and Lebbe would have been surprised to see this shift. In their day, as both pointed out in their writings, Pope Pius XII's papal motto was "Peace as the fruit of justice" with the understanding that justice might have to be fought for with blood. Indeed, Yu even wrote that "the peace that [the Holy Spirit] came to give to the world is bought by the shedding of blood as a witness to justice."[70] Only several decades later this position would come to be at odds with papal pronouncements. By John Paul II's papacy, shaped by yet a different political context in Eastern Europe, the discourse had already shifted substantially: violence was inherently "evil" and "the enemy of justice," while peace has taken precedence as the guiding principle of Catholic reflection on war.[71]

In conclusion, we must acknowledge the ways in which figures like Yu Bin and Lebbe were both "ahead" of their time and "of" their time. In comparison with foreign missionaries still holding on to a sense of European control in China or reticent to see the Chinese Church become too involved in domestic Chinese politics, Yu and Lebbe were forward thinking in orienting themselves toward the domestic nation and its needs. In offering their war-time contextual theology, however, they were also very much "of" their own time, unable to anticipate developments in Catholic social teaching against the participation in violence for purposes of justice. They were transitional figures thinking theologically at a time when it still seemed that, with modifications, the traditional Catholic integration of religious, political and military effort might work in tandem for Christian witness in China.

---

69 Himes, "Peacebuilding," in *Can War Be Just in the 21st Century?*, 279, quoted in Cahill, "The Future of (Catholic) Just War Theory," 25.

70 Yu, "Fructus Justitiae: Pax," 1.

71 John Paul II, Homily at Drogheda, Ireland, Sept 29, 1979, Art. 18–22, https://w2.vatican.va/content/john-paul-ii/en/homilies/1979/documents/hf_jp-ii_hom_19790929_irlanda-dublino-drogheda.html.

Chapter 7

FROM HUMAN SUFFERING TO DIVINE LOVE

The Christian Women's Magazine Nü duo in Wartime China

Zhou Yun, Australia National University

This paper examines discussions of divine love and human suffering in the Chinese Christian women's periodical *Nü duo* 女鐸 during the second Sino-Japanese War. The wartime ordeal served as a collective experience that triggered public theological discussion of suffering among educated Christian women. *Nü duo*, a widely circulated magazine in wartime China, published responses to readers' letters concerning suffering, grounded in biblical interpretation. To address the suffering experienced during the war, the magazine published articles on Christian love that were closely associated with the humanity of Jesus. These discussions pose a sharp contrast to the male-dominated contemporary discourse that centered on the issue of militant resistance. Unlike their male counterparts, Christian women were discouraged from political engagement due to church norms and gendered expectations. An exploration of their voices during wartime China introduces discourse that was personal and yet universal. The advocacy of a humane Jesus in response to the national crisis by *Nü duo* challenges the rigid dichotomous relationship between nationalism and pacifism among male theologians.

Scholarship on Christianity and warfare in early twentieth-century China tends to concentrate on male Christians' ideas and activities. This scholarship shows the concepts of *agape* and just war to be at the center of debate among Christians about approaches to war. The term *agape* is a complex and contested Greek concept that emphasizes the love of the Christian God.[1] Agapism is often

---

1 The Greek noun *agape* has a variety of meanings. According to Thomas M. Finn, the term denotes romantic love, piety, fear, and love of God, and the love of one's neighbor in the Old

interchangeable with pacifism in the discourse of Protestant history in China.[2] In his monograph on the Protestant pacifist movement in China, Yao Xiyi discusses several leading male Christians who initially embraced biblical teachings on love and later grappled with the applicability of pacifism amidst escalating warfare.[3] Wang Zhixi concentrates on the influential Chinese Christian leader Wu Yaozong (1890–1979) and his struggle with *agape*, justice, and hatred in wartime China. With the escalation of warfare, Wu later embraced the advocacy of a just war.[4] Liu Jiafeng has drawn an analogy between two influential pacifist Christians in Japan and China, exploring changes in attitudes to pacifism in the writings and actions of Xu Baoqian (1892–1943) and Kagawa Toyohiko (1888–1960) in the wartime period. With rising Chinese nationalism and Japanese militarism, both encountered seemingly irreconcilable conflicts between Christian pacifism and nationalist sentiments, which Liu argues resulted in their failure to adhere to their pacifist ideals.[5]

Theological discussion among educated Chinese women in wartime China, however, points to a trajectory in thought and concerns that was not confined to questions of nationalism or pacifism. Unlike their male counterparts, Christian women were often discouraged from and deprived of political engagement due to church norms and gendered expectations. From the arrival of foreign missionary

---

Testament. In the New Testament *agape* generally means "self-giving love." The distinctive theology of *agape* shown in the New Testament is that "God, who is love, is embodied in Christ, who, in turn, is embodied in the community of believers, the church, especially in giving of themselves to others." See Thomas M. Finn. "Agape." In *The Encyclopedia of Ancient History*, eds Roger S. Bagnall, Kai Brodersen, Craige B. Champion, Andrew Erskine, and Sabine R. Huebner (Malden, Ma.: Blackwell Publishing, 2013), 166–67.

2 Kevin Xiyi Yao believes that agapism and pacifism are interchangeable but with different emphasis. In Yao's viewpoint, the former stresses motivation and the latter is concerned with action. See Yao Xiyi 姚西伊, 中國基督教唯愛主義運動 [*The Protestant Pacifist Movement in China*], (Hong Kong: Logos Publishers, 2008), 7.

3 Yao, *The Protestant Pacifist Movement in China*.

4 Wang Zhixi 王志希, "Ai hen jiao zhi—Wu Yaozong de weiaizhuyi, fuyinshu wenben yu yesu xingxiang 1918–1948" 「愛恨交織」—吳耀宗的「唯愛論」、「福音書文本」與「耶穌形象」（1918–1948）[Between Love and Hatred: Pacifism, Gospel Texts and Images of Jesus in the Writings of Y. T. Wu, 1918–1948], *LOGOS & PNEUMA Chinese Journal of Theology* 43 (Autumn 2015): 235–66.

5 Liu Jiafeng 劉家峰, 'Jindai zhongri jidujiao hepingzhuyi de mingyun—yi Xu Baoqian yu Kagawa Toyohiko wei ge'an de bijiao yanjiu' 近代中日基督教和平主義的命運以徐寶謙與賀川豐彥為個案的比較研究 [The fate of contemporary Christian pacifism in China and Japan—a comparative case study of Xu Baoqian and Kagawa Toyohiko], *Zhejiang xuekan* 2 (2007): 97–105.

women following the signing of the Treaty of Nanking in 1842 until the early twentieth century, Christian women were governed by gendered ethics that confined women to work with their own sex. Missionary work among women, as Kwok Pui-lan has shown, concentrated in three areas: evangelism, female education, and medical care.[6] Jane Hunter's work shows that missionary women at the turn of twentieth-century China followed a Victorian domestic life and conducted evangelical activities in the domestic sphere that highlighted women's domestic virtues.[7] The emphasis of domesticity in mission work reflected the global Protestant missionary women's movement, which was, as Dana L. Robert astutely points out, core to the global missionary women's movement that consequently provided a rationale for women to engage socially.[8]

Dominant forms of missionary Christianity echoed Confucian ideas of gender segregation, which admonished women to be cloistered in their houses and discouraged them from attending public events. Traditional ethics, however, were greatly challenged by the discourse of modern womanhood that thrived in the 1920s and the 1930s. The notion of the new woman in the Republican era, according to Gail Hershatter and Louise Edwards, was associated with "national modernity" that was essential to reviving the nation.[9] During the Sino-Japanese War, gender discourse was complicated by the Chinese Communist Party (CCP) gender lines based on Marxist class theory. As Ono Kazuko has noted, the CCP worked to "enhance women's political position and cultural level, to improve women's standards of living, and to achieve liberation."[10] This changing social ethos challenged the discourse of Christian femininity that advocated women's roles as wives and mothers. For example, the Christian female activist Liu-Wang Liming (1897–1970) believed women's roles were to be good wives and mothers. In the 1930s, Liu-Wang strongly promoted housework training in schools. Meanwhile she also advocated for women's right to vote and thought that

---

6   Kwok Pui-lan, *Chinese Women and Christianity 1860–1927* (Atlanta: Scholars Press, 1992), 15.

7   Jane Hunter, *The Gospel of Gentility: American Women Missionaries in Turn-of-the-Century China* (New Haven: Yale University Press, 1989).

8   Dana L. Robert, "The 'Christian Home' as a Cornerstone of Anglo-American Missionary Thought and Practice," in *Converting Colonialism: Visions and Realities in Mission History, 1706–1914*, ed. Dana L. Robert (Grand Rapids, MI: Eerdmans, 2008), 136.

9   Gail Hershatter, *Women in China's Long Twentieth Century* (Calif.: University of California Press, 2007), 79–105. Louise Edwards, "Policing the Modern Woman in Republican China," *Modern China* 26, 2 (2000): 115–47.

10   Ono Kazuko, *Chinese Women in a Century of Revolution, 1850–1950*, ed. Joshua A. Fogel. (Stanford, CA: Stanford University Press, 1989), 167.

women's domestic roles did not exclude them from political activism.[11] Regarding the women's feminist movement, Elizabeth A. Littell-Lamb notes that two Christian women's organizations—the Young Women's Christian Association (YWCA) and the Woman's Christian Temperance Union (WCTU)—were two prominent sites of social feminist activity. One prominent figure was the evangelist and revival speaker Deng Yuzhi (鄧裕志 1900–1996), who "joined Shanghai's circle of leftist thinkers" and "was also motivated by political feminism."[12] However, the overall scale of social and political feminist movements, even combining the memberships of these two Christian organizations, remained small.[13] As for views on warfare, the male-dominated discourse that centered on the issue of militant resistance at the time was most likely unthinkable among many Christian women.

By exploring relevant writings in the Christian woman's magazine titled *Nü duo* (1912–51), the first and longest-running Protestant periodical for Chinese women, this paper explores the gendered nature of responses centered on issues of divine love and human suffering. An exploration of educated Christian women's voices during the wartime era introduces discourse that was personal and yet universal. The wartime ordeal was a shared experience that triggered public theological discussion of suffering among educated Christian women. To address the wartime ordeal, *Nü duo* published articles on Christian love that were closely associated with the humanity of Jesus. The writings in the magazine yield a biblical interpretation that had wide implications in wartime China and beyond.

This essay comprises four sections. The first section briefly introduces the magazine, including its editors, purpose, contributors, readership, and circulation. This section shows that the magazine represented dominant church views on gender, which created an intellectual community among Chinese women who were most likely associated with different denominations or church organizations. The second and third sections explore two recurring themes discussed in *Nü duo* throughout the 1930s and up to 1941, when its office in Shanghai was taken over by the Japanese military. In a wartime context where human suffering became appalling, Chinese Christian women started to discuss human suffering. The second section explores readers' letters and the editorial responses in the

---

11 Helen M. Schneider, *Keeping the Nation's House: Domestic Management and the Making of Modern China* (Vancouver: UBC Press, 2014).

12 Elizabeth A. Littell-Lamb, "Going Public: The YWCA, 'New' Women, and Social Feminism in Republican China" (PhD diss., Carnegie Mellon University, 2002), 14.

13 Littell-Lamb, "Going Public," 385.

magazine. Common questions such as "why do humans suffer?" and "where does suffering come from?" underpinned concerns expressed in readers' letters. The magazine responded by upholding God's sovereignty and acknowledging the limitations of human wisdom. The third section examines another crucial theme discussed in wartime *Nü duo*: the humanity of Jesus. This section examines how the magazine promoted a humane Jesus amidst warfare to comfort and strengthen its readers. The unconditional love of Jesus promoted by *Nü duo* was a call for Christians to exercise love and extend it even to the invading foreign enemy. Christian faith thus transformed passive victims of warfare into active agents to live out their faith. The concluding section maps the theological discussions in *Nü duo* of divine love and human suffering in a wider context.

Nü duo and Forming a Community among Educated Chinese Christian Women

Nü duo was published in 1912 by the Christian Literature Society (the CLS), an influential inter-denominational press in Republican China. Its founding editor Laura M. White (1867–1937) was an American missionary who was dispatched to China in 1891 by the Women's Foreign Missionary Society of the Methodist Episcopal Church (WFMS), which was an influential American Protestant women's missionary society from the late nineteenth century to the mid-twentieth century.[14] Priscilla Pope-Levison notes that from 1869 to 1890, Protestant women established home and foreign missionary organizations in several denominations, and points out that "these missionary organizations opened up myriad opportunities for women missionaries to preach, teach, and plant churches on the mission field, the very activities that women were not authorized to do in their home congregations."[15] From the 1890s to the 1920s, historically known as the Progressive Era, missionary women's evangelical work took on a "progressive" color, in contrast to the monotonous Victorian domesticity that confined women to their household duties. American Christian women, according to Pope-Levison, expended considerable effort building institutions during this era, the largest example of which was the WCTU.[16]

---

14 Annual Reports of the Women's Foreign Missionary Society of the Methodist Episcopal Church (WFMS) from 1890 to 1906.

15 Priscilla Pope-Levison, *Building the Old Time Religion* (New York: New York University Press, 2014), 15.

16 Pope-Levison, *Building the Old Time Religion*, 4, 16.

Female missionaries at the turn of the twentieth century were largely a heterogenous group. Some members demonstrated adherence to evangelical work in social causes and others were involved in political education and lobbying.[17] Despite having the freedom to form foreign missions, Patricia R. Hill argues that Western missionary women were restricted by prevailing religious and Victorian cultural ideologies of the time, such as the sanctification of motherhood.[18] White belonged to this group, holding firm belief in women's domestic virtues and motherhood. Before assuming the editorship of *Nü duo*, White had worked in girls' mission schools in Zhenjiang and Nanjing, teaching music, sewing, cooking, mathematics, church history, and Christian classics.[19] Sasaki Motoe identifies two missionary groups conducting education work in China at the time, which she refers to as the "homemakers" group and the "new leaders" group. White belonged to the former group of female missionaries who emphasized homemaking crafts. Matilda Calder Thurston (1875–1958), a member of the "new leaders" group, was disdainful of White, describing her as "full of sentiment" in her support of "mother-craft" rather than higher education for women. From the viewpoint of Thurston, who believed in the importance of Western modernity for the future of Chinese women, White "belonged to a bygone Victorian generation that could not cope with the development of a new form of female subjectivity in China."[20]

When White edited *Nü duo*, from 1912 to 1929, she aimed to eliminate inbred customs (*jixi* 積習) and increase wisdom and morality (*zhide* 智德) among Chinese women.[21] The title of the magazine was written with the Chinese characters *Nü duo* 女鐸 or "women's bell." According to *Zhou li* (*The Rites of Zhou*), wooden bells were used in ancient China to issue proclamations, while

---

17 Barbara Reeves-Ellington, Kathryn Kish Sklar, and Connie Anne Shemo, ed., *Competing Kingdoms: Women, Mission, Nation, and the American Protestant Empire, 1812–1960* (Durham, NC: Duke University Press, 2010), 2, 36–37, 53–54.

18 Patricia R. Hill, *The World Their Household: The American Woman's Foreign Mission Movement and Cultural Transformation 1870–1920* (Ann Arbor: University of Michigan Press, 1985), 23.

19 Annual reports of the WFMS from 1890 to 1906.

20 Sasaki Motoe, *Redemption and Revolution: American and Chinese New Women in the Early Twentieth Century* (Ithaca: Cornell University Press, 2016), 49–51. Motoe quotes this from a private letter, which I was unable to obtain. Motoe's research is based on the letters of Matilda Thurston, 1 March 1914, folder 2854, box 143, RG 11, UBCHEA, Yale Divinity School Library.

21 Laura White, "Nü duo bao bianji dayi" 女鐸報編輯大意 [The editorial message], *Nü duo* (April 1912): 1.

bronze bells were used to announce the outbreak of war. White explained that *Nü duo* was the wooden bell for women, both in the home and at school, to awaken them from the "darkness" and enlighten them with Christian ideals of domesticity.[22] The magazine also advocated modern knowledge to govern everyday home life by publishing many articles on homemaking and popular science. This was reflective of the discourse of domestic science in women's periodicals at the time as well as the efforts of home economics in Christian and non-Christian schools from the 1920s to the 1940s.[23]

Targeting educated women who were soon to be, or were already, housewives, *Nü duo* represented the mainstream church gender norms that featured a notion of domestic femininity. While Christian women were engaged in various activities, domesticity was, as Helen M. Schneider notes, a notable concern of progressive foreign and native Christians, who "contributed to the educational and social efforts to reform families in the late Qing dynasty and the Republican period."[24] Littell-Lamb also notes that the discourse of domesticity advocated by the Progressive-era women of the Chinese YWCA was used to legitimize their public lives "without directly confronting the status quo of the overwhelmingly conservative treaty port and Christian communities where the majority of these women resided."[25] Within the Protestant Christian community, *Nü duo* was viewed as a "sweet, clear voice . . . calling the women of the country to plain home duties, to the care and training of children, to Christian temperance, to social virtues."[26]

Nü duo maintained its advocacy of women's domestic duties particularly under the editorship of White. In the 1930s, the editorship of the periodical was transferred to Chinese Christian women and remained so until the last issue. Li Guanfang (李冠芳 1896–1937?) succeeded to the editorship in 1929 and

---

22 Xu Nailu 許耐廬, "Fakan ci" 發刊辭 [Announcement], *Nü duo* (April 1912): 2.

23 The prominent women's magazine *Funü zazhi* included a column titled *jiazheng* 家政 (domestic science) in the 1910s. See Liu Huiying 刘慧英, "Bei zhebi de funü fuchu lishi xushu—jianshu chuqi de *Funü zazhi*" 被遮蔽的婦女浮出歷史敘述—簡述初期的《婦女雜誌, *Shanghai wenxue* 上海文學 Vol. 3 (2006): 71; Helen M. Schneider, "Raising the Standards of Family Life: Ginling Women's College and Christian Social Service in Republican China," in *Divine Domesticities: Christian Paradoxes in Asia and the Pacific*, eds, Hyaeweol Choi and Margaret Jolly, (Canberra, ACT: ANU Press, 2014), 116–19.

24 Schneider, *Keeping the Nation's House*, 76.

25 Littell-Lamb, *Going Public*, 3, 14.

26 Mrs T. C. Chu, "Magazines for Chinese Women," in *The China Mission Year Book 1917* (Shanghai: the CLS, 1917), 456.

worked as a member on the Board of Directors in the CLS until 1934 when she left the CLS to take up social work.[27] Liu Meili (劉美麗 1906–?, also known as Mary Liu) edited the magazine from 1935 to 1951. Both Li and Liu were White's students and graduates from Ginling Women's College. While *Nü duo* still positioned itself as a periodical for Christian home life, it started to include concerns from Chinese perspectives in the post-White period. From the 1930s onwards, the magazine included a greater portion of writings that portray the active encounters between Christianity and the local environment.

Along with the birth of *Nü duo*, a community of readers and contributors formed among educated Chinese Christian women. Contributors in the initial stages were female teachers and students from Nanjing Huiwen Girls' School, where White was the principal from 1907 to 1913,[28] and other mission schools where she once taught. On an institutional level, contributors came from girls' schools in Beijing, Tianjin, Zhenjiang, Jiujiang, and Guangdong.[29] The WCTU, an organization connected with the editorial board of *Nü duo*, also prepared materials for publication and maintained a long cooperation with the magazine until the late 1930s.[30] During the 1930s, *Nü duo* was impacted by the Sino-Japanese war. Compared with the first two decades, contributors in the last two decades changed frequently and are difficult to trace.

The target readership of *Nü duo* was female students at school and literate girls in homes.[31] Students from mission schools formed one large group of readers. In her report on women's work at Rong xian 容縣 in Guangxi, the missionary Eliza Marshall recorded that the local mission school subscribed to *Nü duo* in 1925, and its fourteen students enjoyed it very much.[32] The popularity of *Nü duo* in mission schools is evident in a survey sent to junior and senior students in fourteen mission colleges and universities in 1925, which listed *Nü duo* as one of the most useful magazines for readers' religious lives.[33] Some missionary

---

27 "Office Bearers for 1928–9," in *The Forty-first Annual Report of the CLS* (Shanghai: the CLS, 1928); *The Forty-seventh Annual Report of the CLS* (Shanghai: the CLS, 1934), 16.

28 Official Minutes of the Central China Annual Conference of the Methodist Episcopal Church held at Nanking China from 1907 to 1913 (Shanghai: Methodist Publishing House, 1907–13).

29 *The Thirty-fifth Annual Report of the CLS* (Shanghai: the CLS, 1922), 22.

30 *The Chinese Recorder* (October 1938): 515.

31 White, "The editorial message," 1.

32 Eliza Marshall, "Women's Work-Junghsien," *The West China Missionary News* (January 1919): 53–54.

33 "What Students are Reading," *The Chinese Recorder* (May 1925): 307–309.

accounts indicated that another group of readers came from the upper social class. One Chinese merchant even claimed, "I read it regularly, as do my wife and daughter."[34]

Among women's periodicals, *Nü duo* enjoyed a relatively wide circulation. The circulation in its launch year was 23,000 copies and continued to be over 10,000 copies a year until the outbreak of the Second Sino-Japanese War.[35] Under Japanese occupation, *Nü duo* published only four issues irregularly from 1942 to 1943. It was not until 1944, when the CLS depot was established in Chengdu, that circulation was revived. Although the scale of its circulation is arguably small, *Nü duo* was among the few sites to document the ideas of educated Christian women from the outbreak of the Second Sino-Japanese War in the 1930s until 1941. It was throughout this mounting crisis that theological discussion took place within the magazine.

Theological Discussions on Suffering amidst Warfare

Scholarship has noted the nationalist and socialist work of the Chinese YWCA in the tumultuous 1930s. From the late 1920s to the late 1930s, the Chinese YWCA became more politicized, carrying out social reform and industrial work. According to Littell-Lamb, the secretaries of the YWCA's industrial work "helped effect a fundamental change in the Association's class identity, social orientation and social perspective."[36] Rather than remaining a simple middle-class women's organization, the industrial work of the Association showed growing

---

34 "The influence of Christian Literature," in Mary Ninde Gamewell, *New Life Currents in China*, (New York: Missionary Education Movement of the United States and Canada, 1919), 165.

35 The regular circulation of *Nü duo* suffered under the outbreak of full-scale war between China and Japan in 1937. In 1938 and 1939 there were, respectively, 590 and 850 subscribers. The magazine had reduced its content from about sixty pages to thirty by early 1938 but regained its former size later that year. Issues remained about sixty pages until late 1941 when war between Japan and the United States resulted in the departure of missionaries from China's hinterland, affecting the magazine's production. With the end of the Isolated Island Era (12 November 1937 to 8 December 1941), British and American members of the CLS in Shanghai were forced to resign and were thrown into detention camps in 1941. See *The Annual Report of the CLS* (Shanghai: the CLS, 1939), 10; Daniel H. Bays, *A New History of Christianity in China* (Malden, Mass.: Wiley-Blackwell, 2012), 142; *The Annual Report of the CLS* (Shanghai: the CLS, 1946), 4.

36 Elizabeth A. Littell-Lamb, "Engendering a Class Revolution: the Chinese YWCA industrial reform work in Shanghai, 1927–1939." *Women's History Review*, 21: 2 (2012): 190.

concern for women in the laboring class. Socialist feminist thinking was evident in the YWCA's work in the 1930s. Some YWCA leaders showed sympathy for Communism and thought some of its message was good for the masses.[37] Leaders including the head of the YWCA Chinese industrial department Lily Haass (1886–1964) criticized "the limitations of the Church as a framework for reform."[38] When the Battle of Shanghai between China and Japan broke out in January 1932, the mouthpiece of the Chinese YWCA, *Nü qingnian yuekan*, published an article on the impact of warfare on Shanghai industries and reported on workers' lives.[39]

In the early 1930s, when *Nü duo* was edited by Li Guanfang, the magazine also demonstrated growing concerns about social issues and the national crisis due to the editor's social concerns.[40] Regarding the Battle of Shanghai, *Nü duo* translated and circulated letters from the Japanese Women's Peace Association (Riben Nüzi Heping Hui 日本女子和平會) and the Japanese YWCA, who expressed deep concerns over current affairs and appealed for collaboration between women of the two countries to promote peace.[41] While the magazine published articles and news on women's voices on anti-warfare as well as their work in national crisis under the editorship of Li, its primary concern on household issues differentiated it from the socialist feminism promoted by the Chinese YWCA. With Li's resignation from the CLS due to her growing investment in social work in 1934, *Nü duo*, under the editorship of Liu Meili, was committed to nurturing the spiritual lives of its readers.

As the Sino-Japanese war intensified, the Chinese YWCA advocated that women played a crucial role in times of national crisis. With Japan's increasing aggression in North China in 1936, the organization added lectures for factory

---

37 For Lily Haass on communism and Christianity, see Littell-Lamb, *Engendering a Class Revolution*, 201.

38 Littell-Lamb, *Engendering a Class Revolution*, 202.

39 "Zhongri zhanzheng duiyu Shanghai gongyejie de yingxiang" 中日戰爭對於上海工業界的影響 [The Impact of the Sino-Japanese War on Shanghai Industry], *Nü qingnian yuekan* 11:6 (1932): 16–17.

40 For a detailed discussion of Li Guanfang, see Zhou Yun, "Christianizing China for the sake of China: Li Guanfang and her Republican Dream," in *Shaping Christianity in Greater China: Indigenous Christians in Focus*, ed. Paul Woods (UK: Regnum, 2017), 83–97.

41 "Riben nüzi heping xiehui zhi Zhongguo funü xiehui shu" 日本女子和平協會致中國婦女協會書 [Japanese Women's Peace Association Letter to Chinese Women's Association], *Nü duo* (April 1932): 58; "Riben jidujiao funüjie fu Zhongguo youren shu" 日本基督教婦女界復中國友人書 [Japanese Christian Women's Reply to Chinese Friends], *Nü duo* (May 1932): 61–65.

women on nationalism and anti-imperialism in addition to literacy and organizational techniques.[42] Regarding the Battle of Suiyuan, where the GMD fought to resist "Japanese incursions from Manchukuo into Chahar" in 1936,[43] the institutional magazine *Nü qingnian* circulated an article calling for the whole nation to unite and fight against imperial Japan.[44] On women's roles in warfare, it reported on the global peace movement among women in other countries in the mid-1930s. The magazine argued that women's roles were essential to the peace movement and appealed for a "united front" (*lianhe zhanxian* 聯合戰線) among women around the world. Regardless of their differences in class and religion, women should join this front and concentrate on objecting to war-provoking criminals. Chinese women, who had demonstrated their bravery in a series of patriotic movements in the 1920s, should fight for China's war against imperialist invasion and secure peace in East Asia.[45]

Amidst the national crisis imposed by Japanese military invasion, *Nü duo*, under the editorship of Liu Meili, turned to the religious interests of its readers and endeavored to address the issue of the war ordeal through biblical interpretation. Everyday life in wartime China stimulated theological discussions on human suffering among *Nü duo*'s readers. The editorial board of this Christian woman's magazine received several letters from its readership touching on questions such as "Why do we suffer?" and "Where does suffering come from?" Some Christian readers even doubted God's supreme power because of the war. Letters showed that their faith was challenged by God's silence in response to their prayers.

In response, the editor Liu Meili co-translated Leslie D. Weatherhead's (1893–1976) work, *Why Do Men Suffer?*, believing that the discussion of suffering in general might be helpful to understanding Chinese peoples' ordeals during the war.[46] From November 1937 to January 1940, *Nü duo* published this

---

42 Littell-Lamb, *Engendering a Class Revolution*, 202–204.

43 Li Xiaobing, ed., *China at War: An Encyclopedia* (Santa Barbara, Calif.: ABC-CLIO, 2012), 128.

44 Xiaoyun 啸云, "You Suisheng zhanzheng shuodao quanguo kangzhan" 由綏省戰爭說到全國戰爭 [From Warfare in Sui Province to National War of Resistance], *Nü qingnian yuekan* 15: 10 (1936): 9–11.

45 Feng Huijun 馮慧君, "Xian jieduan de heping yundong yu funü" 現階段的和平運動與婦女 [The Present Stage of the Women's Peace Movement], *Nü qingnian yuekan* 16: 4 (1937): 31–37.

46 Editor, "Women de xinxin" 我們的信心 [Our confidence], *Nü duo* (July 1939): 1.

serially.[47] While Weatherhead's name might be less well known to Chinese Christians, he was a prolific writer and preacher who had published many books on philosophy of religion by the late 1930s. Weatherhead's book on human suffering, published in 1936 and widely reviewed at the time, was a new collection to counsel people in miserable situations. The urgent need for the editorial board to address the current suffering of Chinese Christian readers made Weatherhead's book a perfect pitch in the wartime period, and Liu Meili started to work on the translation shortly after the book was published. A comparison of the original and translation shows the editor's efforts to provide a faithful literal translation. Central questions included: is God omnipotent; why does God allow suffering; is suffering the will of God; and what is God's attitude to the suffering of human beings? The answer, as addressed in the preface, began with the ultimate sovereignty of God and God's righteousness, justified by the Biblical verses in Psalm 97: 1–2.

> The Lord reigneth; let the earth rejoice;
> Let the multitude of isles be glad.
> Clouds and darkness are round about Him:
> Righteousness and judgment are the foundation of His throne.[48]

The corresponding translation in *Nü duo* is taken from the Union Version of the Chinese Bible.

> 耶和華作王；願地快樂；
> 願眾海島歡喜。
> 密雲和幽暗在祂的四圍：
> 公義和公平是祂寶座的根基.[49]

Weatherhead's book acknowledged the limited wisdom of human beings. It highlighted the friendship of Jesus, who offered himself, and the spiritual power

---

47 Under the title "Ren weishenme shou tongku?" The series was later published in a monograph by the CLS in April 1940. The CLS later published his religious viewpoints on discipleship, psychology, and healing the soul. See "Bianzhe de hua" 編者的話 [Editorial], *Dao shen* 12:7 (1941): 1.

48 Leslie D. Weatherhead, *Why Do Men Suffer* (London: Student Christian Movement Press, 1935), 9.

49 Liu Meili, 'Ren weishenme shou tongku' 人爲什麼受痛苦 [Why do people suffer], *Nü duo* (November 1937): 1.

of God's grace and help, to everyone. The author endeavored to convince Christian readers of the value of prayer in suffering. He wrote, "Its [prayer in suffering] value is seen in the rich fellowship which the sufferer has with God through it." Because of this fellowship, the sufferer can become patient and "is able to co-operate with God so that whatever happens the eyes are lifted to the glory of God and the final consummation of His purposes."[50] Overall, Liu Meili believed Weatherhead's analysis offered "a satisfactory answer to the question 'Why Do People Suffer?'"[51]

The circulation of Weatherhead's work in *Nü duo* evidently failed to meet the needs of readers, who continued to advance discussions of suffering. After reading the series of articles on humanity's suffering, one female reader wrote to the editorial board asking why God treated his children so unfairly. The following is a translation of her letter quoted in *Nü duo* in February 1940.

> If God is indeed our dear father, is he the same as our earthly fathers who show favoritism to their children? If you say "No," then how do you explain why some people are so rich and some are so poor? Why do some people continuously meet with misfortune and some people have no misfortune at all? This evidence demonstrates God's favoritism. If you still say "No," how then can you explain it?[52]

The editor replied that the reader's criticism of God was wrong. With a firm belief in a God whose love and wisdom surpassed that of human beings, the editor advised readers to understand that a person's burden was only known to that individual. The article stated that there were tangible burdens such as illness and poverty, and there were also intangible burdens that troubled the heart, and suggested readers have faith in God and consider suffering as a way of steeling oneself.

Aside from the general questions about suffering, *Nü duo*'s readers raised specific questions about their wartime experience. Many readers' letters were

---

50 Weatherhead, *Why Do Men Suffer*, 180. For the corresponding translation, see Liu, "Ren weishenme shou tongku?," *Nü duo* (July 1939): 9.

51 The cover page of the translated Chinese monograph "Why Do Men Suffer?" See *Ren weishenme shou tongku*, trans. Liu Meili and Ye Bohua (Shanghai: the CLS, April 1940).

52 M C, "Shangdi dui rensheng tongku de taidu" 上帝對人生痛苦的態度 [God's attitude towards human suffering], *Nü duo* (February 1940): 31.

concerned with wartime privations. Some of the letters from the occupied territory mentioned that aerial bombing had destroyed their properties. Some of these letter-writers wrote that they had lost family members. In their flight from warfare, many women were abused, not to mention other difficulties such as losing jobs and suffering from illness. The editor encouraged these readers to share their sorrows with their friends. The article then referred to the last supper, arguing that by sharing food and drink with his twelve disciples, Jesus was sharing his pain with his followers, which brought about the power that changed the world.[53]

On the question of why good people die, the editor Liu Meili responded that many people die of their own "stupidity and ignorance" (*yumei wuzhi* 愚昧無知). As no verse in the Bible promised that good people would have a long life, the editor believed one should not blame God for the death of good people. Noting that Japanese aircraft had killed many civilians, including both good and bad people, the editor considered misery to be something caused by human beings who abused their "free will" (*ziyou de yizhi* 自由的意志). However, she insisted that God would bring goodness out of humans' sins. Although sometimes it was difficult to understand the reasons behind certain matters, she called for continued belief in God's love.[54]

One female reader seemed to be unsatisfied with *Nü duo*'s interpretation of God and humanity's suffering. She wrote to the editorial board,

> You often advise us to believe in God and trust in his almighty power. [You point out that] God is sympathetic to humanity's pain. Much suffering is generated by human beings and therefore one should not blame God. Once pain is caused, it will take a certain period for God to rescue you. God might use this suffering to weave clothing to glorify God. But I think God should be responsible for the suffering of the innocent.[55]

The editor, under the pen name M C, referred to the biblical passage on Jesus and a man born blind, where Jesus explains that the man's illness is not because

---

53 Editor, "Gei shou tongku de ren" 給受痛苦的人 [Message for the suffering], *Nü duo* (August 1938): 1.

54 Editor, "Haoren he yi zao si" 好人何以早死 [Why do good people die at a young age], *Nü duo* (July 1938): 1–2.

55 M C, "Shangdi yu rensheng de tongku wenti" 上帝與人生的痛苦問題 [God and humankind's suffering], *Nü duo* (November 1939): 13.

the man or his parents sinned, but to display God's work in him. The author suggested that readers learn from Jesus and believe in God's love; humans' punishment was often due to the law of cause and effect and not because of God.

Concerning the Sino-Japanese War, the author continued, we Chinese people prayed to God for national victory. So did the Japanese people. As both Chinese and Japanese were God's children, God might be using his powers judiciously to adjust affairs between China and Japan. The editor indicated that God thinks in a way different from human beings. Yet God revealed himself and his love toward us through Jesus so that humanity could understand that God would not punish us through suffering.[56]

In another article titled "Ku'nan yu rensheng" (Ordeals and Life) published in December 1940, *Nü duo* advocated that the suffering of Jesus throughout his earthly life was to prepare himself for the mission of salvation. The author referred to a similar teaching in the twelfth chapter of the book of *Mencius*, which states,

> Thus, when Heaven is about to confer a great office on any man, it first exercises his mind with suffering, and his sinews and bones with toil. It exposes his body to hunger, and subjects him to extreme poverty.[57]

The readers' letters recorded in *Nü duo* point to suffering as the primary concern among educated Chinese Christian women. To address these questions, the magazine concentrated on God's love and supreme sovereignty as well as humanity's limited wisdom and abuse of "free will." In difficult times, *Nü duo* sent out a message that God still cared for humanity and that the ordeal could be transformed into goodness. This evangelical stance formed a sharp contrast to the Chinese YWCA's advocacy of women's engagement in social and political movements. Compared with YWCA's socialist and nationalist stance, *Nü duo* continued to advocate that women's roles were to be a mother and wife at home. It served to address concerns primarily from urban middle-class women about their personal religious struggle during this ordeal. *Nü duo* responded in an evangelical way and promoted showing Christian love even to the enemy.

---

56 M C, "Shangdi yu rensheng de tongku wenti," 14.

57 Wan Shi 頑石, "Ku'nan yu rensheng" 苦難與人生 [Ordeals and life], *Nü duo* (December 1940): 29. Mencius: *Gaozi (xia)*; translation from Legge, see https://ctext.org/mengzi/gaozi-i

Humane Jesus and Universal Christian Love

Nü duo's approach to warfare was to promote a humane Jesus. The magazine portrayed Jesus as one who loved humanity and endured a great deal of suffering to fulfill his plan to redeem humankind. *Nü duo* was not the only voice that advocated Christian love in Republican China. The pacifist movement took place in the 1920s after the end of World War I. It was a shared reflection by Chinese Christians and Western missionaries on the tangled relationship between Christian missions and foreign imperialism. The establishment of The Fellowship of Reconciliation (FoR, *Wei ai she*) in Beijing in 1922 was a landmark in the pacifist movement in China.[58] With the escalation of China's warfare with Japan, however, the pacifist movement partially dissolved into one that promoted resistance. Wu Yaozong, a leading pacifist figure, resigned from his presidency of the FoR around 1937, and a close examination of Wu's thought from the 1920s to the 1930s traces a shift from individual belief to national concern.[59] In the early stages, Wu perceived the practice of Christian love as an individual "spirituality" (*lingxiu chuantong* 靈修傳統) which aimed to improve individual morality. After the Mukden Incident in 1931, which unveiled the Japanese invasion of northeastern China, Wu started to adjust his concept of Christian love and peace in response to the national crisis and acknowledged the necessity and rationality of violent resistance.[60]

Compared with male Chinese Christian pacifists, advocacies and questions documented in *Nü duo* point to an approach that excluded the option of militant resistance and advocated belief in the love of God despite the great sufferings at the time. To advance readers' understanding of Christian love amidst the national crisis, from February 1940 to December 1941, *Nü duo* published a series of articles under the title of "Yesu de renben zhuyi," on the humanity of Jesus, translated from the monograph *The Humanism of Jesus: A Study of Christ's Human Sympathies* by the Scottish biblical scholar Robert Wishart Shepherd (1888–1971).[61] This liberal humanistic view of Jesus was further emphasized in

---

58 Yao, *The Protestant Pacifist Movement in China*, 17–23.

59 See further Qu Li's discussion in chapter 2 above.

60 Yao, *The Protestant Pacifist Movement in China*, 121–60.

61 Shepherd was an ordained minister of the Church of Scotland who began his career as a missionary to South Africa in 1918. Shepherd later worked as the director of the Lovedale Press from 1930 to 1955. During his directorship, the Press published African writings to cater to African needs, making it a crucial press at the time promoting African literature and African consciousness. See *Contemporary Authors: A Bio-Bibliographical Guide to Current Authors and*

Nü duo's translation of humanism into *renben zhuyi*, stressing the humanity of Jesus, not his supernatural aspect. The publication of *The Humanism of Jesus* in 1926 by Shepherd was a manifestation of his belief in God's love across races. The book highlighted Jesus as a humane one who "carried a yearning of sympathy and love for every human being."[62] Comprised of fifteen chapters, the book primarily focused on Jesus's encounters with different groups of people, such as the poor, enemies, gentiles, and children. *Nü duo* faithfully translated thirteen chapters of the book, leaving out the chapter on Jesus and the world of nature, and another about Jesus on the cross, but foregrounding Jesus's humanistic care for different groups of people.[63]

The translation of Shepherd's work in *Nü duo* likewise advocated a Christian humanism that transcended time, space, race, and nationalities. By humanism, Shepherd emphasized the importance of *humanitas*, a love for all humanity. The Latin term *humanitas*, according to Shepherd, was rendered by Jerome in the Vulgate to replace the Greek concept of philanthropy. The term was used to describe the kindness indigenous people showed to Paul when "Paul and his fellow-travelers escaped the storm and landed on Melita" in the *Acts of the Apostles*. Instead of highlighting kindness, both Jerome and Shepherd stressed the depth and breadth of the sympathy of Jesus to all humankind, "Roman, Greek, Samaritan, Canaanite, Jew; rich, poor, learned, ignorant, sickly, healthy, fallen, saintly."[64]

The Chinese equivalent for *humanitas* in *Nü duo* was *ren ai* 仁愛, or "benevolence and humanity." The term *ren* is a cardinal concept in the classics. It features an emphasis on humanity, encapsulated in the Confucian teaching *ren zhe ai ren* ("benevolence means to love people 仁者愛人," from *Mencius*).[65] In his monograph on the study of *ren* and *agape*, Yao Xinzhong examines these two significant concepts in Confucian and Christian traditions and argues that the former was humanistic and universal while the latter was theistic and neighborly love. The primary difference between these two concepts is that the former

---

Their Works, vol. 1, ed., Clare D. Kinsman (Detroit: Gale Research Co., 1975), 573; Tim White, "The Lovedale Press during the Directorship of R. H. W. Shepherd, 1930–1955," *English in Africa* 19:2 (October 1992): 69–84.

62 Robert H. W. Shepherd, *The Humanism of Jesus: A Study in Christ's Human Sympathies* (London: James Clarke, 1926), 9.

63 The monograph titled *Yesu de Renben zhuyi* published the CLS in 1948 in Shanghai, however, included the last two chapters. See *Yesu de Renben zhuyi* (Shanghai: the CLS, 1948).

64 Shepherd, *The Humanism of Jesus*, 9–11.

65 For a summary of the discourse of *ren* and Christian missionaries' attempts in translating *ren*, see Taiyi Kang, "Ci jian ren ai" [love in this world], *Du shu* (November 2015): 168–72.

believes *ren* is a human virtue and the latter holds that *agape* is divine.[66] The compound *ren ai* in writings in *Nü duo* embraced a theistic interpretation of love. It emphasized the universalism of Christian love exemplified through Jesus, and stated that God's love was for all humanity, calling on Christians to follow the example of Jesus.[67]

In addition to delineating Jesus's humanism through the translation of Shepherd's work, *Nü duo* encouraged readers to follow the steps of Jesus and exercise hospitality amidst political and social upheavals. In a wartime context, writings in *Nü duo* tended to categorize non-Christians as strangers. Several articles advocated that readers should provide hospitality to refugees and injured soldiers. For example, an article in the editorial column published in September 1938, one year after the Second Sino-Japanese War escalated into a full-scale conflict, discussed the defining features of a Christian convert. The editor at the time, Liu Meili, stressed that having a caring heart (*you aixin* 有愛心) was the defining feature of Christians.[68] In her estimation, *ai* or love was the foundation of the gospel as well as that of the Christian faith and Christian behavior.

The article referred to Jesus's questioning of his disciple Peter's love for him. The author Liu Meili believed that Jesus's questioning was intended to test whether Peter could be his disciple. She interpreted the passage as showing that if we act based on love and loving others as ourselves, then we obey the divine will and are close to the divine being. Liu stated, furthermore, that Christians should rescue refugees and wounded soldiers in emulation of the loving spirit of Christ. The article urged Christians not to think only of themselves (*du shan qi shen* 獨善其身), but instead, to "go into the midst of the common people (*shenru qunzhong* 深入群眾) and help, relieve, guide, and reform others through persuading them to improve their lives."[69] The author admonished Christian readers not to have a sense of superiority over people with different ideals. Those who isolated themselves from common people, including the poor and the criminal, were, in the editor's viewpoint, disqualified as Jesus's disciples.

---

66 Xinzhong Yao, *Confucianism and Christianity: a comparative study of Jen and Agape* (Brighton: Sussex Academic Press, 1996).

67 "Yesu de renben zhuyi," 耶穌的人本主義 [The Humanity of Jesus], *Nü duo* (February 1940): 26.

68 Editor, "Zenyang cai suan shi jidutu" 怎樣才算是基督徒 [Who is a genuine Christian?], *Nü duo* (September 1938): 1–2.

69 Editor, "Who is a genuine Christian?," 1.

The most challenging group of people for Christians to offer hospitality to was the enemy forces, or Japanese military contingents. On 7 July 1937, the Japanese army provoked the Marco Polo Bridge Incident and conflict with China escalated into a full-scale war. This incident deeply troubled some Chinese Christians' faith in pacifism. Wu Yaozong, a leading pacifist figure, became alienated from the non-resistance approach and started to appeal for intervention from the international community to resist Japan's invasion of China.[70] In contrast to the growing nationalist sentiment and a waning discourse of pacifism among male Protestant Christians, two months after the incident *Nü duo* published an article titled "Do You Love Your Enemy?" The article elaborated on the concept of *ai* (love) from three perspectives: erotic love (*nannü zhi ai* 男女之愛), friendship (*youyi de ai* 友誼的愛), and love for your enemy (*ai nimen de choudi* 愛你們的仇敵). While the first two kinds of love were easy to understand, the article argued that loving one's enemy was the ultimate teaching of Christianity, which was to go beyond hatred and affection and enter a rational state of mind. This type of love was the infallible love of Christ. It stated that the descendants of Christ were to embody God's love for human beings. As God forgave your sins, you should likewise forgive the sins of other people and treat them as God treated you. Loving your enemy, according to the article, did not mean to love their sinful deeds but rather to accept them as God's children and forgive them. While individualism and nationalism encouraged a love for oneself and one's country, the article admonished its readers to love everyone, including one's enemy.[71]

The Chinese term *ai* put forward by *Nü duo* stressed the radical love that resembled the Christian concept of *agape*, "as distinct from *philia*, 'affection' and *eros*, 'passionate love.'"[72] The Greek word *agape* in the New Testament generally denotes the "self-giving love" that was embodied in Christ and is present in the community of believers when they give themselves to others.[73] In her work on Christians' hospitality during war, Caron E. Gentry argues that *agape*, the cornerstone of the Christian faith, features "intrinsic care for others (love of God and neighbor before self)" that "is related to hospitality." Gentry articulates that *agape* "is a purely selfless, obedient, unconditional love" and "brings strangers into

---

70　Yao, *The Protestant Pacifist Movement in China*, 177–79.

71　Xianchao 顯超, "Ni ai ni de diren me" 你愛你的仇敵嗎 [Do you love your enemy], *Nü duo* (September 1937): 36–38.

72　Finn, "Agape," 1.

73　Finn, "Agape," 1.

community via the self's relationship with God and makes others neighbors." Gentry elaborates on "two ways in which neighbor-love is transformative: it loves without self-interest, and it loves the enemy."[74] The advocacy of love in wartime editions of *Nü duo* foregrounds this ideal of Christian humanism even to the enemy forces.

To promote God's love as universal, writings in *Nü duo* referred to the Japanese pacifist Kagawa Toyohiko.[75] Kagawa was a well-received Japanese Protestant in China who promoted love and peace in militarist Japan. In 1934, the CLS published his monograph titled *Love, The Law of Life*. In the preface, Kagawa asked Chinese readers for their forgiveness and appealed to God's love that transcended races.[76] In October 1940, *Nü duo* published an article that resembled Toyohiko's thinking. Under the title "Zhengfu yiqie de shi ai," meaning love conquers all, the article rejected violent resistance and instead advocated the concept of love. It cited Kagawa's attitude on love in his monograph:

> I oppose any knowledge, organization, government, art, or religion that rejects love; I oppose any church that takes pride in faith yet fails to practice love; I oppose any politician that relies on violence and is ignorant of love.[77]

The article mentioned an American film titled *Wanli xunshi* ("Searching for a missionary across thousands of miles;" the original title was *Stanley and Livingstone*) to address the power of love across countries and races. Initially released in 1939 in the United States, the movie was also released in Shanghai in 1940. It depicted a white American journalist who went to Africa to find a missionary doctor and whose racial prejudice toward black peoples was eventually changed

---

74 Caron E. Gentry, *Offering Hospitality: Questioning Christian Approaches to War* (Notre Dame, Indiana: University of Notre Dame Press, 2013), 8, 57.

75 Research shows that Kagawa declared himself no longer a pacifist after the outbreak of the Pacific War in 1941. See Liu, "The fate of contemporary Christian pacifism in China and Japan," 102.

76 Kagawa Toyohiko, *Love, The Law of Life*, translated by Yu Kangde (Shanghai: the CLS, 1934), 2.

77 Cai Yinuo 蔡以諾, "Zhengfu yiqie de shi ai!" 征服一切的是愛！["Love" conquers everything!], *Nü duo* (October 1940): 35. For the original text in the Chinese translation, see Kagawa Toyohiko, *Love, The Law of Life*, 4.

through the love shown by the missionary. The article concluded that love was eternal and all-powerful.[78]

Through promoting Christian love and hospitality to strangers during the national crisis, Chinese Christian women were encouraged to embrace a universal outlook. The advocacy of hospitality and the radical love for the enemy suggest an unconditional love that transcends class, religion, and nationality. Promoting this Christian universalism did not necessarily exclude nationalist concerns, as seen in several articles published in the magazine. For example, an article in the editorial column published in *Nü duo* in April 1938 commended readers to relieve children from warfare and nurture them for the sake of China.[79] When readers recounted their sufferings such as losing property and family members, Liu Meili comforted them with the assurance that they were sacrificing for the whole nation.[80] In another article published in November 1938, the editor referred to the national territory as "ours" (*women de* 我們的) and Chinese people as "our comrades" (*women de tongbao* 我們的同胞).[81] This language can be seen in many other articles in *Nü duo*. The advocacy of a universal Christian love extended to enemies did not contradict Chinese national identity. By promoting the biblical concept of loving strangers and even enemies, the readers of *Nü duo* were invited to actively exercise their religious faith governed by divine love that went beyond races and national borders.

Conclusion

This paper has examined theological discussions on human suffering among a group of educated Christian women through the Christian women's magazine *Nü duo*. In response to the flood of critical questions from readers, the magazine attempted to synthesize the humanism of the Christian God with human suffering. It insisted on God's love while attempting to address the ordeal Chinese people underwent during the wartime period. Frequent contributors on the topic included the editor Liu Meili and Xianchao (the author of "Do you love

---

78 Cai, "'Love' conquers everything!" 36.

79 Editor, "Jiujiu beinan de ertong" 救救被難的兒童 [Save the children], *Nü duo* (April 1938): 1.

80 Editor, "Gei shou tongku de ren" 給受痛苦的人 [To people who suffer], *Nü duo* (August 1938): 1.

81 Editor, "Buyao jupa elie de huanjing" 不要懼怕惡劣的環境 [Don't fear hostile environment], *Nü duo* (November 1938): 1.

your enemy?" There is evidence to suggest that Xianchao was also a pseudonym of Liu Meili.).[82] Another frequent contributor who addressed warfare was Ye Xiaofei, who translated the work of John Sutherland Bonnell, *Pastoral psychiatry*, from 1940 to 1941. Close examination shows that Ye Xiaofei was another name used by Ye Bohua, Liu Meili's male colleague at the CLS.[83] While there is little information on Ye Bohua's theological background, much of his writing was done in collaboration with Liu Meili, who was associated with the WFMS of the Methodist Episcopal Church, an influential Protestant missionary women's society at the time. When Liu joined the CLS staff after her graduation from Ginling Women's College in 1929, she was financially supported by the WFMS (the department of the Methodist Episcopal Church for women's work), which appointed her as its representative in the CLS.[84] *Nü duo* under the editorship of Liu Meili stands as a historical artifact that documented valuable theological thinking among educated Chinese Christian women associated with mainstream dominations.

The advocacy of Christian love that emerged in *Nü duo* in the 1930s seems to run counter to the dominant discourse among the Chinese Christian community. Why did the magazine persist in advocating Christian love in the wartime period, when many male leading pacifists were alienated from the approach of nonviolence? An exploration from the perspective of gender ethics helps to illuminate this enigma. Although the unprecedented warfare was one of the primary concerns for most Chinese Christian churches at the time, it was often male Christians who designed churches' attitudes toward the warfare, since women did not play a leading role in Christian churches. The purpose of *Nü duo* echoed the gendered ethics of the Christian community and designated itself as a religious woman's periodical for home life. The outbreak of warfare with Japan, however, triggered a series of discussions that reflected how educated Christian women interpreted divine love and human suffering in a gendered setting. Unlike their male counterparts, Christian women were not at the center of nationalist movements. Their peripheral position in political activities in turn

---

82 From 1940 and 1941, Xianchao translated the work of Townley Lord titled *Great women of Christian history* and circulated it in *Nü duo*. When this series was published as a monograph by the CLS, the translator's name was given as Liu Meili.

83 When the translated work of John Sutherland Bonnell was published into a monograph by the CLS, the translators listed were Liu Meili and Ye Bohua. Ye Bohua also cotranslated Weatherhead's work on human suffering with Liu Meili, See *Ren weishenme shou tongku*, translated by Liu Meili and Ye Bohua (Shanghai: the CLS, April 1940).

84 *The Annual Report of the CLS in 1946*, 8.

allowed space for them to develop a religious understanding of Christianity that was much less confined by the concept of just war. The magazine also circulated writings of male contributors such as Cai Yinuo who advocated Christian love even when the pacifist movement waned. While many leading male Christians turned away from pacifism and embraced militant resistance in 1940, Cai, a university student of Hujiang University (previously known as Shanghai Baptist College and Theological Seminary), continued his belief in Christian love.[85] *Nü duo* thus also served as a hub for marginalized male Christian voices. Unlike the YWCA's social feminist ideology, the portrayal of Jesus as a humanist in *Nü duo* provided a theological rationale that encouraged women to reach out to strangers and exercise God's love for all.

Discussion of human suffering among educated Christian women was brought to the fore by the war. Readers' search for biblical explanations of human suffering through *Nü duo* indicated the importance of the magazine in their religious life. In response to readers' questions concerning human suffering and God's silence on the subject, the magazine pointed to the authority of God and the limitations of human wisdom. The translation of two male European authors on the topic raises questions of colonialism in the magazine's discourse. It is worth noting that Liu Meili enjoyed more control over the editorial policy than Li Guanfang. Compared with Li, who was on the Board of Directors for only four years (1930–34), Liu had a position on the Publication Committee for a period of twelve years, from 1935 to 1947. Although the Board had the power to elect the Publication Committee, it was primarily concerned with administrative duties rather than dictating editorial policy.[86] When Liu succeeded to the editorship, she demanded of the CLS that "the habit of looking over the material before publication" by "old timers in the Society" must stop, in order to publish the magazine on time. With reduced staff, Liu complained that "there would not be time for this extra checking-up and criticism." She insisted that "either [she would] edit the magazine herself, or [they] must get another editor."[87] In this sense, Liu made her own choice in translating foreign work on themes such as the issue of human suffering. What was embedded in her autonomy of choice,

---

85 Cai Yinuo, "Hujiang daxue hudong gongshe qingnian tuanqi de yici zuotanhui" 滬江大學滬東公社青年團契的一次座談會 [A Discussion of Hujiang University Hudong Youth Fellowship], *Zhenguang zazhi* 真光雜志 39:2 (1940): 35–36.

86 For the editorial policy of the CLS, see the section "Editorial Policy, Editors, and Contributors" in Chapter Two.

87 Edward Hunter, *The Story of Mary Liu* (London: Hodder and Stoughton, 1957), 90–91.

however, was a limitation in the scope of theological references. Facing unprecedented warfare, Republican male Chinese theologians were on the same page as Liu Meili. The urgent need to address readers' questions prompted Liu to seek answers in foreign sources. The male authors point to a lack of theological training for women at the time. In the case of China, as Chloë Starr notes, one could see women's theological essays and reflections published in mission journals and specialized periodical presses, but women were discouraged from careers as theologians or theological educators, as higher level theological training was not commonly open to them.[88]

While Christian women lacked theological training, the shared warfare experience did trigger theological discussions among them. The theological discussion in *Nü duo* during the wartime period of the 1930s and early 1940s showed how local Christian women comprehended and struggled with biblical teachings. The editor Liu Meili attributed human suffering to the abuse of "free will" by some people. Nevertheless, she believed that God would work through the suffering and bring goodness. Under Liu's editorship, the magazine encouraged readers to keep their faith in God's love. From recounting painful individual experiences to advocating Christian universal love, the magazine promoted individual religious life as something with profound implications. Rather than focusing on solutions to international conflict, like male Christian leaders at the time, the magazine reflected a perspective confined by contemporary church gender norms but transcending national boundaries. It shows the shortcomings of assuming a rigid dichotomous relationship between nationalism and pacifism, and advocated an alternative that featured a universal concern for wartime China and beyond.

---

88 Chloë Starr, *Chinese Theology: text and context* (New Haven: Yale University Press, 2016), 53.

Part III

Protestant Denominationalizing

Chapter 8

FROM UNFULFILLED EXPECTATIONS TO CREATIVE ENCULTURATION

Crafting and Communicating Theology in the Chung Hua Sheng Kung Hui 1849–1949

Tim Yung, *University of Hong Kong*

In *Christian Encounters with Chinese Culture*, Chloë Starr discusses the difficulties of establishing an Anglican Book of Common Prayer in late Qing and early Republican China in the absence of vital Church of England infrastructure.[1] This chapter extends the discussion to the broader attempt to craft and communicate theology in the Chung Hua Sheng Kung Hui (Anglican-Episcopal Province of China, hereafter CHSKH), highlighting how the institutional embedding of theology was intimately connected with historical context. Missionaries in the mid-nineteenth century had assumed that Western Christianity and civilization would spread across China unopposed. However, the translation of Anglican theology proved less straightforward than expected due to complicated cultural questions. In the ensuing decades, Anglican missionaries grew in their cultural sensitivity before placing their hopes in missionary cooperation at conferences, synods, and seminaries to create a consistent Chinese Anglican theology. Through the newly-constituted CHSKH general synod in 1912, the goal was to establish consistent church traditions and doctrine. However, the early twentieth century revealed that the transmission of theology was just as complicated as its translation. Moreover, the general synod was now preoccupied with

---

1 Chloë Starr, "Rethinking Church through the Book of Common Prayer in Late Qing and Early Republican China," in *Christian Encounters with Chinese Culture: Essays on Anglican and Episcopal History in China*, ed. Philip L. Wickeri (Hong Kong: Hong Kong University Press, 2015), 81–102.

questions of survival and unable to focus on theology. By the 1930s, CHSKH clergy finally developed viable strategies to adapt to their cultural context and logistical difficulties, resorting to a simplified faith and flexible communication, a legacy that endured throughout and beyond the Sino-Japanese War.

Introduction

In 1849, Bishop George Smith, one of the pioneering Anglican missionary bishops in China, issued a prospectus of plans after the Treaty of Nanjing enabled foreign missionaries to enter Chinese territory, an action that had previously been forbidden by the Qing authorities.[2] Smith's prospectus put forward an elaborate scheme of evangelism involving translating and transmitting Anglican theology throughout China. With the supposedly unstoppable advance of Anglo-Saxon civilization and Christianity worldwide, Smith intended to train Chinese evangelists at St. Paul's College, the Anglo-Chinese educational institution in the newly-established diocese of Victoria (Hong Kong).[3] These evangelists would subsequently translate and propagate Holy Scripture and Christian books, with the ultimate outcome that the gospel would be "understood everywhere." Literati would believe through print, and the masses would believe through the proclamations of young Chinese colporteurs.[4]

A century later at the 1949 centenary service of Smith's diocese, the gospel was still not "understood everywhere." Indeed, the 1949 *Chung Hua Sheng Kung Hui* (中華聖公會 [Anglican-Episcopal Province of China, or Chinese Anglican Church]) bore only limited resemblance to Smith's 1849 prospectus. Christians remained a minority in Chinese society, while the translation and transmission of Anglican theology proved to be far more complicated than Smith's projection. On the surface, the centenary service included essential elements of Anglican faith and order. Outward church practice appeared to be characteristically Anglican in that it combined the insights of the Protestant

---

2 G. F. S. Gray, *Anglicans in China: A History of the Zhonghua Shenggong Hui (Chung Hua Sheng Kung Huei)*, ed. Martha Lund Smalley (New Haven: The Episcopal China Mission History Project, 1996), 6.

3 For further reading about nineteenth-century optimism about Anglo-Saxon civilization and Christianity, see Eugene Stock, *The History of the Church Missionary Society: its Environment, its Men and its Work, Volume I* (London: Church Missionary Society, 1899), 367–81, 486–504.

4 London, Church of England Record Centre, OBF/5/2/7/3/16, George Smith, "Prospectus of Missionary Plans for the Benefit of the Chinese," 1849, 1–4.

Reformation with Roman Catholic traditions.[5] The choir and clergy, all donning vestments, entered St. John's Cathedral in solemn procession. Gospel canticles were sung, Scripture was read in the vernacular, and liturgy was recited by the congregation in unison.[6] However, upon closer inspection, the complicating factors of Chinese Anglican theology were evident. Scripture readings were taken from the 1919 *Shangdi* edition of the Mandarin Union Version, which had been painstakingly compiled over twenty-nine years after extensive debates about particular terms, dialects, and rival translations.[7] Hymns were taken from *Hymns of Universal Praise* [普天頌讚 *Putian Songzan*], a hymnbook jointly published by six denominations in 1936 that consisted of both translated and original Chinese hymns.[8] Hymns notably covered experiences from Chinese daily living such as memorializing ancestors, loyalty to the modern Chinese nation, and family prayers, in a deliberate attempt to become relevant to grassroots believers.[9] Far from nineteenth-century Anglo-Saxon Anglicanism being as all-encompassing as Smith supposed, the development and propagation of theology was not a straightforward process.

The gulf between Smith's prospectus and the centenary service begs the question how and why Chinese Anglican theology was shaped and propagated between 1849 and 1949. The process was inextricably linked to cultural conditions, global encounters, and practice-based reconfiguration.[10] It is helpful

---

5 Justyn Terry, "Theology in the Anglican Communion," in *The Wiley-Blackwell Companion to the Anglican Communion*, eds Ian S. Markham, J. Barney Hawkins IV, Justyn Terry, Leslie Nuñez Steffensen (Malden, MA: Wiley-Blackwell, 2013), 555.

6 Hong Kong Sheng Kung Hui Archive (hereafter HKSKH), 238/18, 中華聖公會港粵教區百週年紀念教區議會：開幕日紀念崇拜聚會禮文 [CHSKH Centenary South China Diocesan Synod: Service for Opening and Dedication of Synod], 21 August 1949, 1–7, 11–15.

7 See George Kam Wah Mak, *Protestant Bible Translation and Mandarin as the National Language of China* (Leiden: Brill, 2018), 15–21.

8 Mak, *Protestant Bible Translation*, 1–2.

9 Chen Ruiwen, "The Protestant Quest for Contextualized Hymnology in Twentieth Century China: A Case Study of the Collaboration Between T. C. Chao and Bliss Wiant in the Contextualization of Chinese Hymns" (Ph.D. diss., Chinese University of Hong Kong, 2014), 225–32.

10 Mark P. Hutchinson, "Glocalized and Indigenized Theologies in the Twentieth Century," in *The Oxford History of Protestant Dissenting Traditions Volume V: The Twentieth Century: Themes and Variations in a Global Context*, ed. Mark P. Hutchinson (Oxford: Oxford University Press), 261. For further reading on the CHSKH, see: Gray, *Anglicans in China*; Philip L. Wickeri, "Anglicanism in China and East Asia 1819–1912," in *The Oxford History of Anglicanism, Volume III: Partisan Anglicanism and its Global Expansion, 1829-c.1914*, ed.

first of all to outline the scope of "theology" in this case study. In the broadest sense, theology refers to the quest for what it means to be Christian in society and the conceptualization of Christ and Christian truth.[11] Yet, existing studies have stressed the distinctly different approaches across cultures in reaching this goal. Hwa Yung argues that among Asian theologians, cultures of cognition are markedly different from those of Western theologians. Asian theology tends to be community oriented, concerned with subjects such as the relation of Christ to social change and verified more through trust-based testimony than factual knowledge. These attributes stand in contrast to the Western post-Enlightenment tradition of individual reason and rationality.[12] Chloë Starr makes a similar point in the afterword of *Chinese Theology*, pointing out that the Chinese theologians she examines do not necessarily follow the same systematic structure of Euro-American theologies involving subjects such as Christology or the Incarnation, but nevertheless attempt to connect society with Christian truth in their own cultural context.[13] For the CHSKH, Chinese Anglicans and foreign missionaries attempted to discover what it meant to be Christian in their surroundings and in so doing, adopted a very broad scope of "theology." The example of the CHSKH thus echoes existing writing on the alternative subject matters and unconventional expressions of Chinese theology.

Two themes that have been extensively explored in existing studies stand out in the CHSKH example—namely, enculturation and textuality. Enculturation refers to the process in which contemporaries translated forms of worship for Chinese Christians, not only with respect to linguistics but also to provide the most natural expressions of worship.[14] In effect, enculturation concerns engagement with existing culture. For instance, Aminta Arrington's recent work on Lisu Christians in southwest China highlights how their faith is mediated by their participatory music and oral culture in a world not dependent on literacy and "abstract theological concepts."[15] Textuality refers to the medium of expression

---

Rowan Strong (Oxford: Oxford University Press, 2017), 320–37; and Wickeri, ed., *Christian Encounters with Chinese Culture*.

11 Chloë Starr, *Chinese Theology: Text and Context* (New Haven: Yale University Press, 2016), 283.

12 Hwa Yung, *Mangoes or Bananas? The Quest for an Authentic Asian Christian Theology (Second Edition)* (New York: Orbis Books, 2014), 1–6, 67–69.

13 Starr, *Chinese Theology*, 279–80.

14 Starr, "Rethinking Church," 99–100.

15 Amina Arrington, "Christian Hymns as Theological Mediator: The Lisu of South-west China and Their Music" *Studies in World Christianity* 21, no. 2 (2015): 154–58.

and dissemination of theology. Across China and beyond, Peter Phan points out the ways in which non-Western theology has been "performed" through new Christologies, visions of catholicity, and pathways of communication.[16] Likewise, the CHSKH wrestled with enculturation and textuality, ultimately adapting its message to meet the felt needs of its members while altering methods of communication to cater to its constrained budget and largely illiterate target audience. By observing the process of enculturation over the course of a century, this case study examines the historical context behind the misguided initial trajectory of 1849 as well as how and why both Chinese Anglican theology and its institutional embedding were adjusted over time up to 1949.

Unfulfilled Expectations, 1849–1895

The narrative of CHSKH theology begins with mid-nineteenth century missionary methods of enculturation and textuality. Bishop Smith's 1849 prospectus essentially conformed to the predominant ways of missionary thinking of the period. In terms of enculturation, the working assumption was that Anglo-Saxon Christianity and civilization was the definitive way forward. Eric Reinders analyzes how most Protestant missionaries essentially dismissed what they regarded as the "doctrinal inarticulacy" of inherited Chinese traditions, looking down on that which could not be rationalized into neat doctrines as per Western post-Enlightenment systems.[17] In 1853, the *Church Missionary Gleaner*, the publication of Smith's missionary society, referred to China as "a stagnant pool" that only needed to be stirred for all to be convinced of its foul nature.[18] Bishop Smith articulated his vision in an address in Manchester, that the gospel of peace would overcome "the most unintelligible people" and "the most impractical government" of China, and that the "providential" extension of the British Empire would "confer on distant races the blessings of Christian civilization."[19]

As for textuality, most were influenced by Robert Morrison, the first Protestant missionary in China.[20] Inspired by his training at Gosport Academy,

---

16 Peter Phan, "Doing Theology in World Christianities: Old Tasks, New Ways," in *Relocating World Christianity: Interdisciplinary Studies in Universal and Local Expressions of the Christian Faith*, eds. Joel Cabrita, David Maxwell, Emma Wild-Wood (Leiden: Brill, 2017), 115–42.

17 Eric Reinders, *Borrowed Gods and Foreign Bodies: Christian Missionaries Imagine Chinese Religion* (Berkeley: University of California Press, 2004), 206–07.

18 Reinders, *Borrowed Gods*, 40–41.

19 George Smith, *Our National Relations with China Being Two Speeches Delivered in Exeter Hall and in the Free-Trade Hall, Manchester, 1857*, 4–5, http://anglicanhistory.org/asia/skh/.

20 See Martha Stockment, "Robert Morrison," bdcconline.net/en/stories/morrison-robert.

Morrison's fundamental approach was to acquire the local language in a primary city, then employ assistants who could translate the Bible and evangelistic texts, and finally establish a seminary to train indigenous evangelists.[21] In an address to Anglican clergy in Shanghai, Smith expressed a similar understanding about the primary mode of conveying theology. Protestant missionaries ought to give the Bible "pre-eminent honor" by translating and circulating it alongside evangelistic tracts such as Liang Afa's *Good Words for Exhorting the Age*, one of the first Christian texts to be composed by a Chinese believer.[22] The assumption was that the Bible was self-interpreting and could be understood on its own terms, therefore converting China would hinge on every Chinese being in possession of a Bible, while evangelists would only need to play a supporting role.[23]

It quickly transpired, however, that the initial task of translation was no mean feat. Bishop John Shaw Burdon, one of the later bishops of Victoria, wrote extensively about the difficulty of even ascertaining a suitable Chinese translation for "God" and "Spirit." To refer to God, Protestant missionaries in China used different terms, including *shen* (神), *Shangdi* (上帝), and *Tianzhu* (天主), but each term had different ramifications for potential misunderstanding.[24] Moreover, "Christian civilization" was not immediately embraced by Chinese society. In Fuzhou, the British Consul observed that women missionaries of the Church of England Zenana Missionary Society insisted on upholding "the European standard of conduct of life" by living alone as single women, brandishing smoothed and braided hair, and wearing shoes and stockings. However, such behavior led local residents to suspect that they were "disreputable women."[25] Where missionaries were not rejected, sometimes they were misunderstood. Pearl Buck recalls an occasion in which her missionary father was preaching to an uninterested and gradually dispersing crowd. As the remnant congregation thinned, an elderly

---

21   Christopher A. Daily, *Robert Morrison and the Protestant Plan for China* (Hong Kong: Hong Kong University Press, 2013), 80–82.

22   George Smith, *China, her Future and her Past: Being A Charge Delivered to the Anglican Clergy in Trinity Church, Shanghae, on October 20, 1853* (London: Thomas Hatchard, 1854), 2–4.

23   George Kam Wah Mak, "The Colportage of the Protestant Bible in Late Qing China: The Example of the British and Foreign Bible Society," in *Religious Publishing and Print Culture in Modern China*, eds. Gustavo Benavides, Kocku von Stuckrad, Winnifred Fallers Sullivan (Berlin: De Gruyter, 2015), 19.

24   J. S. Burdon, *The Chinese Term for God. A Letter to the Protestant Missionaries of China* (De Souza & Co., 1877), 1–11, http://anglicanhistory.org/asia/skh/.

25   London, Lambeth Palace Library (hereafter LPL), Benson Papers 147, fols 365–67, Memorandum by Consul Allen on Fukien Missions, 1895.

woman admonished those in attendance, "Do not offend this foreigner! He is making a pilgrimage to our country so that he may acquire merit in heaven. Let us help him to save his soul!"[26]

Moreover, vernacular print did not result in the Christianization of China. The British and Foreign Bible Society, one of the main agencies distributing Bibles in China in the nineteenth century, noted that the dissemination of Scripture did not lead directly to Christian conversion, contrary to the belief of those who assumed the Bible on its own was both self-interpreting and self-sufficient.[27] For the relatively small percentage who attended mission schools in the nineteenth century, the vast majority became translators and compradors when comparatively profitable career paths existed for graduates with proficiency in English.[28] Wu Tingfang 伍廷芳, one of the early graduates of Smith's Anglican college in Hong Kong, became renowned not for his translation and evangelism, since these were nonexistent, but for his legal and political career, which culminated in him becoming the first Chinese to be called to the bar and eventually Minister of Foreign Affairs for the Republic of China.[29] Later in life, Wu drifted away even further, becoming heavily involved in theosophy as President of the Shanghai Lodge.[30] Over time, Smith became disheartened at the fact that virtually no graduates from St. Paul's College pursued ordination.[31] Despite Anglican missions being established for fifty years, they sorely lacked indigenous church workers. In the provinces of Guangdong and Guangxi, an official survey conducted in 1898 noted that only 26 of the 188 walled cities had some form of missionary presence, and Hunan Province was yet to have any.[32] Toward the end of the nineteenth century, any thoughts of "Christian civilization" being easily translated and transmitted were resoundingly banished.[33]

---

26 Jessie G. Lutz, *Chinese Politics and Christian Missions: The Anti-Christian Movements of 1920–28* (Notre Dame: Cross Cultural Publications, 1988), 14.

27 Mak, "The Colportage of the Protestant Bible," 42–49.

28 George B. Endacott, Dorothy E. She, *The Diocese of Victoria, Hong Kong: A Hundred Years of Church History, 1849–1949* (Hong Kong: Kelly & Walsh, 1949), 20.

29 Vincent H. Y. Fung, ed., *From Devotion to Plurality: A Full History of St Paul's College 1851–2001* (Hong Kong: St Paul's College Alumni Association, 2001), 32.

30 胡學丞 [Hu Xuecheng], "伍廷芳的通神學與靈學生涯" [Wu Tingfang's Theosophy and Career in Parapsychology], 政大史粹 [*Collectanea of History NCCU*] 22 (2012): 2–7.

31 Endacott, *The Diocese of Victoria*, 20.

32 Hong Kong Public Records Office (hereafter HKPRO), HKMS94/1/5/66, Memorandum on the Hong Kong and Kwangtung Mission, 12 August 1898, 1–6, 13–17.

33 For an overview of foreign missions and Chinese opposition between 1860 and 1900, see Daniel Bays, *A New History of Christianity in China* (Chichester: Wiley-Blackwell, 2012), ch. 4.

Toward Enculturated Theology and Unity, 1877–1912

Achieving a comprehensible, consistent theology among indigenous congregations was a shared struggle among churches in China. The equivalent problem across Anglican churches worldwide was met with the formation of the Lambeth Conference.[34] The global expansion of the Anglican Communion had exposed uncertainties in theology, which in turn compelled bishops around the world to search for a consistent standard of theology. Although the first Lambeth Conference in 1867 was more of a knee-jerk reaction to the Colenso Case in South Africa than a carefully planned instrument of communion, subsequent meetings became a platform for Anglican bishops to maintain a "principal bond of union" to overcome "excessive diversities of ritual."[35] The adoption of four fundamental standards through the Chicago Quadrilateral at the 1888 Lambeth Conference thus signaled the move toward more defined statements of faith and order. At the same time, it also implied a move away from the assumption that an obvious, one-size-fits-all Western Christian civilization could be applied to all churches universally.[36]

Not unlike the Lambeth Conference, missionary conferences in China were adopted as a platform to discuss theology. Bishop Burdon took the debate about the term for "God" to the groundbreaking 1877 General Conference of Protestant Missionaries in Shanghai—a conference of 142 members representing 20 denominations—which was a pivotal step toward collective discussion on Chinese theology.[37] By the next conference in 1890, missionaries demonstrated more cultural sensitivity and greater willingness to collaborate. For example, there were extended discussions about Chinese cultural practices such as

---

34 W. M. Jacob, *The Making of the Anglican Church Worldwide* (London: Society for Promoting Christian Knowledge, 1997), 286–95.

35 Robert W. Prichard, "The Lambeth Conference," in *The Wiley-Blackwell Companion to the Anglican Communion*, eds Markham et al., 94–101; Recommendation 7, 1878 Lambeth Conference Recommendations, https://www.anglicancommunion.org/media/127719/1878.pdf.

36 Resolution 11, 1888 Lambeth Conference Resolutions, https://www.anglicancommunion.org/media/127722/1888.pdf. The four standards were Holy Scripture being the ultimate standard of faith, the Apostles' Creed and Nicene Creed, the sacraments of baptism and Holy Communion, and the historic episcopate.

37 *Records of the General Conference of the Protestant Missionaries of China, Held at Shanghai, May 10–24, 1877* (Shanghai: Presbyterian Mission Press, 1878), 8–9; J. S. Burdon, *The Chinese Term for God*, 4; James Thayer Addison, *Chinese Ancestor Worship: A Study of its Meaning and its Relations with Christianity* (Church Literature Committee of the Chung Hua Sheng Kung Hui, 1925), 74–76.

bowing. Some argued for its toleration since one could bow to honor individuals without idolatry, whereas others felt less inclined to accept it given the practice of ancestral obeisance.[38] The 1890 General Conference also involved Bible societies and missionary agencies agreeing to work toward a unified Bible translation in order to eliminate rivalry and enable wider access to the Bible. Zetzsche rightly argues that each missionary translator being paired on equal terms with a Chinese coworker signaled a shift in the relationship between missionaries and Chinese Christians.[39]

The year 1897 was significant for Chinese Anglican theology. First, the Anglican missionary bishops in China convened for the first time to adopt a shared name for their church and initiate the search for uniform theological and liturgical formulae.[40] Second, the 1897 Lambeth Conference called for Anglican missions worldwide not to impress foreign churchmanship upon indigenous communities but to adapt to local circumstances as far as possible without jeopardizing theological orthodoxy.[41] Two years later, the 1899 bishops' conference in Shanghai passed resolutions on church order that targeted common problems among indigenous congregations. This included distinguishing between hearers and catechumens in different stages of preparation for baptism, as well as instructing Christian parents not to betroth their children to non-Christians.[42] The conference also issued common terms for bishop (會督 *huidu*), priest (會長 *huizhang*), deacon (會吏 *huili*), the Lord's Day (主日 *zhuri*), and Anglican (安立間 *anlijian* or 安立甘 *anligan*). At the end of the conference, an ambitious plan was laid out to collect information from every diocese in order to present authoritative statements on Chinese Christian marriage.[43] Chinese Anglican leaders were visibly contextualizing their theology and in so doing, providing coherence across the dioceses.

38　Reinders, *Borrowed Gods*, 115–16.

39　George Kam Wah Mak, "Introduction by Guest Editor George Kam Mak Wah: The Mandarin Union Version, a Classic Chinese Biblical Translation," *Journal of the Royal Asiatic Society* 30, Issue 1 (2020): 8–11.

40　Letter from Conference of Anglican Bishops in China and Korea to Anglican Clergy and Laity, 6 April 1897, http://anglicanhistory.org/asia/skh/.

41　Resolutions 18–20, 1897 Lambeth Conference Resolutions, https://www.anglicancommunion.org/media/127725/1897.pdf.

42　HKPRO, HKMS94/1/5/60A, "Letters and Resolutions of the Conference of the Bishops of the Anglican Communion in China, Hong Kong, and Corea, held at Shanghai," 14–20 October 1899, 3–4.

43　HKPRO, "Letters and Resolutions," 6–8.

The drive to achieve tighter theology in this period is epitomized by the efforts of Bishop Joseph Hoare of Victoria. In 1899, Hoare established a new diocesan periodical, *From Month to Month*, to share local testimonies and reports alongside the international Anglican periodical, the *Church Missionary Gleaner*. In its inaugural edition, he explained that the primary intention of *From Month to Month* was to raise awareness of localized perspectives on theology.[44] For instance, an article in 1902 described the outlook of a Chinese Christian funeral in Shiu Hing as a testimony to evangelistic progress and reinforcement of contextualized theology. The article suggested which cultural expressions of grief could be considered consistent with Christian practice, such as burial in a hillside grave. However, the article also stressed differences from traditional Chinese funerals by the absence of gongs, firecrackers, burnt paper offerings, and extravagant wailing, which were to be regarded negatively since such actions were linked to the belief that dead spirits returned to torment the living.[45] In another article from 1905, Hoare appraised Chinese Anglican gospel knowledge in Fujian Province. Although believers were not aware of major debates about Calvinism and Arminianism, Hoare invited readers to respect their "simple faith" involving belief in Christ's atonement for sin, "warfare with heathenism," and not tolerating drunkenness, opium, and gambling.[46] Hoare thus not only approached Chinese Anglican theology with conscientiousness, but also went to great lengths to make it known across the diocese through periodicals.

In addition to circulating theological knowledge at the diocesan level, Hoare also contributed to the growing theological discourse across China. For example, after asking a number of missionaries about the best translation for "sacrament," Hoare published his findings in the October 1904 edition of *The Chinese Recorder*, a widely-circulated missionary periodical that discussed the relationship between Chinese culture and Christianity.[47] Hoare submitted his publication because almost all to whom he wrote indicated interest in his

---

44 Birmingham, Cadbury Research Library (hereafter CRL), CMS/H/H5/E1/Ch2/3, *From Month to Month* 1 (October 1899): 1.

45 CRL, CMS/H/H5/E1/Ch2/3, Kathleen Hipwell, "A Chinese Christian Funeral at Shiu Hing," *From Month to Month* 24 (May 1902): 3–4.

46 CRL, CMS/H/H5/E1/Ch2/3, "The Bishop's Autumn Tour in Fuh-kien," *From Month to Month* 54 (January 1905): 3–5.

47 彭淑慶，崔華傑 [Peng Shuqing, Cui Huajie], "晚清基督教傳教士與中國上古神話研究—以《教務雜誌》為中心" [A Study of Protestant Missionaries and Chinese Mythology in Late Qing China Through The Chinese Recorder], 民俗研究 [*Folklore Studies*] 03 (2012): 27–32.

findings, which concluded that there was in fact no direct Chinese equivalent for "sacrament." The two most suitable terms were 聖禮 (*shengli*) or 聖事 (*shengshi*). Although the former did not distinguish between sacraments instituted by Jesus and those used in the Anglican Church, Hoare considered it better than the latter, which had "many secular associations."[48] In another instance, Hoare contributed a chapter on Chinese Christianity to Bishop H. H. Montgomery's *Mankind and the Church*, a series of essays that argued in favor of national expressions of Christianity and against purely European approaches to the faith.[49]

The spirit of the age carried over into the following decade. The 1907 Chinese Anglican conference was the first to include indigenous clergy and representatives. Delegates resolved to organize the Anglican Communion in China through a representative assembly that could provide counsel, authoritative decisions, and common policy with regard to church government and theological questions.[50] A week later at the 1907 China Centenary Missionary Conference, 1,186 missionary delegates representing sixty-four missionary societies discussed matters ranging from the state of the Chinese Church to evangelistic methods, from ancestral worship to women's work.[51] Further afield, the 1908 Pan-Anglican Congress in London also demonstrated a shift toward finding a consistent church identity by confronting shared questions in overseas churches and modern society.[52] In 1909, twenty-nine foreign and Chinese Anglican clergy issued a report on local adaptation in response to Resolution 19 of the 1897 Lambeth Conference, outlining approaches to marriage, clergy vestments, architecture, and funerals. Concerning church architecture, the level of thoughtfulness went to the extent of discussing culturally-appropriate designs for doors and shutters, as well as providing benches which could enable congregations to sit, stand, and

---

48 HKPRO, HKMS94/1/5/65, Letter from Bishop Hoare to *The Chinese Recorder* about the Chinese Translation for "Sacrament," October 1904.

49 J. C. Hoare, "The Contribution of the Church of China to the Body of Christ," in *Mankind and the Church: Being an Attempt to Estimate the Contribution of Great Races to the Fulness of the Church of God*, ed. H. H. Montgomery (London: Longmans, Green, 1907), 260–67; Brian Stanley, "Anglican Missionary Societies and Agencies in the Nineteenth Century," in *The Oxford History of Anglicanism, Volume III*, ed. Strong, 135–36.

50 HKPRO, HKMS94/1/6/34, *Report and Resolutions of the Conference of the Anglican Communion in China and Hongkong held in Shanghai*, 15–20 April 1907, 7–9.

51 *China Centenary Missionary Conference Held at Shanghai, April 25 to May 8, 1907* (Shanghai: Centenary Conference Committee, 1907), Front Matter, 769, 807.

52 William L. Sachs, "The Emergence of the Anglican Communion in the Nineteenth and Twentieth Centuries" in *Companion to the Anglican Communion*, eds Markham et al., 39.

kneel, but "not permit lounging when sitting."[53] By the time the CHSKH general synod was constituted in 1912, a generalized Eurocentric and imperialist theology was no longer taken as the standard. Instead, the consistent and conscientious enculturation of Chinese Anglican theology was the goal, while synods and conferences were the proposed means of expounding and propagating such theology.[54] In diocesan synods, Chinese clergy and lay delegates were given voting rights with a view to further the "welfare and progress" of the CHSKH. Foreign missionary clergy had the right to vote, provided they conformed to the canons and constitution of the CHSKH.[55]

The Limits of Synods and Periodicals, 1913–1934

Being aware of the need for enculturated theology was, however, different from forming and disseminating it effectively. Developing a consistent theology required logistical input that was unavailable in the CHSKH. As early as 1913 during the national conference of the China Continuation Committee, which was intended to sustain the missionary cooperation of the 1910 Edinburgh World Missionary Conference, the sixty-odd delegates noted that there was insufficient information to coordinate church work and theological education.[56] It was one thing for the conference to indicate the need for vernacular Scripture and Christian books for family libraries but an altogether different matter for the production and distribution of literature to take place.[57]

For the CHSKH, the second general synod in 1915 directed most of its attention to appointing committees for mission work. With limited time, delegates noted that it was "inexpedient" to resolve theological questions on interdenominational Holy Communion. The preparation of the Prayer Book was delegated to a subcommittee.[58] It was not until the fourth general synod in 1921 that the issue of enriching the Prayer Book was explored in greater depth with

---

53 HKPRO, HKMS94/1/6/33, "Report of the Committee on 'Local Adaptation' Presented to the Conference of the Anglican Communion held in Shanghai," 27 March–6 April 1909, 1, 5–9.

54 LPL, MS2447, fols 1–3, CHSKH General Synod Meeting Minutes, 26 April 1912.

55 HKSKH, 2755, "Provisional Constitution and Canons of the Chung Wa Sheng Kung Hui in the Diocese of Victoria Hongkong, 1913," 1–3.

56 CRL, CMS/G/GZ2/2, *Findings of the National Conference Held in Shanghai, March 11th to 14th, 1913*, 3–12.

57 CRL, CMS/G/GZ2/2, *Findings of the South China Conference Held in Canton, January 30 to February 4, 1913*, 28–30.

58 LPL, MS2447, fols 6–27, CHSKH General Synod Meeting Minutes, 14–22 April 1915.

an enlarged committee consisting of more Chinese members. The committee noted that revising the Prayer Book would first require extensive experiments at the local level in order to figure out how best to incorporate Chinese ideals, before bringing the matter back to consultation with the respective diocesan bishops then the general synod.[59] In effect, Prayer Book revision was a laborious and long-winded process that was not at the forefront of discussions. In view of the priority of church growth, only a few clergymen could dedicate themselves fully to researching theological matters, and the information required to devise such solutions was also lacking.

The quest for a consistent Chinese Anglican theology was complicated further by increasingly intense and widespread discussions about the relationship between Christianity and Chinese national identity in the 1920s and 1930s.[60] In response to China's perceived humiliation at the 1919 Paris Peace Conference and the cession of Shandong to Japan, the May Fourth Movement resulted in "new youth" expressing disillusionment toward the West and placing their hope for China in intellectual cosmopolitanism.[61] These sentiments spilled over into the churches as a number of Chinese Christians questioned the identities of their churches beyond the fiscal and administrative independence offered by mission bodies.[62] Zhao Zichen (T. C. Chao) delivered a speech at the second meeting of the National Christian Council (NCC) that highlighted the main contentions. As the relationship between the Chinese Church and the worldwide Church was being reassessed, Zhao declared that the Chinese Church ought to rise to its special calling to the Chinese people and Chinese culture.[63] In practice, this meant the NCC advocating greater involvement from indigenous church leaders alongside a form of Chinese Christianity that offered "a clear voice on social, economic, and political issues."[64] Although the CHSKH displayed reservations about committing to the NCC in order to abstain from political pronouncements, the influence of republican nationalism led to debates about CHSKH

---

59 LPL, MS2447, fols 69–74, CHSKH General Synod Meeting Minutes, 18–25 April 1921.

60 Chloë Starr, "Maintaining Faith in the Chinese World," in *Relocating World Christianity*, eds. Cabrita et al., 217.

61 Lutz, *Chinese Politics and Christian Missions*, 3.

62 Lutz, *Chinese Politics*, 286.

63 趙紫宸 [Zhao Zichen], "中國教會與世界教會的關係" [The Relationship Between the Chinese Church and the Worldwide Church], 中華聖公會報 [*The Chinese Churchman*, hereafter *TCC*] 16, no. 11 (May 1923): 4–10.

64 CRL, CMS/CHg/O3/1, Ronald Rees, "Some Impressions of the Tenth Biennial Meeting of the NCC," 25 April–2 May, 1935, 2–5.

autonomy, which in turn raised questions about the ultimate source of theological authority in the Anglican Communion.[65]

CHSKH clergy training and theological education also did not go according to plan. After the highly anticipated establishment of the Central Theological School in 1918, logistical problems meant that the school did not open until 1922. From there, the school constantly suffered from high turnover rates among staff and was occupied by military forces in 1927 during Chiang Kai-shek's Northern Expedition.[66] Other theological departments with CHSKH involvement such as the Canton Union Theological College, Huachung University, and Yenching School of Religion enabled a number of standout theologians such as Wei Zhuomin (Francis Wei), Wu Leichuan, and Zhao Zichen to teach and produce Christian literature.[67] Their qualitative impact was undeniable, so much so that their publications have led many to refer to early twentieth-century Chinese Protestantism as the "golden period."[68] At times, they contributed extended commentaries in CHSKH periodicals.[69] However, the number of graduates at the various theological schools was so few that their wider impact on the CHSKH was limited.[70] The cause of theological education was not helped by pressure from the government in the 1920s when colleges were forced to dissociate from theological schools, which set off a vicious cycle between declining student numbers and fewer faculty members.[71]

---

65 LPL, MS2447, fol. 151, CHSKH General Synod Meeting Minutes, 21–28 April 1928. The extensive debate surrounding CHSKH autonomy and conflicting sources of authority is explored in greater depth in Tim Yung, "Keeping up with the Chinese: Constituting and Reconstituting the Anglican Church in South China, 1897–1951," *Studies in Church History* 56 (2020): 383–400.

66 Philip L. Wickeri, "Clergy Training and Theological Education: The Anglican-Episcopal Experience in China," Conference Paper for Yale-Edinburgh Meeting, 30 June–2 July 2011, http://archives.hkskh.org/Page.aspx?id=1067&lang=1.

67 Wickeri, "Clergy Training and Theological Education."

68 Yongtao Chen, *The Chinese Christology of T. C. Chao* (Leiden: Brill, 2017), 2–3.

69 For example, 吳雷川 [Wu Leichuan], "耶穌是我們的夫子" [Jesus is our Master], *TCC* 23, no. 6 (March 1930): 2–5; 趙紫宸 [Zhao Zichen], "受禮十詠" [Ten Odes on Confirmation], *TCC* 34, no. 14 (September 1941): 5–6; 韋卓民 [Wei Zhuomin], "談教會自養" [On Church Self-Support], *TCC* 38, no. 5 (August 1949): 1–5.

70 Wickeri, "Clergy Training and Theological Education." Wickeri provides an extensive survey of theological education in the CHSKH and its enduring challenges, such as balancing denominational identity with ecumenical cooperation, the maintenance of educational standards, and finances.

71 Peter Tze Ming Ng, *Changing Paradigms of Christian Higher Education in China, 1888–1950* (Lewiston: The Edwin Mellen Press, 2002), 66–69.

The next challenge after developing Chinese Anglican theology was propagating it. At the 1907 Anglican clergy conference, delegates decided to initiate a cheap Chinese monthly paper as "the official organ of the Anglican Communion" in China.[72] *The Chinese Churchman* [中華聖公會報] was subsequently established in 1908 and published monthly until 1951. Each volume consisted of an assortment of items, including Sunday school lessons, local church reports, updates from the Anglican Communion, commentary on current affairs, and, notably, reflections on Anglican characteristics and the broader Christian faith.[73] With regard to theology, writers expounded subjects considered important to Chinese Anglican identity. For example, a 1913 article contributed by two catechists in Hankou discussed the importance of apostolic succession from the book of Acts to the present day, and how the growth of the early Church was connected to their undivided belief in one Lord, one baptism, and one faith.[74] In a 1918 commentary on Anglican rites, vestments for priests and the choir were justified by Samuel and David wearing ephods during their "ministry before the Lord" and Psalm 132 respectively, while their use also signaled unity with other Anglican and Episcopal congregations that adopted the same practice. Likewise, the practice of seating men and women on separate sides in church halls was linked to ancient tradition as well as its adoption in Anglican and Episcopal congregations. Finally, the congregation kneeling during prayer was said to be preferable to lying prostrate, which would hinder one from speaking during prayers.[75] For the most part, articles in *The Chinese Churchman* reinforced the use of Bible passages, historical precedent, and common sense to frame Chinese Anglican theology.

This same approach was used to tackle perplexing dilemmas in Chinese Anglicanism. For example, Li Yaoting, a priest in the Diocese of Guangxi-Hunan, offered a comprehensive seven-step guide to how to observe Chinese Christian funerals while honoring God and Chinese custom, but without succumbing to "superstitious" traditions. This began with reading Bible passages to and praying for believers who had become very ill, as indicated in James 5:14–16.

---

72 HKPRO, HKMS94/1/6/34, *Report and Resolutions of the Conference of the Anglican Communion in China and Hongkong held in Shanghai, 15–20 April 1907, 10–11.*

73 *TCC* 2, no. 6 (February 1913): Front Matter.

74 張信一、馬繼堯 [Zhang Xinyi, Ma Jiyao], "我信使徒所立之一聖公會論" [Treatise on the One True Church], *TCC* 2, no. 6 (February 1913): 5–10.

75 "教會常現理解" [An Explanation for Church Rites], *TCC* 11, no. 2 (February 1918): 16–19.

After death, although expressions of grief were permissible, songs to cast away demons were strictly forbidden while Bible readings were suggested as a substitute. Kneeling before the dead was prohibited, as this violated the second of the Ten Commandments. Contrary to existing cultural tradition, the body ought not to be kept too long at the family home to maintain hygiene. During the burial, a gravestone was permitted, but not a level stone for sacrificial offerings. Finally, instead of visiting the dead during Qingming Festival, believers were encouraged to maintain the graves of their loved ones on All Soul's Day. Instead of burnt offerings, believers could share testimonies about the deceased while offering hymns and prayers indicating their hope of resurrection.[76]

The circulation of literature through the periodical press was so conducive to consolidating CHSKH theology that the bishops determined each diocese should send a delegation to meet the editors of *The Chinese Churchman*. Rev. J. W. Nichols, a missionary in Shanghai, was even instructed to relinquish his other duties in order to give his full attention to developing *The Chinese Churchman* from 1921 onwards.[77] In 1928, the CHSKH General Synod formed a dedicated Church Literature Committee, which not only sought to widen the circulation of *The Chinese Churchman* but also promote the use of other printed publications at the diocesan level.[78] In the Diocese of Victoria, statistical tables, uniform certificates of baptism and confirmation, and synod reports were adopted to enable laypeople to develop a sense of belonging to the CHSKH.[79] In 1930, the diocese decided to publish a monthly magazine, *The Kong Yuet Diocesan Echo* (港粵教聲, Hong Kong and South China Echo).[80] In parallel with *The Chinese Churchman*, its purpose was to provide a channel for communication between the three districts in the diocese, as well as a platform for sharing schemes for church development, discussing aspects of Christian living, and reporting local events.[81] In the 1920s and 1930s, the CHSKH Literature Committee also issued its own publications, such as a volume in 1934 about the ideals and order of the CHSKH, which included explanations

---

76 李耀廷 [Li Yao Ting], "喪事規禮" [Rules for Funerals], *TCC* 11, no. 2 (February 1918): 12–15.

77 LPL, MS2447, fols 70–75, CHSKH General Synod Meeting Minutes, 18–25 April 1921.

78 LPL, MS2447, fol. 145, CHSKH General Synod Meeting Minutes, 21–28 April 1928.

79 HKSKH, 2478/46, Diocesan Standing Committee Meeting Minutes, 9 October 1928.

80 HKSKH, 2486/50, Diocesan Standing Committee Meeting Minutes, 3 December 1929.

81 鍾仁立 [Chung Yan-laap], "發刊詞" [Editorial], 港粵教聲 [*The Kong Yuet Diocesan Echo*] 1, no. 1 (March 1930): 1.

of the Chicago-Lambeth Quadrilateral, the Book of Common Prayer, and the essence of Anglicanism being self-governing national churches within the unity of the Anglican Communion.[82]

However, the effectiveness of printed literature was limited by both widespread illiteracy and limited resources. Gilbert Baker, who later became Bishop of Victoria, observed that higher levels of literacy in Republican China were confined to a small number in the cities while the vast majority in rural areas was preoccupied with maintaining their livelihood.[83] Itinerant preachers in South China villages required pictures and magic lanterns since only very few could read and write.[84] Sarah Beattie, a nurse working at a rural CHSKH hospital, observed that despite the chaplain offering to run intensive Bible classes for hospital staff, most preferred to attend family prayers that consisted of simpler teaching and hymns.[85] At the 1933 diocesan synod of South China, the Literature Committee explained that although there was a positive attitude toward church publications, there was still a long way to go for catechists in cultivating the habit of reading among church members.[86] Concerning limited resources, there was always the question of finance. In the first year of *The Kong Yuet Diocesan Echo*'s publication, printing and postal expenses far outweighed income received from subscriptions.[87] For the CHSKH as a whole, the general synod prioritized raising money for Chinese episcopal endowments and new missionary dioceses, since the missionary bishops and CHSKH delegates prized church extension over theological education.[88] By the early 1930s, CHSKH clergy reached the conclusion that enculturation also had to be achieved with textual forms that were both suitable and sustainable. Conferences, synods, and periodicals were not the full answer.

---

82 俞恩嗣、聶高來 [E. S. Yu, John W. Nichols], 中華聖公會概論 [*Chung Hua Sheng Kung Hui: A Brief Explanation of its Ideals and Order*] (Peking: 中華聖公會書籍委員會刊行 [The Church Literature Committee of the Chung Hua Sheng Kung Hui], 1934).

83 New Haven, Yale Divinity School Library, RG8, Box 5, Gilbert Baker's Notes on the Church and Confusing Years in China, 1911–1925 (May 1983).

84 Lai Kei-chong, "Village Work," *Outpost* 11 (January 1925): 23.

85 CRL, CMS/1919–1934/G1/AL/BB-BT, Sarah Beattie Annual Letter, 13 August 1928.

86 HKSKH, 2930/8, South China Diocesan Synod Meeting Minutes, 25–27 April 1933, 8.

87 HKSKH, 2486/54, Diocesan Standing Committee Meeting Minutes, 19 May 1931.

88 LPL, MS2447, fol. 152, CHSKH General Synod House of Bishops Meeting Minutes, 28 April 1928; fols 184–87, CHSKH General Synod House of Bishops Meeting Minutes, 21–28 April 1934.

Creative Enculturation, 1924–1948

The CHSKH faced the ongoing question about how theological materials could percolate from the synods down to church congregations and laypeople, especially those in the countryside.[89] One important move was to adopt simpler materials. For instance, Rev. James Walter Spreckley, a missionary in the Diocese of West Sichuan from 1906 to 1931, made use of simple primers to propagate theological knowledge. For instance, eight-page prayer cycles contained prayers for different levels of church organization. Prayers began with individual congregations, then districts, the diocesan synod, all CHSKH dioceses, and finally, the entire Anglican Communion.[90] In so doing, CHSKH ecclesiology and church organization was taught through prayer. In a similar publication, a gospel primer was condensed to fourteen short lessons in the format of the *Three Character Classic* [三字經] so that even those with elementary education could be taught systematically about God saving sinners through Jesus.[91]

The entire CHSKH soon caught on to such methods, producing simple homilies and prayers about Anglican ecclesiology in shortened format. In 1928 before the General Synod, the Standing Committee issued a homily that not only offered prayers for unity in the CHSKH but also a prefatory statement explaining the position of each believer in relation to the congregation, diocese, CHSKH, and Holy Catholic Church.[92] During the synod itself, delegates agreed to publish and circulate a book of special prayers.[93] Another simplified form of communication was the pastoral letter, addressed to all in the CHSKH. This was first implemented in 1927 as the bishops' response to Chinese Christians forming political associations in the name of the Church, since the bishops believed that political matters should be a matter of individual conscience as opposed to an institutionalized part of church identity.[94] However, the pastoral letter proved to be such an effective means for communication that it was implemented as a permanent part of general synods from 1933 onwards.[95] By

---

89 HKSKH, 2478/41, Diocesan Standing Committee Meeting Minutes, 25 October 1927.

90 CRL, CMS/ACC283/Z3/3, 連環祈禱冊 [Cycle of Prayer], 1924.

91 CRL, CMS/ACC283/Z3/5, 福音初階 [Gospel Basics] (華西聖教會書會 [West China Holiness Church Book Association], 1923). The print and layout of this primer is a testament to creative enculturation.

92 HKSKH, 238/7, *Prayers for the General Synod*, 1928.

93 LPL, MS2447, fol. 151, CHSKH General Synod Meeting Minutes, 28 April 1928.

94 LPL, MS2447, fol. 134, CHSKH House of Bishops Meeting Minutes, 1–4 November 1927.

95 LPL, MS2447, fols. 176–79, CHSKH House of Bishops Meeting Minutes, 21–22 July 1933.

1934, delegates at general synods understood that simplified lists and notices were the most effective method of presenting synod resolutions, so much so that a document entitled Synod Action was to be printed and circulated thereafter.[96]

By the 1930s, all levels of the CHSKH demonstrated greater flexibility in their approach to communicating theology, as indicated by *The Chinese Churchman* advertising short books about Christian living published in both vernacular Chinese (白話文) and classical Chinese (文言文) so that relevant materials could be provided for all types of readers.[97] The NCC similarly began focusing on rural communities in the 1930 Five Year Movement, which was introduced to encourage all churches in China to focus on cultivating literacy and Christianizing daily living at the grassroots.[98] Although the CHSKH was still "not satisfied with everything in the constitution of the NCC" due to its political leanings, it lent its full support to the Five Year Movement, recognizing the importance of revitalizing Christian living through any means necessary, especially among rural communities.[99] Three years later, CHSKH delegates attended the NCC Tinghsien (Dingxian) Conference about rural work. Based on Dr. James Yen's ministry among illiterates in the Chinese Labor Corps in France, the conference suggested churches ought to equip members with a basic level of literacy through "People's Thousand Character Readers" before providing literature in the colloquial language and ministering through relatable means such as pictures, songs, and theatre.[100] Between 1931 and 1936, acknowledging the importance of indigenous praise and worship, the CHSKH became heavily involved in an inter-denominational effort to establish the union hymnal, *Hymns of Universal Praise*.[101] The hymnbook was so highly regarded that the CHSKH even lent money to other denominations that were unable to cover the cost of the new volume, which became a national bestseller alongside the Bible.[102] By 1937, Rev. Robin Chen of Anqing Diocese, later the chair bishop of the CHSKH, led the NCC Commission on the Life and Work of the Churches, asserting that the proclamation of the gospel and religious education should take place through a

---

96 LPL, MS2447, fol. 181, CHSKH General Synod Meeting Minutes, 21–28 April 1934.

97 For instance, *TCC* 23, no. 6 (March 1930), Back Matter.

98 Gray, *Anglicans in China*, 43.

99 LPL, MS2447, fol. 162, CHSKH General Synod Meeting Minutes, 28 April 1931.

100 CRL, CMS/1917–1934/G1/AL/WA-WI, Addendum to H. A. Wittenbach's Annual Letter, 24 July 1933.

101 LPL, MS2447, fol. 193, CHSKH House of Bishops Meeting Minutes, 27 April 1934.

102 LPL, MS2447, fol. 226, CHSKH House of Bishops Meeting Minutes, 29 April–1 May 1938; Chen, "The Protestant Quest," 237.

variety of methods not limited to meetings and printed literature, but also personal witness by character and word, fellowship groups, radio, pictures, music, drama, storytelling, healthcare, education, and other forms of service, including cooperative societies and agricultural improvement.[103]

By the mid-1930s, having realized the difficulties of developing and conveying systematic theology, the preferred approach in the CHSKH was to find alternative, colloquial, and popular methods of communicating simplified but sound theology. This mindset was best expressed by Bishop Mok Shau-tsang (Mo Shouzeng), assistant bishop of Victoria, in his closing address to the 1933 diocesan synod. Earlier in the meeting, Bishop R. O. Hall, who was in his first year of his episcopate, appeared to be discouraged about the shortage of ordained clergy across the CHSKH and by implication, the lack of theological education. Hall's thinking was still fixated on systematic theology rooted in formal education and publications. Mok, however, adopted a different approach to the matter. Mok simply celebrated the progress of the CHSKH over his forty-two years in the ministry, comparing the early days without synods and reports to the planning, procedure, and progress of the present. The twelve clergy at the time were a sixfold increase from the two clergy in the nineteenth century.[104] The diocese had grown leaps and bounds since his early days in the ministry, when church development was so limited that his mother-in-law had to be the first attendee at his evening evangelistic talks in order to attract passers-by to join.[105] Mok accepted the existing situation as it was with optimism instead of assuming the normative state of the Church involving flawlessly crafted and thoroughly communicated theology. Although the CHSKH was yet to reach its goal in achieving widespread theological education, any progress was better than none, whereas any means necessary could be used.

This approach to crafting and communicating theology in the CHSKH was amplified by the Sino-Japanese War. In adversity, CHSKH clergy and bishops focused on what they regarded as the essentials of Chinese Anglicanism. During an emergency meeting in 1943 in Chongqing, the six bishops in Free China reaffirmed the "special contribution" of the CHSKH to Chinese

---

103 CRL, CMS/CHg/O3/1, *Christian Cooperation in China as Illustrated by the Biennial Meeting, Shanghai, May 5–11, 1937: Impressions, Addresses, Recommendations Approved* (Shanghai: National Christian Council of China, 1937), 5–7, 41.

104 HKSKH, 2930/8, South China Diocesan Synod Meeting Minutes 25–27 April 1933, 5, 16.

105 鍾仁立 [Chung Yan-laap], 莫壽增會督傳 [The Life of Bishop Mok Shau Tsang] (香港:聖公會出版社 [Hong Kong: The Anglican Literature Society], 1972), 8.

Christianity in "thoroughness of teaching, dignity and beauty of worship, and Episcopal Church order."[106] At the same time, the experience of operating the CHSKH during the war without missionary oversight gave indigenous leaders a newfound confidence in their expedient methods of crafting and communicating theology.[107] Theological schools also felt more optimistic about the future after experiencing record-breaking enrollment during their temporary relocation to West China.[108] Consequently, CHSKH clergy wrote to missionary societies after the war conveying what they found to be "the most productive" approach to church work, including greater focus on cities instead of villages, conducting weekly family prayer meetings, and circulating simple literature that could simultaneously edify church members and explain the gospel to inquiring friends and family. At the same time, CHSKH clergy also asked for missionaries with "real intellectual acumen" in an effort to support theological training at universities in Canton.[109]

Reconvening for the first time in a decade, in addition to redefining the identity of the CHSKH, the 1947 general synod consolidated their approach to theology after a century of experimentation. The Central Theological School was given renewed backing for further research and writing so that the enculturation of Chinese theology could be given due attention.[110] The synod also instituted a national office to conduct the communication of theology by administering central funds, coordinating common interests, and sustaining regular publications such as the Prayer Book, CHSKH newsletters, annual reports, and *The Chinese Churchman*, which was to be restarted in 1946.[111] Reflecting openness to alternative textualities, the CHSKH also produced a calendar with information about individual dioceses and saints' days.[112] Creative theology was especially encouraged at the synod as delegates dedicated their attention to the unconventional ministry of Rev. Chen Te-heng of Xianyang. Chen had developed "a rather

---

106 CRL, CMS/CHg/O1, "The Crises of the Chung Hua Sheng Kung Hui: A Memorandum from the Chinese and Missionary Bishops of the Chinese Church," May 1943.

107 Yung, "Keeping up with the Chinese," 394–98.

108 Wickeri, "Clergy Training and Theological Education."

109 HKSKH, 2737/1, South China Diocesan Standing Committee to CMS London, 10 December 1945.

110 CRL, CMS/CHg/O1, "Resolutions and Reports: The Tenth General Synod of the CHSKH, Shanghai," 23–31 August 1947, 2–3.

111 CRL, "Resolutions and Reports." 19–33; CRL, CMS/G/AP11, Max Warren, "General Synod in Shanghai: A Report and Commentary," 1947, 4–6.

112 LPL, MS2447, fol. 259, CHSKH Central Office Occasional Newsletter, 31 October 1945.

interesting method of instructing rural folks" by setting church teachings to the tune of folk songs that were familiar to young and old alike.[113]

Finally, the synod also suggested that an experimental canon concerning the ordination of deaconesses to the priesthood be added to the CHSKH canons experimentally until 1967. In 1944, Bishop R. O. Hall had ordained Florence Li Tim-oi to the priesthood, making her the first woman priest in the Anglican Communion. Philip Wickeri notes how the historical context of wartime Macau led Hall to consider it an expedient necessity to ordain Li so that she could administer Holy Communion to the many refugees who had been without a priest.[114] Yet this measure should also be understood in the context of creative attitudes toward Chinese Anglican theology, since the priority of the CHSKH was to survive and serve as much as possible while remaining consistent with what they considered to be the essentials of Anglicanism. The fact that the CHSKH general synod insisted on taking the matter to the 1948 Lambeth Conference before implementing the canon signaled their willingness to uphold the unity of the Anglican Communion over creative enculturation.[115]

Conclusion

Crafting and communicating theology in the CHSKH was not so much a defined obstacle to be overcome at a particular time and place as an ongoing challenge over a hundred years, with a fluid set of parameters. With respect to Chinese theology, this study highlights the importance of the historical perspective, which gives due attention to the processes and practicalities involved in framing theology and embedding it institutionally. The experience of the CHSKH

---

113 CRL, CMS/CHg/O1, "Resolutions and Reports: The Tenth General Synod of the CHS-KH, Shanghai," 23–31 August 1947, 15.

114 Philip L. Wickeri, "The Ordination and Ministry of Li Tim Oi: A Historical Perspective on a Singular Event," in *Christian Women in Chinese Society: The Anglican Story*, eds. Wai Ching Angela Wong, Patricia P. K. Chiu (Hong Kong: Hong Kong University Press, 2018), 110–23.

115 Gray, *Anglicans in China*, 45. The 1948 Lambeth Conference considered the experimental ordination of deaconesses to the priesthood inconsistent with Anglican order, highlighting the potential internal and external consequences of such an action. Despite being asked at Lambeth, Bishop Hall refused to revoke Li's license. However, Li chose to tender her resignation, preferring to continue her ministry quietly and to protect Bishop Hall, who she considered important to the Church in China. See 李添嬡 [Li Tim-oi], 生命的雨點: 李添嬡牧師回憶錄 [*The Raindrops of My Life: The Rev. Florence Tim Oi Li, First Ordained Anglican Woman Priest*], (Hong Kong: Religious Education Resource Centre, 2010), ch. 3.

invites reconsideration of the relationship between the substance of theology and historical context as well as consideration of enculturation and the emergence of theological texts as an ongoing work in progress.

The initial attempt by missionaries to impose preset Euro-American views of theology on China cannot be separated from nineteenth-century imperial assumptions. Toward the turn of the twentieth century, international cooperation led to missionaries and clergy working together to redefine Chinese theology through conferences. After the constitution of the CHSKH in 1912, synods and seminaries were selected as the way forward, alongside an emerging print culture and openness to Western ideals in Republican China. However, the actual development and propagation of Chinese Anglican theology was stalled by the vicissitudes of financial uncertainty, volatile government, and antiforeignism.[116] Finally, indigenous creativity within CHSKH theology in the 1930s and 1940s was accelerated by Chinese assertiveness during the Second Sino-Japanese War and post-war decolonization. By 1949, CHSKH clergy and missionaries were even less sure of what normative theology looked like in comparison with Bishop Smith a century ago, but they were unquestionably more effective in their craft and communication. Their experience might best be summarized by Justyn Terry's argument that the quest for Anglican theology is an ongoing journey, as theologians continually search for the convergence of faith and life, the former having unchanging qualities but the latter being constantly in flux.[117] The journey of crafting and communicating CHSKH theology continued into the Communist period and beyond.

---

116 For more on the fluctuating fortunes of the CHSKH, see Philip L. Wickeri, "The Vicissitudes of Anglicanism in China, 1912–Present," in *The Oxford History of Anglicanism, Volume V: Global Anglicanism, c.1910–2000*, ed. William L. Sachs (Oxford: Oxford University Press, 2018), ch. 6. For further reading on post-1949 CHSKH and Three-Self theology, see Philip L. Wickeri, *Seeking the Common Ground: Protestant Christianity, the Three-Self Movement, and China's United Front* (Maryknoll, NY: Orbis Books, 1988). For further reading on twentieth-century phenomena in communicating theology, see Andy Lord, "Emergent and Adaptive Spiritualities in the Twentieth Century," in *The Oxford History of Protestant Dissenting Traditions Volume V*, ed. Hutchinson, ch. 7.

117 Terry, "Theology in the Anglican Communion," 557–67.

Chapter 9

CHINESE SEVENTH-DAY ADVENTISTS AND SELF-STRENGTHENING

Christie Chui-Shan Chow, *Princeton Seminary*

Introduction

In a 1938 report about the development of the Wuhan Sanitarium, newly established in Hebei Province with the start-up capital donated by Zhang Xueliang (Chang Hsüeh-liang 1901–2001) and Jiang Jieshi (Chiang Kai-shek 1887–1975), the Seventh-day Adventist medical missionary Dr. Harry Willis Miller (1879–1977) related the many challenges he had encountered in running the sanitarium during the tumultuous times of the Japanese invasion. Lacking sufficient funding, medical personnel, and equipment, Miller was overwhelmed by the influx of numerous refugees who came to the sanitarium shortly after the Japanese occupation of Hankow. Notwithstanding the challenges, Miller remained hopeful:

> Christ lived in a restless world as a man. He saw all sides of humanity. When humanity becomes so dangerous that it is unable to live in the environment of human beings, then it is a poor world to live in anyway. We are glad to be able to report these few providences that have resulted in a large and magnificent health retreat being established in the heart of this country. We trust that as a result of the efforts of staff and donors, thousands may find *health and happiness in this life, and the hope of life eternally.*[1]

---

1 H. W. Miller, M.D., "Story of the Wuhan Sanitarium," SDA Bio File M. Miller, Harry Willis & (1) Maude Amelia Thompson (2) Marie Iverson (3) Mary Greer – "China Doctor," Heritage Research Center, Loma Linda University, CA. Author's italics. See also Raymond S. Moore, *China Doctor: The Life Story of Harry Willis Miller* (Mountain View, CA: Pacific Press Publishing Association, 1961, 1969), 113–17. My emphases.

Writing thirty-five years after he arrived in China in 1903, Miller was among the many premillennialist missionaries who aimed to reconcile "the tension between the urgency of the Great Commission and the evidence of the compassion of Christ they sought to emulate."[2] Convinced that the millennial era promised in the Book of Revelation would come after Christ's return, Seventh-day Adventist (hereafter Adventist) medical missionaries regarded the goal of health and healing ministry as both this-worldly and other-worldly: a healthy life on earth was thought to be a preparation for eternal life in heaven. Though the missionary era ended in China during the 1950s, Chinese Adventists adhere to a premillennial eschatology and the denominational vision of the body to this day. Motivated by the belief that the fitness of the body and the mind has implications for entering the divine kingdom, hundreds of thousands of Chinese Adventists are modern health practitioners. They guide their earthly life by following the denomination's teachings on diet, temperance, and lifestyle. They believe that being of good health bears witness to the image of God. Despite the absence of missionary-run sanitariums that Miller built to promulgate the Adventist health practices, today's Chinese Adventists manage private retreat centers in Shenyang, Wenzhou, and Xiamen to promote natural therapy, vegetarianism, and devotional healing for the mind and emotions. An Adventist-owned food supplement business in Beijing has produced an organic "super powder" mix based on over a hundred types of seed claimed by the owner to be found in the Book of Genesis. This Beijing business is one of many Adventist food supplement suppliers across north China.[3]

The relationship between health practices and theology is rarely discussed in studies of Chinese Protestantism. Dominant themes of Chinese Christian healing often center on missionary medicine, such as the founding of clinics, hospitals, and medical schools, and explore the contributions of Western medicine toward China's hygienic modernization.[4] The theology that informs these

---

2 Michael Pocock, "The Influence of Premillennial Eschatology on Evangelical Missionary Theory and Praxis from the Late Nineteenth Century to the Present," *International Bulletin of Missionary Research* 33, no. 3 (2009): 129–35. Quotation is taken from p. 134.

3 Based on the fieldwork I did in China in the provinces of Fujian, Hebei, and Jilin, and in Hong Kong in 2017 to 2019.

4 The most recent monograph on missionary medicine is Chieko Nakajima, *Body, Society, and Nation: The Creation of Public Health and Urban Culture in Shanghai* (Cambridge, MA: Harvard University Press, 2018), chapter 1. See also Angela Ki Che Leung, *Leprosy in China: A History* (New York: Columbia University Press, 2009); Hilary A. Smith, *Forgotten Disease: Illnesses Transformed in Chinese Medicine* (Stanford, CA: Stanford University Press, 2017).

activities is seldom highlighted. This essay first discusses the foundations of a Chinese Adventist theology of health to set a stage for understanding this denomination's engagement of medical mission in Republican and Socialist China. It argues that Adventists' self-identity as the bearers of the end-time "remnants" and their anticipation of the imminent return of Christ underline their advocacy of personal hygiene, dietary reform, and temperance praxis in the mission field. A closer reading of the Adventist messages in denominational magazines and health literature is supplemented by the findings of my fieldwork in 2017, 2018, and 2019. The purpose is to highlight how Chinese Adventists have maintained, preserved, and revived the church's health practices in the post-Mao era.

A Seventh-day Adventist Theology of Health

The Chinese Seventh-day Adventist theology of health has its roots in the teachings of Ellen Gould White (1827–1915), the denomination's American prophetess. During the 1850s and 1860s, White received a number of health-related visions and began to urge members of the denomination to quit an unhealthy lifestyle. In one major vision White had on June 6, 1863, in Otsego, Michigan, she heard God telling her and her husband, James White (1821–1881), that they should "come out against intemperance of every kind—intemperance in working, in eating, in drinking, and in drugging." The vision was more a personal instruction to her, for she was convinced that the Adventists were to be God's "instruments in directing the world to God's great medicine, water, pure soft water, for diseases, for health, for cleanliness, and for luxury."[5] The inspiration had roots in the health reform movements prevalent in mid-nineteenth-century America where Christian physiologists and health reformers advocated for preventive and rehabilitative regimes, remedial treatments, and a simple lifestyle. The modalities through which to safeguard a healthy body broadly included a wholesome, often plant-based diet, sunlight, fresh air, exercise, rest, temperance, cleanliness, and proper clothing.[6] Throughout the late nineteenth and early

---

5 Ronald L. Numbers, *Prophetess of Health: A Study of Ellen G. White*, 3rd edition (Grand Rapids, MI: Eerdmans, 2008), 132; Brian C. Wilson, *Dr. John Harvey Kellogg and the Religion of Biologic Living* (Bloomington & Indianapolis, IN: Indiana University Press, 2014), 26.

6 George W. Reid, *A Sound of Trumpets: Americans, Adventists, and Health Reform* (Washington, DC: Review and Herald Publishing Association, 1982); Ronald L. Numbers, *Prophetess of Health: A Study of Ellen G. White*, R. Marie Griffith, *Born Again Bodies: Flesh and Spirit in American Christianity* (Berkeley, CA: University of California Press, 2004).

twentieth centuries, White advocated for health reform in her extensive writings and sermons. Among her many theological claims on health, White's eschatological insights led to a missiological stance that placed the duty of bodily improvement on both the person and the church. This theological understanding prompted Adventist medical missionaries to promote lifestyle management and professional medicine around the world. Today, Adventists are known for longevity and better health,[7] and the denomination attributes this legacy to White.

An Adventist theology of health centers around creation, eschatology, and identity. Adventists are literal creationists, taking the literal sense of the Genesis stories word by word. Humans, created in the image of God, are vulnerable to disease and sickness because of sin, but God's healing power is dynamic, and a believer can experience this by obeying the laws of nature and the laws of the commandments. Commenting on hygiene and dietary temperance, White wrote,

> Let it ever be kept before the mind that the great object of hygienic reform is to secure the highest possible development of mind and soul and body. All the laws of nature—which are the laws of God—are designed for our good. Obedience to them will promote our happiness in this life and will aid us in a *preparation for the life to come.*[8]

> He [God] instructed me that those who are keeping His commandments must be brought into sacred relation to Himself, and that by temperance in eating and drinking they must keep mind and body in the most favorable condition for service.[9]

Both the laws of nature and the laws of the commandments are meant for the created to be sustained and thrive. For instance, the Garden of Eden foods (vegetables, fruits, and nuts, c.f. Genesis 1:29, 30; 3:18) were God's original diet for humanity. Animal flesh was added only after all plant life was destroyed in the Flood (Genesis 9:1–4). Additional dietary instructions were given to Moses to distinguish "clean" and "unclean" foods (Leviticus 11; Deuteronomy 14:3–20),

---

7 See for example Fatemeh Kiani, Synnove Knutsen, Pramil Singh, Giske Ursin, and Gary Fraser, "Dietary Risk Factors for Ovarian Cancer: The Adventist Health Study (United States)," *Cancer Causes and Control* 17, no. 2 (2006): 137–46.

8 Ellen G. White, *Counsels on Diet and Foods*, 23. Ellen G. White's books cited in this chapter may be accessed at https://whiteestate.org (accessed July 15, 2020). My emphases.

9 Ellen G. White, *Testimonies for the Church*, vol. 9, p. 158–59, cited in Reid, *A Sound of Trumpets*, 117.

and Adventists hold that the biblical bases of all these food laws suggest their universal character. The biblical diets are intended for all humanity. In particular, the practice of eating "clean" meat is thought to be transethnic, not limited to the Jews. Taken together, these various biblical admonitions create a broad Adventist food spectrum, with one end promoting strict vegetarianism, the middle, mild vegetarianism with the use of milk and eggs, and the other end, a diet that included clean meat. Regardless of which diet they follow, Adventists see the body as the temple of God (1 Corinthians 6:19–20), and its physicality as where the soul meets the Holy Spirit.[10]

White's emphasis on "preparation for the life to come" highlights the eschatological notion of the remnant church that informs the denomination's ecclesial identity. Adventist health practice proved integral to the identity of a "remnant." White wrote, "It is for their own good that the Lord counsels the remnant church to discard the use of flesh meats, tea, and coffee, and other harmful foods. There are plenty of other things on which we can subsist that are wholesome and good."[11] Building a remnant people was a step toward building the Kingdom of God, and Seventh-day Adventists, God's remnant people, were to strive to reach the millennial perfection before Christ's return. White asserted, "When the character of Christ shall be perfectly reproduced in His people, then He will come to claim them as His own."[12] Caring for the body and White's emphasis on self-development and perfecting all of one's God-given faculties was essential for preparing not just a Christ-like individual but more importantly, a collective, corporate body of the Christ-like remnant.[13]

Scholars have argued that the ideas of advent and remnant have created a productive tension of being "in the world but not of it" in the denomination's mission practices. Michael Pearson puts it aptly,

---

10 Don F. Neufeld, ed. *Seventh-day Adventist Encyclopedia Second Revised Edition A – L* (Hagerstown, MD: Review and Herald Publishing Association, 1996), 458–59.

11 Ellen G. White, *Counsels on Diet and Foods* (Washington, D.C.: Review and Herald Publishing Association, 1938), 380–81.

12 Ellen White, *Christ's Object Lessons*, chapter three, https://m.egwwritings.org/en/book/15.221 (accessed March 1, 2021).

13 White emphasized that the first duty of the believer was to self-development, "that we may be able to do the greatest amount of good of which we are capable. . . . We cannot afford to dwarf or cripple a single function of mind or body by overwork or by abuse of any part of the living machinery." Ellen G. White, *Temperance* (Mountain View, CA: Pacific Press Publishing Association, 1949), cited in George W. Reid, "Health and Healing," in *Handbook of Seventh-day Adventist Theology*, ed. Raoul Dederen (Hagerstown, MD: Review and Herald Publishing Association, 2000), p. 781.

The idea that Christ is due to return very soon to this earth to bring salvation to those who are faithful, and judgment to those who are not, lends great urgency to the missionary task. It becomes the immediate responsibility of the church to penetrate the world in order to maximize other people's opportunities for finding salvation. The doctrine of the remnant, on the other hand, demands that a pure and faithful community exists to which the redeemed can repair.[14]

This theological tension encouraged the Adventists to embrace a conservative social vision that focuses on personal conversion instead of systemic changes. We see this in China too in the teachings of indigenous preachers such as Wang Mingdao and Ni Tuosheng (Watchman Nee). In describing the apocalyptic turn to premillennialism in American Protestantism in 1870s America, Christopher H. Evans comments, "Instead of seeing millennialism in a socially progressive light, . . . [premillennialism] insisted that societal conditions would grow worse in advance of the second coming."[15] As an apocalyptic movement, Adventism had a social vision different from progressive Protestantism, broadly categorized as the social gospel movement. Moral decline would persist, argued the Adventists, and the Christian duty was less one of pursuing structural changes in social, political, and economic institutions but of spreading the gospel and planting new churches. Although the Adventists agreed with the social gospel activists in their fight against alcoholism and tobacco, they did not call for fundamental societal transformation. After all, social decay was thought to be inevitable and would persist till the end of the world. Yet, as Ronald D. Graybill points out, "Even if they despaired of perfecting the whole world, they were to be paradigms of millennial peace. . . . So Adventists must reach millennial perfection without divine intervention before Christ returns; Christ can only come after that perfection is reached."[16] Health reform was essential for preparing the faithful to emulate the compassion of Christ and to restore the image of God in the personal,

---

14 Michael Pearson, *Millennial Dreams and Moral Dilemmas* (New York: Cambridge University Press, 1990), 26.

15 Christopher H. Evans, *The Social Gospel in American Religion: A History* (New York: New York University Press, 2017), 5.

16 Ronald D. Graybill, "Mrs. Temple: A Millennial Utopian," *Spectrum* 47, no. 4 (2019): 73–80. Quotation is taken from p. 74.

social, and institutional arenas.[17] Anticipating the everlasting kingdom to come, converting the body, mind, and soul was a means of making society inhabitable in the interim.

Dissemination of Adventist Health Messages

Protestant medical ministry in late nineteenth-century China emphasized missionary medicine as a "pathfinder" for the gospel, and missionary doctors such as Peter Parker and William Lockhart cured patients with Western medicine in an effort to lead them to Christ. Like these medical missionaries, when Adventist medical missionaries came to China in the early twentieth century, they used the same strategy to win new converts, but they did this through an integrative evangelistic model that combined the dissemination of popular health literature, the founding of sanitariums and hospitals, and the training of professional health workers. Receptive and creative Chinese then adapted the doctrinal and health knowledge and practice to the local context. Adventist physicians set up small dispensaries in market towns and cities linked by railroads. Over time, these humble clinics developed into sizable sanitariums and hospitals. The first Adventist sanitarium was founded in Shanghai in 1928. By 1948, the numbers of Adventist sanitariums, hospitals, and clinics grew to thirteen, providing free medicine and surgery to the poor and showing the practical benefits of Christianity. Being the denomination's first nursing school in the Far East, the Shanghai Sanitarium Nursing School also trained men and women for medical ministry inside and outside of China.

Adventists differed from other medical missionaries in their extensive use of health publications to reach out to the public. The first American Adventist medical missionaries Harry and Maude Miller (1880–1905) and Arthur (1877–1931) and Bertha Selmon (1877–1975), all graduates of the Adventist's American Medical Missionary College in Battle Creek, Illinois, were familiar with Adventist health printing. The denominational press, the Review and Herald Publishing Association, was a key avenue for promoting Ellen White's health visions and teachings, and one to which the medical missionaries undoubtedly

---

17 Edwin R. DuBose, ed., James W. Walters, rev., "The Seventh-day Adventist Tradition: Religious Beliefs and Healthcare Decisions." https://www.advocatehealth.com/assets/documents/faith/adventist3.pdf (accessed May 21, 2020).

subscribed. As medical students, they also read the professional health journal *Health Reformer*.[18] China's long legacy of religious printing had laid a foundation for an Adventist printing culture in China.[19] When Harry Miller arrived in Henan Province in 1903, he first established a small press that grew into a nationwide Adventist publishing house.[20] The press's health columns in two of the monthly magazines, the *Last Day Shepherd's Call* (末世牧聲 *Moshi musheng*) and the *Signs of the Times* (時兆月報 *Shizhao yuebao*), in addition to numerous health books and pamphlets, marked the Adventist's literary presence in the nation's growing religious print culture. Adventist colporteurs took these health materials to major cities and market towns, and to the Chinese diaspora in Southeast Asia. Some, like *Health and Longevity* (延年益壽 *Yannian yishou* [1916]), authored in Chinese by Arthur Selmon, became bestsellers for years. Adventist colporteur Chen Jinghu 陳鏡湖 (Tan Kia-Ou) recalled meeting Chen Yixi 陳宜禧 (Chan Ngee-Hee, 1844–1929), the famous founder of the Sun Ning Railway Company 新寧鐵路, in the Pearl River Delta during the 1910s. Chen bought a dozen copies of *Health and Longevity* to give to his relatives and business partners.[21] The book covered various practical topics ranging from physiology and control of germs and diseases to first aid and childcare. Arguably the first Chinese Adventist book on public health, *Health and Longevity* was a remarkable success that appealed to readers of all levels.[22] Forty thousand copies were reportedly sold in 1924, and this book was so popular that it ran into thirteen editions by the 1930s. Table 1 lists the distribution of Adventist health

---

18 The founding of the *Health Reformer*, renamed *Good Health*, came with the development of the denomination's first health institute, the Western Health Reform Institute, that was renamed the Battle Creek Sanitarium. The denomination lost control of both the journal and the sanitarium after a power struggle between the denominational leaders and Dr. John Harvey Kellogg, superintendent of the sanitarium. Don F. Neufeld, ed. *Seventh-day Adventist Encyclopedia Second Revised Edition A – L* (Hagerstown, MD: Review and Herald Publishing Association, 1996), 681–82; Malcolm Bull and Keith Lockhart, *Seeking a Sanctuary: Seventh-day Adventism and the American Dream*, 2nd ed. (Bloomington and Indianapolis: Indiana University Press, 2007), 302–15.

19 Philip Clart and Gregory Adam Scott, eds. *Religious Publishing and Print Culture in Modern China* (Boston: De Gruyter, 2015).

20 Joseph Tse-Hei Lee and Christie Chui-Shan Chow, "Publishing Prophecy: A Century of Adventist Print Culture in China," in *Religious Publishing and Print Culture in Modern China 1800–2012*, ed. Philip Clart and Gregory Adam Scott (Boston: De Gruyter, 2015), 51–90.

21 Tan Kia-Ou, *Bibles and Blessings in Old China: A Personal Testimony* (Singapore: Malaysian Signs Press, 1972), 16.

22 Bertha L. Selmon, *They Do Meet: Cross-Trails of American Physicians and Chinese People* (New York: Froben Press, 1942), 14.

publications from 1911 to 1935. Besides *Health and Longevity*, other titles were probably composed of popular articles that first appeared in the health columns of the denominational magazines.

Table 1. Signs of the Times Publishing House Record of Health Book Sales 1911–1935.[23]

English Title	Chinese Title	Year first Published	Previously Sold	No. of Copies Sold 1935	Total No. of Copies Sold
Enemies of Health	健康之敵 *Jiankang zhi di*	1928	96360		96,360
Health & Hygiene	民眾衛生 *Minzhong weisheng*	1934	21199	6756	27,956
Health & Longevity	延年益壽 *Yannian yishou*	1916	136000		136,000
Key to Health *Frederic Lee and Hsu Hwa, compiled	健康要訣 *Jiankang yaojue*	1930		186769	186,769
Way to Health	健康生活 *Jiankang shenghuo*	1932	5057	547	5,594
Way to Health	健康生活 *Jiankang shenghuo*	1932	14763	459	15,222
Way to Health (Leather)	健康生活 *Jiankang shenghuo*	1932	2239	140	2,379
*Decalogue of Health, compiled by L. D. Campbell and Joseph May 梅晉良	強身十律 *Qiangshen shilu*	1938	No. of copy printed: 25,000		

23 Box 34, folder 2, Edwin R. Thiele Papers (Collection 89), Center for Adventist Research, James White Library, Andrews University, Berrien Spring, MI. Information with "*" are drawn from the titles I found in the Center for Chinese Adventist Heritage at Hong Kong Adventist College.

The Content of Adventist Health Teachings

Popular magazines and health literature occupied an essential position in the dissemination of health and hygiene messages in mid-1920s Shanghai.[24] The Adventist-run Signs of the Times publishing house in Shanghai served the entire Chinese world by circulating the *Last Day Shepherd's Call* and the *Signs of the Times* throughout the Chinese diaspora. The *Last Day Shepherd's Call* was the official Chinese Adventist church paper, mainly distributed among members of the church but that also accepted nonmember subscriptions. Covering news of various church ministries and reports of local congregations, the *Signs of the Times* was the denomination's public relations tool. Each issue had a standardized format that included broad evangelical messages, local and international news commentary, biblical prophecies, and lifestyle management. Both magazines had specific health-related columns. Entitled "Health Department" (*weisheng bu* 衛生部) or "Health Compass" (*jiankang zhinan* 健康指南) in the *Last Day Shepherd's Call*, the column published articles written by missionary physicians.

Introducing the purpose of the health column, Dr. W. C. Landis, cofounder of the Shanghai Sanitarium, drew on 3 John 1:2 to link good health with the Adventist end-time duty, "[The Apostle] John understood that for human beings to be useful to a bit of good works for God, they must have a healthy body first. Our church is in the end time now."[25] The magazine was also a doctrinal compass for the denomination's health teachings. For instance, apart from the medical missionaries' writings, the magazine published, in a regular series, the Chinese version of Ellen White's *Ministry of Healing* that discusses the healing work of Jesus Christ.[26] It occasionally reprinted essays taken from Chinese professional health journals. The health column in the *Signs of the Times* was labelled "Hygiene" (衛生須知 *weisheng xuzhi* or 衛生揭要 *weisheng jieyao*) or "Health and Hygiene" (健康與衛生), and discussed a wide range of health-related topics, such as personal hygiene, household cleanliness, prevention against communicable diseases, a healthy (meatless) diet, and a lifestyle of temperance (i.e., the absence of alcohol and narcotic products).[27] Independently, these health

---

24 Chieko Nakajima, "Health and Hygiene in Mass Mobilization: Hygiene Campaign in Shanghai, 1920–1945," *Twentieth-Century China* 34, no. 1 (2008): 42–72.

25 *Moshi musheng* 1, no. 2 (1921): 23–24. "I pray that all may go well with you and that you may be in good health, just as it is well with your soul." (3 John 1: 2 NRSV).

26 See the *Moshi musheng* issues January 1930 to April 1934.

27 Joseph Tse-Hei Lee and Christie Chui-Shan Chow, "Publishing Prophecy: A Century of Adventist Print Culture in China," in *Religious Publishing and Print Culture in Modern China*

columns highlighted health improvement and a hygienic lifestyle, occasionally supplemented by theological reasoning. Putting the "Health Department" and "Hygiene" columns in the magazines' larger context, readers got a sense of the urgency of caring for the body as a key to preparing for Christ's return. Reading the columns alongside other articles that addressed natural and human disasters both inside and outside China, as well as local conflicts and global politics, no one would miss the recurring theme of the impending end of the world. The Daniel apocalypse reading is a case in point.[28] Commenting on the French Prime Minister Aristide Briand's call for the organization of a European Federal Union at the League of Nations in 1930, the Chinese editor Xu Hua 徐華 (Hsu Hua) was skeptical of such integrative efforts in Europe. Through the lens of Adventist apocalyptic vision, Xu compared the half-iron and half-clay toes of the great statue in King Nebuchadnezzar's dream (Daniel 2) with the European states and declared that this political vision of a European union was doomed to fail, as Daniel had prophesied in the past. Xu reminded his Chinese readers that no nation-states could secure a sustainable political union because Jesus Christ, symbolized by the big stone from heaven in Daniel's prophecy, was coming to destroy the world. "Accept Christ as your personal savior now. When He comes, not only will Europe be unified, but the great harmony (*da tong* 大同) will also come." Xu added a spiritual dimension to the Chinese understanding of great harmony and pointed out that the pursuit of evangelization through conversion outweighed the quest for political unity and stability.

Chloë Starr observes that Chinese theological writings were dominated by missionary authors before the 1920s, but this changed when the indigenous Chinese workers were theologically able to take up the writing task.[29] A similar trend happened in Chinese Adventism. During the 1900s and 1910s, missionaries were the major authors of the denominational health writings, and the Chinese staff were translators. Beginning in the early 1920s, the *Signs of the Times* health column expanded its scope to cover the Republican government's public hygiene policies. It also reprinted articles written by non-Adventist Chinese physicians and offered a "questions and answers" sub-column managed by Arthur

---

1800–2012, edited by Philip Clart and Gregory Adam Scott (Boston: De Gruyter, 2015), 51–90. Quotation from pp.74–77.

28 Hsu Hua, "Lun 'ouzhou hezhongguo' de chengbai" 論'歐洲合眾國' 的成敗 [On the Success and Failure of the 'European Federal Union'], *Shizhao yuebao* 25, no. 4 (1930): 12–15.

29 Chloë Starr, *Chinese Theology: Text and Context* (New Haven, CT: Yale University Press, 2016).

Selmon and Chinese physician Hong Shaojie 洪少杰 to address readers' enquiries.[30] The 1920s also saw a proliferation of articles written by Chinese editors and frontline workers. These native authors bolstered the health argument by combining Chinese morality and Adventism with story-telling skills to capture attention. For instance, Goh Djao O (Ge Zhaoé 葛肇諤) used Isaiah 22:13 and Luke 21:34 to critique widespread social ills such as gluttony, alcoholism, and wasteful festivities as signs of the end times.[31] Joseph May's (Mei Jinliang 梅晉良) criticism of Shanghai's materialistic culture struck an Adventist temperance tone when he referred to a friend who squandered his meager salary on theatre trips and expensive restaurants in order to avoid being looked down upon by colleagues.[32] Quoting Ellen White, May urged his readers to use money wisely and to help the poor if one could afford to do so. On another occasion, May promoted the image of a healthy family through the story of a teenage girl, Gi Fong, who got sick after over-snacking and binge-eating unhealthy food.[33] The lesson was that good parenting entailed making wise food choices for children. A woman contributor Chu Hsien Liang 朱賢良 derived her understanding of household cleanliness from the idea of holiness, stating that a proper Chinese home should be orderly, because Adventists were taught to model their earthly family on the heavenly kingdom.[34] It was through the Adventist tradition that Chu came to see cleanliness and pietism as complementary. Finally, Adventists criticized seasonal tonics, a food culture widely practiced among wealthy Chinese, as unnecessary. If a simple diet of vegetables and brown rice was enough to keep peasants strong and energetic, wrote Sing Ginn (Xin Jin 心斤), it did not make sense to spend money on expensive tonics.[35] These examples illustrate the Chinese recipients' capacity to adjust and adapt Adventist health teachings to their immediate context. As might be expected, the Chinese staff did better

---

30 The sub-column, began in January 1921, was titled "Answers to the Difficult Questions Concerning Recuperation" (*liaoyang danan* 療養答難).

31 Goh Djao O 葛肇諤, "Jinhua shidai de zui è 進化時代的罪惡 The Evils of the Evolution Age," *Shizhao yuebao* 25, no. 4 (1930): 4.

32 Joe May 梅馥, "Tantan shehua de wenti 談談奢華的問題 [The Luxury Question]," *Moshi musheng* 9, no. 9 (1929): 26–27.

33 Joe May 梅馥, "Jifang shengbing le 紀芳生病了 [Gi Fong Becomes Sick]," *Moshi musheng* 9. No. 9 (1929: 30–31

34 Chu Hsien Liang 朱賢良, "Qingjie 清潔 [Cleanliness]," *Moshi musheng* 12, no. 17 (1932): 12–13.

35 Sing Ginn 心斤, "Weishime yao chi bupin 為什麼要吃補品 [Why Take Tonic Medicine?]" *Moshi musheng* 17, no. 2 (1937): 28–29.

than the missionaries in contextualizing Adventism in relation to the health and spiritual concerns of native recipients.

As China entered the Nationalist era, a strong China was thought to be made up of a physically strong citizenry capable of fighting against external threats. This conceptualization that linked the fate of the nation to its people in physiological terms dominated the Republican era, as shown in the work of Ka-che Yip.[36] Once established in Nanjing, the Nationalist state set out to develop a modern national healthcare system in October 1928 as part of the broader nation- and state-building process.[37] Strengthening the physical body of citizenry through public health enhancement had significant implications for consolidating Chiang Kai-shek's newfound power. Chiang's keen efforts to prevent infectious diseases, control epidemics, and heighten public awareness of personal hygiene resonated with similar goals long sought by the Chinese health planners and Adventist missionaries in previous decades. Against this backdrop of nation-building through healthcare reform, Chinese Adventist leaders found common ground with the Nationalist state and were keen to adapt their health messages to the official initiatives. It was in this mediating zone that Adventists embedded their doctrinal messages into the state-led public health reform and discovered a larger social role for themselves.

In May 1929, Adventists published a special magazine issue that supported the government's healthcare reform. Notably, the issue began with a number of articles written by Xue Dubi 薛篤弼, head of the Ministry of Health, Wu Liande 伍連德, a renowned epidemiologist, and Zhang Zhijiang 張之江, who led the official anti-opium task force. The editor went on to justify the improvement of public health in theological terms. Citing Philippians 3:20–21,[38] the editor acknowledged the importance of health reform in reducing social ills, but he went further to call on readers to accept Jesus Christ as their savior in order to deal with sin, the very root cause of transmissible diseases.[39] In April

---

36 Ka-che Yip, *Health and National Reconstruction in Nationalist China: The Development of Modern Health Services, 1928–1937* (Ann Arbor, MI: Association for Asian Studies, The University of Michigan, 1995), 36.

37 Ka-che Yip, *Health and National Reconstruction in Nationalist China*, 22.

38 "But our citizenship is in heaven, and it is from there that we are expecting a Savior, the Lord Jesus Christ. He will transform the body of our humiliation that it may be conformed to the body of his glory, by the power that also enables him to make all things subject to himself." (Philippians 3:20–21, NRSV).

39 *Shizhao yuebao* 24, no. 5 (1929).

1930, Adventists connected longevity and happiness with exercising regularly, embracing a plant-based diet, and avoiding stimulants such as tea, coffee, tobacco, and spices. In addition, they urged readers to follow Christ and cultivate Christian character because time was running out and Christ would return soon, according to 1 Peter 3:10–11.[40] Utilizing religious print to endorse the state's healthcare campaign, the Adventists skillfully framed public health and the practice of medicine as a Christian vocation, expressing their love and compassion for non-believers in the end times. Thus, Adventists transcended the divisive template of "China versus the West" and facilitated the exchange and movement of medical knowledge, skills, and practices between sacred and secular domains.

With many years of frontline medical ministry in rural and urban China, Adventist missionaries were aware of the need to improve preventive care of chronic diseases. Nationalist health reform offered an opening for Adventists to advance such educational efforts through their church magazines. Throughout the late 1920s and 1930s, Adventists produced numerous articles to draw attention to general disease prevention strategies. They reminded readers to beware of flies and mosquitoes in spreading malaria, cholera, dysentery, tuberculosis, and typhoid in summer months. They taught people to install mosquito nets at home, cover or keep sewage dry, or put kerosene in it. These measures were designed to keep mosquitoes from laying eggs and spreading diseases. Other popular advice included avoiding buying fruits that were cut open in wet markets, not spitting in public, covering one's mouth and nose when sneezing or coughing, not letting minors play on dirty ground, and securing indoor ventilation when burning coal for warmth during the winter season. While such guidelines for cleanliness were in line with modern hygienic practices, the Adventists added a religious justification to stress that God expected the faithful to follow these preventive and remedial techniques in order to better protect health.

A final example concerns the principle of abstinence. Both the Bible and Ellen White inform the Adventists' theology of self-control. Because the body is a temple of the Holy Spirit, bad habits in eating, drinking, and thinking defile the dwelling place of God. Joining Chiang Kai-shek's "New Life Movement," Chinese Adventist leaders took issue with smoking and alcoholism. These

---

40 "For those who desire life and desire to see good days, let them keep their tongues from evil and their lips from speaking deceit; let them turn away from evil and do good; let them seek peace and pursue it." (1 Peter 3:10–11, NRSV).

practices, widely criticized by the Chinese health reformers as sources of social degradation at the time, had long been condemned in the Adventist temperance movement. *Signs of the Times* special editions on anti-opium and anti-alcoholism appeared throughout the 1920s.[41] A cartoon, published in 1930, imaginatively compared suicide with nicotine and alcohol consumption.[42] Heavy smokers and drinkers destroyed their personal health and caused harm to families and society. Thus, avoiding any hurt to one's health was a step closer to the Kingdom of God.

Practicing the Theology of Health in Socialist China—The Case of Shijiazhuang

Political changes in the 1950s propelled Adventists to face a new reality in their health ministry. By 1951, the Communist government had confiscated the Adventist publishing house, sanitariums, and schools. The absence of a coherent institutional infrastructure had a crippling effect on Adventist health ministry. There was no publisher to produce and distribute health literature, no hospital to promote the church's medical practices, and no school to train ministers who could educate congregants about the denomination's health messages. Nevertheless, individual Adventists held on to the health rules and strove to practice them at a personal level. A simple diet of consuming biblically "clean" food seemed to become the most basic norm among ordinary Adventists. This was not without challenge, given the food ration system in the Maoist era. Because Adventist food culture is similar to that of Muslims, Chinese Adventists drew on the halal rules and official recognition of ethnic minorities' rights to cope with the dietary challenges. A Han Chinese Adventist father in Kunming registered his family as Hui minority, which allowed him to access beef and lamb in the official food distribution system.[43] The Shanghai Adventist religious prisoner Huang Zhaojian 黃兆堅 abstained from pork by convincing the prison guard that his dietary habit was the same as that of Muslim prisoners.[44] By maintaining a biblically "clean" food practice, Adventists did their best to maintain a physically pure

---

41 *Shizhao yuebao* 20, no. 9 (1925) and *Shizhao yuebao* 21, no. 9 (1926).

42 Shan Yingmin 單英民, "Weihe zhisha 為何自殺 Why Commit Suicide?" *Shizhao yuebao* no. 5 (1930): 18–20.

43 A descendant of the family told this story to me when I was at a mission trip in Kunming in 2001.

44 Huang Zhaojian 黃兆堅, *Morning Glory [Qian niuhua 牽牛花]*, unpublished memoir.

body not tainted by "unclean" food when freedom of religious practice was hard to come by.

Relaxation on public religious activities in the post-Mao period permitted greater flows of personnel and ideas among Adventists. As new converts joined the faith, former mission clergy and Ellen White's literature made sure that the new members got their lifestyle right. In Hebei Province, the case of Shijiazhuang is illustrative. During his visit to the Shijiazhuang church, Adventist pastor Duan Yongqian (段雍虔 1904–1991) convinced the congregants, who were former Sunday-worshippers who had recently joined the Adventists, to follow the biblical narrative of Daniel's vegetarian diet. These new converts took Duan's advice seriously, and abstained from any "unclean" foods, but were not fully aware of other Adventist health teachings.[45] Messages from the seminary-educated Duan sounded an orthodox tune to Shijiazhuang Adventists.[46] In 1986, the Taiwan-based Signs of the Times Publishing House published the Chinese translation of Ellen White's *Counsels on Diet and Foods*. The reception of this text was mixed among the Shijiazhuang Adventists, as some congregants wondered whether White's idea of strict vegetarianism, abstaining from eggs, milk and oil, was too extreme. Even though the Taiwanese publisher kept the original preface where the American editor cautioned a contextual application of White's advice, many of the Shijiazhuang Adventists insisted on following this strict diet because "these teachings are from the Lord and from the prophetess," they told me. At a time when alternative proteins such as nuts and beans were not widely available in rural China, the consequence of adhering to strict vegetarianism was dire. Some of the Shijiazhuang Adventists allegedly suffered from malnourishment. A local pastor was physically too weak to preach in the pulpit, and insufficient protein intake caused his son's physical underdevelopment.[47]

Rectification appeared in the 1990s when Adventist public health educators Drs. Beverly and Henri Wiebe came to China as independent missionaries. From 1990 to 1997, the couple conducted a wellness and health program called NEWSTART in the provinces of Heilongjiang, Jilin, Hebei, Shaanxi, and Guangdong. Initially developed by the Adventist-run Weimar Institute in California, the NEWSTART program is derived from eight ingredients, namely

---

45 Interview with Shijiazhuang Adventists, June 6, 2019.

46 Duan Mude 段穆德, "Duan Yongqian 段雍虔," in *Zhonghua shenggongshi* [Chinese Seventh-day Adventist History 中華聖工史], ed. Samuel Young (Hong Kong: Chinese Union Mission of Seventh-day Adventists, 2002), 485–486.

47 Interview with the Shijiazhuang Adventists, June 6, 2019.

Nutrition, Exercise, Water, Sunshine, Temperance, Air, Rest, and Trust in God.[48] Shijiazhuang Adventists learned from the Wiebes that the problem with their strict diet was imbalanced nutrition.[49] The aforementioned pastor took a small bowl of peanuts every day to rebalance his protein intake and revitalize his energy. The Wiebes' wellness training inspired Gao (pseudonym), a woman Adventist in Shijiazhuang, to go abroad to study public health education in the 2000s. Upon completing her education, Gao returned to her hometown and taught the church to use health messages to gain converts. [50]

On a Sunday afternoon in June 2019, Gao invited me to meet a group of women Adventists, the positive outcomes of the NEWSTART program. Over the dining table, I heard extensive dietary advice on how to cure my stomach issues, and one suggestion was to quit animal protein totally. When I said my stomach cramped after eating beans, "Soak the beans and discard the water. It is the used water that causes the gas and upsets your stomach." Gao told me. She then commented on an eggplant dish, "Tomatoes go well with eggplant; you sisters make sure to add tomatoes when you make eggplant next time." After the main dishes, Gao offered me a bowl of nuts. "This is your meat. Don't eat too much because nuts are fatty," cautioned Gao. Her knowledge about the vegetarian diet owed much to the lessons that Shijiazhuang Adventists had learned from the past, and to the professional use of the NEWSTART program for evangelization. In the next two hours, the women Adventists told me that adopting the NEWSTART lifestyle helped cure their chronic illnesses such as migraines, shortness of breath, heart problems, irregular menstruation, nicotine addiction, and being overweight. The treatment entailed a simple change of diet. They ate homemade coarse bread and whole-wheat noodles instead of white buns (*bai mantou* 白饅頭) and white rice, replaced meat with beans and nuts, drank a lot of water, took deep breaths, and exercised daily. The methods resonated with the NEWSTART program promoted by the global Adventist health specialists and educators in the 1990s and 2000s.

In recounting their stories, the women were amazed at the effects of simple behavioral changes in ending their lasting illnesses. Born during the peak of the

---

48 I visited a number of these Adventist sanitariums in 2019. Most of these facilities are built in suburban areas and operated in a low-profile manner to avoid the suspicion of the local authorities. Mainly accepting church members, these sanitariums also admit non-members.

49 Interview with Dr. Henri Weibe on Skype, August 22, 2019.

50 Data of the Shijiazhuang case study is drawn from fieldwork conducted in the region in summer 2019.

Cultural Revolution and growing up in the Reform era, these women are part of China's baby boom. Unless workers are supported by state-owned enterprises' healthcare units,[51] they lack sufficient resources to cope with the physical and mental challenges caused by dramatic changes in the market reforms. When market privatization gradually took over many of the state enterprises in the late 1980s and 1990s, many people struggled to adapt to the harsh reality of cutthroat capitalism. Economic reform policies have expanded job opportunities for women, but traditional gender expectations remain intact. Adventist women are troubled by compelling pressure to meet marital, familial, and professional demands, and find themselves torn between parental stresses and workplace difficulties. The fledgling economy has given them some financial flexibility to live more indulgently, a lifestyle one woman called "craving nothing but good food to compensate for everyday stress." Echoing the Christian message on temperance, they believed that intemperance had compromised their health. By the time they got sick, they realized that their lifestyle had taken a heavy toll on their physical and mental well-being. They spent much money on medical tests and treatments, but the diagnoses and drugs were of little help. A thread that linked the women's stories together was their frustration with the ineffective official healthcare system that offered no viable treatment.

What the women told me fits into the triumphant conversion genre in the global Adventist narrative. But to these women in Shijiazhuang, their health concerns and lived experiences are real and authentic. By joining the church, they become part of an imagined remnant community. When they gather, they embrace and enliven Adventist remnant theology beyond its biblical literalism and the writings of Ellen White. Evidently, this small group of Adventists have accepted, adapted, and passed on the theology of health, and continue teaching potential converts to enact it. They live out this everyday Adventist theology in the mundane activities of eating and drinking healthily in accordance with God's will. This is also a practical theology that comes to life only when it is carried out by believers on a daily basis. The Chinese state still does not allow religious groups, registered or unregistered, to participate in social welfare services, and Adventists lost the medical and educational institutions that they built in the Republican period. Without an infrastructure to promote their health

---

51 Rachel Core, "Institutional Change and Tuberculosis Control: Continuity and Change in Pre- and Post-1949 Shanghai," *American Journal of Chinese Studies* 26, no. 2 (2019): 73–89. Quotation is taken from p. 88.

ministry, the church space registered with the religious patriotic body is pivotal to the denomination's "right arm" reaching out to the public. To the Shijiazhuang women, their steady health improvement after adopting the NEWSTART wellness program manifests the veracity and validity of the church's health theology in the secular domain. This local church is capable of offering vital social support to its congregants and providing them with relevant healthcare knowledge and skills.[52] While relying solely on health messages to proselytize might attract people who would only be interested in health rather than God, the resilience of Chinese Adventist theology lies in its capability to build religiosity and community ties among people and in its practical solutions to common health problems.

Conclusion

The spread of Adventism in China reveals the intersections of theology and health. For Adventists, caring for the body means living faithfully as part of an end-time remnant church. In anticipation of Christ's second coming, the Adventists seek to enact biblical theology and denominational doctrines to envision a perfectible corporeal body. Fundamental to Adventist health theology are the ideas of creation, end time, and salvation. The body is a gift from God, created for a higher purpose and susceptible to excesses. As part of creation, humans ought to follow the laws of nature and the biblical commandments in order to protect, preserve, and promote bodily health. The end of the world is near and Christ will return soon, so the world needs a corporate body of remnants to witness to God's salvation. Here, the spiritual implication for the physical body is significant. The body is a site of knowledge to reveal the nature of God before judgment day. A healthy body communicates what humans ideally should be. It is a bearer of a restored image of God. It is where the soul meets the Holy Spirit.

The concern for individual health and its usefulness for mission could be parochial if bodily practices and prescriptions fail to address sickness, pain, and suffering. Without generating real benefits to the body, a theology of health lacks practicality and loses its appeal. Ellen White's prescriptive texts and missionary medicine gave literal support to the church's health ministry, but it was Chinese practitioners who brought life to these teachings by living them out in daily life. The final destiny of the body is to join God in heaven, Adventists

---

52 The idea of Adventism, health, and social support is drawn from Sherma J. Charlemagne-Badal, Jerry W. Lee, "Religious Social Support and Hypertension among Older North American Seventh-day Adventists," *Journal of Religion and Health* 55, no. 2 (2016): 709–28.

believed. Yet, Adventist health theology does more to lead the soul toward the path of salvation. Despite its eschatological vocabulary, it promises practical steps to vitality and energy in this life, a life enjoyable at the personal level and fundamental to building strong community. Cultivation of health and spirituality is not new in the Chinese religious context. In most of Daoist history, Daoism's inner alchemy (*neidan* 內丹) inspired many to believe in immortality, an element thought to be attainable through a range of bodily techniques.[53] To counter the efficacy of missionary medicine, some wealthy urban merchants organized medical charities to revitalize Confucian worship.[54] It is against this backdrop that Adventism contributed to China's modern healthcare culture by offering a unique Protestant perspective. In tackling the sick and weak, its conservative premillennial concern focuses entirely on producing a converted body without becoming entangled in institutional reasons for the government's failure to deliver healthcare for all.

The demolition of Adventist organizations in the Maoist era stripped the denomination's institutional capacity to heal the sick Chinese body. In subsequent decades, personal resilience preserved Adventist health practices, but at a minimal level. Scarcity of resources posed challenges to the widespread embrace and practice of the prescribed healthful lifestyle. Believers could only hope that the natural therapy of sunshine, fresh air, and water cure would work well in "bare foot" medicine in impoverished rural hinterlands. Adventist health practices persisted and resurfaced in the 1980s, and thrived in the 1990s and 2000s. Unlike the Republican era when Adventists tapped into the rhetoric and policies of the Nationalist government's health reform, Chinese Adventist health practitioners today play no key role in building the nation's healthcare infrastructure. Their care for the body and soul is entirely a private matter for the "self," supported by zealous evangelists full of religious fervor. Following the footsteps of early twentieth-century missionaries, Chinese Adventists still believe that the goals of evangelism, focusing on conversion and a healthful lifestyle, outweigh the quest of social salvation. As healthcare enthusiasts, they continue to position themselves as a Chinese remnant in the making, however little participation they may realize in strengthening the health of the overall population.

---

53 Xun Liu, *Daoist Modern: Innovation, Lay Practice, and the Community of Inner Alchemy in Republic Shanghai* (Cambridge, MA: Harvard University Asia Center, 2009).

54 Angela Ki Che Leung, "Charity, Medicine, and Religion: The Quest for Modernity in Canton (ca. 1870–1937)," in *Handbook of Oriental Studies – Modern Chinese Religion II 1850–2015*, vol. 2, ed. Vincent Goossaert, Jan Kiely, and John Lagerwey (Boston: Brill, 2016), 579–612.

Chapter 10

PREVENIENT GRACE AND REPUBLICAN ERA CHINESE THEOLOGY

Christopher Payk, *National Chengchi University*

In discussing how the Christian message is communicated across cultures, the influential missiologist Andrew Walls wrote:

> Modern Christians should follow the practice of the early Church; Confucius and the other Chinese sages provided the same sort of preparation for the Gospel that Greek philosophy did in the Mediterranean world and offered a similar clothing for Christian thought.[1]

Long before Walls had written these words, John Wesley (1703–1791), the founder of Methodism, recognized that God provides advance preparation for the gospel before the Christian proclamation of the gospel has ever taken place. As Methodist missionaries spread all over the world in the wake of the Methodist revival, they carried the theology of John Wesley into places with previously existing religious traditions. When Methodists encountered the religious traditions of the Chinese world, they found some congruence between their Christian beliefs and Chinese religious traditions. In John Wesley's theology, Chinese Methodists had a theological inheritance that provided positive confirmation that God was at work amongst the Chinese before Christian missionaries ever arrived in the busy port cities of southeastern China. But were any of these new Eastern Methodists listening to Wesley?

When researching Wesley's actual usage of the term "preventing grace," which in modern speech is more commonly rendered "prevenient" or "preceding grace,"

---

1 Andrew Walls, "The Western Discovery of Non-Western Christian Art." In *The Missionary Movement in Christian History: Studies in the Transmission of Faith* (Maryknoll, NY: Orbis Books, 1996), 175.

along with references that Wesley made to John 1:9—"This was the true Light, who lighteth every man that cometh into the world"—which Wesley indicated was the substance of prevenient grace,[2] some interesting facets of his theology become apparent, four of which are particularly important when considering how these implications translate into a Chinese context:

a. Prevenient grace explains the existence of human good works among those who are not justified by faith.[3]

b. After the Fall, the enlightening by the Son, the "true light" which is prevenient grace has re-inscribed the moral law in some measure on every human heart[4] and has restored the human faculty of conscience. Conscience is not "natural" to humans but is one of the benefits of prevenient grace.[5]

c. Prevenient grace is the source of the "light of nature" which reveals God's omnipotence and divine being through the created order.[6]

d. Those who do not have the special revelation of the Old or New Testaments are nonetheless given God's self-revelation in creation, a partial re-inscription of the moral law through prevenient grace, and the restored faculty of conscience through prevenient grace. This grace provides revelation of the existence and power of God and some knowledge of morality, such as the Golden Rule.[7]

---

2 John Wesley, *The Works of Rev. John Wesley*, ed. Thomas Jackson (London: Wesleyan Methodist Book Room, 1829–1831; reprint, Grand Rapids: Baker Book House, 1978), 14:212 (An Extract of the Life and Death of Mr. Thomas Haliburton). The Jackson Edition of Wesley's Works is hereafter abbreviated as Wesley, *Works* [Jackson].

3 John Wesley, *The Works of John Wesley* (Bicentennial Ed.) (Nashville: Abingdon, 1984–), 11:112 (Article of Religion X, Of Free Will from A Further Appeal to Men of Reason and Religion, Part I). The Bicentennial Edition of Wesley's Works will be abbreviated as Wesley, *Works* [BE]. For discussion see further Christopher Payk, "John Wesley's Doctrine of Prevenient Grace and Its Import for Christian Mission in the Chinese World" in *From Everywhere to Everywhere: Methodist Mission in Global Perspective*, ed., David Scott, (Abingdon: Routledge, 2020).

4 Wesley, *Works* [BE], 2:7 (The Original, Nature, Properties, and Use of the Law).

5 Wesley, *Works* [BE], 2:156–57 (The Scripture Way of Salvation).

6 John Wesley, *A Survey of the Wisdom of God in the Creation, or A Compendium of Natural Philosophy*, accessed March 13, 2019, http://wesley.nnu.edu/john-wesley/a-compendium-of-natural-philosophy/a-compendium-of-natural-philosophy-appendix/.

7 See also Wesley's indication in 1750 that the golden rule is engraved on "everyone that comes into the world." *Works* [BE], 1:660–61 (Sermon on the Mount, X). Wesley connects the "true light" with the enlightening of Noah and his descendants, attributing to them "some traces of knowledge, both with regard to the invisible and the eternal world," in his sermon "Walking by Sight and Walking by Faith." *Works* [BE], 4:52.

After John Wesley died, the Methodist Church developed in both England and the United States and subsequently further spread into the countries, including China, where Methodist missionaries of various denominations sowed their theological message.

It was in China that Methodists would develop the idea that God's grace explains the existence of human good works among the Chinese. As described below, these ideas include the notion that the moral law and conscience inscribed on the hearts of the Chinese are the work of the unknown Christ, and that even without the revelation of God in the Bible, God's revelation has been given through creation, through the light of nature, and through *some* aspects of the Chinese religious systems. This development was particularly noticeable in connections that Western missionaries and Chinese Christians made between Confucianism and Christianity. Methodist missionaries such as William E. Soothill and Young J. Allen believed that it was God's grace working through Confucianism that provided the divine light found in some aspects of Confucianism to the Chinese.[8] However, these developments always took place without reference to John Wesley or prevenient grace, despite the congruence between the idea that God was at work in Confucianism and Wesley's ideas about the effects of prevenient grace.

As early as 1863, Wesley's works had been translated into Chinese. In 1863, George Piercy of the Wesleyan Methodist Mission had translated six of *John Wesley's Sermons* into classical Chinese (as 聖經擇要詳論).[9] By 1897, the Publishing House of the Methodist Episcopal Church had published the *Life of Wesley* translated by Sarah Moore Sites[10] and by 1920, a *Life of John Wesley* (unknown translator), and "a volume of Wesley's sermons had been translated into Mandarin by one of the Wesleyan missionaries at Hankow."[11] That the

---

8 See William Edward Soothill, *A Mission in China* (London: Oliphant, Anderson & Ferrier, 1907), 129 and 220. For Allen, see Adrian A. Bennett, *Missionary Journalist in China: Young J. Allen and His Magazines, 1860–1883* (Athens, GA: The University of Georgia Press, 1983), 81.

9 John Wesley, *Shengjing tiyao xianglun* 聖經擇要詳論 [*John Wesley's Sermons*], trans. George Piercy (Canton: Zhengsha Huishi Assembly Hall, 1863). See also, Wu Enyuan, ed., "The 160th Anniversary of Pastor George Piercy Arriving in Hong Kong," *Monthly News*, The Methodist Church of Hong Kong, 2011, September – October, Issue 317.https://www.methodist.org.hk/media/monthlynews/pdf/2011/11/03/2011_iss317-eVersion.pdf, 12. (Chinese).

10 Walter N. Lacy, *A Hundred Years of Chinese Methodism* (New York: Abingdon-Cokesbury Press, 1948), 191.

11 Lacy, *A Hundred Years of Chinese Methodism*, 193.

biography of Wesley and some of his works had been translated is certain. That native Chinese Methodists were reading them is less clear.

Rather, it was through Confucianism that Chinese Methodists who had a Confucian education saw God at work among the Chinese before Christians even arrived in China. By the 1920s, however, Methodists, along with other Christian denominations, were in the midst of a controversy that hijacked efforts to find God at work in the past because the needs of the present were far too pressing. In the early half of the twentieth century, the fundamentalist-modernist controversy had a significant impact on Christians in China, including Methodists.[12] At the turn of the twentieth century, most missionaries in China held to a basic theology that was, in turn, taught to Chinese Christian converts. In the 1920s, however, the former theological consensus among missionaries began to evolve into a spectrum of theological beliefs. The extreme left of the spectrum was dominated by modernists while the extreme right was populated by fundamentalists, with both missionaries and Chinese Christians finding their place along this spectrum.[13]

The majority of Chinese Methodists who would follow Young J. Allen and William E. Soothill's ideas that God was at work among the Chinese before the arrival of Christians likely felt more at home in the modernist camp.

Modernist Methodists and Confucian Heritage—Zhao Zichen

The most famous among these more progressive Methodists thinkers is Zhao Zichen. His works became standard reading among modernist Chinese Methodists in the 1940s and 1950s.[14] After a thorough classical Chinese education, Zhao Zichen (趙紫宸, T. C. Chao) (1888–1979), graduated from Dongwu Methodist College in Suzhou where he converted to Christianity; he later went to Vanderbilt University where he earned M.A. and B.D. degrees. Zhao was a

---

12 See Kevin Xiyi Yao, *The Fundamentalist Movement Among Protestant Missionaries in China, 1920–1937* (Lanham, MD: University Press of America, 2003), 23–54.

13 In 1955, Wang Mingdao described the key beliefs of both modernists and fundamentalists from his perspective as a self-described fundamentalist. See Wang Mingdao, "We Are for the Faith!" 我們是為了信仰! *Lingshi jikan* 霊食季刊 [The Spiritual Food Quarterly] 114 (Summer 1955): 135–36. Translated in Francis P. Jones, *Documents of the Three Self-Movement: Source Materials for the Study of the Protestant Church* (New York: National Council of the Churches of Christ in the U.S.A., 1963), 100–01.

14 Wang Mingdao wrote, for example, that Zhao's *Life of Jesus*, a creative biography of the life of Jesus from a Confucian-Christian perspective, had become a model of Chinese modernist literature. See Wang Mingdao, "We Are for the Faith!" 147.

Methodist until 1941 when he became an Anglican priest[15] and was influenced by what would become known as American Methodist liberal theology,[16] which saw Christianity as open to progress and gradual change. In the early part of the twentieth-century, China was beset by many crises, and various "save the nation" strategies (*jiuguo* 救國) were explored. Some Christians believed that it would be through aligning the development of Christianity with the scientific progress and modern outlook of the early twentieth century that Christianity would be able to provide resources to the nation, particularly by developing a moral populace.[17] However, in order to do that, Christian theology needed to be "updated" in order to remove the "superstitious" elements so despised at the time by modernists like Zhao Zichen.[18] Zhao sought for the reconciliation of his Confucian heritage with his Christian faith, but he thought that "superstition" should be removed from Chinese Christian theology and a "scientific worldview" should be embraced.[19] These "superstitious" elements included the traditional teachings on the deity of Christ, the virgin birth, and the resurrection of Jesus from the dead.[20]

Zhao envisioned Confucianism as working complementarily with Christianity in China as a moral philosophy and not as a competing religious system.[21] He saw God's work among the Chinese through their sages and heroes as being continuous with the later revelation of the incarnate Word in Jesus Christ.[22]

---

15 See Chen Yongtao, *The Chinese Christology of T. C. Chao* (Leiden: Brill, 2016), 70.

16 See Daniel Hoi Ming Hui, *A Study of T.C. Chao's Christology in the Social Context of China: 1920–1949* (Bern: Peter Lang, 2017), 36–39.

17 Ryan Dunch, *Fuzhou Protestants and the Making of Modern China* (New Haven: Yale University Press, 2001), 75–79.

18 Rebecca Nedostup, *Superstitious Regimes: Religion and the Politics of Chinese Modernity* (Cambridge: Harvard University Press, 2009), 6–11. See also Zhao Zichen's biography at "Zhao Zichen," Biographical Dictionary of Chinese Christianity, accessed April 18, 2019, http://bdcconline.net/en/stories/zhao-zichen.

19 "Present Day Religious Thought and Life in China," 1926, repr. in Zhao Zichen, in Xiaochao Wang, ed., *The Collected English Writings of Tsu Chen Chao* (Beijing: Zongjiao Wenhua, 2009), 205; c.f. Chloë Starr, *Chinese Theology* (New Haven: Yale University Press, 2016), 74. However, Zhao's theology would undergo development in the 1940s in a neo-orthodox direction, seeing Christianity as a corrective to Chinese society. See Starr, *Chinese Theology*, 98.

20 "The Chinese Church Realizes Itself," 1927, repr. in Zhao, *The Collected English Writings*, 209; c.f. Kevin Xiyi Yao, *The Fundamentalist Movement Among Protestant Missionaries in China*, 281.

21 "Religious Situation," 1930, repr. in Zhao, *The Collected English Writings*, 304.

22 "A Chinese Delegate Looks at Tambaram," 1939, repr. in Zhao, *The Collected English Writings*, 464.

Consequently, he wanted to conserve these "best elements in Chinese culture" in order to indigenize the Christian message in China.[23] He thought that the church would become indigenous in China if it "conserves and unifies all truths contained in the Christian religion and in China's ancient civilization and which thus manifests and expresses the religious life and experiences of Chinese Christians in a fashion that is native and natural to them."[24]

For Zhao, with his early education in the Confucian classics, to be a follower of Jesus did not hinder him from also being "a faithful student of Confucius and the other Chinese sages." In fact, he saw in Confucius, although only in certain aspects, "a clear revelation of God" who confirmed for Zhao that Jesus is the Son of God.[25] Zhao's Confucian perspective on the person of Jesus brought out an emphasis on the humanity of Jesus, which he saw as a corrective to the emphasis in Western Christianity on the divinity of Christ. The dual nature of Christ was creatively formulated by Zhao in this way: "Heaven was well pleased with sound humanity."[26] Zhao believed that it was the Chinese "cultural heritage," with its discernment of the regularity of the stars in the heavens, that provides the "recognition of the moral law within" each human being on earth. This moral law is best kept by upholding appropriate human relations that are described in the Confucian five fundamental ethical relations. Maintaining these relationships in the proper way is the fundamental task of life. Moreover, Zhao claimed that it was education, which he was so deeply involved in, that provides people with the context to cultivate the ethical nature of humankind.[27] Zhao thought that it would only be through the truths that the ancient Chinese had discovered through their sages that Jesus would be embraced by the Chinese people.[28] Therefore, it was a Chinese Christianity deeply influenced by Confucianism that Zhao put forth as the way Chinese would embrace Jesus. However, at least in his Methodist phase, Zhao thought that Christianity needed to be "updated" by removing the superstitions that he saw as "weak elements."[29]

---

23 "The Articulate Word—The Problem of Communication," 1947, repr. in Zhao, *The Collected English Writings*, 486.

24 "The Indigenous Church," 1924, repr. in Zhao, *The Collected English Writings*, 177.

25 "Jesus and the Reality of God," 1933, repr. in Zhao, *The Collected English Writings*, 343.

26 "Jesus and the Reality of God," 345.

27 "Our Cultural Heritage," 1927, repr. in Zhao, *The Collected English Writings*, 232–36.

28 "Our Cultural Heritage," 242.

29 "Christianity and Confucianism," 1927, repr. in Zhao, *The Collected English Writings*, 252.

Fundamentalist Methodists and Confucian Heritage—John Sung

Meanwhile, some self-described fundamentalist Chinese Christians completely opposed these "updates." They believed that the indigenization of the gospel was not crucial to saving the nation but emphasized the interior spiritual life. For these fundamentalists, the key to life was to adhere to the teachings revealed in the Bible; doing this led to a transformed life.[30] Three of these men are particularly well known in the West. Wang Mingdao was inspired by the Methodist revival in England and, while still in high school in 1919, dreamed of becoming the John Wesley of China.[31] Watchman Nee, or Ni Tuosheng, born of Methodist parents and baptized a Methodist,[32] was later in life inspired by John Wesley's role as a revivalist in England.[33] However, neither of these men remained connected with any Methodist denomination.

The most well-known Methodist Christian among the fundamentalists, but often not recognized as being a Methodist, was John Sung, or Song Shangjie (宋尚節) (1901–44). His father was Song Xuelian, a Methodist Episcopal Mission convert, who became a minister with the church and "a bulwark of Hinghwa Methodism."[34] His son, John, grew up in the Hinghwa[35] Methodist Episcopal Church (MEC) in Fujian Province, occasionally preaching in his father's place while he was away. In 1920, as China was continuing to convulse from the May Fourth Movement in 1919 and beginning to turn its ire against Western missionaries and Chinese Christians as the reason for the deplorable state of the nation, John Sung received a scholarship to study at Ohio Wesleyan University to prepare for Christian ministry. Later, he decided to change majors and subsequently obtained a Master's and a PhD degree in Chemistry from Ohio State University, followed by a period at Union Seminary at New York, a difficult time for Sung's theological development and mental well-being, during which Sung

---

30   See Lian Xi, *Redeemed by Fire: The Rise of Popular Christianity in Modern China* (New Haven: Yale University Press, 2010), 129–30.

31   Wang Mingdao, *Wushinian lai* 五十年來 [The Last Fifty Years] (repr. New Taipei City: CCLM Publishing Group Ltd., 2012), 61.

32   Witness Lee, *Watchman Nee: A Seer of the Divine Revelation in the Present Age* (Anaheim: Living Stream Ministry, 1991), 36.

33   "The Continuation of the Book of Acts, Chapter Twenty," The Collected Works of Watchman Nee, Living Stream Ministry, accessed April 18, 2019, https://www.ministrybooks.org/books.cfm?id=09C754CB0A.

34   Lim Ka-Tong, *The Life and Ministry of John Sung.* (Singapore: Genesis Books, 2012), 32.

35   Hinghwa is known today as Putian (莆田), Fujian Province.

was committed to a psychiatric hospital and spent time recovering from a mental breakdown. Daryl Ireland's research has recounted how Sung later painted a picture of this time as a battle between Sung and theological modernists who sought to suppress his fundamentalist theological beliefs in an attempt to erase the narrative of his mental instability.[36]

After returning to China and resuming his original plan to become a preacher, Sung passed his examinations with the Hinghwa Annual Conference of the MEC in 1928 and was designated "conference evangelist" in 1929.[37] On November 16, 1930, he was ordained as a deacon and admitted to full membership in the Hinghwa MEC Conference and once again appointed as "conference evangelist."[38] Finally, on May 7, 1938, Sung was ordained an elder of the MEC in the Hinghwa Conference.[39] His job designation with the MEC was "evangelist-at-large" until his death in 1944.[40] Daniel Bays writes that Sung "must be considered probably the single most powerful figure in Chinese revivalism in the mid-1930s."[41] Due to his dynamism and the enormous crowds that came to hear him preach, some Methodist missionaries compared Sung's revivals to the revivals of John Wesley,[42] and newspaper reports described him as the "John Wesley of China."[43] His biographer Lim Katong claims that Sung "intentionally followed the models of revival exemplified by John Wesley,"[44] and in his diary John Sung mentions having read a biography of John Wesley (約翰衛斯理傳)[45] and being familiar with Wesley's preaching style.[46] However, it appears that

---

36 See Daryl Ireland, *John Song: Modern Chinese Christianity and the Making of a New Man* (Waco, TX: Baylor University Press, 2020), 21–23.

37 Lim, *The Life and Ministry of John Sung*, 91.

38 Lim, *The Life and Ministry of John Sung*, 105.

39 Lim, *The Life and Ministry of John Sung*, 215–16.

40 Lim, *The Life and Ministry of John Sung*, 136.

41 Daniel H. Bays, *A New History of Christianity in China* (West Sussex, UK: Wiley Blackwell, 2012), 138. Yet Sung is not mentioned in Walter Lacy's *A Hundred Years of China Methodism* written in 1948.

42 Lim, *The Life and Ministry of John Sung*, 148.

43 Lim, *The Life and Ministry of John Sung*, 199.

44 Lim, *The Life and Ministry of John Sung*, 269.

45 Song Shangjie, ed. Song, Tian-Zhen, *Lingli ji guang* 靈歷集光 [The Diary of His Spiritual Life] (Hong Kong: Eng Yu Evangelistic Mission, 1995), chap. 4.4, http://cclw.net/soul/linglijiguang/index.htm. Sung gives no further details as to the author or translator of the biography.

46 Song, *Diary*, chap. 4.2, http://cclw.net/soul/linglijiguang/index.htm. John Sung, dealing with chest pain on April 26, 1931, decided to preach more "serenely" like John Wesley and Charles Finney, both of whom lived long lives, instead of like Dwight Moody who preached vehemently and died young.

Sung did not make his connection to the MEC well known. It is likely that Sung did not want to publicize his connection with Wesley and the MEC due to the increasing nationalist sentiment among Chinese who saw those connected with Western missionaries as the "running dogs of the imperialists,"[47] which was tantamount to a charge of treason in the wake of the May Fourth Movement in 1919 and certainly by the May Thirtieth Movement in 1925 as it connected Christian missions with cultural imperialism.[48]

Although Sung respected the Chinese Classics, and in particular Confucius,[49] he did not find in Confucianism the preparation for Christianity that many modernists such as Zhao Zichen did. In the wake of the fundamentalist-modernist debate, Chinese Christian fundamentalists such as Wang Mingdao, Watchman Nee, and John Sung became suspicious of theological education due to the influence of modernists in theological schools in both America and China. Sung, who had spent time studying at Union Theological Seminary in New York, USA, and had studied under the famous liberal theologian Harry Emerson Fosdick,[50] thought that rejecting liberal theology was essential. As a result, a radical break from China's indigenous religions was necessary: "China does not need the teaching of Fosdick, nor Gandhi. The teachings of Confucius are far better. What the Chinese need is Jesus Christ and his cross."[51] This rejection of modernism and, despite his admiration for the teachings of Confucius, indigenous Chinese religions, was important as well for Sung's personal narrative of being a mentally fit fundamentalist preacher. This emphasis on a radical break with the Chinese past was a significant theological difference between the fundamentalists and modernists before 1949.[52]

---

47 Lim, *The Life and Ministry of John Sung*, 12 and 288 fn. 15.

48 Bays, *A New History of Christianity in China*, 107–13.

49 Sung spent time reading the Chinese Classics to re-familiarize himself with his Chinese context in 1927 upon his return to China from America: see Katong, *The Life and Ministry of John Sung*, 107, 133.

50 Sung speaking to a missionary who admired Fosdick said: "So many people talked about Fosdick. Do you know him? Have you heard him teach or preach? I studied under him and his teachings have been cast out of my life forever." Katong, *The Life and Ministry of John Sung*, 133.

51 Lim, *The Life and Ministry of John Sung*, 133.

52 However, we see a more nuanced perspective of Wang Mingdao after his release from prison in 1980 as revealed in Wang Mingdao, ed. Ying Fuk-tsang 邢福增, *Wang Mingdao de zuihou zibai* 王明道的最後自白 [Wang Mingdao's Last Confession] (Hong Kong: Logos Publishers, 2013), especially with regard to the influence of Confucianism on Wang's theology. See also Christopher Payk, "Revisiting the Life and Theology of the Confucian-Christian Wang Mingdao" (PhD diss., National Chengchi University, 2021).

Another, perhaps even more significant, factor that led fundamentalists to be wary of modernists, in this case Methodists, was their connection to political power. Possibly the most famous Methodist in the modernist camp was Jiang Changchuan (Z.T. Kaung, 江長川) (1884–1958).[53] Jiang Changchuan, a student and teacher (from 1905–09) at the Anglo-Chinese College in Shanghai that Young J. Allen had founded, became the pastor in 1923 of the Allen Memorial Methodist Church in Shanghai. This was where the powerful Song (Soong) family were members, including the patriarch Charlie Song and his daughter, Song Meiling, who would go on to marry Jiang Jieshi (Chiang Kai-shek) in 1927. Jiang baptized Chiang Kai-shek a Methodist Christian in October of 1930.[54] In 1941, Jiang was elected bishop of North China and later, during the Japanese Occupation of China in 1942, he was asked by the Japanese to head the North China Christian Union Group, an organization that the Japanese had created in order to control the Christian churches in China. According to Wang Mingdao, due to Jiang's close connection with Chiang Kai-shek, to refuse would have meant his execution, and so he accepted the role.[55] His connection to Chiang Kai-shek was also the reason, according to Wang, that Jiang accepted a leadership role in the early Three-Self Patriotic Movement (TSPM) as to refuse would surely have resulted in him having been branded a traitor to the new Chinese government.[56] Whether these statements by Wang are correct or not, they do indicate the perception among fundamentalists like Wang Mingdao and John Sung (Sung had died in 1944 with Wang preaching the funeral

---

53 See "Jiang Changchuan," *Biographical Dictionary of Chinese Christianity*, accessed April 18, 2019, http://bdcconline.net/en/stories/jiang-changchuan.

54 Bays, *A New History of Christianity in China*, 125.

55 For a more sympathetic treatment of Jiang during the Second Sino-Japanese war, see Ying Fuk-tsang, "王明道與華北中華基督教團－淪陷區教會人士抵抗與合作的個案研究" [Wang Mingdao and the North China Christian Union Group: Enemy Occupied Area Church Leader's Resistance and Cooperation Case Studies] in *Conflict and Assimilation: Modern Chinese Christian History Research*, (Taipei: Universal Light Publishers, 2006), 138–140. Ying sees Jiang as taking the role in the Japanese-controlled union group in order to keep the Chinese church open during the war years. Had he refused, Jiang believed that the church in China would be forced to close.

56 See Wang Mingdao, *Wang Mingdao de zuihou zibai*, 143–145. More research needs to be done on Jiang's contemporary and fellow Methodist bishop Chen Wenyuan. See "Chen Wenyuan," *Biographical Dictionary of Chinese Christianity*, accessed April 18, 2019, http://bdcconline.net/en/stories/chen-wenyuan. Jiang denounced Chen Wenyuan during the accusation campaigns, which confirmed for the fundamentalists that Jiang was too closely connected to the political power structure in the TSPM.

sermon),[57] that modernists such as Jiang were connected to politicians and thus their commitment to authentic Christian teaching was compromised by their loyalty to those in political power.

With fundamentalist Methodists like John Sung looking at modernist Methodists such as Zhao Zichen and Jiang Changchuan with suspicion, due to their differences in theology and political involvement during the 1930s and 1940s, any talk of continuity with Chinese religions that modernists described in previous decades was not well received by fundamentalists. Much more prevalent among fundamentalists was the teaching for a radical break with the past in order to provide a hope for the future.[58] Also, after the May Thirtieth Movement in 1925, both fundamentalists and modernists did not wish to be connected to what was increasingly seen as Western "cultural imperialism." Justification of theological statements with references to English authorities like John Wesley would not have been seen as authoritative in China after 1925.[59] Consequently, this was not a fruitful time for the direct development of Wesley's ideas regarding prevenient grace in Chinese theology.

Another significant reason for the pause in the search for God at work in the Chinese past through Wesley or Confucianism were the social changes that took place in China near the middle of the twentieth century. After the double blow of the Second Sino-Japanese War and the Chinese Civil War, the orientation to the past was to be put on hold until a more opportune time would arise. Nearing the day when the Chinese Communist Party would take control of mainland China, we find Zhao Zichen writing in 1948 that

> Only in recent years Christians talked about "an indigenous Church" and "China's Spiritual Inheritance." Such voices are now strangely silent— stopped as it were in the face of the collapse of Chinese culture. The literati class has dispersed into various new walks of life and new scholarly pursuits; there is left no solid class of people who understand and protect Chinese culture which consequently falls into oblivion.[60]

---

57 See John Sung, *Wo de jianzheng* 我的見證 [The Testimony of John Sung] (New Taipei City: Glory Press, 1988), 281–82, as well as Wang Mingdao, *Lingshi jikan*, Fall Issue, 1944 (New Taipei City: CCLM Publishing Group, 2013), 149–57. Wang provides the substance of his funeral sermon for Sung in his quarterly journal. The two appeared to share a high regard for one another as well as a similar rejection of modernist theology.

58 See Lian Xi, *Redeemed by Fire*, 129.

59 See Dunch, *Fuzhou Protestants and the Making of Modern China*, 186.

60 Zhao Zichen, *Collected English Writings*, 521–22.

Chinese Christians, including Methodists, had to reformulate their theologies and perspectives of the past in the wake of the formation of the People's Republic of China in 1949. New, more pressing challenges were ahead for the Chinese church.

Within the last decade, an interesting phenomenon has taken place in the Pan-Chinese world. Some leading Chinese Methodists have been part of a "Back to Wesley" trend in various locations in the Chinese world.[61] This corresponds with a larger "Back to Calvin"[62] movement and I think this is, in large part, a reaction to the crisis of meaning in Christian theological education in the wake of post-modernity. Of particular interest for the purposes of this paper is that several of these Methodists have been using John Wesley's doctrine of prevenient grace to explain how God has been at work in the Chinese past and is also now at work amongst all Chinese peoples. Individuals of note include Peter K. H. Lee, or Li Jingxiong (李景雄),[63] of the Methodist Church in Hong Kong and chaplain of Chung Chi College at the Chinese University of Hong Kong;[64] Lin Zhongcheng (林忠誠) from The Methodist Theological School in Malaysia;[65]

---

61 This "Back to Wesley" trend as I have named it appears to have begun in the United States by Albert Outler with the book Albert Outler, ed., *John Wesley* (New York: Oxford University Press, 1964) and his mentorship at various Methodist theological institutions. Outler was an influential Methodist theologian who encouraged Methodists to return to the theology of John Wesley in order to revive Methodist theology and practice. This trend has continued on into the Chinese world in places like the Taipei Methodist Graduate School of Theology and Holy Light Theological Seminary in Kaohsiung, Taiwan. From my personal visits to both schools, I can attest to an emphasis in the curriculum on the theology of John Wesley.

62 For the early developments of this "Back to Calvin" movement on Chinese theology, see Fredrik Fallman, "Calvin, Culture and Christ? Development of Faith Among Chinese Intellectuals," in *Christianity in Contemporary China*, ed. Francis Khek Gee Lim (London and New York: Routledge: 2013), 153–68; Alexander Chow, "Calvinist Public Theology in Urban China Today," *International Journal of Public Theology*, no.8 (2014): 158–75.

63 "Peter K. H. Lee," Chung Chi Chaplaincy, CUHK, accessed April 18, 2019, https://www.cco.cuhk.edu.hk/chaplaincy/chi/1969–1971–7/.

64. See Peter K. H. Lee, "Creation Renewed: Heaven-Earth-Humanity. A Journey in Wesleyan-Orthodox-Confucian Theological Interculturation," The Oxford Institute of Methodist Theological Studies, August 12–19, 2013, https://oimts.files.wordpress.com/2013/09/2013–6-lee.pdf. As well as Peter K. H. Lee, "Virtue Ethics, Confucian Moral Teachings, Wesleyan Spirituality: In a Changing Asian Context," The Oxford Institute of Methodist Theological Studies, August 12–19, 2013, https://oimts.files.wordpress.com/2013/04/2007–6-lee.pdf.

65 See Lin Zhongcheng 林忠誠, "從衛斯理約翰的預設恩典觀看神在救恩中的主權" [Seeing God's Sovereignty in Salvation from John Wesley's Doctrine of Prevenient Grace] (MDiv thesis, The Methodist Theological School, Malaysia, 2014). http://www.mtssibu.edu.my/downloads/wesley/Fr_the_Prevenient_Grace_of_JW.pdf.

Pang Junhua (龐君華), the former dean of the Methodist Graduate School of Theology in Taipei and now the current Superintendent of the Methodist Church in Taiwan;[66] as well as Wilfred Ho (何威達),[67] professor of theology at Trinity Theological College in Singapore.[68]

At various points in history, Chinese Methodists have all looked back and seen God at work among the ancient Chinese. In the early period of Protestant Christianity in China, it was largely through the Confucian tradition that this activity was perceived. In the current period, Chinese Methodists who have become more familiar with the theology of John Wesley have used his doctrine of prevenient grace to explain God's interaction with the Chinese in the past. It seems to me that the correlation of these two ideas, the Christian God at work in the Confucian tradition and the doctrine of prevenient grace—which explains the existence of human good works among those who are not justified by faith, the re-inscription of the moral law in some measure on every human heart, the restored human faculty of conscience, the "light of nature" that reveals God's omnipotence and divine being through the created order, and the universal knowledge of morality such as the Golden Rule in Confucianism[69]—is a significant and overlapping area of both Chinese and Methodist theology and one that deserves further attention. Bringing together Confucianism, Christianity, and the theology of John Wesley offers new insights to foundational Methodist thinking and to the history of Christianity in China. Theologically, as some of the above-mentioned scholars have suggested, there is a common root of God at work among the ancient Chinese that corresponds to Wesley's larger picture of God at work among all people. The implications would be to see, as Walls mentions in the quote at the beginning of this paper, that Wesleyan theologians should feel very comfortable working with the Chinese foundation of Confucian thought as preparation for the Christian message.

---

66 "The Methodist Church's New Superintendent: Pang Junhua," *Chinese Christian Tribune*, accessed April 18, 2019, https://www.ct.org.tw/1338027. See Pang Junhua龐君華"成為真實門徒的群體： 信仰群體的成聖，約翰 衛斯理小組和教會更新運動 [Becoming a Group of True Disciples: The Sanctification of Faith Groups, John Wesley's Small Groups and the Church Renewal Movement] accessed April 18, 2019, http://johnwesleycenter.blogspot.com/

67 "Rev Dr. Wilfred Ho Wai Tat," Trinity Theological College, Singapore, accessed April 18, 2019, https://ttc.edu.sg/english/about/faculty/rev-dr-wilfred-ho-wai-tat/.

68 See Wilfred Ho, 何威達, 思主所思、 行主所行： 衛斯理的救恩教牧神 [Behold, John Wesley: A Soterio-Pastoral Theologian] (Hong Kong: VW Link, 2017).

69 See *Analects* 12.2 and 15.24, "What you do not want done to yourself, do not do to others."

Chapter 11

CHANGES IN THE CONTEMPORARY THREE-SELF CHURCH'S EVALUATION OF REFORMED THEOLOGY

The Theology of Wang Aiming

Yim Tak Leung, *Chinese University of Hong Kong*

Introduction

This paper explores the changes in the Three-Self church's evaluation of Reformed traditions from 1998,[1] the year of the formal launch of "Theological Reconstruction Movement,"[2] through to 2016, when Wang Aiming 王艾明 left Nanjing Union Theological Seminary (NUTS). During these eighteen years, Wang Aiming served in many vital posts, including as vice-principal of NUTS and editor of the *Nanjing*

---

1 Prior to 1998, one important Three-Self leader with a Reformed background was Peter Tsai (蔡文浩 Cai Wenhao, 1913–1993), a graduate of Princeton Theological Seminary who served as president of both the Zhejiang Three-Self Patriotic Movement (TSPM) and Chinese Christian Council (CCC). Tsai was a noted Reformed voice in the Three-Self and influenced the CCC constitution, bringing in Reformed characteristics. See Robert Benedetto, Darrell L. Guder, and Donald K. Mckim, ed., *Historical Dictionary of Reformed Churches* (London: The Scarecrow Press, 1999), 319–20; Philip L. Wickeri, *Seeking the Common Ground: Protestant Christianity, the Three-Self Movement, and China's United Front* (Maryknoll, New York: Orbis Books, 1988), 191.

2 *Shenxue sixiang jianshe* 神學思想建設; as many scholars have pointed out, similar ideas of reconstructing Chinese theology had been expressed during 1980s, but the movement was formally endorsed by the government only in 1998. See Philip L. Wickeri, *Reconstructing Christianity in China: K.H. Ting and the Chinese,* (Maryknoll: Orbis Books, 2007) 345, 347–48; Ying Fuk-tsang, *Dangdai zhongguo zhengjiao guanxi* 當代中國政教關係 [Church-State Relations in Contemporary China] (Hong Kong: Alliance Bible Seminary, 1999), 22, 41, 136–39.

Theological Review (金陵神學志). Although he was subsequently side-lined, Wang had a broad influence within the Three-Self Patriotic Movement and can be seen as a representative Three-Self theologian in that period. Wang is unusual, however, because he worked hard to introduce the Reformation heritage to Nanjing Seminary and made use of Reformed theology to rationalize and legitimize the Theological Reconstruction Movement. Due to his strong language capabilities (Chinese, English, French, German, Hebrew) and academic ability, his theological essays in *Nanjing Theological Review* did not endlessly repeat official political slogans but offered new ideas and built on a Reformation heritage to construct his unique view on Theological Reconstruction, a movement begun by TSPM leader Ding Guangxun. This paper explores the promotion of Reformed theology within the Theological Reconstruction Movement of the Three-Self church.

Brief Biography of Wang Aiming

A brief overview of Wang Aiming's life can help illuminate the theological changes in Three-Self churches.[3] Wang was born in Yancheng, Jiangsu province, in 1963, and obtained his Master of Arts from Nanjing University in 1989 and then taught at Nanjing Normal University until 1992.[4] When Wang was studying, one of his teachers was a Catholic priest, and he became interested in Christian theology. Besides regularly attending mass in Catholic churches, he translated the French Catholic theologian Pierre Teilhard de Chardin's *The Phenomenon of Man* and German theologian Hans Küng's *Does God Exist?: An Answer for Today*[5] into Chinese, leaving a visible trace in Wang Aiming's thinking. Because of the tension in Sino-Vatican relations at that time, the priest recommended that Wang Aiming participate in worship at St. Paul's Church, Nanjing (an Anglican church prior to the unification of denominations) to avoid government surveillance. Coincidentally, Professor Chen Zemin of Nanjing Union Seminary was the senior priest at St. Paul's church (1985–92), so Wang Aiming came to know Prof. Chen.

---

3   For a biography see Chen Zemin, "Xu," (Preface) in Wang Aiming, *Shenxue: Jiaohui zai sikao* 神學: 教會在思考 [Theology: the Church Thinking] (Beijing: China Religious Culture Publisher, 2010), 1–14; Chen Zemin, "Xu," (Preface) in Wang Aiming, *Mading Lude ji xinjiao lunli yanjiu* 馬丁·路德及新教倫理研究 [Martin Luther and Protestant Ethics] (Nanjing: Yilin Press, 2011), 1–6.

4   See Marvin D. Hoff, ed., *Chinese Theological Education, 1979–2006*, 246.

5   Chen Zemin, "Preface," in Wang, *Theology: The Church Thinking*, 1.

In 1992, Wang resigned his teaching post at Nanjing Normal University and went to the University of Neuchâtel in Switzerland to pursue theological studies. He majored in systematic theology and minored in the Old Testament, obtaining a master's degree in theological interpretation in 1999. In the spring of the same year, he was handpicked by Bishop Ding Guangxun (K. H. Ting) for a teaching post at Nanjing seminary. This was also the year in which the Theological Reconstruction Movement was fully launched by Ding. Because of his strong language capacities and theological training from an international university, Wang was often sent to other countries to explain the position and intention of the movement. He was also appointed by Ding to key posts in the seminary, such as director of the research department. In the spring of 2000, Wang Aiming was ordained to the pastorate in St. Paul's Church by Bishop Ding and Professor Chen Zemin, just one year after returning to China.[6] However, because Wang Aiming was not trained at NUTS, his rapid promotion caused suspicion among colleagues.

In 2002, Wang Aiming was promoted to be vice principal and president for academic affairs of the seminary. He was also editor-in-chief of *Nanjing Theological Review*, vice president of Jiangsu Provincial Chinese Christian Council, deputy director of the Chinese Christian Theological Education Committee, and a board member of the Chinese Association for the Study of Religions. In 2003, he went to the University of Basel, an important theology research center on Calvin, to further his studies and received a doctorate in theology in April 2008.[7] In November 2008, he also received an honorary doctorate from the University of Neuchâtel, where he had studied earlier. In 2009, he returned to China to continue his teaching at NUTS and served as the vice principal. His doctoral dissertation was published by Peter Lang Press, entitled *Church in China: Faith, Ethics, Structure: The Heritage of the Reformation for the Future of the Church in China.*[8]

---

6 Wickeri, *Reconstructing Christianity in China*, 354.

7 Marvin D. Hoff points out that in order to improve the academic qualifications of teaching faculty, NUTS uses two ways to train teachers. One is to seek the Southeast Asia Theological Education Foundation's help to invite the world's top theological professors to NUTS and have intensive courses during the summer vacation. The second is to send the teachers to study abroad and return to NUTS to continue to serve. Wang Aiming was the first one to be sent to study abroad. See Marvin D. Hoff, ed., *Chinese Theological Education, 1979–2006*, 341.

8 Aiming Wang, *Church in China: Faith, Ethics, Structure: The Heritage of the Reformation for the Future of the Church in China* (New York: Peter Lang, 2009).

Between 1999 and 2010, Wang Aiming wrote an academic article for each issue of the *Nanjing Theological Review*, the premier publication for Protestant theology in China. His articles were mainly concerned with the theology of Martin Luther and John Calvin. In 2009, to commemorate Calvin's 500th anniversary, Wang Aiming edited a special volume of the journal dedicated to Calvin's legacy. Since 2011, however, Wang's articles have only been published sporadically in the *Nanjing Theological Review* and other papers can only be found online on platforms such as *Consensus Net* (*Gongshi Wang* 共識網), or published in Hong Kong. Informants from the Three-Self Patriotic Movement (TSPM) and the Chinese Christian Council (CCC)[9] have explained that Wang Aiming was slowly becoming a mere figurehead at the seminary due to personnel issues and internal power struggles.[10] He began to spend more time accepting invitations to preach elsewhere, including "illegal" house churches. In 2016, Wang Aiming was forced to leave NUTS and worked for a church in Toronto where he oversaw the Mandarin ministry.[11] He subsequently resigned from the church in 2019 and is now a researcher at the Meiji Gakuin University Institute for Christian Studies in Japan.

Defending the reasonableness of the Theological Reconstruction Movement with Reformed Theology

In early 1999 when Wang returned to China to teach at Nanjing Seminary, the Theological Reconstruction Movement was in its initial stages, and there were a great deal of internal controversies at the seminary. Many teachers who were theologically more inclined toward evangelicalism were (allegedly) dismissed from teaching posts or their contracts were not renewed.[12] Wang Weifan was one such example. These were scholars who criticized the practice of

---

9 These two organizations are closely related and have overlapping functions.

10 Interview with Pastor A in Shanghai, taped December 28, 2016.

11 The Toronto Christian Community Church (TCCC), part of the Association of Christian Evangelical Ministries (Canada).

12 For the internal disputes, see Wickeri, *Reconstructing Christianity in China*, 353–55; Zhou Jiacai 周加才, *Ai wu zhijing: wo suo zunjin de Ding Guangxun zhujiao* 愛無止境: 我所尊敬的丁光訓主教 [Love is Boundless: A Tribute to My Esteemed Bishop Kwang-hsun Ting] (Hong Kong: The New York Theological Education (HK) Center, 2010), 62–63.

"deemphasizing justification by faith"[13] and upheld the importance of biblical authority and the centrality of "justification by faith" to Protestantism.[14] When Wang Aiming returned to Nanjing Seminary, the first problem that needed to be solved was therefore: What kind of rationale was needed for the Theological Reconstruction Movement (TRM) to continue? How should the movement be positioned within the whole Christian tradition? Wang needed to show that the TRM was not just a political movement (required by the United Front), but a natural outcome of the church itself. His academic background was the reason why Ding rapidly promoted Wang, and his academic training was suited to answering questions from the conservative side of the Three-Self Movement.

Faced with the controversy over "deemphasizing" justification by faith alone, Wang Aiming did not immediately express a position. Instead, he went back to the fundamental idea of Ding's proposition: that is, whether the statement "the highest attribute of God is love"[15] conforms with Christian tradition. Wang's answer was yes. He pointed out that God's love was manifest in the whole redemptive history of humankind. God gave God's only begotten son into the world to be crucified and resurrected, in order to complete the plan of salvation, which fully demonstrates the divine grace of God. Therefore, "grace" is the keyword to understanding God's love; as Wang wrote, "grace is God's love for humankind. In this sense, the highest attribute of the Triune God to us is love, which is the most definite expression of God's grace in the context of our faith."[16] Wang Aiming also indicated that this argument for emphasizing grace is seen from the Old Testament to the New Testament, from the Nicene Creed to St. Augustine and inherited in Martin Luther's notion of "Sola Gratia." Furthermore, if Ding's proposition was correct, and God takes love to be the highest attribute, his "providence" does not only consist of judgment and punishment.

---

13 Ting K. H., "Theology and Context," *Chinese Theological Review*, 17: 2 (2003), 125.

14 There are plenty of articles written by Wang Weifan that criticise the TRM, see Wang Weifan, *Shinian juju: Wang Weifan wenji (1997–2007)* 十年踽踽：汪維藩文集 [Walking Lonely for Ten Years: Selected Works of Wang Weifan 1997–2007] (Hong Kong: Christian Study Centre on Chinese Religion and Culture, 2009), 3–16, 97–112, 223–39.

15 Raymond L. Whitehead, ed., *No Longer Strangers: Selected Writings of K.H. Ting* (Maryknoll, New York: Orbis Books, 1989), 70; Ding Guangxun, *Dangdai Zhongguo Jidujiao Fayenren: Ding Guangxun Wenji* 當代中國基督教發言人：丁光訓文集 [Spokesperson of Contemporary Chinese Christianity: Collected Essays of Bishop K. H. Ting] (Hong Kong: Chinese Christian Literature Council, 1999), 93; Peter Tze Ming Ng, *Chinese Christianity: An Interplay between Global and Local Perspectives*, 235–36.

16 Wang, *Theology: The Church Thinking*, 32.

As Wang wrote, "this kind of assertion has already been replaced by the message of the Cross."[17] Moreover, God's providence covers the whole universe, not just Christian believers—a core belief of Ding.

Wang's broad framework for interpreting "justification by faith" allows us to understand why he accused Chinese Christians in the past of taking the words too literally and failing to understand the actual meaning of "justification by faith." For Wang, the first sovereignty of grace is in God's hands;[18] it is God's love for humankind and the reason why humans can be redeemed. It is God's grace that frees from the bondage of sin, and even our faith is initiated by God's grace and not our own will. People cannot be redeemed by doing good deeds and must rely on "grace alone." So, Wang Aiming resorts to the ideas of monergism to explain the doctrine of "justification by faith."

Wang highlighted Luther's view of grace, where "on the deepest level, the highest sovereignty is only with God."[19] In other words, under God's sovereignty, whether the sin of humans will be remitted is not dependent on the human will to confess but should be "considered and answered in the whole creation and redemption plan of God." No one knows "whether, in the end, God will save every sinner after the Last Judgment, the final power of judgement is only in God's hands." He further stated that "whether human sins can be forgiven, or whether God's grace can be applied to everyone, is not a matter of human choice and the various merits and deeds encouraged by the church, but lies in God's innate loving nature."[20]

Secondly, Wang Aiming tried to reinterpret the relationship between faith (*xin* 信) and works (*xing* 行). He pointed out that Luther's upholding of "justification by faith" was highly contextualized and mainly to oppose scholasticism, as the Middle Ages had relied too much on reason as the criterion for making judgments. For this reason, he emphasized that the sovereignty of redemption lay with God and nothing else was a prerequisite for salvation.[21] Nonetheless, this did not mean that one could just have "faith" without "works." Wang shows how the view of freedom in Luther's ethics complements this. If people are to

---

17 Wang, *Theology: The Church Thinking*, 95.

18 As Troeltsch also stated, under the doctrine of predestination, "it is the Nature of God to give salvation to some without any merit on their part, purely on His own freewill and choice . . ." See Ernst Troeltsch, *The Social Teaching of the Christian Churches*, vol. 2 (New York: Harper Torchbooks, 1960), 582.

19 Wang, *Theology: The Church Thinking*, 32.

20 Wang, *Theology: The Church Thinking*, 42.

21 Wang, *Theology: The Church Thinking*, 244.

be responsible for their actions, they must affirm free will; however, for those who believe in Christ, so-called freedom is not absolute but is a "bondage."[22] "Faith" and "works" are bound together, two sides of a coin. Therefore, Luther emphasized that "because of Jesus Christ's obedience to the established moral standards of the society . . . this requires us also to follow, like a servant, the moral and legal order of society."[23] Wang even affirms the significance of secular work, thus expanding the meaning of "faith" and tightly linking it to "works." This understanding coheres with the claim of Ding Guangxun that many Chinese Christians used the doctrine of justification to separate faith from works.[24]

Although these two points are present in Luther's theology, his life-and-death struggles did not allow for nuance or development and they had to be realized by second-generation reformers. By the time of John Calvin, the Protestant church had begun to establish an order and a system. The contradiction between Catholicism and Protestantism had eased a little, so the relationship between "faith" and "works" could be better expressed. Therefore, when Wang Aiming commenced on Calvin, he emphasized that the sovereignty of grace is in God's hands. Anyone who pretends to be God and proclaims that non-believers will not be saved has greatly misunderstood "Sola Gratia."[25] "Faith," moreover, entailed not only being justified by God but being willing freely to choose to be a servant to serve others—thus was closely associated with the road of sanctification.[26] Wang wrote various further articles to illustrate how Ding's theology is based on Christian tradition and conforms with apostolic succession and the church's catholicity.[27]

These arguments, however, show only that the Chinese church's misunderstanding of the doctrine of "justification by faith" in the past had led to misjudgments over Theological Reconstruction and were not enough to explain the need for "deemphasizing" the doctrine. Therefore, Wang Aiming further cited Thomas S. Kuhn's "paradigm shift" of 2004 to illustrate the need for "deemphasizing." He underlined that Luther's proposal of "justification by faith" was of great significance in sixteenth-century Germany and the subsequent Reformations in

---

22 Wang, *Theology: The Church Thinking*, 245.

23 Wang, *Theology: The Church Thinking*, 245.

24 Ting, *Spokesperson of Contemporary Chinese Christianity*, 22; Wickeri, *Reconstructing Christianity in China*, 343.

25 Wang, *Theology: The Church Thinking*, 82.

26 Wang, *Theology: The Church Thinking*, 127.

27 Wang, *Theology: The Church Thinking*, 44.

Europe[28]—but that when Luther's paradigm entered into the Chinese context, it was easily misunderstood and negatively influenced the Chinese church, provoking an irrational anti-intellectualism.[29] "Justification by faith" can therefore no longer answer the questions raised by the Chinese church today but has become an obstacle to the present development of the Chinese church; what is needed now is to "run the church well," as John Calvin might have put it. Wang used the Reformed tradition to offer a comprehensive reinterpretation of the doctrine and transform "justification by faith" into "justification by faith through grace." The ambiguity of doctrine in the Chinese context has been erased, enabling a more accurate grasp of the meaning of Luther through the lens of Calvin.

From this, Wang Aiming helped Ding's theology to find footnotes in Christian tradition. However, Wang Aiming did not stop here, and he worked hard to construct links between the Reformation and Theological Reconstruction. Ultimately, this was not just to increase the legitimacy of the movement but to guide it back to a deeper form of Christian tradition. He imagined that "to return to the core issues of the Reformation era, we can transcend the limitations of the ninteenth-century missionary heritage left by different Western Protestant denominations in China."[30] In other words, if the Three-Self Churches could move beyond the theological traditions left by Western denominations and directly accede to the origins of Protestantism, this would gain the understanding and trust of churches outside the TSPM/CCC.[31] The Reformation heritage, for Wang, provided the most authentic nondenominational Protestant theology. If the Three-Self Churches could succeed in this, they could dialogue with different churches across the world as equals and be admitted as a member of the ecumenical church and not just a puppet controlled by an atheist government.[32] This assertion is the unique contribution of Wang to the development of Theological Reconstruction.[33] However, Wang's assertion was not welcomed by the house churches and few people agreed with it even in the Three-Self churches.

During the period from 1999 to 2005, Wang Aiming's main focus was on how to rationalize the Theological Reconstruction Movement and to affirm the

---

28 Wang, *Theology: The Church Thinking*, 200.
29 Wang, *Theology: The Church Thinking*, 202.
30 Wang, *Theology: The Church Thinking*, 6.
31 Wang, *Theology: The Church Thinking*, 118.
32 Wang, *Theology: The Church Thinking*, 220.
33 Wang, *Theology: The Church Thinking*, 412–15.

movement within the scope of ecumenical tradition—or to "rectify the name" (*zhengming* 正名) of the movement. At the same time, Wang hoped to reconcile a Reformation heritage with the propositions of the Theological Reconstruction Movement, to enable the movement to associate with a broader Christian tradition. Wang Aiming failed, however, to systematically promote the significance of Christian tradition to the contemporary Chinese church. A more systematic response would only be formed after a year's break from writing duties.

Back to Protestant Origins

From 2005 onwards, Wang Aiming tried to present the Reformation heritage to the Three-Self church more systematically by publishing a series of articles about Luther and Calvin in *Nanjing Theological Review*. Wang went beyond defending the reasonableness of the movement and showed a keen interest in exploring its teaching about Christian ethics. He hoped the TRM could accord more closely with the Reformation spirit, and not just at a superficial level, while also meeting the Chinese national policy requirements. Wang dug into the theology of Luther and Calvin and tried to correlate their heritage with the Chinese context [34] in a series of articles that became the primary content of his doctoral dissertation and subsequent two books, *Martin Luther and Protestant Ethics*[35] and *The Theology of John Calvin and the Church in China*.[36] Elsewhere, Wang Aiming paid particular attention to Calvin's discussion of "the third use" of the law (*tertius usus*) and regarded this as an excellent dialogue platform between the Three-Self church, the ecumenical church, and the house churches.

Luther's paradigm: "Law and Gospel"

Before explaining the "third use" of the Law, it is necessary to understand the danger caused by a one-sided understanding of Luther's theological notions. This is the key to seeing why Wang Aiming so emphasized the importance of the use of the law in Calvin's theology. Wang summarizes Luther's theology as a

---

34 Wang knew that there are different types of Reformation in Europe, like the Anglican tradition. However, he argued that the most significant were Luther and Calvin's reforms; See Wang, *Mading Lude*, 104–31.

35 Wang, *Mading Lude*.

36 Wang Aiming, *Jia Erwen shenxue yu zhongguo jiaohui* 加爾文神學與中國教會 [The Theology of John Calvin and the Church in China] (Hong Kong: Christian Study Centre on Chinese Religion and Culture, 2011).

"Law and gospel" paradigm,[37] with the problems caused by Luther's interpretation forcing Calvin to transform it into a "gospel and Law" paradigm.

What is the difference between "law and gospel" and "gospel and law"? In Luther's understanding, Wang points out, the law is to convict people and generate confession inside the heart. This enables people to understand the gospel and be justified by God[38] (that is the first use of the law, as a theological use, in Calvin's understanding). As Wang says:

> Luther started with inner repentance and confession to God, but paid much more attention to the direct communication and exchange between the individual and God, which created a shock of historic proportion for the whole reform movement: before God, everyone could confess directly, and the highly institutionalized millennial theocracy and papal authority would have to fade and dissolve.[39]

Although Luther made a significant contribution to Christianity as a whole, Luther's followers upheld his principles without fully acknowledging their context and caused severe misinterpretation.

These contextual factors that needed consideration include, firstly, that Luther was an Augustinian monk before becoming a reformer. In Luther's mind, people were always bound by sin and not free. "Faith" led people to believe that justification could only be generated by God's grace, a causal relationship that is the presupposition of Luther's understanding of justification.[40] The laity, without this presupposition, will "treat this [justification by faith] as the source of authority for upholding individuals' absolute sovereignty and subjectivity."[41] Such a misunderstanding of "justification by faith" also took place in the Chinese context and quickly became the notion that a person can be justified by faith.

---

37 Wang also held that the best way to understand Luther's theology is not by the doctrine of "justification by faith" but by the "Law and Gospel" paradigm; Wang, *The Theology of John Calvin*, 260.

38 Wang, *The Theology of John Calvin*, 51.

39 Wang, *The Theology of John Calvin*, 326.

40 Wang, *The Theology of John Calvin*, 327; Ernst Troeltsch also pointed out that in Lutheran doctrine, "Faith is not a human faculty at all, it is a perception given by God as an absolute miracle; at the same time the human element in the shape of all human 'merit' and all 'natural' human activity is excluded." Ernst Troeltsch, *The Social Teaching of the Christian Churches*, vol. 2, 581.

41 Wang, *The Theology of John Calvin*, 328.

Secondly, it is easily forgotten that Luther faced a robust Catholic church in putting forward his interpretation of justification, and therefore personal faith was stressed because of the urgency of the Reformation. "The reality of Reformation made Luther seem to raise personal confession of faith indefinitely and deny the institutionalization and doctrinal definition and restraints of the church."[42] When personal faith is promoted as the center of Christian belief, other doctrines, like believers' worldly responsibilities are subordinated and become secondary.[43] Later generations of followers extended this tendency and fostered a deviation that obscured believers' responsibility for the world. Under Luther's doctrine of two kingdoms, secular powers have a certain degree of legitimacy from God, yet the misinterpretation of Luther caused a retreat from believers' responsibility to society, a tendency that culminated in the German church's failure to prevent the rise of the Nazi regime and even to endorse theologically its tyranny.[44]

Luther's "law and gospel" paradigm broke the barriers between believers and God that had existed since the Middle Ages[45] and allowed people to become free because of the gospel. His groundbreaking understanding also laid out the theological principles for the Reformation. However, the lack of institutional norms for believers' sanctification[46] might easily lead to "a type of belief that one is convicted under the law and saved in the gospel," leading to a preference for "the pursuit of inner conscience and peace,"[47] and underplaying the church's responsibility in the world. As the Reformation reached the second generation, John Calvin needed to correct the imbalance while retaining Luther's theological principles. This imbalance is the background to the "gospel and law" paradigm.

Calvin's paradigm: "Gospel and Law"

For Wang Aiming, the importance of Luther is to highlight the fundamental difference between Protestantism and Catholicism and to establish the theological

---

42 Wang, *The Theology of John Calvin*, 259.

43 Wang, *The Theology of John Calvin*, 210.

44 Wang, *The Theology of John Calvin*, 346.

45 Wickeri, *Reconstructing Christianity in China*, 350.

46 As Ernst Troeltsch commented, Lutheranism ceased to advance further because of "its stress on personal piety, its acceptance of the existing situation, its acquiescence in the objectivity of the means of grace, as well as to its lack of capacity for ecclesiastical organization, and its non-political outlook," and it was left to Calvinism to extend the Reformation. See Troeltsch, *The Social Teaching of the Christian Churches*, vol. 2, 576.

47 Lin Hong-Hsin, "Preface," in Wang, *The Theology of John Calvin*, xxi.

identity of Protestantism.[48] As a second-generation reformer, Calvin inherited the theological principle of "justification by faith," affirmed that redemption is not due to human good deeds, and aimed to ensure that Protestantism did not return to the way of Catholicism. However, Calvin did not just stop at this but continued to develop the doctrine and such guiding questions as: How should a person, having been selected by God and born again, respond to such amazing grace? As Wang points out, Calvin's ecclesiology framed his thinking on justification.[49] The church is a group of sinners called by God; therefore the role of the law is undeniably to maintain church order. Although salvation is not the consequence of the law, keeping God's commandments is the inevitable result of one's being saved, because the gospel makes it possible for people to escape their bondage from sin, and the law means that "we know the order and will of God's creation." Those who receive the gospel naturally want to participate in God's creation and fulfil his commandments in order to glorify God.[50]

The paradigm of "Gospel and Law" refers to those who have received the gospel and live under the guidance of the law, who actively "commence their moral obligations and responsibilities in the secular world"[51] in order to glorify God.[52] While maintaining Luther's theological principles, Calvin balanced the relationship between the gospel and the law in the church's practice,[53] so as not to let church become a group of self-righteous antinomians. The Chinese church crucially needs to understand the paradigm of "Gospel and Law" because it is the only way indeed to inherit the spirit of the Reformation heritage from Luther. As Wang comments, Luther was the originator of the Reformation but was limited by his times, and the legacy of the German National Church submitting to the Nazi government in following early Lutheran tradition shocked theologians into a greater understanding of the advances Calvin made and an appreciation of the distinctive nature of Calvin's legacy. "The appearance of Karl Barth and Dietrich Bonhoeffer confirmed Calvinism as the dominant form and successor to Luther's Reformation undertaking, and only on the basis of this can the Chinese church break through the fences and ravines of Protestant denominationalism in Europe and the Western world, and validly

---

48 Wang, *The Theology of John Calvin*, 347.
49 Wang, *The Theology of John Calvin*, 178.
50 Wang, *The Theology of John Calvin*, 348.
51 Wang, *The Theology of John Calvin*, 347.
52 Lin Hong-Hsin, "Preface," in Wang, *The Theology of John Calvin*, xxi.
53 Wang, *The Theology of John Calvin*, 317.

draw on the whole precious heritage and spiritual witness of the saints, to lay a foundation for the future institutional development and theological tradition of the Chinese church."[54] In other words, although Luther and Calvin created two denominations, it was Calvin who inherited Luther's reformation spirit and promoted it. Therefore, Chinese believers need to understand Luther through the paradigm of "Gospel and Law," and this is the better way to understand "justification by faith."

Calvin on "The Third Role of the Law"

Advocating the law is scarcely contrary to Luther's theological principles, and Wang highlights Calvin's ethical "third use of the law" as his contribution to its development. As Wang writes:

> For human beings, the law generally contains three functions. The first is its theological function, just like a mirror that reflects sin, so that humans can understand what is the justice of God, what injustice is in the world, and other such evils.
>
> The second function of the law is its political or civil use; to make those who commit crimes constantly fear and worry about punishment and sanction in the face of the justice of God . . .
>
> The third use of the law is disciplinary, explicitly directed towards believers. In terms of church belief, this function acts as an ethical directive, to cause Protestant churches in the Calvinist tradition to begin to pay much attention to doctrine, regulation, order and conscience in restraining church members' behavior, particularly church leaders and those with church administrative power. For the ordinary laity, this will also have the effect of causing them to continuously reflect, remain alert and watch themselves.[55]

Wang's quotation above shows that Luther's "law and gospel" paradigm already includes within it the first and second functions. On this foundation, Calvin emphasized the third use, that is, the use of the law specifically within the church. Although the third use of the law is not a necessary condition for a "true

---

54 Wang, *The Theology of John Calvin*, 266.
55 Wang, *The Theology of John Calvin*, 325–26.

church,"[56] it is essential for church members' sanctification.[57] For this reason Calvin devoted much energy in Geneva to establishing the church's law and order. He instituted church courts to deal with violations by members. It is evident that the emphasis for Calvin shifted from stressing the difference between Protestantism and Catholicism to the effort to establish good institutes for the church, which coincides with Ding's maxim (and the state-church policy slogan) of "running the church well" (*ban hao jiaohui* 辦好教會).[58]

Church regulation is not only a problem of sanctification, because church laws have the function of regulating the daily lives of church members and are often stricter than the moral standards of society, and so church law is a role model for society. When the church can restrain its members in this way, government and society will undoubtedly believe that the laws of the church are beneficial to the order and morals of society.[59] Moreover, the church can become more independent by being self-disciplined and not requiring the government to intervene.[60] To maintain order in the church, Calvin linked holy communion with the morality of believers, making it an explicit mark that allowed the world to monitor the moral life of believers. The gospel unquestionably sets the Christian free from the bondage of sin and gives the liberty to live by conscience. Calvin was not content, however, with Christians remaining at the level of personal conscience and hoped for them to affect the public domain.[61] The third use of the law is thus not only inward sanctification but also has outward significance. As Wang Aiming writes:

> Calvin further developed the reform traditions of Luther, Zwingli, and Melanchthon, mainly reflected in institutional levels of development, to ensure that the progress of reforms were beneficial to evangelism and the formation of regular and reasonable church-state relations.[62]
>
> . . . from a historical perspective, if [order in] the church is seen as natural as living under national law and order, then the Reformation possesses

---

56 Generally, the marks of the true church in Protestant theology refers to the preaching of the holy word and the administration of the sacraments.

57 Wang, *The Theology of John Calvin*, 220–21.

58 Ting, *The Spokesman of Contemporary Chinese Christianity*, 117–27.

59 Wang, *The Theology of John Calvin*, 273.

60 Wang, *The Theology of John Calvin*, 52–53.

61 Wang, *The Theology of John Calvin*, 272.

62 Wang, *The Theology of John Calvin*, 277.

legitimacy. This was Calvin's aim and sincere intention in stressing church discipline and the strict management of the church according to law.[63]

If the Three-Self Church can give full play to the third use of the law, it will indeed receive greater recognition and support from the public domain.

Likewise, Christians abide by laws and regulations "and take the initiative on ethical and spiritual responsibility for the nation's stability and social development."[64] In this way they can "mutually adapt" (*xiang shiying* 相適應) to "harmonious society" (*hexie shehui* 和諧社會), a notion vigorously promoted by the Chinese government.[65] As Wang explained:

> In sum, taking an overall view of the significance of Calvinist heritage for the Chinese church, the perspective of the development of church polity happens to conform well to the national policy of pursuing a harmonious society, in which China is governed by law and virtue. Besides, using ancient Chinese civilization to interpret the unique church polity of the Calvinist heritage is itself of great global significance and of cultural value to humanity.[66]

Furthermore, drawing on this heritage not only increases social stability but also helps China's modernization. Wang writes:

> One of the revelations from Calvin's heritage is that the beliefs and principles established during the Reformation were turned into law and order in reality in church polity. This is the most critical step that China's modernization needs to take. Therefore, if Chinese theologians are able to take the lead in realizing this point, and study extensively innovation and design in church polity, that would be the significance of our commemoration of Calvin's birthday.[67]

One can see that Wang Aiming actively uses Calvin's views on the use of the law as a dialogue platform with broader culture. Ding's idea of "running the church well"

---

63 Wang, *The Theology of John Calvin*, 235.
64 Wang, *The Theology of John Calvin*, 234.
65 Wang, *The Theology of John Calvin*, 196.
66 Wang, *The Theology of John Calvin*, 291.
67 Wang, *The Theology of John Calvin*, 298.

and its challenge to the fundamentalist idea that "faith had functioned to dilute works" (*yinxin faxing* 因信廢行) could find support in the "third use" of the law." High moral standards in the church allowed it to extend its moral influence on society and increase its legitimacy. Wang's hope was that the Three-Self church could inherit the Reformation heritage from Martin Luther and enjoy a better dialogue with the ecumenical church and with house churches within China. Through it, the Three-Self church could hope to dispel fears of being labeled "unbelievers" or seen as a religious group manipulated by the government and rejected by others.

In sum, the period 2005–2012 saw Wang Aiming tirelessly introduce Reformed theology to China, not just as his own theological interest, but as a response to the actual needs of the Three-Self church. The TSPM/CCC had promoted the Theological Reconstruction Movement for years but failed to achieve the intended results, and been rife with conflict and accusations both inside and outside China. Wang believed that the reason for this situation was the TSPM/CCC attempt "to replace all Christians' normal thinking with political expressions and propaganda slogans,"[68] as it became more of a political organization than a structure to serve the church's needs. Church leaders wanted to follow government instructions and require the church to back government policy with theological reasoning,[69] while fundamentalists and conservatives also used political reasoning to reject all suggestions of the Theological Reconstruction Movement, simply labeling the movement "political slogans and propaganda in theological clothing." In a situation where conservatives were accusing open-minded pastors of being the "party of unbelievers[70]"—such accusations often lacking theological grounds and reasoning—Wang hoped the issue of Theological Reconstruction could become again a matter of theological discussion rather than being mired in politics. However, his suggestions have not been well received and discussions about Reformed theology within the Three-Self church remain inadequate.

2012 to 2016: Thinking independently about the Way Out for the Three-Self church

Wang Aiming's emphasis on Calvinism contradicted official claims that China had entered a post-denominational era, and his assertions threatened to deepen

---

68 Wang, *The Theology of John Calvin*, 410.
69 Wang, *The Theology of John Calvin*, 414.
70 Wang, *The Theology of John Calvin*, 411.

the Three-Self church's internal theological differences. At the same time, since the year 2000, Reformed traditions have been welcomed by many house churches and claimed as the theological basis for house churches' acts of resistance, such as the outdoor worship of Beijing's Shouwang Church and Chengdu Early Rain Church in 2009,[71] making the government even more suspicious of this theological trend.[72]

Theological development within the Three-Self church has become increasingly politicized since the Beijing Olympics in 2008, a tendency that displaced Wang further from his academic training and made it harder for him to live within the system. Once Ding Guangxun passed away in November 2012, one of the Three-Self theologians most admired by Wang Aiming was no longer present. These changes made him think further and be more openly critical about the status and future of the Three-Self church. Some informants have indicated that Wang's marginalization was due to many factors, including internal power struggles and financial disputes. His critical stance undoubtedly further marginalized him in Nanjing Seminary, and Wang's articles were rarely seen in official journals after 2012, with many only found on unofficial online platforms managed by liberal intellectuals.

After Wang Aiming returned to China, he gradually realized that the main problems of the Chinese Protestant Church were political. The unfriendliness between the Three-Self and the house churches left no room for theological discussion. Government hostility toward any global connections that Christianity held made it more challenging to connect the Three-Self church with ecumenical Christian traditions. Wang hoped to introduce the concepts of "Magisterial Church" and "Free Church"[73] to facilitate the transformation of the Three-Self and the house church and reconcile the relationship between them. These two concepts are critical for understanding his theology in this period.

Wang Aiming defined the "magisterial church" as one that succeeded from a medieval theocracy in which the state and church relationship were closely connected;[74] while "free church" meant "refusing all forms of control, funding and

---

71 Carsten T. Vala, *The Politics of Protestant Churches and the Party-State in China: God Above Party* (New York: Routledge, 2018), 163, 185.

72 Wang Aiming, *Tizhi jiaohui yu ziyou jiaohui* 體制教會與自由教會 [Magisterial Church and Free Church] (Hong Kong: Centre for the Study of Religion and Chinese Society, 2017), 95.

73 For the relationship between Free Churches and Calvinism, cf. Ernst Troeltsch, *The Social Teaching of the Christian Churches*, vol. 2, 656–61.

74 Wang, *Magisterial Church and Free Church*, 8.

connection from the government."[75] The former for Wang includes Lutheranism in Germany and the Anglican Church in the United Kingdom,[76] while the latter includes churches such as the Baptist, Brethren, and Presbyterian churches in the United Kingdom.[77] Since the "magisterial church" is part of the nation, its church polity and theology will often become a reference for national spirit and administrative order. Here the church is required to become a role model for nonbelievers and encourage them to understand their civic responsibilities and moral requirements. Such churches usually claim to adhere to the Catholic tradition. The "free church" is a community formed by people with strong religious beliefs and an emphasis on individuality but includes the basic creeds and doctrines of the church catholic. The relationship between the magisterial and free church is not mutually exclusive,[78] however, the "free church" usually separates from the state to maintain its spiritual purity, while the "magisterial church" is easily "tempted by the world. Therefore, the purified and introverted nature of the free church plays an important role in restraint and balance."[79]

However, the crucial question is, who in China represents the "magisterial church" and who represents the "Free Church?" Wang Aiming's answer is that the churches under TSPM/CCC are the only Protestant churches that can operate legally but are becoming more "bureaucratized and yamenized (*yamen hua* 衙門化[80])." The officers in charge of church affairs in China often lack basic theological training, which makes the church under the TSPM/CCC more like an organization to help the state control the laity.[81] Its existence is often maintained by state power from the State Administration of Religious Affairs (SARA).[82] The TSPM/CCC cannot however perform the functions of the "magisterial

---

75 Wang, *Magisterial Church and Free Church*, 9.

76 Wang, *Magisterial Church and Free Church*, 18.

77 Wang, *Magisterial Church and Free Church*, 9.

78 Wang, *Magisterial Church and Free Church*, 21.

79 Wang *Magisterial Church and Free Church*, 22.

80 The Yamen was the administrative office in imperial China; "yamenization" usually means that the management of an organization becomes less efficient; see Wang, *Magisterial Church and Free Church*, 76, 86.

81 As Wang Aiming notes, "According to the legacy of the Reformation, if the church had only good relationships with the authorities of the state, without the ecclesial essence based on the Scripture, the Creeds, and the principles of the reformation, this kind of church will rely and depend on the political authorities without any autonomy in the secular order," see Wang, *Church in China: Faith, Ethics, Structure*, 485.

82 SARA, 國家宗教事務局, formerly known as Religious Affairs Bureau (RAB) is now the National Religious Affairs Administration.

church" and finds it hard to "inherit the tradition of creeds and doctrines from the catholic church."[83]

Meanwhile, a large number of "illegal" churches outside the establishment "have committed to inheriting the traditions and denominational principles from the historical churches." [84] These churches can therefore be said to possess more features of the mainstream magisterial church than the Three-Self church.[85] If this is the case, the development of Protestantism in China will be aberrant.[86] The one possessing legal status cannot become the "magisterial church," while the one without legal status appears identical to the "magisterial church." These facts demonstrate that the Chinese government's management of Protestantism has reached a point where change is inevitable.[87]

How to solve this problem? Wang Aiming boldly suggested that the State Administration of Religious Affairs should no longer dominate the management of the TSPM/CCC or any faith-based organization. The government should allow the church to register directly under the state Ministry of Civil Affairs (*min zheng bu* 民政部) without the intermediary of the TSPM/CCC—something house churches have long requested. The government should only act when the church is breaking the law, allowing the church to operate with the highest degree of autonomy. The TSPM/CCC need to be slowly phased out, so the church can be governed within the legal framework (and not directly under the state).[88] After the depoliticization of church management, the church could then focus on religious affairs and enhance its ecclesiology. The Three-Self and house churches should be actively "preparing to inherit the theology and polity of the 'magisterial churches'" and distinguish themselves from the "free church," extending doctrinal tolerance and understanding to the free church, along with legal status and protection.[89] The government should allow the reestablishment of denominations and churches to operate according to their denominational traditions.[90] Churches should be permitted to form some kinds of nongovernmental "national Christian council

---

83 Wang, *Magisterial Church and Free Church*, 75.

84 Wang, *Magisterial Church and Free Church*, 72.

85 Wang, *Magisterial Church and Free Church*, 83–84.

86 Wang, *Magisterial Church and Free Church*, 173.

87 Wang, *Magisterial Church and Free Church*, 80, 82, 91, 102.

88 Wang, *Magisterial Church and Free Church*, 23. This is also something which house church pastors have called for.

89 Wang, *Magisterial Church and Free Church*, 191.

90 Wang, *Magisterial Church and Free Church*, 112, 171.

or coalition" rather than the current TSPM/CCC system. If this were implemented, the government could give church and religious groups autonomy, based in the law, and this would help solve the only "controversial issues of religious freedom in China."

Given such a perspective, it is easy to see why Wang Aiming suddenly became interested in the cases of the Christian Assembly (*jidutu juhuichu* 基督徒聚會處)[91] or the Local Church (Little Flock Church, *zhaohui* 召會)[92] founded by Watchmen Nee (倪柝聲) and Witness Lee (李常受). Over the past thirty years, "evil cults" (*xiejiao* 邪教)[93] were severely suppressed by the government, especially after the Falun Gong incident in 1999. The Shouters (*huhan pai* 呼喊派) was one such religious group defined by the government as an "evil cult."[94] However, since the Shouters were closely related to the Local Church tradition, the Christian Assembly and Local Church were also implicated and persecuted by the government. Wang Aiming pointed out that the Christian Assembly and Local Church are "theologically similar to the Congregational traditions, such as Mennonite, Quaker, and Brotherhood," and as such, it is difficult to conclude they are heretical. Besides, their "church system, especially viewed from their prayers, fellowships, ministries, and expression of faith, all showed that they belong to the category of free churches . . . in the West." However, Wang was not really interested in Watchmen Nee's ecclesiology or the polity of local church. Instead of a detailed examination of Nee or Lee's theology, Wang simply concluded that the Christian Assembly and Local Church were not "evil cults." For Wang, the cases of Christian Assembly and Local Church were a touchstone to prove that China enjoyed a higher degree of religious freedom than before.[95] If the Christian Assembly and Local Church could restore their reputation and gain legal status, this meant that whether a church is identified as

---

91 Sometime, the name *Juhuichu* is literally translated as "meeting place" and it was commonly known as the Little Flock (*xiaoqun* 小群) also.

92 The term *Zhaohui* 召會 is the Chinese translation of "church" and adopted in the local church tradition, meaning "an assembly of the called ones"; see Fenggang Yang, Joy K.C. Tong and Allan H. Anderson, ed., *Global Chinese Pentecostal and Charismatic Christianity* (Boston: Brill, 2017), 162

93 The Chinese government official English translation of *xiejiao* 邪教 is "evil cults," however, the more correct way to translate it is "heterodox teachings"; see Massimo Introvigne, *Inside the Church of Almighty God: The Most Persecuted Religious Movement in China* (New York: Oxford University Press, 2020), 18–19

94 Wickeri, *Reconstructing Christianity in China*, 341–42.

95 Wang, *Magisterial Church and Free Church*, 213.

an "evil cult" or not could be defined on theological not political grounds.[96] Their legal existence would significantly enhance the development of the "free church tradition" in China.

Moreover, if the "free church" could legally and freely exist in China again, the real "Sinicization" (*Zhongguohua* 中國化) of Christianity could take place, with the "free church" restraining and balancing the secular tendencies of the "magisterial church." The danger of Sinicization is that it quickly becomes an expression of extreme nationalism,[97] especially under the current party-state political system. The Three-Self church lacks autonomy and can only follow government instructions, which results in "a group of cadres and so-called representatives from the religious sector who are appointed according to the cadres' own interests, who have rejected all the fine traditions of the historical church and the basic principles and concepts that have long been part of universal values," whose actions are done "in the name of 'Sinicization' of Christian theology."[98] In Wang's opinion, such Sinicization would limit "ultimate belief" to real political notions and positions and lead the Chinese church to repeat the problem of the German church during World War II. The government ought rather to allow the church autonomy and protection under the law, as in Geneva's tradition. Allowing the church to have autonomy is the only possible way for Christianity to localize or contextualize without being reduced to a tool of politics.[99] Once the church is self-governed, believers can freely express, seek, and interpret the truth according to their situation. Then, the true meaning of Sinicization can be realized.[100]

Wang Aiming's attitude toward the theological movement proposed by the TSPM/CCC has changed significantly. In 2013, when Xi Jinping proposed "Chinese Dream" as a guiding slogan for his rule, the TSPM/CCC could only copy and follow in promoting the "sinicization of Christianity."[101] This theological movement was promoted in a top-down manner without any vitality, eventually becoming a collection of political slogans and theological "model articles" (*yanban wenzhang* 樣板文章), something Wang could no longer support. Wang Aiming has been transformed from someone actively using Reformed theology

---

96 Wang, *Magisterial Church and Free Church*, 206.

97 Wang, *Magisterial Church and Free Church*, 179.

98 Wang, *Magisterial Church and Free Church*, 193.

99 Wang, *Magisterial Church and Free Church*, 214.

100 Wang, *Magisterial Church and Free Church*, 185–87, 195.

101 See TSPM and CCC, ed., *Jidujiao Zhongguohua yantaohui lunwenji (2): Jinian Ding Guangxun zhujiao danchen 100 zhounian* (*Papers from the Forum on the Sinicization of Christianity Vol. 2: Commemorating the Centennial of the Birth of K.H. Ting*) (Shanghai: TSPM & CCC, 2016).

to rectify the Theological Reconstruction Movement to using "free church" traditions to resist "sinicization."[102] From vice-principal of Nanjing Seminary to persona non grata, Wang's change in status also reflected the non-acceptance of Reformed theology in the TSPM/CCC.[103]

Concluding Remarks

This article has pointed to three stages in Wang Aiming's theology from 1998 to 2016. In the first stage, as a leader at Nanjing Union Theological Seminary, he attempted to support the rectification of the Theological Reconstruction Movement, drawing on Reformed traditions to provide a rationale for the movement. In the second stage, Wang further integrated the theological heritage of the Reformation with the Theological Reconstruction Movement, explaining why Luther's "law and gospel" paradigm needed to shift toward Calvin's "third use of the law." Wang was gradually marginalized in Nanjing Seminary and came to realize that the main problem for Theological Reconstruction was the outdated nature of the church system. In a third stage, therefore, Wang Aiming used the concepts of "magisterial church" and "free church" to formulate a way forward for Three-Self and house churches. He showed great hostility to the project of Sinicization and was afraid that the concept would be quickly reduced to extreme nationalism. However, Wang's suggestions failed to bring any substantial changes to the Three-Self church: Reformed theology, like Wang Aiming, was both introduced and then marginalized within the church.

---

102 Wang, *Magisterial Church and Free Church*, 162–63.

103 Most Chinese house church members I have met, even those closer to Reformed traditions, do not agree with or heed Wang Aiming's theology. Although Wang left Nanjing Theological Seminary in 2016, most house church leaders still regard him as a Three-Self church leader, his departure interpreted as a result of NUTS internal power struggles rather than theological differences.

Part IV

Reform Era Thinking

Chapter 12

CHRISTIAN SOUND AND HOSTILE STATE

Radio Evangelism and Theological Reasoning in Maoist China[1]

Joseph Tse-Hei Lee, *Pace University*

Introduction

In Maoist China (1949–76), sound and power met intensely, building up and tearing down communities in the name of strengthening a centralized, authoritarian state. Despite being an official tool of political propaganda and mobilization, the popularization of radio offered an opening for the Far East Broadcasting Company (遠東福音廣播公司, hereafter as "FEBC"), a Chinese evangelical organization in Hong Kong. By airing programs in Mandarin and various dialects, the FEBC created an invisible, electronic platform for isolated Christians to transform their clandestine gatherings into a listening community of believers, studying doctrinal and theological issues, and seeking spiritual guidance from the outside. Listening to Christian broadcasts became an important part of the Chinese faith practice when the Maoist state permitted only very limited church services within the officially-run religious patriotic organizations' public religious activities throughout the 1960s and 1970s. Accessing valuable religious and secular information abroad through these programs not only emancipated the listeners from the ideological remnants of Maoism, helping them to make sense of the fast-changing world, but also allowed them to engage in theological exchange through correspondence with the FEBC staff in Hong Kong. Chloë Starr argues that the evolution of Chinese

1 This work is part of the General Research Fund Project entitled "In Search of Popular Christianity: A Study of Audience Responses from Mainland China to Christian Gospel Broadcasts (1959–2004)," (Project CUHK 453113), supported by the Research Grants Council of Hong Kong. I thank Prof. Fuk-Tsang Ying of the Chinese University of Hong Kong for leading this project.

theology must be understood through the lens of indigenous literary expression.[2] When Chinese believers appropriate their literary and philosophical frameworks to theorize a Christian God and publicize their insights through native platforms, they seldom adhere to the rigid structure of Western logical analysis. Their theological reasoning is relational and dialogical, engaging theologians, church leaders, and ordinary believers as spiritual peers to explore the commonalities between Christianity and Chinese culture. This is also true for the FEBC radio audiences who embedded theological reflection in their everyday religious practice. Consulting a variety of Chinese listeners' letters from the 1960s to the 1970s, this study highlights the significant qualitative change in China's cultural landscape, from one monopolized by the one-party state, to a more pluralistic domain semi-regulated by the government and the market. Because the letters are constructed source materials at a particular moment in history, it is important to treat the listeners' accounts as indicative of their efforts to theologize personal struggle and faith experience and to seek new modes of self-expression.

This investigation builds on the latest research by Lei; Lei and Sun; Ying; and Ying and Guo about the influential role that radio broadcasting played in China's transition from an authoritarian society to a semi-liberalizing entity.[3] A closer look at the impact of Hong Kong's Christian radio programs on Chinese identity configuration advances our understanding on two levels of dramatic attitudinal and behavioral changes in 1980s China. First, throughout the Cold War, global Christian missionary movements became pluralistic in terms of theological outlook, evangelistic methods, and reception, largely because the institutional makeup of independent nation-states differed from continent to continent. Communist nations in Asia, such as the People's Republic of China, North Korea, Mongolia, Vietnam, and Laos, followed in the footsteps of the Soviet Union, expelling foreign missionaries and co-opting native Catholics and

---

2 Chloë Starr, *Chinese Theology: Text and Context* (New Haven, CT: Yale University Press, 2016).

3 Wei Lei and Wanning Sun, "Radio listening and the changing formations of the public in China." *Communication and the Public* 24 (2017) 320–34. Wei Lei, *Radio and Social Transformation in China* (New York: Routledge, 2019). Fuk-Tsang Ying, "Voices from the bamboo curtain: A study of the audience response to the Christian broadcasting in Maoist China (1959–1968)," in *Unfinished History: Christianity and the Cold War in East Asia*, ed, Philip L. Wickeri (Leipzig: Evangelische Verlagsanstalt, 2016), 111–131. Fuk-Tsang Ying 邢福增 and Guo Fei 國斐. "Unheard voices from China: The 'second society' as seen from the audience letters of Christian Radio Evangelism during the Cultural Revolution" 未聽到的中國聲音：文革時期福音廣播聽眾來信所見的「第二社會」. *Bulletin of the Institute of Modern History, Academia Sinica* 107 (2020): 1–35.

Protestants into state-controlled patriotic religious institutions. Christianizing efforts had to adapt and adjust to new and hostile local realities. It was in the radio landscape where an intense encounter between Christian sound and secular power took place.

Second, China's radio landscape witnessed a phenomenal shift from collective listening as a mode of socialist indoctrination to private listening as a personal choice in the 1970s and 1980s.[4] Frustrated by the excesses of Maoist rule, individuals were determined to pursue personal dreams over national interests, a process characterized by Yan Yunxiang as a Chinese pursuit of individualization.[5] What is under-explored is the paramount role that international Christian radio enterprises played in advancing this psychological shift of the Chinese populace from collective self to personal self. When countless people listened to Christian programs from Hong Kong, they tapped into a transnational Chinese-speaking religious radio landscape that operated outside the surveillance of the Communist state. By utilizing Christian insights to reorient themselves, they accessed new information about the global Church and gained spiritual and practical guidance from non-state actors.

The Far East Broadcasting Company is one of the major international radio organizations based in the United States, with offices in Hong Kong and Manila. Founded in Los Angeles in 1945, the FEBC launched its religious broadcasting to China and most of Southeast Asia from the Philippines in 1948. It soon established its studio and office in Hong Kong in 1958.[6] Incorporated in British Hong Kong in 1971, the executive board of the local FEBC was composed of Chinese pastors. The FEBC's Hong Kong office received the first listener's letter in 1958, but between 1959 and 1978, only a few hundred letters arrived per year. The situation dramatically changed when the Chinese government launched economic reform programs in 1978 and permitted citizens to communicate with people abroad via regular mail. Subsequently, from 1979 onwards, the Hong Kong office received over 10,000 letters annually. In total, over 350,000 letters came from different parts of China (including Tibet and Xinjiang) to Hong Kong from between 1959 and 2004. In 2005 alone, this China component has contributed significantly to a total of 4,087 hours of weekly religious programming managed by the FEBC and its affiliated local offices, in 161 languages at 147

---

4 Lei and Sun, "Radio Listening and the Changing Formations of the Public," 329.

5 Yunxiang Yan, *The Individualization of Chinese Society* (Oxford: Berg, 2009).

6 Jean DeBernardi, *Christian Circulations: Global Christianity and the Local Church in Penang and Singapore, 1819–2000.* (Singapore: National University of Singapore Press, 2020), 348.

radio outlets, including one in Hong Kong, and in 89 cities and fourteen countries around the world.[7]

Methodologically, several questions arise in consulting the Chinese listeners' letters: Why did listeners risk sending letters to Hong Kong during the Maoist period? Why did they continue to do so in the Reform era? How did the Christian radio enterprises process, classify, and preserve these letters? What are the limitations of these source materials for scholarly analysis? The length of the audiences' letters varies. Most are very brief, expressing appreciation for the religious radio programs and asking for copies of Bible, hymnals, and English learning materials. Some letters include testimonies of individual conversion, accounts of clandestine congregational gatherings, and comments on local politics and the economy. Ignoring government bans, the listeners were eager to express their opinions and stories in these letters, with which one can piece together the everyday experience of Chinese Christians and faith inquirers. Initially, the listeners mailed letters to a postal address in Hong Kong, but the FEBC staff found out from some listeners during the late 1960s and early 1970s that this official address looked politically suspicious to Chinese censors. Eventually, the FEBC used multiple residential addresses in Kowloon to receive correspondence. Because more letters were allegedly confiscated by postal censors, the stories to be told here are just the tip of the iceberg.

Furthermore, from the colonial era to the present, Hong Kong has been a Chinese gateway to the world. Because of the long history of Chinese migration, some letters were hand-delivered by Hong Kong residents who visited relatives and friends in their ancestral hometowns. During the 1970s these visitors served as crucial informants for the FEBC to evaluate the popularity of their religious programs in China. The FEBC took the letters seriously and its staff considered each letter to be a spiritual cry from the wilderness. It mobilized and trained local Christians to be pen pals in order to reply to every single letter it received. Like their colleagues in the traditional religious print media, the Christian radio broadcasts relied heavily on listeners' feedback and interviewed listeners who had fled to Hong Kong and Macau. They filed the letters, year by year, for the purposes of internal study, fundraising, and potential evangelistic outreach. Before the British handover of Hong Kong's sovereignty to China on July 1,

---

7 Timothy H.B. Stoneman, *Capturing Believers: American International Radio, Religion, and Reception, 1931–1970.* Unpublished Ph.D. dissertation. Georgia Institute of Technology, 2006, 3.

1997, the FEBC microfilmed the letters and destroyed the original copies. Then, it changed its plan and preserved hundreds of boxes of the undestroyed original letters.

While consulting the listeners' letters, scholars must combine the methodologies of textual and contextual analysis with the latest interpretive and hermeneutic paradigms. Texts and contexts are interrelated. The letters have to be consulted in relation to other sources, such as the Chinese Christian writers' autobiographies, field reports written by international visitors, and ethnographic data collected by researchers in China today. Empirically, the letters are constructed source materials at a particular moment from the late twentieth century. Their reliability should be assessed against the changing relationship between radio producers and listeners. René Wolf states that the radio broadcasts control the transmission yet know little about "the number of recipients and reception of contents," whereas the audiences "can only receive, but by making reception a matter of choice, feel authoritative."[8] There is also an issue of "time lapse" in which the audiences' memory of the programs fade when they receive replies from the radio stations. Rather than taking the letters as a mere reflection of the listeners' daily reality and struggle, this research explores the reception history of radio ministry and treats the materials as indicative of the writers' efforts to contextualize their experience through the lens of Christianity. "I listen, therefore, I am!" is a powerful thread that throws light on the construction of one's "private religious self" via aired radio programs, and this analytical focus parallels the current scholarship on emotionality and identity formation in modern China. Looking at the instrumental, spiritual, and emotional dimensions of the listeners' religiosity, this article explores how ordinary listeners constructed their spiritual "self" in an ideologically charged environment, how they sought outside support to consolidate their faith and build autonomous churches, and how they encountered specific moral and emotional challenges as they came to terms with Christianity.

Beginning with a general account of the development of China's radio landscape and Christian radio evangelism, the following analysis argues that Christian radio evangelism challenges many of our preconceptions of religious conversion, indigenous agency, everyday faith practice, and church-state relations. Transmitting the Gospel in ways different from the missionary era, the

---

8 René Wolf, *The Undivided Sky: The Holocaust on East and West German Radio in the 1960s* (New York: Palgrave Macmillan, 2010), 153.

radio ministry proved to be a powerful tool to transcend ideological, temporal, and spatial boundaries. Even when the Chinese state eradicated religion from the public and, to a certain extent, private domain, religious broadcasting followed distinctive patterns and networks when crossing territorial boundaries and reaching out to local audiences in unexpected ways.

China's Radio Landscape

Ever since 1949, the People's Republic perceived radio as a vital instrument for political propaganda and agitation, strengthening official efforts to eradicate unsanctioned ideas and to mold the new socialist citizens. To advance these state-building objectives, the Maoist government increased the production of radios dramatically while expanding broadcasting and relay stations nationwide to penetrate all levels of society. Before the age of television and social media, state-built radio reception stations, across rural and urban areas, reached the great mass of the population by introducing the practice of collective radio listening in public.[9] As a sound medium, radio broadcasting enjoyed a monopolistic status, because organized collective listening to official announcements was a common social ritual, contributing to the formation of a socialist citizenry. China had developed an extensive network of radio reception facilities across the interior and nurtured an entire population who knew how to obtain, process, and analyze information through sound.[10]

Popularization of radio made headway during the 1950s, as the state utilized daily political broadcasts to build up and tear down people in the name of constructing a socialist utopia. Regular political broadcasting contributed significantly to the state-building process, and occupied a major part of (or place in) people's everyday lives. Public radio broadcasting was a constant presence in many listeners' upbringing, as local work units in cities and villages, as well as public institutions such as municipal buildings, schools, and hospitals set aside certain hours of the day to air major political speeches of Mao and other national leaders. Radio stood out from traditional print media due to its remarkable capacity to spread information over long distances and to connect isolated audiences with national events that were unfolding in real time. While radio trained people of all stripes to be sensitive to the ideological signals and messages from

---

9 Lei and Sun, "Radio Listening and the Changing Formations of the Public," 330.

10 See Li, Jie, "Revolutionary Echoes: Radios and Loudspeakers in the Mao Era." *Twentieth-Century China* 45, no.1, 2020: 25–45.

above, it sowed the seeds of curiosity among the populace about the outside world.[11] When China gradually transformed itself from the collectivized and communally oriented society of the Maoist years to one featuring privatization, individualization, and globalization during the 1980s, the radio infrastructure offered an opening for overseas Christian radio broadcasting agencies. Thus, religious broadcasting benefited from the change of China's religious landscape, from one monopolized by the Maoist state, to, since the 1980s, a more pluralistic domain semi-regulated by the government and the market.

Radio Evangelism in China

A handful of early twentieth-century American Protestants envisioned the power of religious radio, and after the Second World War, they invested in global radio broadcasting infrastructure. Marketing this vision to most of the former China missions that were expelled by Beijing following the outbreak of the Korean War on June 25, 1950, they collaborated with Chinese churches in Hong Kong, Taiwan, and North America to design and prepare religious and educational programs, without knowing the immediate effects of their efforts. The success of proselytization was no longer measured by the numbers of conversions, baptisms, and church planning as had been the case during the missionary era. Against this backdrop, the FEBC radio ministry manifested the combination of transnational and indigenous evangelistic efforts.

Technically, the global expansion of international religious broadcasting benefited from the growth of reception facilities in countries across the Global South that followed decolonization in the 1950s and 1960s, and the diffusion of portable transistor radios. Since the 1980s, American Protestant-affiliated radio stations have dominated the international airwaves, dwarfing the world's major political voices, broadcasting more hours of religious programs a week in more languages than the BBC, Voice of America, China Radio International, and Voice of Russia combined.[12] More importantly, these Protestant radio stations, especially the FEBC's Hong Kong office, have operated and thrived outside the United States for the sole purpose of penetrating political, geographical, and linguistic barriers to spread the Christian message among foreign audiences.

---

11 Lei, *Radio and Social Transformation in China.*
12 Stoneman, *Capturing Believers,* 2–3.

In addition, the FEBC took advantage of the legal autonomy in British Hong Kong, the expansion of the local commercial radio industry, and the spread of an urban consumer culture. Broadcasting its Chinese Christian programs from the Philippines and Guam, the office did not need a government license to operate using official airtime. Keenly aware of the political turbulence in Hong Kong during the 1960s and early 1970s, the FEBC recruited its staff from local evangelical churches and took no action that might jeopardize the colony's volatile relationship with Beijing. Striving to ensure the neutrality of their religious mission, the office avoided criticizing the British colonial governance, local Communist underground activities, and growing economic inequality. Instead, the program producers encouraged listeners to embrace values such as individualism and volunteerism, of a more inward-looking form of evangelical Christianity, which were in line with the free-market ethics and norms welcomed by the British.

Throughout the 1960s and 1970s, the FEBC offered three types of religious broadcasts, in Cantonese, Mandarin, and Shanghainese, to hundreds of thousands of listeners in coastal and inland provinces. Daily broadcasts in Shanghaiese were brief, with no more than twenty minutes, but Cantonese and Mandarin programs lasted over two hours.[13] The first type of program was evangelistic and included "Golden Age of Life," a popular show about basic Christian doctrines and universal values, ethical problems, human relationships, etc., that went on for decades. The formats entailed sermons, lectures, songs, and reading selected biblical passages. The second type of program concerned the dissemination of current events. The FEBC provided daily summaries of the news from around the world, especially international news on China. The last type of program focused on English-language education. Recognizing the growing interest in English among disillusioned youth at the end of the Cultural Revolution, the radio producers worked with professional language instructors in Hong Kong to develop shows on beginner and conversational English. Other popular formats that were introduced in the late 1970s and 1980s included religious dramas, lectures by theologians, and answering listeners' questions and prayer requests. The FEBC model of radio ministry represented a more diffused approach of evangelization that relied on the financial and personnel support of overseas Chinese and Hong Kong Protestant churches.

---

13 Letter, April 8, 1968, Hong Kong to Guangzhou, Document #00128.

What follows are some personal narratives discerned in the audience letters, shedding light on the subjects of spiritual counseling, faith consolidation, and religious conversion in a deeply isolated environment. In particular, this study highlights the overlapping modes of faith practice and explores the commonalities and differences of Christianization in the old missionary and Maoist eras.

Spiritual Counseling and Faith Consolidation

Chinese Christians quickly recognized the religious nature of the broadcasts and were the first listeners to write to the FEBC. After the Chinese state monopolized the religious sphere, many listeners complained about the abolition of institutional churches from the 1950s to the early 1980s, and elderly audiences expressed fond memories of the former mission schools and hospitals. In Guangzhou, the Red Guards occupied the famous Cathedral of the Sacred Heart of Jesus, locally known as the Stone House Church. They cut the hair of a handful of Catholic nuns and priests and posted a large banner, "Execute the Lord," in the churchyard.[14] The first school for the blind, founded by the American Southern Baptist missionaries in Guangzhou and confiscated by the municipal officials after the Korean War, became a factory during the Cultural Revolution, but many of the students listened to the religious programs to seek psychological comfort and study doctrine.[15] Rather than being just passive listeners, they attended clandestine religious activities at home.[16] Some of the former missionary-trained Bible women (i.e., women evangelists) led these scattered house gatherings of listeners in Guangzhou. Despite the official crackdown on ecclesiastical institutions, there was a transition from a vertical leadership to a horizontal one. Gone was the old top-down ecclesiastical hierarchy among Chinese Christians. A cluster of loosely organized prayer groups and youth fellowships emerged in urban neighborhoods and production units across Guangdong Province, offering an informal, alternative social space for isolated Christians to seek spiritual counseling and support each other.

---

14 Letter, Guangzhou to Hong Kong, No.1966–216.

15 Letter, Guangzhou to Hong Kong, No.1975–16.

16 Si-Wen, Guangzhou, May 15, 1968, Document #00168.

Christian listeners who could not get any pastoral counseling turned to religious radio for help. Wu Guanlan (吳觀蘭), a middle-aged woman, found herself in an abusive marital relationship. When she got married in the late 1940s, her husband had never mentioned that his first wife ran away from home. They bore a few children, and many years later, the runaway wife returned, causing much stress to the family. Wu's husband and in-laws never supported her conversion to Christianity, and this made her feel isolated at home. She worried about being "a victim of black magic" as her husband had allegedly hired a shaman to curse her. In December 1967, Wu's eldest daughter was abandoned by the son-in-law's family after a miscarriage, and her daughter's mother-in-law reclaimed the wedding rings and other possessions. Sympathizing with the misfortune of Wu and her daughter, the FEBC staff offered a broad conceptualization of biblical teachings on divorce, rather than a narrow, moralistic interpretation of the Bible. They drew on the Christian idea of compassion to encourage Wu to focus on her daughter's well-being and resilience, and to celebrate the end of an abusive relationship.[17]

Another similar situation was that of Zhan Jiezhen (詹結貞), a Christian who was trained, in 1939, by the British as an emergency rescue worker in Hong Kong in preparation for Japanese military attack. During the Japanese occupation of the colony, she recalled the acts of Christian charity that took care of the vulnerable elderly and associated the idea of heaven with the humble service for the poor. She later moved to Guangzhou and settled there. After 1949, her medical background made her an outcast in the eyes of the Communist municipal officials. She was "given a black mark by others" in numerous mass campaigns. In late 1968, she was falsely accused of "being a bad woman" and stealing from others. According to Zhan, the accusers were "some bad men wanting to get the leading positions" in a production unit. Zhan wondered if "God has some way of taking away the black spot in order to make me innocent." She regarded the radio as "a guiding lamp to show me the way in the dark so that I may not stumble" and hoped to receive a Christian magazine in order to "get some spiritual water to drink." Troubled by much discriminatory harassment, she was eager to know biblical teachings on karmic justice: "Why in this world is it that those people with sinful conduct have comfortable lives while those who are honest

---

17 Wu Guanlan, Guangzhou, July 1, July 8, and August 13, 1968, Document#00268; June 29, 1968, Document#00278; October 17, 1968, Document#00428; November 2 and 8, 1968, Document#00458.

and obey the law have miserable lives? Is there any day of justice in the world? Does God treat us human beings unjustly? I feel resentment in this kind of a situation."[18] When the principle of fairness and justice failed, a genuine hope for divine justice often took root. Zhan hoped that God would judge those who mistreated her.

Some listeners with better biblical knowledge viewed the same desire for God's intervention in human affairs through a theological lens. On June 3, 1968, Liang Bing-lih wrote of the government's anti-Christian policies as "the hands of Satan" obstructing the spread of the Gospel. "What we can see here is only the tyrannical rule of men and I am horrified whenever I think of this."[19] The only way for him to counter the antireligious propaganda was to meditate on some memorized biblical verses and hymns. The story of Peng Mingzhong (彭明中) is also illustrative. As a new convert, he was involved in a house gathering in Guangzhou. He wrote on January 2, 1968:

> I am afraid that you don't know much about the problems that we are facing now. We do pray for our Father to lead us, guide us and keep us. Some of us pray that He can lead us across the Red Sea. Pray for brothers Chan, Sih and Fang, sisters Kao and Ng, and also Doctor Tse. We pray that God will lead them out of Egypt.[20]

Peng pleaded with the FEBC for help with their escape to Hong Kong. Like many Christians who did not have the Bible, Peng talked about the benefits of meditating on the biblical verses on the calendar given by the FEBC:

> After reading your letter and the Scripture verses printed on the calendar, I feel so sweet that it seems that I have come beside still waters. The whole family [house church] misses you. There is some warfare here and yet many brethren feel calm. They all have their own longings and hopes, and many a time, they feel so depressed that they think they are under the repressions of Pharaoh. I am sympathetic with their desires of crossing the Red Sea. Please pray for it. . . . Enemies are around us and anything

---

18 Zhan Jiezhen, Guangzhou, August 31, 1968, Document#00378; August 10, October 10, 1968, Document#00438; November 1968, Document#00468; January 4, 1969, Document#00518.

19 Liang Bing-lih, Guangzhou, June 3, 1968, Document#00288.

20 Peng Mingzhong, Guangzhou, January 2, 1968, Document#00018.

can happen. I pray that I will be in the hands of our Father instead of our enemies. Our Father is always victorious and so we can attain our goal if it is His will. Emmanuel.[21]

Peng drew on many biblical metaphors to critique the Maoist rule as "the repression of Pharaoh" and to justify his decision to attempt to flee to Hong Kong as "crossing the Red Sea." A few months later, he talked about the "moments of weakness and of sin" when members of his house group had "many dissensions, quarrels, etc." and lacked "forgiveness and love" toward one another.[22] In times of chaos and instability, Christians often use such metaphors to criticize injustice.

In February 1968, Peng was determined to "leave Egypt." At that time, it was common for young escapees to swim across the waters of Deep Bay to Hong Kong's New Territories, spending "four to eight hours in the water, dodging Chinese gunboats and battling the tides."[23] Unfortunately, Peng "failed and lived [imprisoned] in a violent and cruel place for a month." During his incarceration, he reflected on "the posterity of Adam" and recalled relying on God's grace as he "passed through the Red Sea."[24] He wrote:

> A line in the Psalms: to whom can I impart my sorrow . . . ? Dear brother, in the past 26 years, how many cups of bitterness have I drunk! But now I can understand what it means by " . . . and not be conformed to this world, and am consoled!" May I one day say, like Paul, "I have fought a good fight, I have finished my course. . . ." Yes, everything is ultimately, in the hands of God. After my release, I was bodily weak for a period of time, but now things are going well again, and I have returned to school [house group] already. My colleagues [other Christians] are good to me.[25]

His radio was confiscated, but he relied on the memories of biblical verses and hymns to sustain him. Peng assisted in organizing several Christian youths to talk about the faith clandestinely: "Surrounding me are young people. Though

---

21 Peng Mingzhong, Guangzhou, May 29, 1968, Document#00178.

22 Peng, Document#00178.

23 Ian Stewart, "Chinese Refugees Swim Across a Perilous Bay to Hong Kong," *The New York Times*, June 22, 1972: 2. Retrieved on June 13, 2020 from https://www.nytimes.com/1972/06/22/archives/chinese-refugees-swim-across-a-perilous-bay-to-hong-kong.html.

24 Peng, Document#00178.

25 Peng, Document#00178.

we all have different hardships, we are very happy when we gather together. We encourage one another. Please remember us in your prayers so that we may grow in faith, hope, and charity. Also please pray to the Father that He may fulfil our desire of leaving Egypt." Peng always felt ill-equipped to teach them anything except prayers, even though he was encouraged by a Bible woman named Cheong Wah-On.[26] His determination to participate in a house fellowship was strengthened via the radio. At a time when public church activity was banned, Christian broadcasts played a crucial transitional role in sustaining the spiritual interest of faith-seekers and helping them to find a supportive community. Isolated listeners, being unable to attend institutional churches, found the radio messages resonated with their theological, moral, and emotional sentiments. It was through the letters that we can trace the fragments of their thought on hardships and pain, and their hope for God's deliverance during dark and trying times. Evidently, the FEBC could not craft the religious programs to satisfy the specific needs of individuals such as Wu, Zhan, and Peng, but it strove to empower a growing community of clandestine believers.

Religious Conversion and Pastoral Support

With the opportunity to visit their ancestral hometowns in China, some Hong Kong Christians proved a valuable source of information to the radio program producers. One woman named Liu was born in Guangzhou and moved to Hong Kong during the 1950s. When visiting Guangzhou in 1971, she found it common for her relatives and classmates to tune in to the Christian radio programs at home, as they were disillusioned with the Communist propaganda. She advised the FEBC to avoid philosophical discussion about differences between Marxism and Christianity, to talk about the celebrations of Christmas and Easter in other parts of the world.[27] Another Christian named Xie visited Chaozhou City in the summer of 1971. His relatives and friends listened to the radio programs regularly. Because the programs were in Cantonese, not in the Chaozhou dialect, they did not fully comprehend the content. His relatives asked Xie about the identity of Jesus, and Xie utilized the opportunity to proselytize among them.[28] Using kinship and peer networks to convert people was an old evangelistic strategy, and radio actually helped overseas Chinese Christians to reactivate the same approach.

---

26 Peng, Document#00178.

27 Interview with Sister Liu, no date given, Hong Kong.

28 Interview with Brother Xie, September 7, 1971, Hong Kong.

On some occasions, the radio attracted unexpected audiences. Baptized in Indonesia in the early 1960s, Pan Guoxing (潘國興) was among hundreds of thousands of ethnic Chinese who were repatriated to China following mass killings that broken out in Indonesia in 1965–1966, targeting Communists, Javanese Muslims, Chinese, and alleged leftists. Upon his return to Guangzhou, he found all the churches to be closed and worried that God had abandoned him. The FEBC consoled Pan by referring to John 10:28–29, reminding him of the meaning of eternal salvation, a gift given to all Christians that cannot be taken away by any external power. They cited John 4:24, "For God is Spirit, so those who worship him must worship in spirit and in truth." The Chinese literal translations of "spirit" and "truth" mean "heart and soul" (心靈 *xinling*) and "honesty" (誠實 *chengshi*), respectively. These biblical verses helped to consolidate Pan's faith.[29]

To people who were haunted by political turmoil, the Christian idea of heaven and hell invoked their imagination to see beyond the harsh realities and to set their minds on eternal things. Shim Kit-Ching was keen to know the qualifications that people "need to have to enter Heaven," and the knowledge to identify "the Devil's words and deeds."[30] Lin Richeng (林日誠) expressed his hope to "only live a life without worries and sorrows," because he recalled seeing "several scores of carcasses flowing past on the river [from Guangxi Province to Guangzhou]. These people, young and old, men and women, who have been made a fool of by Devils will now meet their eternal damnation. What can we do except to pray to God, and wish them to obtain their ultimate rest?"[31] It was a trauma for Lin to see countless victims of factional violence at the peak of the Cultural Revolution and to mourn the loss of innocent lives.

In some remote production units in rural Guangdong and Fujian provinces, curious listeners tuned into radio transmitters under the cover of heavy bedding to avoid suspicion. This was quite unbearable in the hot, humid summer months.[32] By the early 1980s, many religious inquirers who first learnt about Christianity from the programs wrote to the radio host, asking for copies of

---

29 Pan Guoxing, Guangzhou, January 27, 1968, Document#00068.

30 Shim Kit-Ching, Guangzhou, July 4, 1968, Document#00278.

31 Lin Richeng, March 24, 1968, Document#00158; March 31, 1968, Document#00198.

32 Gene Wong Kim-Lai Ng. 黃吳劍麗. "Opening the Iron Curtain: A Closer Look at the Chinese Church Before and After the Reform Era through the Lens of Christian Radio Audiences' letters (1959–1983)" 竹幕升起: 從良友電台內地聽眾來信 (1959–1983) 看大門重開前後的中國教會. Unpublished M. Div. dissertation. The Chinese University of Hong Kong, 2010, 33.

Christian literature and hymnals. A young Han listener in the Muslim-majority Xinjiang Autonomous Region requested a copy of the Bible and religious pamphlets so that he could study the doctrines with his close friends, even though his parents warned him not to receive parcels from abroad.[33] Inspired by the martyrdom of her grandfather in the mid-1950s, a woman named Wu asked for some visual illustrations of Jesus Christ because her family lost all their Christian icons, hymnals, and Bible in the Cultural Revolution.[34] In 1979, a middle-aged man named Liu from Guangzhou regarded the Christian radio as the sympathetic "Other." Persecuted as a rightist in 1958 and jailed for four years, he had difficulty finding proper employment and lived in poverty. He found much comfort in listening to the Christian sermons and music.[35]

The FEBC's staff in Hong Kong were from diverse denominational backgrounds. By introducing the core beliefs of Christianity to arouse the listeners' curiosity, they worked to promote doctrinal ideas of creation and salvation, commonalities between faith and science, Christianity and progress, etc. While assessing the quality and state of broadcasting infrastructure in order to reach out to more areas of China, they took advantage of the fact that radio had become part of people's daily life and designed programs easily accessible to "sent-down youth" (知青 zhiqing), peasants, officials, senior citizens, and children. Because of the technological limitations of the 1960s and 1970s, they taped the radio programs in stereo. Religious broadcasts might lose the "live" quality, but the reliance on recorded programming meant that the programs could be designed with greater rigor.

Transcending geographical, class, and cultural differences, the religious programs offered a Christian-informed moral sensitivity to which Christians and non-Christians could relate. This new moral outlook manifested in the listeners' critique of the lack of trust and integrity among post–Cultural Revolution youth and their deep desire for the construction of a Christian ethical order on Chinese soil. The decades-long Maoist ritual of revolutionary practices actually prepared young listeners to be more receptive to religious radio programs. The listeners were more appreciative of Western and Chinese hymns than the conventional propaganda songs; they found taped sermons more personal than political speeches; they saw a behavioral parallel between acting on one's Christian faith

---

33 Letter, Urumqi to Hong Kong, No.1983–375.
34 Letter, Guangdong Province to Hong Kong, 1979–7079.
35 Letter, Guangdong Province to Hong Kong, 1979–1690.

and living a revolutionary life. The stories of the following Red Guards illustrate some of these themes.

A former Red Guard named Yao was typical of the post-1949 generation of students, workers, and intellectuals who grew up in an atheistic environment and experienced little of Christian and traditional religious rituals.[36] Yao was from Zhejiang Province, and his parents were government cadres who settled in Guangdong Province after 1949. He grew up in a privileged family in Dong-guan (東莞). Born in the 1950s, he lost his schooling after the outbreak of the Cultural Revolution. He joined the Red Guards to tour the country, fomenting the revolution and destroying temples and churches in the interior. He was also involved in countless attacks on what the state termed "class enemies," forcing them to confess their political sins and confiscating their possessions. As time passed, he became one of the "sent-down" youths experiencing poverty in resource-stricken production units. The emigrant village where he resided was a long way from his comfortable home and worlds away from the hustle and bustle of Dongguan. It was Yao's first exposure to boredom and monotony, and was quite a culture shock to a city boy. In emigrant communities where people received remittances from relatives in Hong Kong and Macau, peasants had radios at home, even though it cost two-months of a worker's salary to purchase one. Listening to Hong Kong's commercial and religious radio programs, and chatting with returning emigrants who were in Hong Kong and Southeast Asia before 1949 were the only comforts common to Yao. With little money at their disposal, many sent-down youths built their own radios and listened to the religious broadcasts at night. Young audiences found the official radio programs to be dreary and unconvincing and were inclined to avoid broadcasts laden with propaganda. They were interested in the international news about the latest developments in China and the outside world, and in the programs on Western classical music. Lacking the opportunity to gain a formal education, Yao did not see much opportunity for upward mobility. Without much hope and freedom, he fled to Hong Kong in March 1971. He took days to walk across the mountains from Guangzhou to the border and swam across the Daya Bay. Three of his five companions unfortunately drowned. Although Yao had never heard of the Gospel, he came across some references to God in translated European and Russian novels. At that time, the peninsula of Kowloon was the hub of the Chinese population. Its overcrowded streets and alleys teemed with all kinds

---

36 Interview with a Red Guard, no date given, Hong Kong.

of family-run businesses and most of the tenements where people lived. On the edges of Kowloon clustered squatter shantytowns for newly arrived Mainlanders such as Yao. After settling down, he visited the YMCA meeting hall on Waterloo Road and asked to be taken to a church.

Two discontented youths named Zhang and Hu fled to Hong Kong in 1971. They were deeply dissatisfied with the Maoist system:

> Because of control and intimidation tactics used by the state, people lived in fear. Everyone feared everyone; everyone informed on everyone; everyone suspected everyone; everyone mistrusted everyone; everyone spied on everyone else. . . . This is a common habit in China. People has [*sic*] individual thought. Humans are different from pigs and dogs. People with a few years of education can think for themselves. They know that there is a much larger world, and there is so little we know. The Communists always worry that people have independent access to information and knowledge.[37]

As with other sent-down youths like Christian writer Shi Tiesheng, both Zhang and Hu perceived themselves as victims of the Cultural Revolution, and questioned not just official privilege and corruption but the entire totalitarian system.[38] They recalled seeing many anti-government flyers posed by disillusioned youths in schools and other public buildings in Guangzhou. They were frustrated with the Hong Kong leftists hosted by municipal authorities. These Hong Kong leftists went on special tours of government offices and factories, embraced by local officials. They never had the opportunity to interact with ordinary people. Seeing these naïve Hong Kong leftists in Guangzhou, Zhang and Hu ridiculed them, yelling at them "to treasure what they had in the British colony." They found Maoist China to be a caste society, without upward mobility for former Red Guards. Coming from an atheistic background and growing up without exposure to religious traditions, they understood very little of religious radio programs but enjoyed listening to the hymns and music. Religious sites had become government warehouses and offices. Without freedom, it was impossible for people to practice and appreciate religious faith. It was through listening to

---

37 Interview with two exiled youths, no date given, Hong Kong.

38 Chloë Starr, "Shi Tiesheng and the nature of the human." *Christianity and Literature* 68 no. 1 (2018): 100–116.

the broadcasts that these listeners first encountered Christianity, imagined new possibilities for themselves outside China, and eventually fled to Hong Kong.

Accessing the Outside World

A major unintended consequence of radio evangelism was the propagation of outside knowledge. The religious programs provided a wealth of information on current world affairs, religious messaging, musical entertainment, etc., for non-Christians who participated in a global imaginary of cultural integration and who kept returning to the same religious channel because radio offered them an imaginary world to think beyond the Maoist state and its socialist entertainment. They pictured and experienced the outside world through listening, and the varieties of religious and secular knowledge consumption created images of hopes and opportunities, giving rise to a global imaginary of integration.

The educated youths and intellectuals were always curious about the outside world. After US President Richard Nixon's historic visit to China on February 21, 1972, the religious program producers recognized the appeal of English and decided to utilize the English learning programs to promote basic understanding of Christianity. According to Ng, from 1974 to 1983 the most popular program was "Beginners' English."[39] In 1979, 9,000 out of 10,781 letters asked for English learning materials, with some letters coming from the remote frontiers of Xinjiang, Tibet, or Qinghai. Some listeners, including medical and engineering majors coming to grips with a post-Maoist society felt that they should acquire new linguistic and professional skills to engage with the world.

Radio Church Service and Pastoral Advice

Many house churches organized worship according to the broadcast schedule. Listening to sermons and hymns together became a key liturgical practice among underground Christians who upheld their faith and sought guidance from the global Church. They saw themselves as being part of a listening community of faith, when they could not organize public religious life. The radio provided a symbolic meeting place for people who found themselves isolated and disillusioned with political upheaval. They retreated to a daily sacred moment in order to focus intensely on God. The practice of contemplative listening embodied a

---

39 Ng, "Opening the Iron Curtain," 43–44, 49.

sense of self-denial, surrendering one's desires and anxieties, and welcoming the presence of God to reside in one's soul. Similar to Christian prisoner Lin Zhao (林昭 1932–68), they contextualized their ordeals as part of a larger spiritual battle against the atheistic state. The biblical lessons, devotional practices, and hymns that they had learnt from radio became "the imaginary bricks" of an imagined chapel for daily worship.[40] Even though the mighty Communist state demolished countless physical churches, what really sustained the faithful was an invisible spiritual fortress on the airwaves. The listeners' experience reveals the characteristics of a historically grounded spirituality that emerged in China as a theology of defiance. This reflected their spiritual transformation toward a personal relationship with the Christian God and kept them from abandoning the faith.

Upon hearing some of the broadcasts, listeners asked existential questions about themselves and questioned the socialist discourse that they inherited from the government. They meditated on the sermons, wrote down inspirational biblical verses and hymns, and read aloud letters sent by the FEBC. Despite tremendous political pressure, many Christian listeners exercised limited agency to reach out to churches in Hong Kong. One Christian named Liu in Guangzhou described China as "a spiritual desert without a single drop of water" and praised the radio broadcasting for filling the spiritual void of society.[41] Access to religious broadcasts varied across the country. Most listeners came from cities such as Guangzhou, Shanghai, Xiamen, Shantou, etc., but radio reception seemed to be better in rural townships in the Pearl River Delta and along the southeastern coast because of the spacious landscape without mountain barriers.

Listeners reported many tales of the cosmological battle between Christianity and popular religions. Even though the state abolished religious institutions and took over religious properties, there were growing numbers of atomized individuals who rejected Maoism and turned to religion for solace. On November 4, 1968, Wang Enhui wrote, "The way to pray that you taught me in your letter is rather easy to follow. It is not like the Chinese style which needs sacrifices and fruits as an accompaniment to the prayer."[42] Fully believing in the power of the prayer to protect and heal, Zhu Zhiming (朱志明) praised the guardian angel that saved him from being stoned by thugs in Guangzhou's suburbs,

---

40 Xi Lian, *Blood Letters: The Untold Story of Lin Zhao, A Martyr in Mao's China* (New York: Basic Books, 2018), 19.

41 Letter, Guangdong Province to Hong Kong, No.1979–1601.

42 Wang Enhui, Guangzhou, November 4, 1968, Document#00448.

and three female traditional medical practitioners from Shaoguan (韶關) asked the FEBC to pray for the conversion of their husbands and children during the broadcasts.[43]

An independent evangelist called Ling'en learnt about Christianity from his mother, but he never took it seriously until the Cultural Revolution. Living in hardship, he found much comfort in Christian radio broadcasting. During the 1960s, he often visited his sister, a devoted convert and an active evangelist, and they listened to the religious programs together.[44] Although Christians had no public religious life, they still liked to socialize and marry one another. One of Ling'en's relatives was a pastor before 1949. This pastor taught children the Lord's Prayer. Collective reading of the Maoist writings actually prepared Ling'en and his friends to be more receptive to the liturgies of congregational singing, Bible study, and group prayers. The revolutionary rituals were quite similar to these faith practices, with the only difference that the object of worship was God, not a political figure. Ling'en argued that the old Buddhist, Daoist and popular religious institutions lacked the same broadcasting infrastructure to rebuild themselves. He perceived the FEBC as a prophet, an evangelistic pioneer utilizing advanced technology to design good religious and musical programs to spread the Gospel. He recalled meeting a female popular religious specialist who listened to a Christian broadcast. Seeing herself as "an orphan finding her mother," she discovered the Christian God from these programs. She confessed to Ling'en, "One understands the warmth of the fire in cold winter, and appreciates the beauty of snow in hot summer."[45]

Rural Christians who had never met any missionaries before 1949 turned to religious broadcasters for advice. Without access to the Bible, they copied biblical passages and hymns from the broadcasts, and relied on the program contents to consolidate the faith.[46] Upon receiving replies from the FEBC, the listeners often shared the letters among themselves, and even read aloud the replies in their own worship.[47] Many self-appointed house church leaders in mountainous regions turned to religious broadcasts for inspiration. Because so many new

---

43 Zhu Zhiming, Guangzhou, May 14, 1968, Document#00164; Wu Aqin (吳阿勤), Wang Fuyin (王富英) and Zhang Jiebing (張潔冰), Shaoguan, December 1973, Document#00013.

44 Interview with Brother Ling'en, Hong Kong, May 1, 1972, Hong Kong.

45 Interview with Brother Ling'en, Hong Kong, May 1, 1972, Hong Kong.

46 Ng, "Opening the Iron Curtain," 62.

47 Ng, "Opening the Iron Curtain," 60.

converts had never seen the Bible, they simply reflected on and preached what they heard on the radio. Sometimes, they even listened to religious programs together during evening worship.[48] In 1984, a Christian in Xinjiang passed away at the age of 81. This believer had worked as mission staff when he was young. He moved to stay with his children in Xinjiang when he became old. Deeply moved by his convictions, his children marked a "cross" on his tomb.[49]

A Christian named Zhong from Zhejiang Province wrote, "Even though all the Protestant churches were demolished in the Cultural Revolution, our hearts were not demolished. We did not lose heart. We were scattered across the wilderness, and were determined to use different ways to spread the gospel."[50] In the 1980s, many Christians felt suspicious toward the state-controlled Three-Self patriotic churches and would rather turn to the religious radio programs for spiritual instruction. As Jiang from Shandong Province wrote in 1986, "Because the church is just a religious institution in name only, it is a secular entity, not a spiritual body. There is no church revival locally. It may be better to listen to your radio for the Gospel."[51] What is shown here is a remarkable transition from the conventional understanding of a Three-Self Church to a Four-Self faith community: self-propagating, self-governing, self-supporting, and self-theologizing (developing their own understanding of the Christian God when being denied access to a proper theological education).

Mediating Theological Disputes

Throughout the 1980s, the Chinese official discourse of "Reform and Opening Up" played to the advantage of Christian radio producers in Hong Kong. Learning from the West and Hong Kong to transform China's backwardness became a norm in rural and urban areas. Before the socialist state reinstated the institutional mechanism of ecclesiastical surveillance and control in the late 1980s, Christians in inland provinces communicated with Hong Kong radio producers, expressing their frustrations in cases of doctrinal and church conflicts. They turned to Christian radio stations as pastoral advisors. Through postal correspondence, the listeners bypassed the state-controlled patriotic churches and granted authoritative legitimacy to the Christian radio producers as mediators of church disputes and theological disagreements. Making the FEBC a parallel

---

48　Ng, "Opening the Iron Curtain," 65.
49　Ng, "Opening the Iron Curtain," 91.
50　Ng, "Opening the Iron Curtain," 62.
51　Ng, "Opening the Iron Curtain," 73.

mode of theological authority beyond the official one, this development contributed to the bifurcated division between patriotic churches and house churches. When house churches in Hunan Province encountered the Shouters, people affiliated with Witness Lee's Local Assembly Movement in Taiwan and the United States, in 1981, they sought theological advice from the FEBC. Congregants debated fiercely whether they should shout "Amen" during worship. While the Shouters criticized the silent congregants for betraying the biblical primitivism, the latter condemned the Shouters as theologically heterodox.[52] In the mid-1980s, church members in Guangdong also debated what sacraments ought to be practiced in the Church, such as celebrating Christmas, admitting infant baptism, etc.

In areas with a rich tradition of home-grown Christian sectarianism, the theological discussion touches on the diverse expressions of Protestantism in Chinese society. In 1982, in Jiangsu Province, a listener named Ma claimed to have received supernatural powers from God, just like the mid-nineteenth-century Taiping Christian leader Hong Xiuquan. Ma proclaimed that he had followed biblical instructions to perform miracles, using his breath to heal the sick, writing Christian prayers to perform exorcisms and save people's souls.[53] In Shandong, some people proclaimed to be Yahweh, with the power to revive the dead, and did not adhere to the Ten Commandments.[54] Responding to these Christian-inspired sectarian practices, the radio producers consulted prominent theologians in Hong Kong, and sought their advice to address these doctrinal concerns on their programs. The radio broadcasters invited these scholars to serve as arbitrators in theological debates, striving to introduce doctrinal orthodoxy among listeners. In the 1980s, after receiving letters from listeners, radio producers began to make the programs more interactive. They read aloud letters and answered audience questions.[55] In the absence of clerical leadership, Chinese religious actors drew on the limited biblical message they heard from the broadcasts to theologize their non-belief in Maoism. The socialist upbringing, together with the state's rituals of ideological propaganda and indoctrination, actually prepared mainland listeners to be receptive to Christian radio programs. Beginning in the early 1980s, the FEBC staff sent evangelists to visit those listeners who expressed a keen interest in conversion. In fact, other Christian

---

52 Letter, Jiangsu Province to Hong Kong, No.1982–2129.

53 Letter, Jiangsu Province to Hong Kong, No.1982–2129.

54 Letter, Shandong Province to Hong Kong, No.1982–2964.

55 Ng, "Opening the Iron Curtain," 38.

enterprises such as China Ministries International, Seventh-day Adventists, and Trans-World Radio in Hong Kong sent people to visit their listeners, collected feedback, and designed new programs to cater to their needs. The late Jonathan Chao partnered with Trans-World Radio to broadcast a program called "Seminary on Air" (空中神學院), focusing on doctrinal instruction and leadership training. Chao later published the program materials as *Handbook for Training Church Workers* (教會工人培訓手冊), educating a new generation of Chinese Christians.[56]

Conclusion

After several centuries of proselytization, Christianity has clearly transformed itself from an alien faith into a Chinese religion. This process of indigenization has not only built on the courage and candor of countless believers who adhered to their faith and organized covert congregational activities throughout the Maoist years, but has also benefited from the innovations of transnational Christian radio broadcasting enterprises, utilizing the strategic location of Hong Kong to air religious radio programs to China's coastal peripheries. The failure of the Communist state to dominate the radio landscape gave rise to a truly self-propagating and self-theologizing church on Chinese soil. The radio's ability to transcend physical boundaries between Hong Kong and China represented an immeasurable opportunity for the continuation of Christian influence. The interplay between radio broadcasts and audiences gave rise to a meaningful process of theological dialogue that developed, hour by hour, minute by minute, on the Chinese airwaves. The theological engagement was embedded in the everyday religious practice of Chinese listeners. This development has made underground Christians less vulnerable to state persecution and has allowed them to respond quickly and be flexible to change.

Equally significant is the incremental formation of personal spirituality among the listeners that corresponded to a larger phenomenon of the shift from collective radio listening to private listening as a matter of individual choice. The Maoist and post-Maoist authorities tried to block foreign broadcasts, but since the 1980s, the state has tolerated the transmission of religious broadcasting from Hong Kong, loosening restrictions on people tuning to the programs. The

---

56 I thank Dr. Tak Leung Yim of the Chinese University of Hong Kong for sharing this information.

old loudspeakers and public broadcast stations built by the government enforced the top-down circulation of propaganda for the wider listening public.[57] Public listening had become mandatory as an expression of loyalty to the state. When China refashioned itself as a market-driven consumer society, countless listeners searched for different programs that interested them personally. Since foreign radio broadcasting was not completely banned, people used shortwave radio sets to access the BBC, VOA, and Radio Australia for news, English learning, and music appreciation.[58]

It was through effective religious broadcasts from Hong Kong that Christianity had emerged as an attractive moral-ethical system among people who were dissatisfied with the ideological excesses of Maoism. Because the transnational radio landscape was outside the confines of state control, Christian broadcasts transcended national borders and geographical distances, reaching the private homes of listeners and the realm of house churches. It was through listening that Chinese Christians joined a transnational public community of faith and reimagined themselves as part of global Christianity, even though they had not yet obtained the opportunity to go abroad. They constantly tuned in to the same programs that were consistent with their spiritual sentiments. Operating as much as an agent of opinion reinforcement as a force of change, the FEBC radio ministry captured the audiences' attention and gave them an outlet to support their strongly held personal opinions. In the final analysis, radio was a material and technical object that was widely praised as a catalyst of modernity in the twentieth century. Yet, through this powerful medium, religious broadcasting created a daily sacred moment for Chinese listeners from 1958 to the present, empowering them with new modes of re-imagination, and enabling them to access the outside world for faith consolidation, theological discourse, and pastoral support.

References

Unpublished and Unclassified Listeners' Letters and Transcripts of Interviews of the Far East Broadcasting Company

Interview with Brother Xie, September 7, 1971, Hong Kong.
Interview with a Red Guard, no date given, Hong Kong.

---

57 Li, "Revolutionary Echoes.
58 Lei and Sun, "Radio Listening and the Changing Formations of the Public in China," 330.

Interview with two exiled youths, no date given, Hong Kong.
Interview with Sister Liu, Hong Kong.
Interview with Brother Zhou from Xiamen, Fujian Province, July 28, 1972, Hong Kong.
Interview with Brother Fu, Hong Kong, January 31, 1972, Hong Kong.
Interview with Brother Ling'en, Hong Kong, May 1, 1972, Hong Kong.

Chapter 13

DANCING WITH COMMUNISM

A Comparative Study of Wu Yaozong and Bishop Ding Guangxun's Contextual Theologies[1]

Zhong Zhifeng, *Renmin University*

Introduction

With the shift of gravity of Christianity from the Western world to other parts of the globe, theological developments in the rest of the world have belatedly caught the attention of Western academia. Several monographs have recently appeared dedicated to Chinese theology as well as two English-language journals.[2] However, most research on Chinese theology focuses on the dialogue between Christianity and various other Chinese cultural expressions (such as Confucianism, Buddhism, and Islam),[3] while

---

1 This article is a product of the project "The Political Attitudes of Religious Leaders in Transitional China," funded by the National Social Science Fund.

2 See Chloë Starr, *Chinese Theology: Text and Context* (New Haven: Yale University Press, 2016); Yongtao Chen, *The Chinese Christology of T. C. Chao* (Leiden: Brill, 2016); Alexander Chow, *Chinese Public Theology: Generational Shifts and Confucian Imagination in Chinese Christianity* (Oxford: Oxford University Press, 2018). English journals concentrating on Chinese theology include: *Yearbook of Chinese Theology* edited by Paulos Z. Huang of University of Helsinki, and *Chinese Theological Review* published by the Foundation for Theological Education in South East Asia.

3 John D. Young, *Confucianism and Christianity: The First Encounter* (Hong Kong: University of Hong Kong, 1983); Lai Pinchao (Lai Pan-chiu), *Yefo duihua: jindai zhongguo fojiao yu jiduzongjiao de xiangyu* 佛耶對話: 近代中國佛教與基督宗教的相遇 [Buddhist-Christian Dialogue: Buddhist-Christian Encounter in Modern China] (Zongjiao wenhua chubanshe: 2008); Ralph Covell, *Confucius, the Buddha, and Christ: A History of the Gospel in Chinese* (New York: Orbis, 2004); Liu Yizhang and Huang Yuming, eds., *Butong erhe: jidujiao yu yisilanjiao zai Zhongguo de duihua yu fazhan* 不同而和：基督教與伊斯蘭教在中國的對話 [A Cordial Divergence: Christian-Islam Dialogue in China and its Development] (Hong Kong: Alliance Seminary Press, 2010).

relatively little scholarship has concentrated on the dialogue between Christianity and communism.[4]

The rise of communism and the establishment of its ruling power since 1949 posed a great challenge to Christianity. How to respond intellectually to the challenge of communism became an important issue of theological contemplation for Chinese Christians. Various studies have tackled the issue of Christianity and communism,[5] but these have tended to approach the relations between Christianity and communism from a very general, philosophical perspective. A number of case studies have examined influential Christians' responses to communism,[6] but these have tended to pay more attention to their actions than their thought.[7] Such studies have also often held very negative opinions of Three-Self

---

4 Exceptions include: Roland Boer & Kenpa Chin, "Chinese Christian Communism in the Early Twentieth Century," *Religion, State and Society* 44 (2016): 96–110; Chin Kenpa 曾慶豹,"Minguo jidujiao yu makesi zhuyi de duihua: yi Zhang Shizhang de yesu zhuyi weili 民國基督教與馬克思主義的對話—以張仕章的耶穌主義為例 [Early Twentieth Century Chinese Christian-Marxist Dialogue: A Case Study on Zhang Shizhang]," *Logos & Pneuma* 51 (2019): 121–54; Li Zhixiong, "Jian yu shizijia: renwen shiyu xia makesi zhuyi yu jidujiao zhi bijiao 劍與十字架—人文視域下馬克思主義與基督教之比較 [The Sword and Cross: A Comparative Study on Marxism and Christianity Within the Humanistic Field of Vision], *Shanghai daxue xuebao* 18 (2011): 128–40.

5 See M. S. Bates, *Jidujiao yu gongchanzhuyi* 基督教與共產主義 [Christianity and Communism], trans., Zhang Shizhang (Hong Kong: Association Press, 1939); John Lewis, Karl Polanyi, and Donald K. Kitchen, eds., *Christianity and the Social Revolution* (London: Victor Gollanca, 1937); David M. Paton, *Christian Missions and the Judgment of God* (New York: Eerdmans, 1996). Although these books all consider Communism as a major challenge to Christianity, some view this negatively while others have a more positive judgment. For example, Paton argued that Communism was God's judgmental hand to push the missionaries to repent for their imperialist sins.

6 On Wu's involvement in the TSPM and his legacy, see Leung Ka-lun and Ying Fuk-tsang, *Wushi niandai sanzi yundong yanjiu* 五十年代三自運動研究 [A Study on the Three-self Movement in the 1950s] (Hong Kong: Alliance Seminary Press, 1996); Leung Ka-lun, *Wu Yaozong sanlun* 吳耀宗三倫 [Three Essays on Y. T. Wu] (Hong Kong: Alliance Seminary Press, 1996); Philip L. Wickeri, *Seeking the Common Ground: Protestant Christianity, the Three-Self Movement, and China's United Front* (New York: Orbis, 1988), 113–53. For Ding's involvement and impact, see e.g. Philip L. Wickeri, *Reconstructing Christianity in China: K. H. Ting and the Chinese Church:* (New York: Orbis, 2015).

7 Ye Jinghua, *Xunzhen qiuquan: Zhongguo shenxue yu zhengjiao chujing chutan* 尋真求全：中國神學與政教處境初探 [Seeking truth and perfection: A Preliminary study on Chinese theology and the church-state context] (Hong Kong: Christian Study Center on Chinese Religion and Culture, 1997).

Patriotic Movement (TSPM) leaders, to the point of doubting the authenticity of their Christian identity.[8]

More literature has emerged that reevaluates the legacy of controversial figures such as Wu Yaozong (Y. T. Wu) and Ding Guangxun (K.H. Ting),[9] yet even this often still pays more attention to their political than their theological endeavors, underplaying their influence on Chinese theology. Both Wu and Bishop Ding were important figures in the dialogue between Christianity and communism. They were not only influential political leaders who steered the church to find a new space for herself in the new China but important theologians who worked painstakingly to reconcile Christianity and communism.

This paper takes Wu Yaozong and Ding Guangxun as case studies and compares their various approaches to reconciling communism and Christianity. Wu and Ding were influential TSPM leaders who made distinctive contributions to Chinese theology. Wu (1893–1979) was a liberal Christian who was greatly influenced by the social gospel movement. He converted to Christianity after attending public lectures by Sherwood Eddy (1871–1963), a prominent missionary from the Young Men's Christian Association (YMCA) of the USA, in 1918. Wu later became a secretary of the national YMCA in China and was responsible for the Christian Student Movement (SCM) and YMCA publications. He received his theological training from Union Theological Seminary in New York. In the 1950s, Wu launched the Three-Self Patriotic Movement and became the main promoter of this movement. Trained in the Anglican tradition, Ding Guangxun (1915–2012) received his B.D. from St. John's University in Shanghai and his M.A. from Union Theological Seminary in New York. Before he became principle of the Nanjing Union Theological Seminary in 1953, he had worked for the SCM of the YMCA (both in China and Canada), and for

---

8 Starr, *Chinese Theology: Text and Context*, 186.

9 Ying Fuk-tsang, ed., *Da shidai de zongjiao xinyang: Wu Yaozong yu ershishiji Zhongguo jidujiao* 大時代的宗教信仰: 吳耀宗與二十世紀中國基督教 [Abiding Faith for A Nation in Crisis: Y. T. Wu and Twentieth Century Chinese Christianity] (Hong Kong: Christian Study Center on Chinese Religion and Culture, 2011); Ambrose L. Y. Tse (謝龍邑　Xie Longyi), Weiqu qiuquan? Wu Yaozong de shengping yu jiuguo qinghuai 委曲求全: 吳耀宗的生平與救國情懷 [Compromise for Survival? Y. T. Wu's life and National Salvation] (Hong Kong: Tiandaoshulou, 1995); Liu Huajun 劉華俊, Tianfeng ganyu: Zhongguo jidujiao lingxiu Ding Guangxun 天風甘雨—中國基督教領袖丁光訓 [Heavenly Wind and Seasonable Rain: Ding Guangxun as the Leader of Chinese Christianity] (Nanjing: Nanjing University Press, 2001).

the World Students' Christian Federation in Geneva. Ding was consecrated as the Anglican Bishop of Zhejiang in 1955. After the Cultural Revolution, Ding became the second-generation leader of the TSPM and remained at the helm for several decades.

Wu's main intellectual reconciliation with communism can be found in his books *No One Has Ever Seen God* and *Darkness and Light*.[10] The former is a monograph in which Wu endeavored to reconcile Christianity and communism. The latter is a collection of essays written between 1942 and 1949, which presents Wu's reflections on Christianity in the context of political transformation (from the aggressive Japanese invasion to the founding of new China). The main themes of this book are a corrupted church, repentance and reform, and embracing the dawning new era. Ding's main intellectual reconciliation with communism can be found in *The Selected Works of K. H. Ting*,[11] and in numerous journal articles published in church magazines and journals such as *Tianfeng* (Heavenly Wind) and *Nanjing Theological Review*. Central themes in these publications include God's universal love, Cosmic Christ, "downplaying justification by faith (淡化因信稱義)" and reconstructing the church.

My assumption is that both Wu and Ding are sincere Christians who believed that there is common ground between Christianity and communism, a belief that motivates them to harmonize these two contentious entities. The main arguments of this paper are as follows: although under political pressure, yet out of their belief in the common ground between communism and Christianity, both Wu and Ting toiled painstakingly to reconcile these two value systems. Despite quite different political settings at their time of writing, both achieved only very limited success in their reconciliation projects. In term of results, Wu and Ding shared more similarities than differences. The following sections first provide an overview of the dynamic relations between communism and Christianity, examining how Wu and Ding's common theological training in Union

---

10 *No One Has Ever Seen God* 沒有人看見過上帝 (Shanghai: Qingnian Xiehui Shuju, 1938). In the 1948 version (fifth edition) of this book, Wu added two essays as appendices: "Christianity and Materialism: A Christian's Confession" and "Is it possible to reconcile truth?" *Darkness and Light* 黑暗與光明 (Shanghai: Qingnian xiehui shuju, 1949).

11 There is one Chinese edition of *Ding Guangxun wenji* 丁光訓文集 (Nanjing: Yilin, 1998), and several English editions of selected works, including Janice Wickeri, ed., *Love Never Ends: Papers by K. H. Ting* (Nanjing: Yilin Press, [1991] 2000); Raymond L. Whitehead, ed., *No Longer Strangers: Selected Writings of K. H. Ting* (Maryknoll, N.Y.: Orbis Books, 1989). An edition of *Love Never Ends* published by Cook Communication Ministry International in 2004 also incorporates some of Ding's later articles and speeches.

Theological Seminary and encounters with communism influenced their theological thinking. I then examine how they formulated their ideas of God and developed their thinking on church reform to ease the tension between theism and atheism and to provide a theological basis for the TSPM. Finally, I evaluate the results of their efforts to harmonize communism and Christianity. The paper hopes to shed light on church-state relations as well as contextual theology under communism.

The Dynamic Relations Between Communism and Christianity

The dynamic history of communist–Christian encounter in China may be divided into three periods: from the 1920s to mid-1930s, from the mid-1930s to 1949, and from 1949 to the present. During the first period, Communism and Christianity were largely in conflict, partly due to the prevailing anti-Soviet mentality among missionaries, and partly due to Christians' own experiences. Since the founding of the Communist Party of China (CPC) in 1921, there had been enormous tension between communism and Christianity, and a war of souls flared between the nascent CPC and the Student Christian movement, as each wanted to draw the youth into their camp.[12] The representatives of Communist International (Comintern) in China who guided the CPC in its early days believed they needed to eliminate the widespread yearning of youth to adopt American models, in order to mobilize young people to adopt the Russian model.[13] At that time, most missionaries came from the United States, and the missionary enterprise exerted a great influence on the youth. It was this competition of influence that brought communism and Christianity into conflict. Christianity was regarded as a vanguard of scientism (科學主義) and despised by some communist leaders as superstition.[14] Under the banner of nationalism, the CPC also attacked the imperialist face of Protestantism by launching the Anti-Christian Movement (非基督教運動) and the later anti-religion

---

12 Tao Feiya 陶飛亞, "'Wenhua qinlue' yuanliu kao" 文化侵略源流考 [A Textual Study of "Cultural Aggression], *Wenshizhe* 5 (2003): 33–34.

13 Zhongguo Shekeyuan Xiandaishi Yanjiusuo, ed. and trans., *Weijingsiji zai zhongguo de youguan ziliao* 维经斯基在中國的有關資料 [Source Materials for Voitinsky's Activities in China] (Beijing: Zhongguo Shehui kexue chubanshe, 1982).

14 Chen Duxiu, "Jidujiao yu Zhongguoren" 基督教與中國人 [Christianity and Chinese] *Xin qingnian* 7 (1920): 15–22.

campaign.[15] The Communist Party and its Chinese Youth League were the initiator and active promoters of the Anti-Christian Movement.[16] From the 1920s to mid-1930s, a number of church buildings were confiscated and missionaries kidnapped by radicals in revolutionary bases (革命根據地), part of a survival strategy developed by the encircled CPC.[17] Christianity was one of the main targets of radicalized farmers, because of its connections with foreigners and warlords. During this period, Wu Yaozong published an article entitled "Why does the Communist Party try so hard to make trouble with us?"[18] In time, the failures of the CPC's radical policies as well as the Japanese invasion in the 1930s led the CPC to renounce this aggressive approach and adopt a more moderate United Front policy, opening a new page in communist–Christian encounter.[19]

During the second period, from mid-1930s to 1949, communism and Christianity worked in partnership. With Japan's nationwide invasion, China experienced unprecedented pressure. In this situation all parties began to put aside their internal conflicts and built an anti-Japanese United Front. With the help of several successful communication campaigns, the CPC's repositioning reshaped its image within the Christian community. Many progressive Christians began to view communism positively, and they started to treat CPC as a liberator and force for national salvation rather than a ruthless instigator of disruption. For

---

15 Local histories of the CPC reveal that the CPC was the initiator of this campaign, see Zhonggong Beijing Shiwei Dangshi Yanjiushi, *Beijing geming shi dashiji* 北京革命史大事紀 [Important Events in the History of Beijing Revolution) (Beijing: Zhonggong dangshi ziliao chubanshe, 1989), 26; Zhonggong Shanghai Shiwei Dangshi Yanjiushi, *Zhonggong Shanghai dangshi dadian* 中國上海黨史大典 [History of the CPC in Shanghai)(Shanghai: Shanghai jiaoyu chubanshe, 2001), 4.

16 Tao Feiya, "Gongchan guoji daibiao yu zhongguo fei jidujiao yundong 共產國際代表與中國非基督教運動 [The representatives of the Communist International and the Anti-Christian Movement in China)," *Jindaishi yanjiu* 5 (2003): 114–36.

17 Jack R. Lundblom, *On the Road to Siangyang: Covenant Mission to Mainland China 1890–1949* (Wipf & Stock, 2015), 179–206; R. A. Bosshardt, with Gwen and Edward England, *The Guiding Hand: Captivity and Answered Prayer in China* (Hodder and Stoughton, 1973); Arnolis Hayman, *A Foreign Missionary on the Long March: The Memoirs of Arnolis Hayman of the China Inland Mission* (Merwin Asia, 2011).

18 Shucheng (Wu Yaozong's pen name), "Gongchandang weishenme pinming de yu women daoluan" 共產黨為什們拼命的與我們搗亂 *Zhinan* 41 (1928): 2–3.

19 There were also some regional variances. For example, in Shanghai, due to the failure of the radical labor movement and the repression of GMD, the underground CPC shifted its policy and began to collaborate with the YWCA in Shanghai in the late 1920s. See Emily Honig, *Sisters and Strangers: Women in the Shanghai Cotton Mills, 1919–1949* (Stanford, CA: Stanford University Press, 1992), chapter 8.

example, in the foreword to the translation of M.S. Bates's *Christianity and Communism*, Wu Yaozong maintained that:

> Since the establishment of the anti-Japanese United Front between the CPC and the Nationalist Party (*Guomindang*, GMD), the CPC has obtained legal status. Its policy orientation has greatly shifted; its method of building new China with the Three Principles of the People was not bloody struggle, but peaceful means. The leaders of the CPC have also shown a friendly attitude towards Christianity. . . . Therefore, if we were to neglect these new realities and continue to apply our general attitude towards communism to the present CPC, it would be most unfortunate.[20]

The corruption of the GMD and its suppression of the democratic movement during the civil war also alienated many intellectuals.[21] As a result, the Communist Party and certain progressive Christians built up an anti-Civil War, anti-dictatorship united front.[22] The Christians' Seminar on Democracy in China was established by twenty-six progressive Christians in Shanghai in 1945.[23] Some believers not only established good collaboration with communists but also joined the CPC and became communist Christians (or "red Christians").

In the third period, from the late 1940s onwards, communism and Christianity were in constant tension. That is why the state pushed Christian leaders to remold Christianity in the 1950s, and why Christianity was pushed to reconstruct itself even after Opening Up and Reform (1978–). Once the CPC expelled the GMD from the mainland and established itself as the new ruler of China, the tradition of state-dominated religion was fully resumed, and Christianity came under constant pressure. Compared to traditional dynastic courts, the CPC was more modern and more powerful. Scholars use terms such as "totalitarian" to describe the nature of communist regimes.[24] Christianity was

---

20 Wu Yaozong, Foreword, in M.S. Bates, *Christianity and Communism*, trans. Zhang Shizhang (Shanghai: Qingnian xiehui, 1939), 4. Translated by the author.

21 Luo Weihong, ed., *Zhongguo jidujiao shi* 中國基督教史 [A History of Christianity in China] (Shanghai: Shanghai renmin chubanshe, 2014), 623–28.

22 Wickeri, *Seeking the Common Ground*, 122–27; Wong Wai-yin Christina, "Expanding Social Networks: A Case Study of Cora Deng and Y. T. Wu on their Roles and Participation in the National Salvation Movement in 1930s," in *Da shidai de zongjiao xinyang*, 291–340.

23 Luo Weihong, ed., *Zhongguo jidujiao shi*, 625.

24 Zou Dang, *Ershi shiji zhongguo zhengzhi* 二十世紀中國政治 [Chinese Politics in the 20th Century] (Hong Kong: Oxford University Press, 1994).

problematic not only due to its imperialist faults and political incorrectness (that is, its closeness to the Nationalist GMD), but also because of its ability to act as an alternative source of power and ideology. The CPC tried to consolidate its rule by domesticating the church, a process greatly accelerated by the outbreak of the Korean War in the early 1950s.

Scholars usually divide the history of People's Republic of China into two periods: the Maoist era and the post-Mao era (or the Reform Era).[25] Although there are noticeable differences between these two periods in terms of church–state relations, the differences are in degree rather than in type. Relations fluctuated, sometimes for the better, sometimes for worse.[26] It is not difficult to identify a pendulum of tightening control and relaxation in the CPC's religious policies. This is the main context of Wu and Ding's reconciliation projects.

It was not only the macro context that had an impact on the relationship between communism and Christianity, however. Personal experiences and institutional connections with the Communist Party also mattered. Before 1949, Wu had several personal conversations with Premier Zhou Enlai and other high-ranking communist leaders such as Wu Yuzhang (吳玉章), Zhu De (朱德) and Dong Biwu (董必武).[27] These conversations not only eased his doubts on communism but also established some level of collaboration. Wu was convinced that there was common ground between communism and Christianity, and that the CPC's policy of religious freedom was sincere. For Wu, the common ground was to "build the country, defend peace and advance the happiness of humanity."[28] Ding had also established a working relationship with Zhou Enlai through the Gong sisters (Gong Pusheng and Gong Peng), Zhou's secretaries

---

25 Martin T. Fromm, *Borderland Memories: Searching for Historical Identity in Post-Mao China* (New York: Cambridge University Press, 2019); Xiao Donglian, *Lishi de zhuangui: cong bo-luan fanzheng dao gaige kaifang* 歷史的專櫃： 從撥亂反正到改革開放 [Turning Point in History: Re-examination of the Cultural Revolution and the Policy of Reform and Opening] (Hong Kong: Chinese University of Hong Kong Press, 2008).

26 Zhong Zhifeng, "Bodong de zhengjiao guanxi yu jidujiao zai dangdai Zhongguo de fazhan 波動的政教關係與基督教在當代中國的發展 [The Fluctuation of Church-State Relations and the Development of Protestantism in Contemporary China]." *Logos and Pneuma* 44 (2016): 123–50.

27 Zhao Xiaoyang, "A Short Chronicle of Y. T. Wu," in *Wu Yaozong juan* 吳耀宗卷, ed., Zhao Xiaoyang (Beijing: Renmin University of China Press, 2014), 494–95.

28 Y. T. Wu, "Guanyu guance zongjiao zhengce de yixie wenti" 關於觀測宗教政策的一些問題 in *Wu Yaozong wenxuan*, ed., China Three-self Patriotic Movement Committee (Shanghai: TSPM Press, 2010), 380.

for foreign relations.[29] For both Wu and Ding, their encounters with communists shaped their theological reconciliation with communism.

Besides these personal connections, institutional channels helped build up relationships with the CPC. Both Wu and Ding trained at Union Theological Seminary in New York; both served in the progressive Student Department of the YMCA. Influenced by the social gospel movement and the national salvation movement, it was not difficult for them to connect with communists. The Student and Labor departments of the YMCA were important Christian organizations that connected Wu Yaozong with the CPC. He also collaborated with the CPC through national salvation movement organizations such as the Fushe (Revival Society) and Jiuguo Hui (National Salvation Association). As a leader in the Student Department of the YMCA, Ding also had the opportunity to meet with left-wing students. Due to the repression from the GMD and foreign authorities in the concession areas, the Communist Party in Shanghai had operated underground from the 1920s to the 1940s. In order to influence students and workers, the underground CPC had penetrated universities, corporations, and Christian institutions so as to find some fellow travelers. Among these, St. Peter's Church and St. John's University were two cardinal platforms for connecting with the CPC and well-known "red" institutions.[30] St. Peter's Church was an important venue in the history of communist–Christianity encounter, and many progressive leaders came from this church. Rev. Dong Jianwu 董健吾 and Rev. Pu Huaren 浦化人 even joined the CPC. St. John's University was also a hotbed of radical students.[31] The CPC not only used these institutions as

---

29 Both Gong Pusheng (龔普生 1913–2007) and Gong Peng (龔澎 1914–1970) were Zhou's secretaries. Both graduated from Yenching University (a mission-founded institute) and joined the CPC in the 1930s.

30 For more information about these two institutions' connection with the CPC, see Chin Kenpa, *Hongxing yu shizijia: zhongguo gongchandang de jidujiao youren* 紅星與十字架：中國共產黨的基督教友人 [Red Star and the Cross: CPC's Christian Friends] (Taiwan: Zhuliu Chubanshe, 2020), 79–112. In his memorial essay to Zhao Fushan, Wu Zongsu provides an important clue on crossover activity: Zhao, a left-wing TSPM leader, shifted from his anti-Japanese and anti-Chiang Kai-Shek position to join the Communist revolution during studies at St. John's University. See Wu Zongsu, "Luohua youyi, liushui wuqing" 落花有意流水無情 [While the falling flowers have great passion, the heartless brooks were ruthless] in *Da shidai de zongjiao xinyang*, 562.

31 According to Edward Yihua Xu's research, there was an underground organization established at St. John's by the CPC in 1938. In 1946, there were more than one hundred CPC members at St. John's University. For more detail, see Edward Yihua Xu, "Religion and education: St. John's University as an evangelizing agency" (Ph.D. diss., Princeton University, 1994), 178–82.

a shield to protect their comrades amidst the repression of the GMD, but also exploited them as secure platforms to promote patriotic and democratic activities. Through such collaboration, both Wu and Ding developed some sense of comradeship with communists, reinforcing their belief that there was common ground between Christianity and communism.

The constantly changing relations between communism and Christianity encouraged an attitude shift among some progressive Christians. Wu's attitude toward communism moved from antagonism to sympathy and then to admiration.[32] This change was accompanied by a theological turn: from pacifism to a limited synthesis of communism and Christianity (in the social gospel).[33] Wu maintained that communists had educated him.[34] Ding also acknowledged that his attitude toward communism had shifted from blind animosity to respect.[35] Admiration and congenial feelings thus motivated their reconciliation of Christianity and communism.

The Origin and Nature of the Reconciliation Projects

Before diving into their theological reasoning, we need to first examine the nature of the reconciliation projects. The tensions between communism and Christianity were great: most missionaries, pastors, and Christian intellectuals considered them to be incompatible, with great divides in the binaries of atheism vs. theism, God-centered vs. human-centered, militant vs. peaceful, political vs. spiritual, earthly utopia vs. heavenly kingdom. Most Christians at the time considered communism a challenger to religion. If reconciliation was just one option in the early twentieth century, it had become an urgent task for the survival of Christianity in the new China, as the CPC compelled the churches to adjust Christianity to the new reality. If Christianity and communism shared common ground, and had established

---

32　For more information about Wu's left turn, see Ying Fuk-tsang, "Y. T. Wu's life, thought and times," *Heian yu guangming*, xii–lix; Zhong Zhifeng, "When Religious Freedom Was under Attack: A Study of Four Christians' Responses in Modern China," in *Human Dignity, Human Rights, and Social Justice*, ed. Xie Zhibing et al. (Springer, 2020), 59–61.

33　Although Wu embraced communism, he did not give up the idea that Christianity transcended communism. He believed Communism a useful tool to diagnose the contemporary situation and expel the invaders, while Christianity remained a better solution to the problem.

34　Wu, "Gongchandang jiaoyu le wo 共產黨教育了我 [The Communist Party Educated Me]," in *Wu Yaozong wenxuan*, 255–59.

35　K. H. Ting, "Forerunner Y. T. Wu," in *Love Never Ends*, ed., Janice Wickeri (Nanjing: Yilin Press, 2000), 75.

points of collaboration in the past, how could they be reconciled theoretically in the new era?

Neither Wu nor Ding were opportunists. Their efforts to reconcile communism and Christianity were not primarily the outcome of irresistible external pressure. Both were, rather, sincere Christians who believed in the common ground between these contentious entities, and neither changed their beliefs over time. (This was confirmed by the CPC: at Wu's memorial service held in 1979, for example, Zhang Chengzhong, the director of Shanghai's United Front Work Department praised Wu's unswerving loyalty despite many political hardships.[36]). There was a dual aspect to the reconciliation project: both to prove their patriotism to the CPC and to prove the authenticity of the TSPM to conservative Christians. Both Wu and Ding needed to convince the communists that a reformed Protestantism was compatible with socialist society and convince the CPC that Christians were patriotic and could benefit the regime. They needed to downplay the differences between communism and Christianity, and to articulate the ideological resonances with Christianity.

There were internal tensions too. Tension was greater between the CPC and conservative Christians, since the CPC disliked autonomous Christian groups operating outside of the sanctioned TSPM. In the 1950s, Christianity was not only divided into many denominations but also divided along modernist/fundamentalist lines, which the CPC considered to be an obstacle to its unified leadership. During the Reform Era (1978–), the CPC regarded conservative theology as unsuitable for a socialist society. Therefore, in order to be reconciled with communism, Wu and Ding also needed to integrate the conservatives into the TSPM, and transform their theology—but this would need the understanding and cooperation of conservatives. They also needed to convince them that the TSPM's political campaign was compatible with Christian faith and would be good for the church in the long run. This in return required reconciliation between modernists and fundamentalists, a topic beyond the scope of this essay.

---

36 Zhang Chengzong, "Zhang Chengzong tongzhi zai Wu Yaozong xiansheng zhuidaohui shang suo zhi de daoci [Speech Delivered in Wu Yaozong's Memorial Service]," in *Huiyi wu yaozong xiansheng*, ed., China Three-Self Patriotic Movement Committee (Shanghai: TSPM Press, 1982), 4.

Reformulating the Concept of God
to Accommodate Communism

The doctrine of God is a cardinal component of Christian theology. The tension between communism and Christianity begins with the very concept of God, in atheism versus theism. Both Wu and Ding reformulated the idea of God to accommodate communism. Wu reduced God to an objective force in the universe and portrayed Jesus Christ as a revolutionary.[37] Ding used the analogy of a mother to portray God, eliminating God's anger and punishment.[38]

In the 1940s, Wu published *No One Has Ever Seen God*, an attempt to reconcile Christianity and materialism. The main thesis of the book is that both communists and Christians evidence strong faith and devote their lives to truth, and that the idea of an immanent yet invisible God is very similar to the idea of universal law cherished by the communists. Borrowing from Spinoza, Wu argued that from a horizontal perspective, the eternal will of God was the same as the universal law of the universe. He maintained that there was no conflict between belief in God and materialism, because Christians also believe that "all things in the universe exist objectively and are knowable and can be experienced by scientific methods."[39] He pointed out their similarities:

Although it [revolutionary belief] seems to be quite different from that of a religious person, they are the same. For both of them believe that there is a force in the universe to shape history and guide life according to certain rules. This power, whether we call it God or dialectics, has the same effect on life.[40]

Facing criticism from communists, Wu also adjusted his idea of Jesus. In the past Wu held that Jesus was someone of great personality, whose most prominent attribute was love.[41] In 1946, Wu received a letter from a reader of *Tianfeng* lamenting that Christianity used to be a proletarian movement, and Jesus

---

37 Wu Yaozong, "Wo suo renshi de yesu 我所認識的耶穌 [The Jesus I Know]," in ed., Ying Fuk-tsang, *Wu Yaozong quanji* [*The Collected Works of Y. T. Wu*] (Hong Kong: Chinese University of Hong Kong Press, 2017), 633.

38 Ting, "The Cosmic Christ," in *Love Never Ends*, 416–18.

39 Wu Yaozong, *Meiyou ren kanjianguo shangdi* 沒有人看見過上帝 in *Wu Yaozong juan*, 85. Translated by the author.

40 Wu, *Meiyou ren kanjianguo shangdi*, 74.

41 Wu, "Wo suo renshi de yesu," *Tonggong* 81–82 (1929).

a revolutionary leader, but later Christianity separated from the proletariat and became a tool of rulers. In his reply, Wu confirmed that Jesus was a revolutionary, although he also pointed out that his revolution was both political and religious.[42] Looking at Jesus through the filter of (social) class, Wu Yaozong stressed that Jesus had only love and pity for the masses, but only hatred for his enemies.[43]

Wu's formulations of God and Jesus were quite different from conventional doctrine of God and Christ. In fact, when publishing his essay "Christianity and Materialism: A Christian's Confession," his communist editor pointed out it was "a concession to materialism" and "a revision of Christian doctrines."[44] Wu understood that such a synthesis would be treated as an absurd heresy by both orthodox materialists and orthodox Christians.[45] Although the communist editor praised his courageous efforts in his editorial, he was dissatisfied with the reconciliation, dismissing it as metaphysics and criticizing Wu's evasive and unscientific attitude. The editor argued that although both aimed for the happiness of human beings, they did not share common ground on truth, pointing out that truth was not reconcilable, nor should it be reconciled.[46]

Ding took another approach to reconciling Christianity and communism. For him, the moral goodness of revolutionaries outside the church challenged Christians to re-examine their idea of God and salvation.[47] He used the concept of the cosmic Christ, drawn from Teilhard de Chardin and Alfred North Whitehead, to formulate his idea of God. For him, Wu's method that reduced Jesus to a moral model and a social reformer, and the self-isolation of conservative Christians, were both counterproductive because they both drove believers away

---

42 Wu Yaozong, "Yesu shibai le ma" 耶穌失敗了嗎 [Did Jesus Fail]?" *Tianfeng* 55 (1947): 10–11.

43 Wu Yaozong, "Wo yijing shengguo shijie: zhanwang 1948" 我已經勝過世界： 展望 1948 [I have surpassed the world: looking forward to 1948]," *Tianfeng* 105 (1948): 7. Wu also mentioned the CPC had changed his understanding of Jesus's teaching on loving one's enemies. See Wu, "Gongchandang jiaoyu le wo" 共產黨教育了我 in *Wu Yaozong wenxuan*, 255–59.

44 Editorial "Jidujiao yu weiwulun" 基督教與唯物論 *Daxue* 6 (1947): 25. Wu's essay was "Jidujiao yu weiwulun: yige jidutu de zibai."

45 Wu, *Meiyou ren kanjianguo shangdi*, 74.

46 Editorial "Jidujiao yu weiwulun," 25. Li Quan (a pseudo-Christian, most likely a communist) also wrote a lengthy comment on Wu's confession, restating that Christianity and Materialism were not reconcilable. See Li Yaoquan, "Jidujiao yu weiwulun: lingwai yige jidutu de yijian 基督教與唯物論： 另外一個基督徒的意見 [Christianity and Materialism: Opinion from Another Christian]," *Tianfeng* 106 (1948): 4–8.

47 Ting, "The Cosmic Christ," in *Love Never Ends*, 409; Ting, "Talk at a Theological Forum," in *Love Never Ends*, 513–15.

from the church.[48] Ding wanted to find a new way to adjust to communism. He believed the concept of the cosmic Christ was a better solution and argued that it emphasized the following two aspects:

> (1) the universal extent of Christ's domain, concern and care, and (2) the kind of love which we get a taste of in Jesus Christ as we read the Gospels being the first and supreme attribute of God and basic to the structure and dynamic of the universe, in the light of which we get an insight as to how things go in the world.[49]

In other words, God not only cares about believers but also non-believers. Further, God is the cosmic lover rather than a cosmic tyrant or punisher, whose love extends to atheists.[50] Ding used Catholic theologian Karl Rahner's idea of an "anonymous Christian" to incorporate many communist moral models in his writing (such as the communist hero Lei Feng).[51] He also used the image of a mother instead of father to describe God.[52] These sorts of moves eased the tensions between communism and Christianity, since the cosmic lover did not condemn the communists merely on account of their nonbelief and accepted that atheists could also be anonymous Christians.

There are subtle differences between Wu and Ding's reformulations. Although both recognize universal love as one important attribute of God, their treatments of Jesus are quite different. Wu paid more attention to Jesus's humanity while Ding emphasized Jesus's divinity. Wu paid more attention to God's justice and portrayed Jesus as a moral prophet, while Ding emphasized God's love and portrayed Jesus as a priest who interceded for others.

Reconstructing the Church to Adapt to the Socialist State

It is not difficult to understand why a religion entangled with feudalism, capitalism, and imperialism faced trouble in the New China. Internal reform was

---

48 Ting, "The Cosmic Christ," in *Love Never Ends*, 409–10.

49 Ting, "Cosmic Christ," in *Love Never Ends*, 411.

50 Ting, "God's Love Extends to the Atheists." In *God Is Love*, 171–77.

51 Ding Guangxun, "Zenyang kandai jidujiaohui yiwai de zhenshanmei?" 怎樣看待基督教會以外的真善美 [How to View truth, goodness and beauty outside the church?], 252–53.

52 Ting, "The Cosmic Christ," in *Love Never Ends*, 416–17. The idea of a maternal God is also in Ting, "Womanhood, Motherhood, Divinity," in *Love Never Ends*, 259–62.

necessary to adjust to the new reality. The TSPM can be seen as a movement to reconstruct the church in order to show its merits to the state, and ensure its toleration.[53] However, given its controversial political nature, Wu and Ding needed to legitimize the movement by adding a theological rationale, though with differing tactics. They tried to convince their Christian audiences of biblical examples of self-reform movements, and that the painful process of self-denial during the reconstruction campaign would lead to a bright future to the church. Both Wu and Ding gave many speeches on the theological foundation of the TSPM. In this section, I will compare their different approaches to reconstructing the church in terms of reconciling communism and Christianity.

Wu's Reform Ideas

Wu's ideas on church reform can be found in his anthology *Darkness and Light*, and in particular in the essays "Christianity's Mission" (基督教的使命), "Christianity and Contemporary China" (基督教與今日中國), "The Tragedy of Christianity in Our Time" (基督教的時代悲劇), "The Reform of Christianity" (基督教的改造) and "Christianity under the People's Democratic Dictatorship" (人民民主專政下的基督教).[54] Wu's ideas of church reform were also articulated in another important essay published in 1950, where he systematically examined the context, rationale, and method of self-reform.[55]

For Wu, self-reform was necessary due to the miserable reality of the church, which had become a "reactionary" force, polluted by capitalism and imperialism. He pointed out the tragedy of Christianity:

In the past hundred years, it has unconsciously become a conservative force. Furthermore, in the present world, it degraded even further into a reactionary force. . . . Christianity did not use its prophetic spirit to protest. Rather, it united itself with the reactionary project.[56]

---

53 For more detail on the TSPM, see Daniel Bays, *A New History of Christianity in China* (Oxford: Wiley-Blackwell, 2012), 158–82; Leung and Ying, *Wushi niandai sanzi yundong yanjiu.*

54 Wu Yaozong, *Heian yu guangming* 黑暗與光明 [Darkness and Light], ed., Ying Fuk-tsang (Taiwang: Huaxuan chubanshe, 2012), 32–37, 41–43, 218–26, 279–87, 314–28.

55 Wu, "Zhankai jidujiao gexin yundong de qizhi" 展開基督教革新運動的旗幟 [Unfurl the Banner of the Christian Reform Movement] in *Wu Yaozong wenxuan*, 219–34.

56 Wu, "Jidujiao de shidaibeiju" 基督教的時代悲劇 in *Wu Yaozong wenxuan*, 157.

Due to this decay and corruption, the Chinese church has "committed many sins," of which Wu summarized seven cardinal ones as follows:

1. Many of the unequal treaties were products of church legal cases (教案).
2. Most Christian messages preached by foreign missionaries were shaped by capitalist ideology.
3. Christian schools established by the churches exhibited an imperialist, anesthetizing, enslaving tendency.
4. In turbulent times, most Christian leaders and scholars in various countries had taken an ambivalent attitude toward the revolution, and even defended the status quo.
5. Although the church in China is nominally independent at present, it is still directly or indirectly influenced and controlled by Western missionary societies.
6. Much of the gospel preached by the church is no longer the revolutionary gospel of Jesus that aims to emancipate humankind, but the gospel of personal salvation with anesthetizing elements, the icing on the cake that gives the bourgeoisie and the leisured classes a little emotional warmth and comfort. This gospel has been separated from the working masses.
7. The church cannot offer a way out for suffering human beings. Even if it does some charitable work, this is just a kind of reformist method that is not helpful and brings little change to the world.[57]

For Wu, the church had degraded herself and become "the dregs of the times" despised by the people. Therefore, under the People's democratic dictatorship, this corrupted Christianity must repent and reform, otherwise it would not be tolerated by the new regime. For Wu, the only way forward for Christianity was for it to "join in the current of the times and cooperate with it to fulfill the mission of the times."[58] He laid out the main tasks of reform: to decouple from capitalism and imperialism, become an independent Chinese church, repent and let the old body die and new life come; throw itself into the fight against imperialism and exploitation, and build a new China.[59] Wu argued that such self-directed reform was not only based on political necessity but was also in accord with

---

57 Wu, "Jidujiao de gaizao" 基督教的改造 in *Wu Yaozong wenxuan*, 167–73.

58 Wu, "Renmin minzhuzhuanzhengxia de jidujiao" 人民民主專政下的基督教 in *Wu Yaozong wenxuan*, 193.

59 Wu, "Jidujiao de gaizao," 170–71.

biblical teachings and Christian traditions. Wu used Jesus's example of cleansing the temple to justify his reform campaign, pointing out that "Christianity had always protested against Roman hegemony, the church's corruption and dictatorship, slavery and the indifference and cruelty of modern industry."[60]

For Wu, Jesus was a revolutionary prophet who tried to restore a corrupted religion to purity. Wu tried to argue that both Jesus and communists shared a revolutionary zeal, and were eager to turn a corrupted world into paradise on earth. He maintained that "only progressive, revolutionary Christianity can truly represent Jesus Christ's spirit. Christianity's contemporary mission is to turn a world which enslaves people and treats them as tools into a world which fully respects the value of humanity, where there will be no division or war due to conflicting interests and class stratification."[61] Although many Christians worried about the fate of Christianity under a democratic dictatorship, Wu believed that the hardship was temporary, for a purified church would be compatible with communism. He maintained that:

> Christianity is a religion that cherishes love. The meaning of love is to respect each individual's personality, get rid of all things that restrict humanity and enable it to develop freely. This love is completely consistent with the current trend of "emancipation (解放)" and "deliverance (翻身)."[62]

For Wu, the Communists' mission to emancipate human beings was also a work of supreme love. He believed that after a baptism of fire, the church would be redeemed and resurrected, and the common ground between Christianity and communism would be strengthened.

Ding's Reform Ideas

The radicalization of the CPC following a series of political campaigns in the 1950s and 1960s prevented Wu from realizing his vision of the Chinese church in the Maoist era.[63] Only after the Cultural Revolution could the church reinstate

---

60 Wu, "Jidujiao de shiming," 110.

61 Wu, "Jidujiao de shiming," 109. Translated by the author.

62 Wu, "Renmin minzhu zhuanzheng xia de jidujiao," 189.

63 In the final report of the second national conference of TSPM, Wu laid out the "Three Witnesses and Ten Tasks" of the TSPM. See Wu, "Guanyu Zhongguo jidujiao sanzi aiguo yundong de baogao" 關於中國基督教三自愛國運動的報告 [Report on the Chinese Christian TSPM] in *Wu Yaozong wenxuan*, 360–74.

herself, when churches were reopened and TSPM organizations reinstated. The torch had been passed on to Ding, now the leading figure charged with restoring the church. Ding tried to continue and advance Wu's project of reconciliation in the new circumstances.

Echoing Wu, Ding maintained that the TSPM was not only a political necessity but was also in accord with the Bible and church history,[64] and had far-reaching "practical, historical and ultimate significance."[65] He articulated the rationale of the TSPM in a speech delivered at Doshisha University in 1984, commending its inculturation principles as the means by which Christianity had transformed from a Jewish sect to a world religion and the way the Chinese church could achieve catholicity, arguing that the Bible also supported the TSPM and its core spirit of patriotism.[66] Yet, the radical campaigns that the TSPM participated in (such as the Denunciation Campaign from 1951 to 1954) and their deleterious results severely undermined the reputation of the institution. In the Reform Era, Ding needed to reinstate the organization and also restore its legitimacy. At the third National Conference of the TSPM held in Nanjing in 1980, Ding delivered an opening speech setting the tone for the future development of the TSPM. He stated that while it had made great achievements, its mission was not yet over and the church should not only be self-governed but also be run well.[67] On the 45th anniversary of the TSPM in 1995, Ding summarized the seven great achievements of the organization:

1. It has raised the patriotic consciousness of believers so that they can love their country and join in the socialist construction.
2. It has basically accomplished independence, self-government, self-support, and self-propagation so that after the Cultural Revolution, we have been able to run the church well.
3. It has improved the image of Christianity.
4. It has promoted concord and harmony among denominations.
5. It has offered a model of independence and self-government for Christians in the Third World.

---

64 Ting, "Unchanging Faith, Evolving Theology," in *God is Love*, 449–50.
65 Ding Guangxun, "Sanzi zai renshi" 三自再認識 [Another Look at the Three-Self] in *Ding Guangxun wenji*, 322. This sentence was deleted in the English version.
66 Ting, "Why the Three-Self Movement," in *God is Love*, 398–409.
67 K. H. Ting, "Retrospect and Prospect," in *Love Never Ends*, 293.

6. It has exposed colonialists and imperialists' use of evangelism in their invasion of China.
7. It has raised the status of the Chinese church in the global Christian community.[68]

Ding's theological reflections on Christianity and communism can be found in English in various editions of *The Selected Works of K. H. Ting* and essays published in the *Chinese Theological Review*. In his speeches on the legacy and future of the TSPM, he tried to shift its center of gravity from the political to the religious. When Ding declared the TSPM had achieved great success, the implication of this statement was that it needed to go beyond its historical heritage. At the third national conference of the TSPM in 1980, Ding made some important remarks summarizing the legacy and contemporary mission of the TSPM:

With respect to the church, the main question which the TSPM asks is: Who should run the Chinese church? The answer is quite clear: it must be self-run; Chinese Christians ourselves have to take over its management. Once this question has been settled, we are faced with a second: How can we make it a well-run church, that is, how shall we build up the body of Christ? The emphasis in self-governing, self-supporting and self-propagating is on the "self"; this means ourselves. Now we must go one step further. The church must be well-governed, well-supported, and do the work of propagation well.[69]

In this same speech, he also proposed a new analogy: the TSPM and China Christian Council (CCC) as scaffolding—a support framework for church work. Since then, "from Three-Self to Three-Well (从三自到三好)" has become the leading slogan of the TSPM. Ding's initiatives on reordering the relationship between the TSPM and the church, and separating out the religious function and the political function of the TSPM by establishing the China Christian Council to operate as the ecclesial wing of the church,[70] and safeguarding

---

68 Ting, "Running the Church Well," in *Love Never Ends*, 410.

69 Ting, "Retrospect and Prospect," in *Love Never Ends*, 64.

70 Ting, "Three-self and the church: Re-ordering the Relationship," in *Love Never Ends*, 339–47.

religious freedom through religious legislation, were important aspects of the policy of "running the church well."[71]

In the late 1980s and early 1990s, Ding even maintained the hope of getting rid of the scaffolding in due course, if the TSPM should become an obstacle to running the church well.[72] However, the shifting political situation changed the direction of the TSPM, and the Tiananmen Incident in 1989 led to the tightening of religious regulation. Legislation on the protection of religious freedom proposed by Ding and Zhao Puchu (then President of the China Buddhist Association) was halted, and Document 6, issued by the Central Committee of the CPC and the State Council in 1991, set a new direction in the regulation of religions. In the 1990s, a number of religious cults flourished, as natural disasters and social anomie increased. As a result, the CPC pressured all religions to actively adapt to socialist society. In 1993, Jiang Zemin, the then General Secretary of the CPC, laid out three guiding principles of religious administration at the National Conference of the United Front, including to "actively guide religion to adapt to socialist society." In 1998, the task of adaptation became more urgent, as flooding in 1996 and 1998 triggered end-time prophecies among conservative Christians, and the regime was nervous about the threat of sectarian and popular religious movements such as the Shouters or Falun Gong, with renewed calls from Jiang Zemin for the active adaptation of religions. Thus, retuning theology to adjust to the new reality became the central task of the TSPM, and the basis for the Theological Reconstruction Movement (神學思想建設運動).

For Ding, who instituted this new movement, theological reconstruction was necessary firstly "for the survival and witness of the church."[73] Without such reconstruction, the church would begin to resemble Falun Gong or other cults banned by the state and would have no future.[74] Yet, society had also changed. The church needed to keep pace with the times. As the CPC updated its ideology with a new focus on the "Three-representatives" (三個代表思想),[75] and

---

71 Ting, "Religious Liberty in China: My Perspective," in *God is Love*, 550–61.

72 Wickeri, *Restructuring Christianity in China*, 270–71.

73 K. H. Ting, "Adjustments in Theology are Necessary and Unavoidable," *Chinese Theological Review* 17 (2001): 122.

74 K. H. Ting, "Theology and Context: Speech on the 50th Anniversary of the Three-Self Patriotic Movement of the Protestant Churches in China," *Chinese Theological Review* 17 (2001): 127.

75 Ed. note: formally written into the Party constitution in 2002, the Three Represents or Three Representatives indicate the representative leadership of the Party in economic production, cultural progress, and the fundamental interests of the masses.

Western churches updated their theology, the Chinese church also needed to update, and, in Ding's words, "to raise our level to that of our culture and intellectual circles."[76]

In analyzing Ding's reconciliation project, we need to take both the religious and political dimensions into consideration. For example, his "downplaying justification by faith" and mention of a "Cosmic Christ" spoke both to the CPC and the conservative Christians. For the CPC, these moves downplayed the gap between believers and nonbelievers, and brought unity to the body politic. Ding tried to convince conservative Christians that the move could bring more space for the development of Christianity and offer a witness of unity to the people. As for emphasizing the moral dimension of Christianity, although some dismissed it as another version of the social gospel, it was intended to demonstrate the usefulness of Christianity in the construction of a "spiritual civilization" (精神文明建設), another key government aim. This in return would earn more space for both liberal and conservative Christians. "Downplaying justification by faith" was a necessary step toward theological reconstruction for Ding, who worried that emphasizing justification by faith would damage the unity between believers and nonbelievers, and foster a tendency of denying morality.[77] By downplaying this doctrine, Ding aimed to bring nonbelievers to God's universal love and enable Christianity to better contribute to socialist China's construction of spiritual civilization.

By launching the Theological Reconstruction campaign, however, Ding veered away from his previous approach of mutual respect that tolerated the house churches and allowed both the modernist and the conservative theologies to coexist in his Nanjing Union Theological Seminary, which in the end undermined the campaign. He had wanted to use the campaign to challenge and transform a conservative but sectarian Christianity. Although Ding tried to argue that Theology Reconstruction did not aim to change the basics of faith, conservatives did not view it this way. For Christians who held high the slogan *sola fide*, downplaying justification by faith amounted to heresy. Although Ding did not intend to replace "justification by faith" with "justification by love," his opponents claimed this was the underlying intention. The campaign triggered much controversy, with opposition from both the left and right.

---

76 Ting, "Theology and Context," 127.

77 Ting, "On a Profound Christian Question," in *Love Never Ends*, 507–10; K. H. Ting, "Old Style Theological Thinking Needs Revision and Renewal," *Chinese Theological Review* 17 (1998): 22.

If we compare Wu and Ding's efforts and results: both attempted in word and deed to reconcile Christianity and communism. Wu's main interventions included establishing patriotic organizations to fight against the Japanese and the GMD and to rescue democratic comrades in danger; hosting democracy seminars, publishing a series of *Tracts of the Times*, and launching the TSPM by publishing the Three-Self Manifesto and building up the organization. Ding's project covered two quite different periods: the Maoist era and the Reform and Opening Up era. In the earlier period, Ding joined in the counter-revolution campaign, publishing a denunciation essay to criticize Wang Mingdao, and amalgamating the smaller seminaries into Nanjing within a reformulated Nanjing Union Theological Seminary.[78] In the Reform Era, Ding tried to rebuild the church, make room for religious freedom, and reconstruct the church to make it fit for a socialist society. In this period, his main efforts include restarting the TSPM, engaging in religious diplomacy, and launching the Theological Reconstruction campaign.[79]

Although the political atmosphere in the current Reform Era has been much friendlier toward the church, there is still tension between Christianity and communism. What should the main goal of religious legislation be: protecting religious freedom or strengthening religious regulation? and where should priorities lie: adhering to TSPM principles or running the church well? Some criticized Ding for the political tenor of his theological reconstruction and his evenhanded approach to religious legislation—but such critiques were often made out of context. Apoliticism was the cardinal sin of charismatic and separatist Christians in the 1950s. How could we expect the political leader (or spokesperson) of the TSPM to be apolitical? We should also be cautious when using Three-Self as a label for Wu's project and Three-Well for Ding's endeavor, since these two interrelate. For Wu, Three-Self is a path toward running the church well. He argued that there were ten tasks to labor at in order to run the church well, and one of them was to advance theology.[80] For Ding, running the church well came under the principle of Three-Self.

---

78 Ding Guangxun, "Zhenggao Wang mingdao" [Warning Wang Mingdao] *Tianfeng* 477–78 (1955): 16–20.

79 For more details, see Wickeri, *Reconstructing Christianity in China*, 201–369.

80 The ten tasks are: consolidating unity, building up institutions, forming a self-support committee to achieve self-support; establishing a self-propagation committee to research this issue; publishing more Christian literature; more research on theology, church history, and ministry; training more leaders and preachers; participating in socialist construction, defending the peace of the world; and stimulating the learning of socialism. See Wu Yaozong, "Guanyu zhongguo jidujiao sanzi aiguo yundong de baogao," 371–74.

Under better conditions, Ding had more opportunities to push the pendulum toward the religious side. However, his achievements were limited. In this regard, "a student is not above his teacher."[81]

While Falling Flowers Have Great Passion, the Heartless Brooks Were Ruthless

Wu and Ding were sincere Christians who believed they could bridge the gap between Christianity and communism, and peacefully coexist with more conservative Christians. The belief in common ground between Christianity and communism did not come from a vacuum but was based on personal conversations with high-ranking CPC leaders and past collaboration. Stimulated by this belief, both worked assiduously to reconcile these two contentious entities. However, both were frustrated. From the perspective of the CPC, Christianity remains politically suspect, and Wu and Ding's efforts were rejected by the left, while both were condemned as non-believers (or even heretics) by certain conservatives. As Wickeri points out, Wu's efforts to seek the common ground between Communism and Christianity were rejected by both the left and the right, a conclusion also applicable to Ding.[82]

In a conference held in Hong Kong in 2010, Wu Zongsu (Y. T. Wu's elder son) presented a lengthy paper on his father's life and legacy. The title of his paper was "While falling flowers have great passion, the heartless brooks were ruthless (落花有意, 流水無情)." He clarified the meaning of the title as follows:

> "Having great passion" refers to my father's wishful belief, without any reservations, in the socialist system and the Party, and his consistent, uncomplaining, support for all of the CPC's policies.
>
> "Ruthless" refers to the tragic result: the torrent of revolution had broken down the Chinese church, and my father in the end was also destroyed by it.[83]

---

81 Matthew 10:24. On many occasions, Ding spoke of Wu as his teacher. See Ting, "Y. T. Wu: A Lasting Influence for Marxism and Christianity," in *God Is Love*, 485–514.

82 Wickeri, *Seeking the Common Ground*, 157–78.

83 Wu, "Luohua youyi, liushui wuqing," 610.

Wu Zongsu lamented that although his father was a thoughtful and idealistic Christian "who bore the burden of saving the country and her people, and stepped onto the socialist path from a Christian position, he was not received by his people, but rejected and protested against by both the left and the right, and by people inside and outside the church."[84] He used the term "tragedy" to conclude his evaluation of his father, echoing Wu's self-evaluation in 1951 when the TSPM was launched. In that assessment, Wu lamented that he was denounced by his Christian colleagues.

> In the past twenty years, due to the influence of communism, I forbore enormous struggle within the Christian community. I was misunderstood, criticized and even attacked by many Christians. With the shift in my social thought, my theological thinking also changed significantly, which elicited much judgment. My thinking was not only condemned as radical but also heretic.[85]

Ding was more fortunate than Wu because he lived through a gentler era; yet his fate was no better. Wu Zongsu's conclusion at his father's reconciliation project is also partly applicable to Ding, and Ding was also condemned by conservative Christians as a nonbeliever and heretic.[86] Due to his tough stance in the Theological Reconstruction Movement, Wang Weifan, for example, (Ding's loyal student and an important evangelical theologian in Nanjing Seminary) also distanced himself from him. Wang believed that downplaying justification by faith was an attack on conservatives and would distort the Reformation basis of Protestantism.[87]

Ding was also challenged and criticized by the left. Had he not been rescued by Zhou Enlai, Ding might have been humiliated by radicals in the 1960s and 1970s.[88] He was interrogated and temporarily removed from public gaze due to

---

84 Wu, "Luohua youyi, liushui wuqing," 611.

85 Wu, "Gongchandang jiaoyu le wo," 259.

86 Li Xinyuan 李信源, *Yige buxinpai de biaoben: ding guangxun wenji pingxi* 一個 "不信派" 的 標本： 《丁光訓文集》 評析 [A Non-believer's Representative: Analysis of the Theology of K. H. Ting], (Deerfield, Ill: Life Press, 2003).

87 Wang Weifan, "Zhuiyi Ding Guangxun zhujiao 追憶丁光訓主教 [Remembering Bishop K.H. Ting]," *The Center for Christian Studies at the Chinese University of Hong Kong Newsletter* 18 (2013): 1–13.

88 Wickeri, *Reconstructing Christianity in China*, 172–75.

his support of the student protests in 1989.[89] Cao Shengjie, a recent president of the China Christian Council, also criticized Ding's Theological Reconstruction movement, lamenting:

> I feel that he was over confident at the end of his life. He rushed to achieve something. It is a pity that some of his speeches did not consider the audiences' response, and deviated from the mutual respect principle he cherished.[90]

Why did projects endeavoring to reconcile communism and Christianity end in this dual rejection? Perhaps the tension is too great to reconcile and their failure resulted from an underestimation of the differences between communism and Christianity. When Wu argued that there was a 99 percent similarity between communism and Christianity, and their minor differences were not important, Zhou Enlai corrected him, emphasizing the differences.[91] As discussed in the previous section, the relationship between communism and Christianity has always been dynamic, and the common ground is contingent on circumstances. As Luo Zhufeng succinctly pointed out, in discussing Wu's attempt at the near-impossible mission of seeking ideological common ground between communism and Christianity:

> Wu tried to connect Christian doctrines to socialist values. For example, he tried to seek common ground between loving others as yourself and the Chinese notion of selfless common good (大公無私). However, there were many obstacles, including significant differences in terms of world view, morality and value systems. In the face of stark reality, these kinds of efforts were suspended.[92]

There was, furthermore, internal tension and politicking over differences between "holding firm to the TSPM principle" (堅持三自原則) and "running

---

89 Wu Zongsu, Foreword, in *Da shidai de xinyang*, xix.

90 Cao Shengjie, *Cao Shengjie koushu lishi* 曹聖潔 口述歷史 [Oral History of Cao Shengjie] (Shanghai: Shanghai shudian chubanshe, 2016), 225.

91 Zhou Enlai, "Guanyu jidujiao wenti de sici tanhua" 關於基督教問題四次談話 [Four conversation on the issues related to Christianity] in *Zhou Enlai tongyi zhanxian wenxuan*, ed., Central Committee of the United Front Work Department of the CPC (Beijing: Renmin chubanshe, 1984), 180–81.

92 Luo Zhufeng, *Huiyi wu yaozong xiansheng*, 204.

the church well."[93] In a period that downplayed ideological purity, it has been much easier to balance the political and the professional. However, the experience of the 1960s and '70s demonstrated that it was almost impossible to simultaneously build up the economy and further the revolution. This is also true for the TSPM. It was difficult to hold to Three-Self principles and run the church well at the same time. When Ding tried to dismantle the scaffolding of the TSPM, he met with strong opposition. In a speech delivered to mark the sixtieth anniversary of the TSPM in 2017, Wang Zuoan, the director of the State Administration of Religious Affairs (SARA), pointed out that the TSPM had many tasks outstanding and a long way to go.[94]

According to Luo Zhufeng, after many ruthless political campaigns, Wu Yaozong ultimately reached the conclusion that it was better to separate Christianity and communism because religious belief and communism were two different value systems that could not be mixed.[95] Ding also gave up the wishful thinking of replacing the TSPM with the CCC. Given this situation, reordering the relationships between the TSPM and the church also has a long way to go.[96] As can be seen, mingling religion with politics is not easy in communist China; it is not easy to serve two masters. The failure to win over the trust and tolerance of the CPC hindered internal Christian unity. The dual tasks of reconciliation proved hard to achieve in tandem.

Conclusion

.How to engage Christianity with communism was a cardinal theme of theological reflection for much of the twentieth century. Based on past collaboration, good relations, and a belief in common ground between Christianity and communism, both Wu Yaozong and Ding Guangxun labored assiduously to harmonize Christianity and communism. These efforts to reconcile Christianity and communism form an important part of the development of Chinese contextual theology.

---

93 Wang Weifan, "Tan banhao jiaohui yu shenxue sixiang jianshe" 談辦好教會與神學思想建設 [On Running the church well and the Theological Reconstruction Movement] in *Shinian juju: Wang Weifan wenji* (Walking Lonely for Ten Years: Selected Works of Wang Weifan) (Hong Kong: Christian Study Center on Chinese Religion and Culture, 2009), 457–65.

94 Wang Zuoan, Speech in the Sixtieth Anniversary of the TSPM, http://www.ccctspm.org/cppccinfo/9684, accessed July 1, 2020.

95 Luo Zhufeng, in *Huiyi wu yaozong xiansheng*, 204.

96 Ting, "Three-self and the Church: Re-ordering the Relationship," in *Love Never Ends*, 339–47.

Facing challenges from communism, both Wu and Ding refashioned their ideas of God to accommodate communism. Wu reduced God to an objective force in the universe and portrayed Jesus Christ as a revolutionary, while Ding used the analogy of a mother to portray God and transformed God into a deity who does not punish. Wu's Jesus as a proletariat revolutionary and Ding's Christ as a cosmic lover were quite different from the conventional teachings on God and Jesus prevailing in the Chinese Christian community. Although both Wu and Ding tailored Christianity to communism, there are subtle differences in their approaches. Wu paid more attention to God's justice and regarded Jesus as a moral prophet, while Ding emphasized God's love and regarded Jesus as a priest who interceded for others. Both sought to reconstruct the church to serve the state. Wu portrayed Jesus as a revolutionary prophet who tried to restore the corrupt church to purity. Following Jesus, Wu also launched the TSPM campaign to clean up a reactionary church. He believed that after a baptism of fire, the church would be redeemed. However the radicalization of CPC in the Maoist era prevented Wu from realizing his vision of the Chinese church. Later, in the Reform Era, Ding reinstated the TSPM and launched the Theological Reconstruction Movement to continue and advance Wu's project. Although he tried to follow the government directive to "run the church well," the belief that Ding advocated "downplaying" justification by faith caused fractious rifts and severely undermined his legacy.

Although the two church leaders took different approaches and undertook their reconciliation projects in quite different political settings, the results of their efforts were similar in that both achieved limited success and were rejected by left and right alike. Both remained controversial. Despite their passion, neither could prevail against the divergent forces of the CPC and conservative Christians—and in this regard, their differences were in degree but not in type. To the present, much tension still exists between Christianity and communism.

Chapter 14

LI ZHIZAO, WANG WEIFAN, AND THE THEOLOGICAL INTERPRETATION OF CHINA'S PAST

Chloë Starr, *Yale University*

Introduction

When the "Xi'an Fu Stele" (or "Nestorian Monument") was unearthed near the city of Xi'an in the 1620s, there was great jubilation among Roman Catholic Chinese and resident Jesuits. The stone stele recorded the (long lost) early history of Christianity in China, documenting events from the arrival of Aluoben, a monk of the Church of the East, in 635 CE, to the time of writing in 781 CE. This great stone monument remains today one of the most important sources on early Chinese Christianity.[1] The joy at the archaeological discovery, carved in classical Chinese with Syriac, stemmed in part from a sense of deep relief at the recognition and belonging it brought to Christians. There is little more Chinese than a huge slab of granite on a turtle back, standing among a forest of lapidary documents. The finely carved calligraphy of a stele is at once aesthetic monument, historic text, and signifier of cultural import. For Ming Christians, newly evangelised by Jesuit missionaries, the stone confirmed the presence of Christians in the Chinese historical record and their welcome under a renowned Tang emperor. It stood as witness to the value placed on history in society, conferring a certain gravitas on Christianity and place in the national record, and seemed to offer proof of God's abiding presence and plan.

1　The stone stele still stands in the Beilin ("Forest of Steles") museum, in Xi'an, China, with an inscription that gives the year according to the Chinese, Persian, and Greek calendars. The exact location and year of its rediscovery (1623 or 1625) are debated.

This essay looks at one of the earliest, and one of the more recent, Chinese interpretations of the Jingjiao stele text, Li Zhizao's (1565–1630) "On Reading the Jingjiao Stele" of 1625 and Wang Weifan's (1927–2015) "Theology of Unceasing Generation" of 1997, to consider how theological method has been shaped by its reading of China's past. Questions of theology, contextualization, and the reading of church texts are too often considered separately. Any attempt to consider theological readings of Jingjiao Christianity[2] by later Chinese shows why the three cannot be separated and points to the notion that for many late imperial and twentieth-century Chinese theologians, theology was a practice of text reading. To date there has been a concentration on archaeological and linguistic studies of Jingjiao material. Together with the academic divide between Syriac studies and contemporary theology, and a popular narrative tracing European use of the "Nestorian Monument,"[3] this has left Chinese theological reflection on the Jingjiao tradition obscured in the stone's shadow. Yet theological reflection on China's Christian past offers a vital reclamation and a decidedly indigenous method.

The reading of China's Christian past offered an important theological opportunity to those sent early rubbings of the stone in the late Ming—as well as a pragmatic one, to petition for imperial translation funds and permissions similar to those afforded to the seventh-century church. Questions of the stele

---

2　景教, literally "Luminous Teaching," i.e., the Church of the East/East Syrian Church, often referred to as "Nestorians" in older Western texts.

3　A recent series of articles in Chinese and English has considered the different histories of the "Nestorian stele" as object, appropriated, translated and relocated, and the "echoes" and "mirrors" it provides for those studying the monument. It is clear that different questions filled the European imagination than inspired Chinese scholarship at points along the way: as Saeki notes, for example, it is a little bizarre that Western scholars of the eighteenth and nineteenth century determined the stone to be "a Jesuit forgery" without having seen the original or being able to read its inscription (see P. Y. Saeki, *The Nestorian Monument in China* (London: SPCK, 1916), 33.) "Meta-studies" of studies of the monument and its text include Michael Keevak's monograph *The Story of a Stele*, which argues that "the stele was always a reflection of European concerns rather than Chinese ones" and Philip Leung's study of stone as physical object, translation, and symbol. See Michael Keevak, *The Story of a Stele: China's Nestorian Monument and Its Reception in the West, 1625–1916* (Hong Kong: Hong Kong University Press, 2008); Leung, Philip Yuen-sang 梁元生, "石頭記——一塊玄碑的幾重故事" [Notes on the stone: stories on a mysterious stele], in 十字蓮花——基督教與中國歷史文化論集 [Cross Lotus—Selected Essays on Chinese Christianity: Historical and Cultural Perspectives] (Hong Kong: Christian Study Centre on Chinese Religion and Culture, 2004), 1–18; Timothy Billings, "Jesuit Fish in Chinese Nets: Athanasius Kircher and the Translation of the Nestorian Tablet," in *Representations* 87 (2004).

are questions of contemporary Christianity: To what degree is acculturation accommodation or syncretization? How should Christian terms be translated into Chinese? The Xi'an text of the eighth century was itself already a history and a historical reading of the church and its theology. In his essay, Li Zhizao engages in comparative theology and reflection on contextualization, as well as commending the stone as a good omen for the dynasty. Several centuries later, the church theologian Wang Weifan reads though the stele text to the Chinese classics it cites. In doing so, he reinscribes the Christian stele into Chinese tradition, and the classics into theological history. The reading of China's classical heritage—of God's presence in the early Chinese textual world—offered a native Chinese Christian history, a challenge to missionary history and to the prevalent narrative of Christianity as a foreign, Western religion. This alternative Chinese Christian history was a theological history, a textual history. Its focus is not the missionary Aluoben but the historian Jingjing (Syriac: Adam), and in particular, how Jingjing drew on earlier, non-Christian Chinese texts for his understanding and representation of God. The role of Chinese culture in theology has long been a prime theological question, but here Wang Weifan, an evangelical Christian, offers a move more usually associated with liberal theology. Wang affirms Chinese pre-Christian culture as a central source of theological reflection—and classical text reading as methodology for "modern" theology.

Graven Wrangling

The last twenty years have seen a resurgence of Jingjiao studies, with new historical, archaeological, and textual research, as well as new academic concentrations and centers devoted to Tang Christian studies. Much of the research has been social scientific, linguistic, or philological, and relatively little has pertained to Jingjiao theology.[4] Growth in scholarship and interest in Jingjiao has coincided with archaeological finds over the centuries. These include the stele text, monastery ruins, and a silk painting, as well as numerous tombstones, tablets,

---

4 As Benoît Vermander writes, "The corpus of academic references to Nestorianism in contemporary Chinese theology is a very limited one," see "The Impact of Nestorianism on Contemporary Chinese Theology," in *Jingjiao: The Church of the East in China and Central Asia*, ed. Roman Malek with Peter Hofrichter (Sankt Augustin: Institut Monumenta Serica, 2006), 181–96. This section draws directly on Chloë Starr, "Jingjing," in *A Reader in Chinese Theology*, ed. and trans. Chloë Starr, 3–8. ©2022. Reprinted with the permission of Baylor University Press. All rights reserved.

and bronze crosses from the Mongol Yuan period.[5] Written sources on Tang Christianity include references to Jingjiao in official Chinese documents; Syriac and Arabic sources, including church synod records; and the "Dunhuang documents." These last brought a second moment of great excitement to the study of early Christianity in China, when several Jingjjiao documents came to light among a cache found in 1907 in caves in Dunhuang, in the northwest of China, including two composed before 638 CE.[6] The documents show how contingent findings and knowledge have been—it was only in 2006, for example, when a Christian funerary pillar from Luoyang dating to 815 CE was discovered, that one of the Dunhuang texts, long considered a forgery, was proven to be original.[7]

The Xi'an stele text begins with an exaltation of God, "our eternal true Lord God, triune and mysterious," and a brief doctrinal section describing God's creation and the human feuding that necessitated the appearance of the Messiah. God and humanity are touched upon in Christ and the church, with brief descriptions of Jesus's life, salvation, the books of the New Testament, and basic rituals of the (Eastern) church. This theological overview is followed by a substantial historical account of the missionary-monk Aluoben's arrival and a transcription of Emperor Taizong's edict of 638, affirming the excellence of the Jingjiao religion and permitting the construction of a church in Chang'an.[8] The summary of Jingjiao history in China over its first hundred and fifty years is threaded through with a laudatory description of imperial benevolence toward the religion, framed within a Confucian worldview, where right rule brings peace and prosperity. A third section of the text starts by praising the donor and benefactor Yisi (Syriac, Yazdbuzid) of the monument, followed by a hymn extolling "the luminous religion" of Jingjiao, a colophon, and a list in Syriac of bishops and monks of the Chinese church.

The language of the stele text is difficult but provides us with important information about the church, the organization of clergy, and details of edicts such as that of 745 CE authorizing the establishment of monasteries in all

---

5 See Nicolas Standaert, ed., *Handbook of Christianity in China Vol One* (Leiden: Brill, 2001), 10–15 and 52–61.

6 For an English translation of the Chinese Nestorian documents (excluding the Xi'an stele), see Li Tang, *A Study of the History of Nestorian Christianity in China and its Literature in Chinese* (Frankfurt: Peter Lang, 2004), 145–204.

7 See Matteo Nicolini-Zani, Hidemi Takehashi, "The Dunhuang *Jingjiao* Documents in Japan: a Report on their Reappearance," in *Winds of Jingjiao*, eds. Li Tang and Dietmar W. Winkler (Wien: LIT Verlag, 2016), 15–26.

8 The original edict of 638 reproduced on the stele is lost, but the *Tang hui yao*, a collection of imperial edicts completed in 961, largely corroborates its accuracy.

prefectures. The style of the text shows its adaptation to a Chinese worldview (in valorizing a particular imperial perspective on history, for example) and to the political context of its day (in its strategic reference to the Syriac patriarch Henanisho II, despite his successor having been consecrated[9]). The inscription makes numerous references to Chinese classics, showing the deep familiarity with Chinese culture of the author, the monk Jingjing. Since the time of the first missionary Aluoben, the language used in Christian texts had evolved—discarding problematic terms such as Buddha *fo* 佛 for God, or a phonetic transcription of "Jesus" *Yishu* 移鼠 that literally meant "get rid of the rat"—but a sizable number of Buddhist and Daoist loanwords were retained, and the stele text draws on a Buddhist inscription for its literary model.[10]

The Jingjiao texts offer one model of inculturation in a multi-religious society, with a particular resonance between contemplative texts across traditions. Their creativity came from having been formed in collaboration with Chinese traditions and scholars, making Jingjiao Christianity "a Chinese synthesis as well as a Nestorian one."[11] This mode of deep cultural exploration through which Chinese Christianity finds its language and self-understanding is picked up by the two essayists Li and Wang.

Li Zhizao and an early Chinese interpretation of Jingjiao

Li Zhizao's (1565–1630) role as high-level patron and mediator with the Ming court for missionaries like Matteo Ricci or Giulio Aleni, and as sponsor and editor of anthologies of Christian texts, gave him an instrumental role in the survival and spread of the early Jesuit mission.[12] Portuguese missionary Álvaro

---

9　See Max Deeg, "An Anachronism in the Stele of Xi'an—Why Henanisho?" in Tang and Winkler, eds., *Winds of Jingjiao*, 243–51. Deeg and others have suggested that this anachronism is not because news had not reached China of the new patriarch, but because Henanisho was a safer name for the memorial, given his successor's contested election and the factional affiliations of priests in China.

10　The model being *Toutuo si bei* 頭陀寺碑 [Stele Inscription of Dhûta Monastery] composed by Wang Jin (d. 505), and found in the *Wenxuan*, see Paul Pelliot, *L'inscription nestorienne de Si-ngan-fou*, ed. Antonino Forte (Paris: Collège de France, 1996), 189, and extensive explanation by Forte, 473–81.

11　Vermander, "The Impact of Nestorianism on Contemporary Chinese Theology," 193.

12　For biographical details, see Arthur W. Hummel, ed. *Eminent Chinese of the Ch'ing Period* (Washington, DC: United States Government Printing Service, 1943), 452–54. The

Semedo wrote in 1645 that hardly one "of the fifty works which the Fathers have translated into the Chinese tongue, both of Divinitie and other Sciences" had not passed through Li's hands, as he edited, helped correct and revise texts, and composed prefaces or prologues to ensure the books were received as valued writings among Chinese literati.[13] Li was extremely well read in Roman Catholic thought as it existed in translation and personally contributed to the development of that thought in Chinese.

Li, who obtained his *jinshi* degree in 1598, was also a rare science enthusiast among scholars and developed close friendships with several missionaries, including Ricci and Giulio Aleni, begun through collaboration on scientific translations. He memorialized the emperor several times, including in 1610, 1613, and 1621 over matters concerning missionaries, from the question of burial plots to scientific translations to issues of state security, and was visionary in seeing the potential use of western scientific and technical instruments for the Chinese state, and in persuading more skeptical Chinese officials, arguing that Jesuits should be employed to translate Western calendrical and scientific texts. In 1610, a little before Ricci's death, Li Zhizao was baptized by him (taking the name Leon/Leo), and subsequently devoted much time to the Christian cause.

During a second period of retirement in the mid-1620s, Li used his retreat from political life to write prolifically. He composed prefaces, such as one for a work of geography by Diego de Pantoja, he translated texts, such as Aristotle's *De caelo et mundo* together with Francisco Furtado, and wrote pieces such as his response to the "Nestorian Stele," "On Reading the Jingjiao Stele." Li would go on and publish in 1629 the first major anthology of missionary and Chinese Christian writings, the *Tianxue chuhan* (天學初函 First Collection of Works on Heavenly Studies). The breadth of works included in "Heavenly Studies" (such as hydraulics, geometry, astronomy, and trigonometry) shows how the pursuit of science was, for Li as for his Jesuit confrères, at one with the pursuit of God.[14]

---

introductory paragraphs in this section draw directly on Chloë Starr, "Li Zhizao," *A Reader in Chinese Theology*, ed. and trans. Chloë Starr, 65–67. ©2022. Reprinted with the permission of Baylor University Press. All rights reserved.

13 Semedo's 1645 text was published in English in 1655 under the title *The history of that great and renowned monarchy of China. Wherein all the particular provinces are accurately described . . .* Passage quoted in Chen Min-Sun, "T'ien-Hsüeh Ch'u-Han and Hsi-Hsüeh Fan: the Common Bond between Li Chih-Tsao and Giulio Aleni," in Lipiello and Malek, eds., *Scholar from the West: Giulio Aleni S. J. and the Dialogue between Christianity and China* (Sankt Augustin: Monumenta Serica Institut, 1997).

14 On the Jesuit curriculum that progressed to theology via philosophy, physics, geometry, and astronomy see e.g., Gianni Criveller, *Preaching Christ in Late Ming China* (Taipei: Ricci

Li Zhizao's 1625 essay on the monument provides as near to a pristine Ming encounter with Jingjiao Christianity as we can imagine. His contact with the text of the monument predates later philological work, Syriac studies, and the debates on authenticity and inculturation. Yet in this short piece, Li works through a whole series of responses to the stele, from theological to linguistic, textual and aesthetic, through to imperial eulogy and contemporary application. Li was one of the earliest in the Christian community to see a full transcript or rubbing of the text, which came with an accompanying question from his correspondent Zhang Gengyu: "Nobody has heard of this religion before: is it the Heavenly Studies that the Western scholars are propagating?"[15] Li's first approach is to settle the identity question, arguing that the Jingjiao (Church of the East) religion known in China in the Tang and Yuan dynasties was the same religion as Catholicism—a move that led numerous Ming-Qing believers to identify with Jingjiao and claim an older and more authentic-seeming Chinese heritage for their religion.[16]

Li's method of reading the monument text is a form of linguistic eisegesis, interpreting what he reads in light of his own understanding. As he writes, "Where it says "[existing since the] beginning of beginning and without origin; [through] succession of succession yet mysteriously still extant," and speaks of an artisan who opened out heaven and earth, created all things and established the first humans, the true Lord, worshiped first above all divinities—if this were not God, the Lord of Heaven, who could it be?"[17] By the time that Li wrote the introduction to his anthology of Christian writings, he was even more assured of the identification of Jingjiao with Roman Catholicism, and opens that text with the declamation "Heavenly Studies is what used to be called Jingjiao in the Tang."[18]

Institute, 1997). While Li Zhizao may have wanted his readers to ingest a knowledge of God along with their study of western instruments and logic, many of his secular critics among Chinese literati were much less sanguine about the inclusion of "unorthodox doctrines" in such texts and the attempt to teach readers to worship of the Lord of Heaven. See further Min-Sun Chen, "Li Chih-Tsao and the T'ien-Hsüeh Ch'u-Han," in *Echanges culturels et religieux entre la Chine et l'Occident* (San Francisco: Ricci Institute, 1995) 35–44, 41.

15 Tianxue chuhan 天學初函, Peking University Library Edition (Taipei: Xuesheng shuju, 1965).

16 See Min-Sun Chen, "Li Chih-Tsao and the T'ien-Hsüeh Ch'u-Han," 42–43.

17 "所云'先先無元，後後妙有'開天地匠，為萬物立初人，眾聖元尊真主，非天主上帝，疇能當此?"

18 "天學者，唐稱景教."

In his essay, Li proceeds by a method of direct equivalences, explaining phrases for the Trinity or Incarnation by translating them into contemporary Christian theological terms.[19] As Li writes "The 'three-in-one mysterious body' (三一妙身) denotes the Trinity; . . . 'the same as humans he was born' and 'a virgin gave birth to the holy one in the Roman Empire,' mean that the nature of the Lord of Heaven joined with human nature, and he was born from the womb of a Judean virgin, Maria . . . 'When it reached mid-day he ascended to the truth' (亭午升真) refers to Christ, who having successfully completed the work of saving the world and spreading the gospel, at noon ascended on high . . . Today we say 'Deus' where the stele has 'Aluohe [Elohim],' and we say 'great haughty devil' where the stele has 'Satan,' since these were all the language of the ancient scriptures of Judea . . ." Li anticipates future debates, echoing through the works of sinologists and theologians like James Legge by his clear mapping of Tang Buddhist-inflected language onto orthodox Catholic terminology. On the contentious point of "三一分身," for example, which could be read as suggesting two persons in Christ, Li writes unambiguously "where it says 'the three-in-one divided itself' this refers to the *filius* coming down to be born on earth."[20] Li demonstrates an unwavering belief in his own ability to parse Tang Jingjiao and set it against Roman Catholic texts; the expertise is textual as much as theological, but the two are scarcely distinguishable.

Li Zhizao's mapping is not just semantic but geographic, as he also layers the place names of the Jingjiao text onto Biblical lands to strengthen the associations, aligning Da Qin with Judea via the authority of the Tang History.[21] Li selects what is most clear and straightforward in the stele text and foregrounds references to readily known historical figures and places. He re-narrates at length,

---

19 Michael Keevak suggests that "it was not necessarily a simple task to equate an eighth century Sino-Syrian inscription with the doctrines of early modern European (Catholic) Christianity" and the text requires much interpretation (*The Story of a Stele*, 11) but Li, whom Keevak discusses while placing Zhang Gengyu's question into his mouth, seems to have found it relatively straightforward to make these correspondences.

20 On James Legge's ambivalent response (seemingly arguing both ways in different places) as to whether the language of 分身 confirmed or avoided the Nestorian heresy, see Billings, "Jesuit Fish in Chinese Nets," 21.

21 "It does not say "Judea" but "Daqin (the Roman Empire)," and if you examine the *Tang History*, there it says "the country of Fulin, another name of which is Daqin, lies forty thousand *li* to the West of China." If we further consult the *Topographical Map of the Western Oceans*, it also says "The name of the district to the east of Judea's imperial domains is Qin, and the area within the district is approximately the same as it." Alopen and his generation nearly all came from that country, and so that is why it is called "Daqin."

with commentary, the description of the Imperial Edict regarding the establishment of a Jingjiao church and contrasts the reception of foreign believers by Taizong with that of Empress Wu, interweaving externally corroborated history with the stele text. Li's praise of the Tang emperors also acts as commentary on the present, a move he strengthens by linking the "divine founders" of the Ming directly to the cause of Matteo Ricci and the Catholic missionaries. By praising the Tang, Li appeals to the Ming rulers for the same treatment to be extended to the heirs of the Jingjiao monks, the Jesuits. This historic context of the text is as important as the theological message for Li, since the context authenticates that message.

Two of Li Zhizao's observations are particularly astute: one is an intercultural commentary on the fact that the Syrian monks, according to the stele, "preserve the beard to symbolize their outward actions" and "shave the crown to indicate the absence of inward affections,"[22] which Li uses to explain the pre-accommodation faux-pas of Matteo Ricci in taking "the same confused track" and not distinguishing between the religious (monks) and the secular (Confucian scholars). Ricci's mistake, in Li's view, matched exactly the errors of the earlier Christians in China, but imperial graciousness enabled Ricci to see a more inculturated light. A second prescient point is in anticipating the retrieval of other Jingjiao texts and translations from the description of the twenty-seven *jing* (scriptures/classics 經), which were transmitted by the Church of the East. It would be 282 years before some of these were found, secreted among Buddhist texts as Li presaged, in Dunhuang.

For much of his commentary on the Jingjiao monument, Li triangulates between the historic witness of the stele, the authenticity of the message (and its bearers) that it testifies to, and the continuities in the mandate of Heaven and the wisdom of rulers. In this latter Li follows Adam, or Jingjing, the author of the stele, who was "interested in one thing: what kind of relation the emperor has to the new religion from the west."[23] In Jingjing's narrative of history, praise is directed to the series of emperors who favored the new religion, and a direct link is made between their benevolent attitude toward Christianity and the well-being and prosperity of the empire. Li may not have found Jingjing's Tang history wholly credible—but the message of the stele is remarkably germane to his

---

22 Translation from A. Wylie, in Paul Carus, ed., *The Nestorian Monument* (Chicago: Open Court, 1909), 12–13.

23 Jürgen Tubach, "Deuteronomistic Theology in the Text of the Stele of Xi'an," in Malek, ed., *Jingjiao*, 177.

own.[24] Li's main thrust in his essay is the applicable nature of the text and its potential impact on contemporary mission policy, the status of the Christian Dao, and the pressing need for a decision on stock-piled texts awaiting imperial permission for translation. Li's writing here is in line with the capital the Jesuits would make of the stone in due course, and with their delight in the long-awaited artifact and its evidence of God's early providential blessing on China. Li chides those, however, who would make false or misleading textual associations between Christian texts and the Chinese classics, and warns that the stele acts as a tool of judgment, a stone probe or acupuncture needle (砭), enabling accurate comparison. In chastising his own generation of scholars for their narrowmindedness, and relativizing the eminence of Confucius and Mencius, Li pleads for a greater intercultural understanding ("What separates Chinese and barbarian?"[25]).

To parse the Jingjiao memorial and harmonize it with Roman Catholicism, Li draws on all of his textual reading skills, using knowledge of histories and gazetteers, of custom and calligraphy. He has a clear agenda: to shore up the status of the Jesuit missionaries, authenticate their message, bring to light the unknown history of imperial reception of early medieval Christianity, and use this to call for a favorable reception of missionaries and the translation of newly arrived Christian texts. The couching in imperial terms and the laudatory language embeds Christianity in the Chinese state-scape, and Li is keen to present Christianity as a benevolent influence for the nation. It is clear, moreover, that Li feels close to the Jingjiao religion as presented by the text in good part because of shared religious *and textual* preoccupations. It is, we might argue, because the stele reads as a Chinese text, inscribed into the Chinese textual landscape and patterns of transmission, that Li feels as close to the Jingjiao writer as he does to Roman Catholic texts.

Li anticipated the genre and history of reading the "Nestorian stone" as object. He takes note of the physical text, praising the elegance of the language and style of characters, and thereby acclaims it as a Chinese text. But more than this, he suggests the stone brings its own auspicious testimony to Ming rule: "as if awaiting times of peace" in which to appear from the ground. The millennium-old

---

24 For example, he elaborates on the disastrous stretch of the Shengli reign, and Empress Wu's immorality. Tubach suggests that the source for Jingjing's description of history and imperial panegyrics, linking the spread and status of Christianity to the well-being of the empire, is the Deuteronomistic histories, yet we can safely say that for Li Zhizao there is ample precedent in Chinese histories for such a move.

25 "何隔華夷."

stone testifies to the ancient authority of the religion inscribed on it: "Now this elegant and informative text has the seal of the ancient church . . . this teaching has been known from ancient times." The stone could scarcely have advanced his cause more if Li had written the text himself. Li is able to point to the links between the "the bright order of the Supreme Ruler of Heaven" and protecting sages so that "frontier passes shall be no hindrance to them" to make strategic suggestions about treatment of the Jesuit missionaries. Moreover, the elision of Jingjiao and Catholicism allows broad claims to be made about Christianity; in the introduction to the *Tianxue chuhan* collection, Li writes "It has been called the earliest, the truest and the most widespread religion: even if the sages were to arise again, they would not change it. Our sacred and divine imperial dynasty has inherited it" allowing the historically-verified religion to resonate with the earliest Chinese philosopher-sages.

In his article "Towards a New Translation of the Chinese Nestorian Documents from the Tang Dynasty," Max Deeg argues that twentieth-century translators of the stele text, including P. Saeki, A. Moule, Chiu, Li Tang, and Martin Palmer are all "more or less guilty" of Christianizing the translation.[26] The problem lies, Deeg suggests, in "identifying Christian terms in texts without sound philological reasoning and foundation" and a shallow understanding of Daoist and Buddhist terminology. This ties in with Keevak's and others claims that the Jesuits were "never able to see that it was fundamentally different from themselves."[27] Yet it would be difficult to fault a reader like Li Zhizao for a weak philology or lack of appreciation of Buddhist or Daoist terms. Both Li and Wang Weifan challenge Deeg's assumption that Chinese texts do not translate quotations from the Jingjiao texts, since both provide extensive translation and comment. The question of translation principles remains, however. Deeg starts out from the questions "Why retranslate?" and "How retranslate?" the stele. As he writes, "Because the documents we are dealing with are supposed to be Christian on the basis of content or terminology, the translation tries to render them in a Christian idiom in the target language even by losing the connotational meaning of the original."[28] A prime example he gives is translation of 三威 as

---

26 Max Deeg, "Towards a New Translation of the Chinese Nestorian Documents from the Tang Dynasty," in ed. Malek with Hofrichter, *Jingjiao: The Church of the East in China and Central Asia*, 117.

27 Keevak, *The Story of a Stele*, 2.

28 Max Deeg, "Towards a New Translation of the Chinese Nestorian Documents from the Tang Dynasty," 120

"Trinity" rather than "Three Majesties" (Deeg translates 景教三威蒙度讚 as "Praise of the true pāramitās of the Three Majesties of the Illustrious teaching"). If Buddhist terms are signifying a Christian reality, should they be translated as if Buddhist? (and in whose conception—the Jingjiao writer, that of the Daoist or Buddhist translator into Chinese, or a Chinese or Syriac Christian reader of the day?).

Li Zhizao, for whom the text represents a known concept in an archaic terminology, has no hesitation in claiming that the elements of Christian ritual and history "all tally with the practices and procedures that Mr Ricci has spread from the West." While Deeg accepts that "translating Chinese Nestorian documents is not the same as translating Chinese Buddhist texts," not least because without a bigger corpus we are "ignorant" about the underlying context, the effect of translating Jingjiao terms into Buddhist terminology (in English or whatever language) seems equally problematic regarding intention and reception. Li Zhizao, for one, regarded the text as deeply Chinese, as *jing* 經 (scripture, classic, or sutra), and as congruent with his own faith and his understanding of church-state relations. The flurry of activity among his Jesuit friends that would soon attempt to prevent a misleading impression from the Jingjiao text (on such theological tenets as creation ex nihilo[29]) had yet to present itself to Li, who carried much less dogmatic baggage and had already internalized a working fusion of the Syriac faith in Chinese cultural form with his own.

Wang Weifan

Wang Weifan (1927–2015)[30] studied theology during the turbulent years of the 1950s and emerged holding firmly to his evangelical roots while embracing the new Three-Self Patriotic Movement and the social aspirations of the church.[31] His role models were intellectual evangelicals like Jia Yuming, Xie Fuya, or the

---

29 On Aleni's 1628 pamphlet 萬物真原 as counterpoint to Jingjiao theology of creation, see Billings, "Jesuit Fish in Chinese Nets," 12.

30 For biographical details, see Yuan Yijuan 袁益娟, *Shengsheng shenxue—Wang Weifan shenxue sixiang yanjiu* 生生神學 — 汪維藩神學思想研究 [Unceasing Generation Theology: research into Wang Weifan's theological thought] (Beijing: Jincheng Press, 2010), 3; Janice Wickeri, Preface, to Wang Weifan, *Lilies of the Field: Meditations for the Church Year* (Nashville, TN: The Upper Room, 1993).

31 This section draw directly on Chloë Starr, "Wang Weifan," in *A Reader in Chinese Theology*, ed. and trans. Chloë Starr, 277–80. ©2022. Reprinted with the permission of Baylor University Press. All rights reserved.

later Zhao Zichen. Wang's career as a preacher was abruptly interrupted when he was labeled a Rightist in 1957 and renewed only at the start of the Reform era. His twenty most productive years of theological writing and education thus came toward the end of his life as he preached, pastored, and taught New Testament at Nanjing Union Theological Seminary. Wang's research was mainly in the field of Biblical Studies and Chinese Christian history, but his oeuvre spans biblical commentary, theology, and spiritual writings. His publications include *Chinese Theology and its Cultural Sources* (Nanjing, 1997), *Leviticus* (Chinese-language Bible Annotations) and *Lilies of the Valley*, a devotional work, as well as anthologies of his essays and collected works published since his retirement.[32] Since Wang's retirement in 1999, his work has attracted increasing interest in China, and since his death in 2015, in the English-speaking world.[33]

Chinese Theology and its Cultural Sources 中國神學及其文化淵源 is a major and innovative text.[34] The second chapter of the volume presents Wang Weifan's "Theology of Unceasing Generation" (生生神學), a bold theological proposal in which Wang uses Tang and Yuan Christian documents to commend the theological reasoning of the Jingjiao church (both Tang Syriac and Mongolian Arkagun[35]) and its use of early Chinese canonical, mainly Daoist, texts. This move does two things: it re-inscribes the Christian Khans into Chinese history, offering the "alien" Yuan dynasty as a model of leadership and of faith, and, more importantly, it presents a methodology for a Chinese Christianity, as Wang reads the Tang and Yuan Jingjiao re-readings of early canonical texts. In the classics, in

---

32 Wang Weifan, *Shinian juju: Wang Weifan wenji (1997– 2007)* 十年踽踽： 汪維藩文集 [*Ten Years of Walking Alone: Selected Works of Wang Weifan (1997–2007)*] (Hong Kong: Christian Study Centre on Chinese Religion and Culture, 2009); Wang Weifan, *Nian zai cangmang: Wang Weifan wenji (1979–1998)* 廿載滄茫： 汪維藩文集 [*Two Decades in the Wilderness: Selected Works of Wang Weifan (1979–1998)*] (Hong Kong: Christian Study Centre on Chinese Religion and Culture, 2011).

33 Recent articles include Kevin Xiyi Yao's study of Wang as a major evangelical figure in the Chinese Protestant church, one subdued, if not silenced, by more liberal voices, and Alexander Chow's exploration of Wang's "cosmic theology" and Christ as "Lord of the Cosmos" and "Lord of History." Kevin Xiyi Yao, "Wang Wei-fan's Evangelical Theology: Its Significance for the Church in China Today. *Yearbook of Chinese Theology* 2016: 3–16; Alexander Chow, "Wang Weifan's Cosmic Christ." *Modern Theology* Volume 32, Issue 3. July 2016: 384–96.

34 For a much fuller study and analysis, see Yuan Yijuan, *Shengsheng shenxue*, which presents a chronology of Wang's thought; traces the influences on Wang; and analyses his theological thought in separate sections on his theology, Christology, pneumatology, ecclesiology, etc.

35 Or Yelikewen, in Chinese. Wang specifies that the theological writings of Güyük Khan, Möngke Khan and the founding Emperor of the Yuan dynasty, Kublai Khan can be researched alongside the stele text and the Dunhuang finds.

ancient Chinese theories and concepts, and in the divination oracles of the *Zhou Yi* (Yijing, I-Ching) in particular, Wang finds ideas that help conceptualize and add to knowledge of God.

Wang Weifan's reading of Jingjiao is evidently more developed and extensive than Li Zhizao's. God is, for Wang, first of all a God who ceaselessly generates and creates life (in God the Creator), redeems life (in Christ), and continuously remakes life and bestows life (through the Spirit).[36] This creation is the life of the universe, and not just of humanity. Life is at the very center of Wang's theology: the English "ever-generating" or "unceasing generation" translates the binome *shengsheng* (生生 "gives birth to life");[37] God is the God of life; God is life. In this we hear echoes of early Daoist texts and cosmologies—in the continuous flourishing and expansion of nature—as well as Christ's words. (Wang argues, moreover, that "life" was central to the *Zhou Yi*'s version of the Chinese virtue of benevolence, *ren* 仁, unlike its later Confucian reading.[38]) For Wang, God will only cease from generative activity when all creatures enter eternal rest: "He can find rest only when mortals find rest," as Wang wrote elsewhere, citing Jesus's quotation from Isaiah: "My father is always working."[39] Redemption for Wang is a continuation of creation, part of creation; the Biblical antonym of creation is not destruction but renewal.[40] In his essay on "The Lord of Sorrows," Wang emphasizes the ceaseless nature of creation and salvation: since "the whole of human history" recounts God taking on the burden of human sin and suffering.

The Christian narrative in Wang's Theology of Unceasing Generation is veined through with language and concepts derived from early Chinese thought.

---

36 Wang's classic Nicene pneumatology (with filioque) also emphases the life-giving aspects of the Spirit, who gives all life its breath. The spirit enables humans to recognize Jesus as Lord; moves people; causes them to pray; makes people holy; gives the ability to love, gives power, and gives knowledge of God. The Spirit is also intimately involved in church unity, and in Wang's Trinitarian (and very Orthodox) mode of salvation, in divinization, or making Christians holy. See Yuan Yijuan, *Shengsheng shenxue*, 111–14.

37 Archie Chi Chung Lee translates this as "Life-Birthing God" in "Contextual Theology in East Asia." In Ford, David F.; Muers, Rachel. *The Modern Theologians: An Introduction to Christian Theology since 1918* (3rd ed. Blackwell, 2005), 527.

38 Wang Weifan, *Zhongguo shenxue ji qi wenhua yuanyuan* 中國神學及其文化淵源 [*Chinese Theology and its Cultural Sources*] (Nanjing: Jinling Xiehe Shenxueyuan, 1997), 17. A "God of life," incidentally, also stands as a counterpoint to Wang's colleague Ding Guangxun's "God of love."

39 Wang Weifan, "The Lord of Sorrow," from the *Nanjing Theological Review*, No 10 (1989), trans. Janice and Philip Wickeri. and *repr.* in *Chinese Theological Review*, 1989: 113–17.

40 Cf. Yuan Yijuan, *Shengsheng shenxue* 95, 89.

For Wang, the Jingjiao stele has one overriding feature: its citation from the classical Chinese corpus. He writes that:

> the brief text of the *Memorial Commemorating the Propagation of the Luminous Religion in China*, which is not quite two thousand characters, refers to the *Yijing* in thirty places, the *Book of Odes* in thirty places, the Spring and Autumn Annals twenty times, as well as various other Confucian classics in a hundred and fifty places, the histories in more than a hundred places, and other ancient philosophical texts in thirty places.[41]

Wang's theology follows the same pattern and models itself on Jingjiao's use of classical texts. Wang's study begins from the *Zhou Yi*: he takes the last two trigrams as his starting point to show that "the philosophical base of the Chinese people" is a cyclical, rising spiral, a spirit of constant progression and striving. In creation, the primeval wind (here glossed as the Holy Spirit) gives birth to the two *qi*, and the cardinal directions (or compass points) map out the universe. God displays the same binary, or complementary aspects envisaged by yin-yang thought: God is active and passive, boldly creating, yet also immanent and still. God is "parent," just as early Chinese emperors were parent to the people. Wang finds support for his prime motif of a God of life in the theological writings of the Church of the East as it thrived in China between the seventh and thirteenth centuries, writings that conceive of the Christian God in Chinese religious and cosmological ideas. Wang's praise for the Jingjiao Church offers support to those who think that Orthodox theology (especially in its ideas on Original Sin, atonement, and divination) might be closer to traditional Chinese views, and a better model for Chinese Christianity, than Protestant or Roman Catholic thought,[42] but also offers an account of a theological methodology that Wang holds up as quintessentially Chinese: a text reading (or here, a reading of texts reading texts), where God is apprehended afresh through insights from the Chinese classics.

This was not an unthinking or untested application of the Chinese to the Christian or vice versa. As Wang writes in the first chapter, "The use of 'already 既濟' and 'not yet 未濟' as the title of this essay shows what it will expound: the areas in which Chinese Christianity is already in harmony with traditional Chinese culture, and those areas that still await attention." Some connections are

---

41 Wang, *Zhongguo shenxue ji qi wenhua yuanyuan*, 7.

42 See, e.g., Alexander Chow, *Theosis, Sino-Christian Theology and the Second Chinese Enlightenment: Heaven and Humanity in Unity* (New York: Palgrave Macmillan, 2013).

theologically fruitful; others are not. Elsewhere Wang has written scathingly of those who make unqualified cultural connections between *Tian* (Heaven) and God, or Dao and Logos.[43] Wang offers rather "revelation, tradition, culture, and reality or experience"[44] as the four pillars of Chinese Christianity. Wang's hermeneutical theology as exemplified in his Theology of Unceasing Generation has affinities with Archie C. C. Lee's Cross-textual reasoning, and with Yang Huilin's construct of Chinese Scriptural Reasoning. Wang's elevation of "classical" culture and implicit assumption of, if not the superiority, then the foundational nature of the early canonical texts, fits with traditional views on the golden age of China's past, but does raise questions about exactly what he means by "traditional Chinese culture;" how it is to imbue Christianity in the late twentieth century; and the nationalist project it entrains.

If Li Zhizao's use of the Jingjiao stele was for the good of the mission church, Wang Weifan's programmatic use of Jingjiao experience aims at the building up of a Chinese theology. For Wang, the rises and falls of Christianity in China, from the Tang-Yuan onwards, provide praxis and experience out of which:

> "we ought to be able to abstract rich material for theological reflection and work it into a theological theory with Chinese characteristics, using this to guide the Chinese church and its believers during the process of China's modernization, as well as offering it as a gift to the universal church"[45]

If Li Zhizao takes Chinese cultural pride as a given, for Wang Weifan the longevity and power of Chinese culture needs spelling out (and reclaiming, against the "fault-line" rupture of the Cultural Revolution). For Wang, the central concepts of "the mean" and "harmony" enable Chinese culture to absorb others' cultures without itself being readily assimilated—which means that any religion *must* become inculturated to survive in China.

---

43 "Quite a few researchers working on the integration of Christianity and Chinese culture who came after Wu Leichuan and T. C. Chao (Zhao Zichen) often seized upon the Confucian concept of 'Heaven' (*Tian*) with great relish as being identical to the Christian concept of 'God,' or Laozi's 'Dao' (*Tao*) as the Christian 'logos' and so on. In terms of the comparative study of religion, these people painted themselves into a corner without realizing it." Wang Weifan, "Summoning Personality and Spirit," *Chinese Theological Review* 5 (1989): 76–83.

44 Wang Weifan, "The 'Already' and the 'Not Yet,'" trans. Starr, *A Reader in Chinese Theology*, 281.

45 Wang, "The 'Already' and the 'Not Yet,'" 281.

In arguing that the Church of the East writers (as well as Ricci and other Jesuits) ascribed import to Chinese culture (unlike the later Protestant missionaries), Wang steps in to the debates on translation and Buddhist and Daoist influence wearing rose-tinted glasses. While most scholars see necessity, or the requirement of collaboration with local monks to prepare translations as the cause of "Buddhist clothing" of Jingjiao texts, Wang sees a positive choice for an inculturated Christianity. In this he is supported by the work of other twentieth-century Jingjiao scholars like the French Jesuit Yves Raguin, who regarded the (enforced) cooperation with Daoist and Buddhist monks as a blessing that enabled a theological synthesis, allowing Jingjiao thought also to permeate the religious beliefs and ideas of its translators.[46] For contemporary Jesuit Benoît Vermander, the key question here is whether a borrowing of others' concepts and worldviews enhances one's own self-knowledge (so "Nestorian 'theology' can legitimately be seen as a most exciting, maybe prophetic Christian theology of its own"[47]) or whether it weakens the institution and message, even to the point where the church disappears, as it did in the ninth century.

Wang Weifan sees the more syncretic language of Jingjiao texts not as a necessary evil brought about by the expression of Orthodox religion within the context of a Daoist and Buddhist world, but as homage to the Chinese canon and culture. He sees a continuous development of Chinese theology as the "baton" (接力棒) has been passed on from Jingjiao to the present, with different cultural/religious influences dominant in different periods. In discussing the creative activity of God described in the Jingjiao stele, for example, Wang writes:

> In this passage Jing Jing skillfully assimilates the Daoist theory of production from the *Zhou Yi*, that is, the co-production and co-existence of yin and yang and their mutual transformation in the "Great Ultimate," in order to record the work of God in creation in the first chapter of Genesis and make it into a theological construction with Chinese cultural traits, projecting an active God of unceasing generation.[48]

There are several complex steps in this description: from assigning so much agency and to the monk Jingjing in text composition and in the intention to

---

46 See Vermander, "The Impact of Nestorianism on Contemporary Chinese Theology," 191.

47 Vermander, "The Impact of Nestorianism on Contemporary Chinese Theology," 193.

48 Wang Weifan, "Unceasing Generation Theology," trans. Starr, *A Reader in Chinese Theology*, 290.

create a culturally-Chinese theology; in making the connection to Tang readings of the Zhou Yi in the stele text; in the particular reading of those Daoist texts as celebrating "unceasing generation"—and further, in then making this central to a program of "revitalizing" Chinese theology *and* Chinese culture nationally. This example shows in brief both the genius and the flaws of Wang's method.

Where Li Zhizao glides over any potential tension between Buddhist language and Christian concepts by assimilating or Christianizing it, Wang assumes an underlying compatibility. In advocating that Chinese theology should "seek out and recover" the lost spirit of "self-strengthening without rest, unceasing generation and drawing on heavenly strength," Wang Weifan has no qualms about promoting the Four Ways to spiritual peace of the Dunhuang text *Zhixuan anle jing* (志玄安樂經)[49] (that is, non-desire 無欲, non-action 無為, no-virtue 無德, no-demonstration 無證) and praising their deep spirituality as the basis for "life," arguing that "although the author has assimilated some Daoist and even Buddhist, language and sentence structures, its spirituality is Christian."

In other words, Wang Weifan does not pause at the Daoist- or Buddhist-inflected language of the stele text but pushes it back to its "source," which he locates in the early classics, and he sees this process as a deliberate part of the theologizing of the Jingjiao writers. These methodological traits, moreover, guide the whole of his theological treatise. In the following chapter, *Haoqi pian* 浩氣篇, for example, Wang presents an idealistic view of Chinese *shi* 士 (scholar, knight-gentleman), comparing them to Hebrew prophets, and considers the Chinese pursuit of "character" in the classics as the basis for their perfection, before proceeding to outline a Christology that is heavily dependent on this formulation of character from the classics, as moral perfection and good action. If sometimes the connections seem forced (as when Wang finds the roots of Chinese mystical theology in Southern Song *lixue*[50]), a more pressing problem for contemporary Christians in locating the source of "revitalization" of Chinese culture (and Chinese Christianity) in the classics and in Yuan Jingjiao ideas, is their highly gendered and socially stratified concept of the human person. Wang was visionary in both the reclamation of traditional culture and in his ecumenical or inter-religious outlook, but the dangers of applying the past to the present are also clear.

---

49 P. Y. Saeki translates as *The Sutra on Mysterious Rest and Joy*; A. C. Moule as *The Book Devoted to Hidden Peace and Joy*.

50 Wang, *Zhongguo shenxue ji qi wenhua yuanyuan*, 66.

Conclusions

At the outset of his volume, Wang Weifan suggests that his work will not be systematic theology in a western fashion but "a Chinese way of thinking and style of expression." This "Chinese way of thinking" indicates a textual history and method, tracing the early textual sources behind the Jingjiao stele text, and seeing in this relationship a valorization of "traditional" Chinese culture, which for Wang offers both a theological method for the present and a hope for cultural revival. Through the Yuan Jingjiao readings in particular, Wang sees the possibility of a more "robust" model of the Chinese past.

Wang Weifan's theological readings of early Chinese classics are remarkable. They accomplish much, directly and indirectly. Wang is able to defend Ding Guangxun against charges of weakening justification by faith by showing the Chinese contribution to faith in action through classic texts and the importance of faith-and-works, as reinterpreted by an earlier evangelical like Jia Yuming. In this move he also gives evangelical support for the TSPM, and the notion of one church, that can overcome theological splits and hold together different positions on the spectrum of belief. Defending Ding via Chinese-inflected Christian thought valorizes Chinese culture as a medium for theology. This enables other moves: Wang draws on the "ideal spirit" of Mencius, unshaken by riches or poverty, power or violence—as parallel to, and entirely compatible with, our God-given human nature, *imago dei*—to open up Christian theology to those of the wider culture, by foregrounding common elements. Creating a genealogy of Chinese scholarship in his references and readings of classical texts via Xie Fuya, Zhao Zichen and others forged an intellectual history that is solely dependent on Chinese scholarship, with not a westerner in sight, and is also a methodological nod to Chinese traditions of learning and citation. While Li Zhizao absorbed Tang Church of the East elements, including their Buddhist terminology, into his own view, Wang finds Christian-compatible truths in the classical corpus that allows for earlier wisdom texts to be used in Christian discourse.[51]

---

51 It is not just, as Chow suggests, that Wang's Christ as "Lord of the Cosmos" is "not so much formulated as the mystery of Christ behind other religions as it is about how other religious and philosophical traditions can guide the articulation of Christian faith and theology,"— which suggests an emphasis and interest in other religions per se—but that Wang actually sees the Dao and the *Yijing* etc. as part of the same truth, and reads Christianity in light of these Chinese cultural expressions of that one truth. See Alexander Chow, "Wang Weifan's Cosmic Christ," *Modern Theology* 32: 3 (2016): 384–96, 393.

Despite their many differences in approach, both Wang Weifan and Li Zhizao perform a similar historicizing of the stele for contemporary readers, using it to comment on the present: for Li, this is with the Jesuit mission in mind, for Wang, with the reclamation of Chinese culture after the Cultural Revolution and the revitalization of the Chinese people. Both use the text to speak to the church and the state and broader social issues. The question of translation does not arise for either in the way it has exercised non-Chinese readers of the stele and histories of its reception: both writers assume their own capability in reading what the text meant in its time and in relating that to their own Christian understanding. Ecumenical questions—moving between the church of the East/Orthodox theologies and their own traditions—did not disturb Li or Wang, whether through ignorance or choice, and both bridged many hundred years of divide (and language, and ethnicity). Traditions of text reading and scholarship provide a shared language and shared habitus for these scholars, and the practice of text-reading as a Chinese method of theology unites seventeenth-century Catholic with twentieth-century Protestant.

Chapter 15

CHINESE CATHOLIC NUNS AND THEIR THEOLOGY OF MINISTRY

Michel Chambon, *National University of Singapore*

This paper presents the role that nuns have played in the Catholic Church in China and discusses their underlying theology of ministry.[1] As numerous as diocesan priests, and belonging to diocesan orders that share similar structures and functioning from place to place, nuns are deeply involved in the pastoral care of Chinese dioceses. But how can one best describe their ecclesial role? What does it say about the Church as a whole?

To answer these questions, this article elaborates on ethnographic material collected between 2015 and 2017 and presented in an article "Chinese Catholic Nuns and their Organization of Religious Life in Contemporary China."[2] In continuity with this socio-historical analysis of Chinese religious orders, the present article argues that the Church in China has generated a consensus on ministry that is quite distinct from the rest of the worldwide Catholic Church and rooted in its particular history and context. In the People's Republic of China, nuns are a constitutive part of the diocesan clergy and their collective position is best described as a diaconal ministry. This Chinese consensus on ministry does not necessarily contradict the Catholic Tradition but manifests one localization of the Church.

The article proceeds in five steps. First, I briefly summarize how the Catholic Church in China has gradually developed quite distinct religious orders. After presenting an overview of how Catholic religious orders usually operate around

---

1 I would like to thank sisters Janet Caroll, Marinei Pessanha Alves, Theresa Shi, Mathias Guo, and other Chinese nuns who supported me during my research. This paper has also greatly benefited from the encouraging support of Chloë Starr and Stephanie Wong.

2 Chambon, "Chinese Catholic Nuns and their Organization of Religious Life in Contemporary China." *Religions* 10 (7), 2019: 447.

the world, I underline how Chinese ones have tended to become uniformly multivalent, regional, and diocesan. Then, I explain how as a French Catholic theologian I position myself in this effort to uncover the theology of ministry in which Chinese nuns serve their communities. This clarified, I connect this paper with broader ecclesial debates and revisit conversations about women's ministry that, over the past fifty years, have occurred at various levels of the Catholic Church. The following section discusses how in China, there is an ecclesial consensus about the permanent existence of a formally institutionalized, officially blessed but not ordained diaconal ministry that women belonging to diocesan religious orders fulfill. I conclude by connecting this theology of ministry to the discipline of sacraments in order to suggest further adjustments to strengthen the involution[3] of the Church in China.

An Overview of Catholic Religious Orders in China and Elsewhere

Catholic Religious Orders

In the Catholic Church, religious orders are usually formed of Christians who take vows of poverty, chastity, and obedience. In contrast to the "secular clergy"[4] serving local dioceses, consecrated people are not necessarily ordained. Their vows constitute their core identity, and often, their religious congregation is their primary community of belonging. Over the past centuries, Western Christianity, and later Roman Catholicism, has constantly encouraged religious orders to specify their identity and spirituality. Often, they identify a charism—such as contemplative prayer, a particular spiritual tradition, *ad gentes* missionary work,

---

3 To characterize the changes and complexification of a social system, the American anthropologist Clifford Geertz uses the notion of "involution" to avoid terms like "evolution" or "revolution." In a modern context, those terms are politically and ideologically loaded. By contrast, "involution" emphasizes how a cultural system necessarily relies on internal resources to address external forces and challenges, and how through this integrative process, it successfully adapts and perpetuates itself. Thus, continuity and change are not a mere opposition between internal and external elements but the integrative collaboration of the two. See Clifford Geertz, *Agricultural Involution the Process of Ecological Change in Indonesia.* Monographs and Papers, 11. (Berkeley: Published for the Association of Asian Studies by University of California Press, 1963).

4 The notion of "secular clergy" is a medieval category distinguishing between clerics belonging to religious orders and governed by a "rule"—the regular clergy—and those who serve under the authority of a local bishop—the secular clergy.

preaching, and so on—as being the core foundation of their religious commitment. Thus, this charism becomes their distinct marker within the vast diversity of Catholic orders.

Unlike the secular clergy devoted to the pastoral and multifaceted service of the people of God present within the delimited territory of a diocese, religious orders are not bound to a territory nor a population—they operate at a transregional level—even though they may cultivate specific ties with particular places.[5] Benedictines, Dominicans, Jesuits, Carmelites each hold to a specific rule defining their spirituality, framing their apostolic activities, and outlining the power structure of their institutions. Therefore, they are often called "regular clergy" in reference to the rule that defines their religious life, belonging, and charism.

Yet, Catholic orders are tremendously diverse. While most have a superior general holding authority on the entire network of local communities or convents, the Order of St. Benedict does not. Each Benedictine abbey is autonomous. The identity of orders can evolve over time. For example, the Sisters of St. Andrew were contemplative nuns during the medieval period. Later, they embraced Ignatian spirituality and committed themselves to school-based education. Today, they closely collaborate with the ecumenical Taizé community and engage with various apostolates worldwide.

Finally, in addition to the variety of their charism and structures, Catholic religious orders are highly irregular in their local presence. In certain regions of the world, the historical role and the pastoral leadership of some orders is extremely important in the daily life of the faithful. Yet, elsewhere, their existence is barely known. In other parts of the world, the diocesan clergy is almost alone and local Catholics have very limited interactions with monks and nuns. Thus, the variety of orders lies not only in their nature but also in their local significance for the Church.

In sum, Catholic religious orders are characterized by three specific features. First, their effort to embrace evangelical life produces extremely diverse lifestyles and structures. Second, they each seek to specify their contribution and spirituality. Finally, most of them have a worldwide or regional presence, and yet this presence is often unevenly distributed.

---

5 For instance, Franciscans care for specific sites of the Holy Land and Assisi, Trappists for sites in Normandy, and Salesians for sites in Turin.

Catholic Orders in China

In my article "Chinese Catholic Nuns and the Organization of Religious Life in Contemporary China," I detail how Chinese consecrated women rely on two specific traditions to shape and define their religious life today. The first tradition is that of the consecrated virgins—or more properly named the *beatas*, the blessed ones.[6] This ancient institution was widely present in Europe from the thirteenth to the sixteenth century,[7] and during the seventeenth century, it was introduced in multiple parts of China to support the rapid growth of the Church.[8] In this model of religious life, individual women chose not to marry but under the blessing of their bishop, served local communities. After taking private vows, they lived with their relatives or within a distinct building of the village to help with pious activities, children's education, and religious rituals. Without belonging to a religious order or embracing conventual life, they created horizontal associations to train new beatas.

In China, beatas were crucial for the apostolate among Chinese women who, in late imperial China, were often segregated from public life.[9] During periods of persecution, they gained more importance by taking care of religious education, administering baptism, visiting the sick, and gathering people for prayer meetings. Most of the time, they lived within their parents' household and did not wear specific clothing.[10] Today, this model of religious life is still alive either

---

6   In "Chinese Catholic Nuns," I argue that the term "virgin"—and its sexual connotation—should be avoided and replaced by the traditional term "beata."

7   See, e.g., René Lagier, "Une Institution Vellave: Les Béates." Cahiers de La Haute-Loire, Revue d'Etudes Locales, 1979: 131–68; Intxaustegi, Nere Jone. "'Beatas,' 'Beaterios' and Convents: The Origin of the Basque Female Conventual Life." *Imago Temporis: Medium Aevum*, no. 11, 2017: 329–341; Laurey Braguier, *Servantes de Dieu. Les Béatas de La Couronne de Castille (1450–1600)*, (Rennes: Presses Universitaires de Rennes, 2019).

8   Robert E. Entenmann, "Christian Virgins in Eighteenth-Century Sichuan," in *Christianity in China, From the Eighteenth Century to the Present*, ed. Daniel H. Bays, (Stanford, CA: Stanford University Press, 1996), 180–94; Eugenio Menegon, "Child Bodies, Blessed Bodies: The Contest Between Christian Virginity and Confucian Chastity." *Nan Nü* 6 (2) 2004: 177–240; R. G. Tiedemann, "Controlling the Virgins: Female Propagators of the Faith and the Catholic Hierarchy in China." *Women's History Review* 17 (4) 2008: 501–20; R. G. Tiedemann, "Chinese Female Propagators of the Faith in Modern China: The Tortuous-Transition from the 'Institute of Virgins' to Diocesan Religious Congregations." *Religions & Christianity in Today's China* VIII (2) 2018: 52–72.

9   Kang Zhijie 康志杰, *Jidu de xinniang: Zhongguo Tianzhujiao zhennü yanjiu* 基督的新娘：中國天主教貞女研究 (Beijing: Zhongguo Shehui kexueyuan, 2013).

10   See Nadine Amsler, *Jesuits and Matriarchs: Domestic Worship in Early Modern China* (Seattle: University of Washington Press, 2018).

in its traditional form in places like Fujian or through its exemplary influence on contemporary religious life.[11] Yet, the number of beatas has drastically declined over the last twenty years and vocations are rare.

After the Opium Wars (1839–1842 and 1856–1860) and the creation of European charitable organizations funding Catholic missions, the number of Western missionaries in China increased quickly and the role of the beatas had to be reshaped. While missionaries were reestablishing hierarchical control over the Church in China and implementing a post-Tridentine approach to Catholicism, they also worked at redefining and regulating the apostolate, training, and spirituality of the beatas. "Given the virgins' [beatas] relative independence, religious initiatives and weak corporate identity, it is not surprising that from around the middle of the nineteenth century the European clergy promoted the idea of establishing Chinese religious sisterhoods to cultivate their religious lives and establish proper ecclesiastical control over them."[12] Thus, the beatas were usually encouraged to form new communities and follow a Westernized model of religious life. This involution was inspired by the second main tradition that informs religious life in China: the missionary congregations. From the late nineteenth century until the end of World War II, many Catholic missionary congregations planted themselves in China and reshaped the ways the Church manifests itself. In partnership with male missionaries, female religious orders from the Western world sent countless groups of nuns to establish schools, orphanages, hospitals, leprosaria, and other "modern" institutions. While colonial powers were pointing at foot binding, polygamy, and female infanticide to portray Chinese civilization as oppressive toward women,[13] the Catholic Church worked at reconfiguring the ways Chinese women embrace religious life and access to ecclesial leadership. Nonetheless, as Tiedemann writes, "the long and sometimes tortuous road toward the creation of indigenous institutes of women . . . did not produce any fully recognized indigenous female congregations before 1949. Instead, a great variety of Chinese Catholic religious communities of women had come into being, ranging from rather loose pious unions of virgins [beatas] to a few

---

11 See Maria Jaschok and Jingjun Shui, *Women, Religion, and Space in China: Islamic Mosques & Daoist Temples, Catholic Convents & Chinese Virgins* (New York: Routledge, 2011), 143; Chambon, "Chinese Catholic Nuns."

12 Tiedemann, "Chinese Female Propagators of the Faith in Modern China," 61.

13 See Kang, *Jidu de xinniang*, 494.

properly constituted institutes of diocesan right, on the verge of full papal approbation."[14]

After 1949 and the departure of foreign priests, nuns, and bishops, Chinese religious sisterhoods and institutes were soon dismantled by the new regime. Many Chinese nuns returned to a life similar to the one of the beatas. While conventual and collective institutions disappeared, Chinese nuns went back to their hometowns to discreetly support religious practice and education within local Catholic communities. Based at their parents' home without any distinctive sign, they were critical in maintaining an ecclesial continuity. After 1979 and the reopening of China, one of their tasks was often as a kind of liaison officer guiding foreign ecclesial visitors who circulated in China and searched for Catholic communities. During the late 1980s to early 2000s, various lay patrons, priests, and bishops also encouraged the beatas to regenerate religious orders in order to support the rebirth of the Church. With the increase of female vocations, many dioceses created a religious order, a congregation of diocesan right devoted to the service of local parishes.

Some thirty years later, 3,170 Chinese women belong to eighty-seven registered religious congregations, and 1,400 more belong to thirty-seven unregistered congregations.[15] This means that most dioceses have their own order, each hosting an average of thirty-six nuns. A vast majority of these women are in their forties to fifties and vocations are now dropping. While individual beatas, sometimes organized in informal sisterhoods, continue to exist, diocesan congregations of various sizes have tended to become the dominant form of religious life in contemporary China. Some may have only a dozen members while others count up to two hundred nuns.

Depending on their size, the local socio-political context, their financial resources, and the relation with the bishop—four aspects that can greatly impact the reality of Chinese religious orders—these congregations engage with a variety of apostolic work. Most of the time, they support nearby parishes where a few nuns live and help with catechism, religious services, and housekeeping. But a growing number of congregations have a majority of their members performing non-parish-based apostolates as well. In the same congregation, some nuns may serve in a parish, some run an elderly home for laypeople, some offer informal healthcare service, and others preach at retreats for laypeople in search

---

14 Tiedemann, "Chinese Female Propagators of the Faith in Modern China," 71.

15 See *Religions & Christianity in Today's China*, 2018, Vol. VIII, No. 2, pp. 26–51, ISSN: 2192–9289, www.china-zentrum.de. At the same time, the country counts a total of 3,800 priests and 112 bishops.

of spiritual renewal. Most of these relatively new apostolates are done from their convents where an increasing proportion of nuns reside. Consequently, on the one hand Chinese nuns have tended to strengthen conventual life and to increase the devotional and spiritual life of their community. As a congregation, nuns spend more time together and in their chapel. On the other hand, nuns have diversified their interactions with laypeople and non-Catholics, spending more time outside of traditional parishes.

Consequently, China is witnessing the emergence of a distinct type of religious order present within each province of the country as a stable ecclesial entity. These institutions of diocesan right operate at a regional level usually defined by the territory of the diocese they belong to. They are multivalent in their apostolate and perform an increasing number of highly specialized services.[16] Within these orders, various generations of women have different aspirations and sensibilities that they negotiate together. Younger members are often searching for deeper spiritual and communal life while older nuns insist on the importance of insuring the material autonomy of the order and on the necessary religious proximity with the faithful. This intergenerational diversity combined with a rapidly changing society has encouraged Chinese congregations to remain engaged in parishes, increase their conventual life, and diversify their apostolates. These multiple commitments not only secure various sources of financial and social capital but also help nuns to express their many interests and skills.

In terms of power structure and authority, these female corporations stand under the leadership of their local bishop. His personality can greatly impact the ecclesial, financial, and spiritual situation of an order. Yet, Chinese congregations manifest a rather fluid, egalitarian, and democratic approach to authority and obedience. When the bishop does not interfere, nuns stand as an autonomous community that elects a superior and council members every four years. Since those persons can be reelected only once to the same office, Chinese orders tend to frequently rotate who stands as Mother Superior. Unlike elsewhere in the Catholic world, there is therefore no long-lasting matriarchal figure within Chinese religious orders. These institutions rather remain horizontal in their functioning, and responsibilities circulate among members.

Yet, Chinese nuns often face institutional misogyny. Relationships to priests and bishops are often marked by tensions and condescension. In some places, the bishop may try to enforce a certain agenda upon his diocesan congregation

---

16 Jaschok and Shui, *Women, Religion, and Space in China*, 223.

without consulting its members. Some abusive and scandalous examples have even made the news.[17] At the same time, many priests tend to position themselves as a hierarchical superior and to ignore the voice of nuns. But institutional misogyny can also come from the state and works in favor of diocesan orders. State officials easily disregard the role played by nuns that are often perceived as naive and uneducated. Compared to the priests who are closely scrutinized by the state, nuns are less monitored and enjoy a higher political autonomy. However, the scope of their action is often limited by their financial resources. The faithful, who are not freed from misogyny either, usually prefer to make donations to their priests and bishops. Nuns often struggle to secure a minimal income.

Finally, we need to bear in mind that the Church in China has almost no national or international religious orders.[18] Due to political constraints, the vast majority of Chinese religious orders and priests are attached to a particular diocese, and exchanges between dioceses are closely monitored by civil authorities. Unlike in other parts of the world where Catholic communities can benefit from transregional religious orders, the Church in China operates under diocesan clergy only. Various circulations within the country and abroad do occur, but they remain informal and do not diminish the preeminent role of the secular clergy.

Chinese nuns, therefore, do not constitute a juxtaposition of individual figures, and their orders are not reducible to a series of local particularities. Even though a variety of situations exists—including cases where a diocesan order is in conflict with its bishop or where financial resources are so limited that nuns are entirely dependent on local priests—the Church in China is generating a distinct type of religious life that needs to be acknowledged. Without that, Chinese nuns vanish behind the diversity of their situations, their ecclesial ministry remains mostly unacknowledged, and foreign observers are left with the preconceptions they already had on Catholic orders. This being said, we also need to underscore how the ecclesial position of Chinese nuns is neither self-defined nor simply predetermined by universal Canon Law. Rather, it emerges within a network of negotiations, expectations, pre-existing ministries, and in relation to socio-ecclesial needs. The status and roles of Chinese nuns result from an

---

17 See https://www.ucanews.com/news/chinese-nuns-end-hunger-strike-still-seek-compensation/ 79597 — accessed on July 1, 2020.

18 There are only a very few exceptions, fewer than five for the entire country.

ongoing conversation sustained by the many actors of Chinese Catholicism. Together, they define a certain consensus on the nature and functions of Chinese religious orders. While most Catholic orders across the globe are trans-regional, shaped around a singularizing charism, and diverse in their organization and identity, Chinese ones tend to be homogenously regional, multivalent in their apostolates, and quite similar in their organization and identity.

This gap between Chinese and non-Chinese orders has been noticed by numerous ecclesial observers. The fact that Chinese congregations engage with multiple apostolates simultaneously without defining a specific charism seems puzzling to many. Thus, two schools of thought seek to make sense of these Chinese characteristics. Some approach Chinese ecclesial differences as the mere result of political interference, and in other words, as a distortion that should ultimately disappear.[19] This interpretation, however, carries many underlying assumptions, among which are that Catholic institutions should be everywhere the same and the Chinese state is necessarily antagonist to the Church. Other observers argue that Chinese ecclesial particularities come from the cultural distinctiveness of Chinese civilization.[20] Thus, they may stand as a gift of the Holy Spirit mediated through the history of this nation.[21] Again, most ramifications of this approach remain unsatisfactory because their underlying notions of culture are extremely diverse and often arbitrary. Who gets to define "Chineseness"? Nonetheless, these two approaches are questionable because they assume that changes and differences within the Church are primarily coming from outside of ecclesial communities. Variations are likewise initiated outside of the Church (the communist state or the Chinese culture). Is there not a risk in presenting the body of Christ as fundamentally "passive" or even merely "resistant?" How do we consider the generative action of the Holy Spirit within the Chinese ecclesial community itself?

---

19 Ze-Kiun Joseph Zen, *For Love of My People I Will Not Remain Silent: A Series of Eight Lectures in Defense and Clarification of the 2007 Letter of Pope Benedict XVI to the Church in the People's Republic of China* (San Francisco: Ignatius Press, 2019).

20 Some may wonder whether those particularities are rooted in or inspired by other Chinese religious traditions (e.g., Daoist and Buddhist monastic traditions). However, the data collected during interviews and participant observations do not suggest such a parallel. I personally consider that historical legacy and socio-political constraints have been much more significant factors in the particularizing involution of the Church in China.

21 Edmond Tang, "The Cosmic Christ—the Search for a Chinese Theology." *Studies in World Christianity* 1 (2) 1995: 131–42; Lo, Lung-Kwong. "The Nature of the Issue of Ancestral Worship among Chinese Christians." *Studies in World Christianity* 9 (1) 2003: 30–42.

Consequently, this paper proposes to reassess the theological significance of Chinese religious orders and to elaborate an alternative interpretation of their particularities. How, from a Catholic standpoint, to describe their position in the Church?

Responding from a Situated Standpoint

As a layperson trained in Catholic theology, a cultural anthropologist, and a non-Chinese man, my goal is to reflect on what the Church in China has collectively produced regarding the contribution of religious women to the Church and the world. I intend to theologically characterize the consensual and shared practices of the Church in China. Thus, I do not seek to solely summarize the theological discourse of some Catholic nuns or professional theologians, nor the various statements made by Catholic institutions. The core interest of my theological enterprise is the action of the Church in China, the Body of Christ. In other words, my theological work is built upon ecclesial practices understood as the primary textual corpus—a thick web of meaning—of investigation.

Knowing that the Church is a mother giving life to many practices and institutions, I approach theology as an effort to dialogically question, discern, and designate these actions and structures. While giving birth is one thing, naming is another. It propels a child to a new degree of legitimacy and belonging. Similarly, by helping to name what the Church is actually doing, theologians participate in the collective effort of the Church who seeks to welcome, sustain, and acknowledge the fruits the Holy Spirit is giving to her. Thus, my starting point is the many religious orders that the Church in China is deploying. If social science helps to characterize them, theology seeks to evaluate how they speak of the Church, the Body of Christ, and how they reflect something of the triune God. Furthermore, it goes without saying that this naming enterprise comes in dialogue with the Scriptures, the Magisterium,[22] and the Tradition.

Ethnographic investigation suggests that the particularities of Chinese congregations are shaped by various actors such as historical models of religious life, younger and older generations of Chinese women, male bishops and priests, as well as broader socio-political constraints. Thus, the ecclesial service and position of consecrated women is neither self-arrogated nor antagonistic

---

22 In the Catholic tradition, the Magisterium refers to the teaching capacity of the Church and to her ability to discern the authentic interpretation of the Word of God. It is enacted by the authority of the Church, the college of bishops paired with the bishop of Rome, the pope.

to other ecclesial entities. On the contrary, it emerges through a broad ecclesial discernment involving the many parts of the body of Christ. Their ministry is a multi-vocal reality that emerges through encounter and dialogue, but also through occasional tensions and contradictions. Consequently, I argue that there is a dynamic but rather stable Chinese consensus about how to share responsibilities, services, and duties among the various members of the Church, including the nuns.

To reflect on this consensus that shapes female religious life, I propose to elaborate on the notion of the *sensus fidei fidelium*—the sense of faith. This theological notion of the Tradition claims that the whole people of God have a capacity that unfailingly adheres to the true faith, penetrates it more deeply with right judgment, and applies it more fully in daily life.[23] Even without verbalizing it or without the explicit approval of the Magisterium, the Body of Christ guided by the Holy Spirit has the capacity to intuitively discern and follow the calling of the only Heavenly Father. Often applied to notions related to dogmatism and morals, I suggest applying the *sensus fidei fidelium* to theology of ministry.[24] Which kind of theology of ministry does this Chinese consensus manifest? What does it say about the nuns' ministry?

To acknowledge and articulate how this Chinese consensus participates in the Catholic Tradition, I also suggest elaborating on Pope Francis's reflection on the polyhedron.[25] Several times Pope Francis has highlighted that the more we see and talk about the world as a sphere—a globe—the more we risk reinforcing processes of standardization and homogenization. Unquestioned discourses on a "globalized world" threaten to foster a single worldview that denies regional variations and particularities. In contrast, the polyhedron, a multi-sided geometric figure, acknowledges the unity of the human family yet does not erase the particular angles of its many facets, cultures, and socio-political traditions.

Similarly, my present effort to name the emerging theology of ministry that the Church in China is collectively generating seeks to better perceive how Catholicism is not a mere "global Church," an institution made of supposedly homogenous discourses and practices. Rather, I argue that it might be best apprehended as a polyhedron shaped by many traditions centered on the unique incarnated Christ. For instance, it is common knowledge that multiple personal ordinariates

---

23 Catechism of the Catholic Church, 92–93.

24 *Lumen Gentium*, 12.

25 Pope Francis, *Evangelii Gaudium* (2013), 236; *Amoris Laetitia* (2016), 4.

and autonomous Churches coexist within the same Catholic Church. In this concert of Churches and communities, a sign of ecclesial diversity is that most Catholic priests of Eastern Catholic Churches and ordinariates are usually married. Another example of ecclesial diversity comes through local history. As mentioned earlier, history creates quite different equilibriums between secular and regular clergies. In some regions, the diocesan clergy is the backbone of ecclesial life while in others, religious orders may have a much more significant influence. Finally, variations are also present within the ordained clergy itself. While Vatican II and Pope Paul VI have restored a permanent diaconate, vast regions of the Catholic world do not have such deacons.[26]

In other words, ecclesial diversity—and different theologies of ministry—are not a specificity of peripheral communities. They are the core identity of the Catholic Church because distinct liturgical traditions, particular ecclesial histories, and cultural differences can together manifest the creative and triune nature of the Christian God. Yet, these variations remain a challenge for the communion and unity of the Church. There is a permanent and dialectical tension between diversity and unity. Thus, theological investigation remains necessary to discern how to articulate the relation of particularities to the whole mission of the Church.

The Catholic Magisterium and the Question of Women's Ministry

To participate in this effort to name what the Church in China is manifesting and to situate it within the larger communion of the worldwide Church, a second background factor involves broader and recent conversations that Catholic entities have developed about women's ministry. Although I do not intend to offer a comprehensive overview of the question, one cannot ignore the vast discussion to rethink the contribution of women to Church ministry underway since Vatican II.[27]

A first involution occurred in 1970 when Pope Paul VI granted saints Theresa of Avila and Catherine of Siena the title of doctor of the Church. Until then, no women had ever received this formal recognition. A doctor of the Church—an

---

26 See the decree *Ad Gentes* 16, and the motu proprio published in June 18th 1967, *Sacrum Diaconatus Ordinem*.

27 Mary J. Henold, *The Laywoman Project: Remaking Catholic Womanhood in the Vatican II Era.* (Chapel Hill: The University of North Carolina Press, 2020).

antique title given to a few figures who have made a significant contribution to theology and doctrine—was implicitly a man. Later, Pope John Paul II did the same with Thérèse de Lisieux, and Pope Benedict XVI with Hildegard of Bingen. Thus, four women are now officially recognized as the highest theological authority of the Catholic Tradition. They are not anymore considered as mere "mystic" figures, a relatively loose term that acknowledges the spiritual influence of a saint, but as significant and normative contributors to the formal and intellectual teaching of the Church. Thus, gender roles within the Catholic Church do involve.

In this effort to revisit the specific contribution of women, Pope John Paul II and his successors have repeatedly talked about "the genius of women." This expression suggests that women bring something particular to humankind and the Church, something that should be praised and acknowledged. This new formulation aims in particular at not reducing women to an idealized figure of Mary nor at diluting them into broad humankind.[28] Yet, the biblical theologian Anne-Marie Pelletier has questioned this growing tendency of the Magisterium to praise women without engaging in a real dialogue with them.[29] While an increasing number of laudable statements about women are produced, the clergy remains exclusively masculine, and until recently, most ecclesial responsibilities were given to men. Pelletier points out that in Genesis 2:23, when Adam comes to speak for the very first time, he talks about his new wife. But he does so by referring to himself—"my bones," "my flesh." He speaks about her as a third person as if she is not fully present. Meanwhile, Eve remains silent. Clearly, this first encounter between Adam and Eve is not yet a dialogue. The creatures, image of God, still have to complete the work of their creator to let the human couple reflect the dialogical nature of the triune God. In a similar vein, Pelletier argues that the men-shaped Magisterium does not engage yet in a real dialogue with women. More precisely, it does not let them truly participate in the magisterial dialogue of the Church.

In this effort to reconsider the role of women within the ministry of the Church, the ordination of women has been one of the most recurrent and debated questions. While the recent Magisterium has been very clear about the

---

28 See *Congregation for the Doctrine of the Faith*, Collaboration of Men and Women in the Church, July 31, 2004.

29 See Anne-Marie Pelletier, "Femmes Dans Une Ecclésiologie Intégrale." *Transversalités* 133 (2) 2015: 95–115; "Des Femmes Avec Des Hommes, Avenir de l'Église." *Études Janvier* (1) 2017: 47–56.

impossibility for women to receive priestly ordination, debates about diaconal ordination remain open.[30] In August 2016, Pope Francis established a pontifical commission in charge of investigating the historical existence of female deacons. After two years of work, participants agreed that female deacons existed historically until the Gregorian period,[31] but members of the commission disagreed about the significance of this historical tradition for the Church today. Thus, in April 2020, Pope Francis announced the creation of a new pontifical commission to continue this study of the possibility of women deacons. With this background, let us now return to the Church in China and to the roles that nuns play within it.

How to Name the Ministry of Chinese Nuns?

Since the 1980s—and despite a real variety of situations—the Church in China has nonetheless generated religious congregations that tend to become uniformly diocesan and multivalent. What does that say about the Church in China, the Body of Christ, as it manifests and honors the presence of the Heavenly Father through the action of the Holy Spirit?

Standing within the diocesan clergy

In contrast to international congregations, Chinese religious orders avoid an industrial Taylorism of ministry and religious life. Instead of focusing on one distinctive charism—as if an order should commit itself to a specific task only—enacted across large territories, each Chinese congregation engages with a variety of services within a defined territory. During the 1980s and 1990s, nuns were mostly serving local parishes. But, the more the Church has recovered from the traumatic Maoist era and the more that Chinese society has evolved, the more Chinese nuns are engaging with relatively new forms of apostolates such as elderly care, medical service, social service with disabled persons, and so on. Administrative constraints are still important but nuns find creative ways to respond to socio-political changes without neglecting the importance of the parishes and

---

30 See John Paul II, *Ordinatio Sacerdotalis*, May 22, 1994. For in informed introduction to the question of diakonia, see the document published by International Theological Commission, *From the Diakonia of Christ to the Diakonia of the Apostles*, 2002.

31 Phyllis Zagano, Bernard Pottier, Guy Jobin, Bernard Collette-Dučić, and Cory Andrew Labrecque. "Que Savons-Nous Des Femmes Diacres?" *Laval Théologique et Philosophique* 74 (3) 2018: 437–45.

the prayer of the hours. Depending on the local context, each religious order discerns where to orient its efforts. Thus, Chinese convents—usually located near the cathedral—are becoming a hive for social and pastoral care. Nuns teach, clean, preach, cook, counsel, and provide medical care.[32] For them, the service of the Church and society is not limited to a single task or spirituality that would set them apart, even within the parishes. Inspired by the tradition of the beatas, their sense of care is highly holistic.

While specific apostolate and charism do not define Chinese religious orders per se, the boundaries of their diocese are gaining more significance. During elaborate liturgies widely publicized, nuns take vows within the hands of their local bishop or his delegate. Through this crucial moment of their religious life, but also throughout the regular functioning of their order, nuns associate with their local Church. They form the religious order of a particular diocese. Even though some nuns may circulate across provinces as priests do, religious orders are not outside the support of the local Church. Under the authority and protection of the bishop, they are a part of the ministry of the diocese, serving in most parishes and diocesan apostolates. In the face of financial adversity or internal crisis, it is the bishop—and the diocese as a whole—who is responsible for the integrity of the order. There is a shared consensus that nuns and their diocese must pray and care for each other.

In view of this diocesan belonging, as well as the multivalence of the services fulfilled by the nuns, one must acknowledge that these women belong to the diocesan clergy. Usually, the Catholic Church keeps the term "clergy" for ordained ministers only—a group of men who stand in a dual relationship with the laity and who receive through the sacrament of Holy Orders a formal and permanent service to fulfill.[33] However, in China, the nuns engage with the wholeness of diocesan pastoral care as well. Their service is obviously different from the priestly ministry, but their commitment is no less multivalent, permanent, and absolute. They take public vows promising perpetual chastity and poverty, but also obedience to their order—and subsequently, to their bishop. Furthermore, the faithful perceive them as being part of the "professional and "consecrated" body of people who take care of the diocese. With the priests, they are the other arm of the bishop.

---

32 Chambon, "Chinese Catholic Nuns," 12.

33 (Canons 232–93). Yet, this theoretical approach promoted since the Tridentine period remains at odds with religious orders. Nuns and monks officially belong to the laity and yet, in practice, remain clearly distinguished from lay people.

Unlike in other countries where a rapid decline in religious vocations has led nuns to disappear from the shared life of local Catholic communities, Chinese ones remain remarkably present and visible within the day-to-day activities of local parishes and dioceses. Like priests, nuns are a familiar part of the Church in China. Both under the authority of the bishop, priests and nuns are set apart to serve and nurture local communities. They both wear distinctive clothes[34] and commit themselves to celibacy and obedience. Both come from the local community of faithful and compose the group of "religious professionals" who permanently care for the Church. Thus, it is appropriate to say that, in China, nuns belong to the diocesan clergy.

Enacting the diaconia of the Church

In their shared service to the diocese, Chinese priests and nuns are still different, and their differences are not denied. Rather, they continue to be reassessed and institutionalized.

Government cadres, for instance, ask priests to spend a significant part of their time joining various official meetings and training, and the administration itself subsequently reinforces priests' leadership role. Meanwhile, nuns are usually disregarded by local officials and can devote themselves to the pragmatic service of the population. Then, inside parishes, priests continue to stand as the source of authority. Because of their importance for sacramental life, they remain an *alter Christus*, another Christ. When a priest and a few nuns serve within the same parish, a hierarchical relationship exists between them. The priest is the pastor. Yet, at the diocesan level, this relationship is far subtler than a vertical one because the bishop remains the ultimate reference, the only head of the diocesan community. The presbyterium as a whole has no authority over the nuns. Ultimately, female diocesan orders respond to their bishop. In other words, the ecclesial ministry of the nuns is shaped by a whole network of relationships in which the administration, bishops, priests, and faithful take part.

At the diocesan level, Chinese nuns and their orders provide the means to gather the necessary human and material resources to effectively assist those in need. Freed from a leadership role fulfilled by the priests and the bishop, as well as the administration of the sacraments, they pay attention to a humanity that often remains fragile, broken, and poor. In relation to the various figures and resources of their diocese, nuns generate actions to assist those in spiritual,

---

34 In some Chinese dioceses, nuns may wear secular clothes but with distinctive "modesty."

intellectual, material, and medical needs. Sometimes bold in their approach, often courageous and thoughtful, religious women humbly engage with elderly care, home visits, medical work, and spiritual counseling.

Consequently, it is important to recognize how Chinese nuns dedicate themselves to works of charity and enact the *diaconia* of the local Church. What they do is not merely the Christian charity that every Christian is called to perform. Nuns act within a network of responsibilities and reliability to sustain a collective answer to the difficulties of their society. Their cooperative action, tailored to assist those in need, speaks on behalf of the whole Church. Their charitable action is highly institutionalized and speaks on behalf of their diocese. Thus, Chinese religious orders fulfill a formal ministry that is primarily diaconal.

This Chinese enactment of ministry is not necessarily in contradiction to the Magisterium. In October 2009, Pope Benedict XVI revised several canons concerning the sacraments of holy orders and marriage. In a *motu proprio* named *Omnium in Mentem*, the bishop of Rome provided an alternative understanding of the three ranks of the ordained ministry. While Vatican II and the subsequent 1983 Code of Canon Law have considered them intrinsically linked so that, each according to his grade manifests Christ the Head, Pope Benedict has brought the Canon Law to differentiate the diaconal ministry. *"Those who are constituted in the order of episcopate or presbyterate receive the office and faculty of acting in the person of Christ the Head, while deacons receive the power to serve the people of God in the diaconia of liturgy, word and charity"* (canon 1009). In this configuration, the diaconate is understood as something quite distinct and autonomous from the rest of the ordained ministry. This allows one to envision diaconal ministry as being something apart from the rest of the Church's institutionalized ministry. Consequently, I argue that the Church in China is following a rather similar theology of ministry that recognizes a distinction between deacons and the paired priests-bishop. In the People's Republic of China, there is already an ecclesial consensus about a formally institutionalized, officially blessed but not ordained, diaconal ministry that stands next to the ministries of ordained priests and bishops. This *diaconia* is fulfilled by consecrated women organized in diocesan religious orders and obedient to their local bishop.

Yet, Chinese nuns do not apply this technical term to define their own religious life. Rather, women I have interviewed prefer to insist on the importance of service. When I asked about their vocational journey, a vast majority of my interviewees explained that, as young women, they wanted "to serve the Church and the society." A nun is a person who takes care of people around her through her actions and prayers. Nun Shi of Nanping reiterated that "nuns are not here to rule but to serve."[35] Clearly, Chinese nuns prefer to describe themselves as "servants of the Church" who enact a life of service and prayer. They do not call themselves deacons and would not claim this title for themselves. Nonetheless, because of the way they link service and prayer while engaging with a diversity of needs, the ministry of the nuns remains the most institutionalized and visible *diaconia* of Chinese dioceses.

Reflecting the triune nature of the Christian God

To honor the diversity of their apostolates, Chinese nuns usually form small groups of coworkers and take turns to fulfil their missions. While a few nuns are primarily assigned to the elderly home, others take care of the convent and others of the adjacent dispensary. After a few years, groups are redefined and apostolates reassigned. In some cases, nuns may recruit paid lay workers or volunteers. But, either within their convent or outside, teamwork characterizes the way Chinese nuns serve. Religious women do not act alone. Instead, collaboration is a distinctive feature of their diaconal ministry.

By contrast with a parish priest or a bishop who often stands as the only episcopal or priestly minister of the community, nuns are typically encountered as a collective figure. Usually, they work two by two, or more. They all dress the same way and engage in the same work. In China, while a typical Catholic priest would appear as a singular figure, nuns stand as a plural one. In their daily apostolate and life of prayer, they depend on their consecrated colleagues and remain under the authority of their congregation and bishop. For the sacraments, they rely on the willingness of a priest or a bishop to celebrate mass and give them the sacrament of reconciliation. If priests and bishops can appear as independent and self-supporting ministers of the Church—with the risk of being self-referential—nuns are always situated within a network of dependence, authority, and accountability.

Consequently, there is an ecclesial consensus in which Chinese priests and bishops are manifesting one side of the ministry of the Church while nuns incarnate the other. The bishop and his scattered priests, acting in the person of Christ the only Head, are serving unity and authority while groups of nuns are committed to collaboration and institutionalized charity. Throughout this duality, priests and bishops testify that God is only one, nuns testify that God is the

---

35 See Chambon, "Chinese Catholic Nuns," 7.

communion of three cooperating persons, one and three, two facets of the same Christian God. Thus, the dynamic equilibrium between bishops, priests, and nuns shows that their two fundamental ministries are not in opposition. Rather, they manifest the two sides of the triune God who is permanently teaching, sanctifying, and ruling, as well as assisting, nourishing, and healing the Church.

Woman and Man, image of God

Although the style of every single bishop, priest, and nun may vary, they each often borrow from contemporary gender norms of Chinese society. In fact, members of the Chinese clergy know how to appear either masculine or feminine in order to fulfill and strengthen their apostolate. Subsequently, one may underscore how the ministry of the Church in China is gendered in a quite distinct way.

During fieldwork, I was surprised to see how the beatas navigate between different appearances. On some occasions, they would not hesitate to wear elegant and feminine outfits combined with a stylish purse and pair of shoes. Whether they walk the streets of a modern city like Fuzhou or circulate through the countryside of northern Fujian, they willingly match with local women of their generation. Similarly, nuns I have encountered in their convents and apostolates take great care of their physical appearance. Wearing a mandatory uniform made of a religious dress and a veil does not prevent them from proudly displaying signs of femininity through their ways of walking, laughing, and behaving. Indeed, Chinese nuns use cultural codes associated with charm, female discretion, and motherhood to support their diaconal ministry and the agenda of their order. In a similar vein, priests and bishops elaborate on Chinese notions of fatherhood and masculinity to strengthen their position. Through their virile body motions, as well as their way of presiding at large meals and speaking with authority, they stand as the patriarch of their Catholic community. Consequently, we need to recognize how Chinese ecclesial ministers borrow from the two main genders of their society, femininity and masculinity, to fulfill their missions. In other words, there is a genderization of the ministry.

The Tradition shows that there are many ways to let gender identities intersect with ecclesiology and theology of ministry. Localized masculinization and feminization are not the only options. For instance, generating a third gender has been a pretty common strategy to overcome tensions that lay between sexual identity, gender roles, and ecclesial ministries. In monastic traditions within which female and male communities each embrace the exact same lifestyle and rules, and wear rather similar outfits, surrounding gender norms are not only challenged but surpassed. For example, Benedictine communities of male monks and female nuns structure their communal and religious life the exact same way. Yet, the biological sex of their members still matters while their related gender role vanishes before the coming of the Kingdom. Without denying sexual identity, the monastic rule makes a third gender possible. Another example comes from situations where only men represent the clergy and, at the same time, wear distinctive uniforms borrowed from what would be considered as the opposite related gender. The cassock is the most well-known example, a dress-like coverage of the celibate male body. Again, this paradoxical situation brings clergymen to belong to something other than mainstream masculinity. Those ministers collectively create a unique gender proper to their function.

Clearly, consecrated people have long shown how they can belong to something else than the masculinity or femininity of their time. There are many ways to gender ministers of the Church. However, in Chinese dioceses and parishes, the presence of feminine nuns and masculine priests at most levels of ecclesial structures suggests that ministry is made of the two sexes, and at the same time, gendered with Chinese characteristics. Instead of going for a third gender which would merge all clergy members into an alternative and eventually "neutral" category, the binary genderization of their ministries underlines the presence of the two sexes. And this can bear theological significance. The collaboration of men and women to perform an institutionalized service of the Church echoes biblical statements. It is together, in their acknowledged sexual differences, that man and woman are the image of God (Gen. 1:27). Thus, when Chinese ministers, male and female, work and serve together for the wellbeing of the diocesan Church, they are moreover the image of God.

To recap, I would like to offer a metaphor summarizing the ways the Church in China calls its nuns to participate in ministry. Rooted in a long and rich history, Chinese Catholicism has quietly developed a distinct consensus in which bishops act as the head of the diocesan community, the local Church, assisted by two hands, the priests and the nuns. Although those two groups of ministers are equal in dignity, they remain clearly distinct and hierarchized in practice. The dominant and masculine hand participates in the leading role of the bishop. With a single finger pointing to heaven, it gives direction and blessing. Meanwhile, the non-dominant and feminine hand has its five fingers fully opened to embrace, assist, and comfort the people of God. In coordination with the right hand, the feminine hand assists the head in bringing the Gospel to the Chinese nation. Thus, the subtle—and often unspoken—power relations and collaborations occurring between Chinese bishops, priests, and religious women manifest the pastoral care of the Church. Without overloading this metaphor, I want to highlight how the Chinese approach to ministry is, despite appearances, not specifically unilineal and vertical. Echoing the trinitarian nature of God, it is also circular and dialogical. Ministry in China is made of the two sexes, it is bi-gendered, and it manifests how men and women, both, are called to dialogically served the Church.

Concluding Suggestion

This article has investigated the ecclesial role of Chinese nuns and unveiled its related theology of ministry. Based on ethnographic data, it appears that Chinese Catholicism seeks to both embrace and adapt the norms of the worldwide Catholic Church. On the one hand, it follows the modern, and post-Tridentine, normativity of Catholicism in a sense that ecclesial communities are structured along with a binary relationship between clerics and laypeople. The two are clearly distinguished and the number of ministries is relatively limited. Furthermore, the Chinese clergy is predominantly a secular and diocesan one. All ministers embrace celibacy and promise obedience to their local bishop. This contemporary structuration contrasts with other regional and historical periods of Catholicism where a wide spectrum of institutionalized ministries would blur the boundary between clerics and laypeople, and where actors like abbots, local sovereigns, or universities would have a more prominent role in the leadership of the Church.

On the other hand, the Church in China does not simply replicate contemporary norms of the worldwide Catholic Church. Rooted in a long ecclesial experience marked by its own challenges, history, and cultural expectations, Chinese Catholicism has generated female religious orders that are quite different from the rest of the world. These congregations tend to become homogenously diocesan and multivalent in their apostolates, standing within the diocesan clergy to perform a diaconal ministry. Consequently, the Chinese clergy is made of the two sexes and informed by the two dominant gender roles of its society.

Sometimes, an excessive emphasis on the homogeneity of the Catholic Church brings certain observers to assume that the specificities of the Church in China are primarily due to political oppression and to a lack of ecclesial maturity. While these explanations are important to consider, one cannot ignore that God is always walking with God's people. By focusing only on what the Church in China is supposedly missing, one risks dismissing what God is doing in China. In fact, ecclesial specificities may equally come from the *sensus fidei fidelium* reflecting the grace of God given to Christian communities in their particular cultural, economic, and political contexts. Therefore, without idealizing or absolutizing the subtle and moving consensus on ministry that the Church in China has generated, its particularities call for benevolent solidarity and critical attention.

Still, naming what the Church is generating in order to better recognize and strengthen what God does among God's people is not enough. Theology has also the mission to counsel. This is what this conclusion would like to offer. If the Church recognizes the Chinese theology of ministry discussed in this article as faithful to the Tradition, what could the Magisterium do to support it? How can it be even more fruitful for the Church in China and beyond? Knowing that many things have been done for and by the Church in China, I would like to propose just one suggestion. The Tradition has always approached ministry as being intimately related to the discipline of the seven sacraments. The two are mutually dependent, both standing as living realities that involve within an organic relationship. Therefore, to acknowledge and strengthen the particular diaconal ministry that Chinese religious women are effectively doing, the Church in China—in obedient dialogue with the Apostolic See—could explore the possibility, for example, to let them dispense baptism.

In practice, baptism is already deeply related to the actual ministry of Chinese nuns. In their apostolates, they constantly manifest the new life and salvation that God gives to his people. Furthermore, there is no absolute theological obstacle that would prevent such permission. Contemporary examples of Catholic women giving baptism already exist.[36] And in the past, Chinese beatas had often baptized children when no priest was available.[37] Of course, contemporary circumstances and conditions under which nuns could administer baptism would have to be defined by the Chinese conference of bishops in dialogue with the Holy See. However, an involution of the discipline of the sacraments may not only show how Chinese bishops and the Magisterium value what nuns bring, but more importantly, it may help Chinese Catholics to better acknowledge how God nourishes his people through the action of consecrated men and women. Additionally, this involution may help to manifest how the Catholic Church is not afraid to both stand as a polyhedron and to welcome Chinese characteristics.

---

36 Pope Francis, *Querida Amazonia* (2020), 99.
37 Tiedemann, "Chinese Female Propagators of the Faith in Modern China," 58.

Chapter 16

THEOLOGY AND CHURCH-BUILDING IN SHANGHAI

Divine Love *Monthly*

Benoît Vermander, *Fudan University*

In January 2018, a Catholic monthly, *Sheng'ai* (聖愛 *Divine Love*), sponsored by the research and publication center of the Shanghai diocese, Guangqishe 光啟社, circulated its first issue as an "internal" (*neibu* 內部) publication. The present essay takes as its material the first thirty issues of *Divine Love* (January 2018 to June 2020). It aims to show how the monthly magazine participates in an ongoing process that is the crafting of a renewed style of Catholic Chinese thinking and worshiping, a style fostered both by the cultural climate specific to Shanghai and by the appearance of a new generation of intellectuals within the Church.

The first part of this article will focus on the purpose of the publication, its format and its editorial team. The second will study the style progressively elaborated on by the editors. Part three will endeavor to read several contributions found in *Divine Love*, focusing on contrasts that can be found within the publication as a whole. Part four reflects on what the reading of the monthly may suggest as to the theological and pastoral issues faced by the Chinese Church today.

Background: Purpose, Format and Team

The editor-in-chief of *Divine Love*, Father Yuan Wei 袁偉, graduated from Sheshan Seminary in Shanghai and has an MA in religious studies from Renmin University in Beijing. Although Fr. Yuan is the editor of the monthly, his mentor, Fr. Tian Yuanxiang 田愿想, a parish priest who is also the Chief Editor at the Guangqi Center, has played a central role in the launch of the magazine, defining its overall mission and recruiting a good part of the team. The vision sponsored by Fr. Tian first came to him through his studies around twenty years ago at the Institut Catholique de Paris. The team conceived of the positioning of this publication by noting that there were two types of publications issued by the Catholic Church in China. One was popular in scope, aimed at the traditional core of the faithful and centered on Church-based news, the clearest example of it being *Faith* (*Xinde* 信德) published by the Hebei Xinde News Agency. The other was research-oriented, such as the academic essays gathered in *Catholic Studies* (*Tianzhujiao yanjiu* 天主教研究) by the Beijing Institute of Catholicism and Culture. There was no publication in between. The original idea for *Divine Love* was thus to target young and middle-aged people with a certain educational level, so as to enable readers to balance theological knowledge and general culture in such a way as to help them to deepen their faith.

Launching the monthly was also seen as necessary to revive the mission of the diocese's research and publication unit, *Guangqishe*, which had ground almost to a halt after Bishop Ma Daqin 馬達欽 had been forbidden to exercise his functions for political reasons.[1] *Divine Love* has somehow become the substitute for the six different publications that *Guangqishe* had sponsored in the past. At the same time, the restrictions that led to the closure of these publications effectively worked as an incentive toward the invention of a new editorial model. Contacts were made with Shanghai's Religious Bureau, so as to make sure that this endeavor would be permitted and fully legitimate. The Bureau conducts a check on the monthly's content before each issue appears, but, up to the present, the mutual knowledge existing between the partners has allowed for minimal screening.

On the basis of the expertise of people willing and able to contribute, a number of "columns" (*zhuanlan* 專欄), or subject areas, were determined (see below). The hope was that, through a diverse range of topics and writing styles, people of different backgrounds could enrich their faith life and find material of interest in each issue. The Guangqi Center benefits from funding that presumably comes from income provided by diocesan real estate—the fruit of the very active policy of reconstruction of the Shanghai Church pursued during the time of Bishop Aloysius Jin Luxian (1916–2013). This in turn benefits *Divine Love*. The monthly is gifted to the priests and nuns of Shanghai, to every parish in the Diocese, and to every church institution in China, as well as to other institutions that request it, such as some Protestant seminaries. Subscriptions began in 2019, but ascertaining circulation figures is difficult. In addition, the monthly

---

1 Bishop Ma had announced his intention to resign from the Catholic Patriotic Association during his episcopal ordination Mass.

has a WeChat public account that publishes some of the magazine content, an account with about 3,000 followers at present, with the most-read article generating 8,600 viewings.[2]

The general feedback for *Divine Love* has been positive, but no robust survey has been conducted, and readers' opinions have not been consistently collected. Most comments have to do with the layout and the printing quality and are highly appreciative. Specific praise has been forthcoming, however, from some Protestant pastors and a few believers of higher educational levels. The approbation coming from these authorized voices often underlines the fact that, compared with the national Protestant magazine *Tianfeng* (天風), or the local *Shanghai Christianity* (上海基督教), *Divine Love* is free from political influence and shows depth as well as offering educational value.

A team of dedicated contributors

The strength of *Divine Love* lies primarily in the team that has gathered around the magazine. Apart from the cover story, which mobilizes one of the main contributors each time, each column is managed by a dedicated writer:[3] Shanghai has been the intellectual center of the Roman Catholic church for several centuries, and the journal draws on the city and its seminary graduates for the majority of contributions. The "Bible" column, however, is written by Father Ma Xiangqin (馬向欽) born in the 1970s, and trained in exegesis at the Catholic Institute of Paris. Fr. Ma currently teaches at the National Seminary in Beijing. His declared aim is to diversify the way of looking at the Bible and to foster a group of ordinary believers whose passion for the Scriptures leads them to drive others to share in the experience.

The Doctrine column is mainly staffed by Fr. Fang Buke 方補課, born in the 1970s, a graduate of Sheshan seminary (Shanghai). Fr. Fang obtained a Master's degree in theology from the Department of Theology of the Catholic University of America and another Masters in religious education from the same university. After returning to China, he received a doctorate in education from the Institute of International and Comparative Education of East China Normal University. He taught moral theology at Sheshan Seminary and served there as the Dean. Currently he serves as the pastor of the international community gathered at the

---

2 Very recent figures have been difficult to obtain; there has been a gradual increase in online consultation, while subscriptions to the paper publication remain stable.

3 My presentation of their background and, at times, of their expectations, is partly based on WeChat exchanges.

Sacred Heart church in Pudong, Shanghai. His avowed hope is that his column will help believers to approach the core beliefs of the Church in a way both direct and systematic. Besides Fr. Fang, another contributor to this section is Father Gao Chaopeng 高超朋, another graduate of the Sheshan Seminary, who has a PhD in Ethics from the Catholic University of America and is the current Dean of Sheshan Seminary.

The column on Liturgy is staffed by Father Pan Xiaoping 潘小平, born in the 1970s in northern Fujian. After graduating from Sheshan Seminary, Fr. Pan obtained a Masters in liturgy in the Philippines and is now studying for a PhD in Macau. He alternates with Father Tian Lei 田磊, born in the 1960s, of the Hohhot Diocese, who holds a Master of Religion from Renmin University and has served as Dean of the Inner Mongolia Seminary. Father Tian has been teaching Liturgy in training courses in major seminaries and the Diocese of Hong Kong for many years.

The Theology column is the responsibility of Father Chen Kaihua 陳開華, born in the 1970s, who obtained a Master of Patristics at the Jesuit Faculties of Philosophy and Theology of Paris (Centre Sèvres) and a doctorate in Sacred Theology from Fu Jen University (Taiwan). He once taught at the Sichuan Seminary and now teaches at the National Seminary. His contributions, he asserts, aim at showing the continuity of theological development in time, his current focus being on the Church Fathers.

Spirituality is the domain of Ms. Xie Hua 謝華, born in the late 1970s, who holds a PhD in Philosophy from Fudan University (on St. John of the Cross) and a Master of Theology from Centre Sèvres. Xie Hua is currently teaching at the East China Theological Seminary (Shanghai), one of two Catholic teachers active in this institution. She conceives her column as an introduction to various spiritual traditions, an inspiration for readers' spiritual lives, and a guide for further research. The column on the Church is written by Zhou Yong 周永, a lay person who is the other Catholic professor at the East China Theological Seminary. He holds a Master of Biblical Theology, Catholic University of Leuven, and a PhD in religious studies from Fudan University. The column is primarily concerned with emerging movements before and after Vatican II, helping readers to recognize how the Church continuously evolves under the impetus of the Holy Spirit.

There is also a column on inspirational figures, under the responsibility of Li Teng 李騰, born in the 1980s. After a Master of History from Shanghai University, Li Teng, a lay person, went to the University of Liverpool, completing a PhD in Medieval Church history. He is now an Associate Researcher in the World History

Department of Shanghai Normal University.[4] The way he states it, Li aspires to narrate the development of the Church during the Middle Ages and to relate it to issues now facing the Chinese Church: providing readers with insights on the relationship between Church and state and internal Church reform in the belief that this will nurture hope and courage among the faithful. Other authors contributing to the column include Fr. Ruan Xiwu 阮希鹢, born in the 1980s, from Mindong Diocese in Fujian, whose Master of Religious Studies (Renmin University) was dedicated to Yves Congar; and Fr. Tian Weishuai 田煒帥, from Xianxian 獻縣 Diocese (Hebei), born in the 1970s, who holds a doctorate in History from Sorbonne University and currently directs a local Church-based research institute.

A further column introduces and reviews books, mainly publications on Christianity written from an historical or cultural perspective. Zhou Yuqi 周郁琦 majored in economics, and currently works in the medical industry. She was baptized in 2013, and her love for reading led her to accept responsibility for this column. Two other women, Xu Yan 徐彦 and Yang Hongfan 楊虹帆, have taken charge of the Arts column. Xu Yan creates sacred iconography in her own studio in Wuhan. Yang Hongfan, a specialist in comparative literature, holds a PhD in Religion from Peking University and has recently been a post-doctoral student at Leuven University. A column entitled "Stories" focuses on oral history, based on interviews with older faithful. Hu Xuewei 胡雪瑋, a female freelance writer born in the 1980s, acknowledges the difficulties she meets in maintaining this column. Zhang Yuanyuan 張淵源, a male Catholic born in the 1980s, with a passion for Shanghai history, maps, and illustrations, writes articles on the Church buildings of the metropolis. Through his active social accounts, he documents urban development seen from the grassroots level. A final column on Pilgrimage is staffed by different authors, who share their experience at home and abroad. Additionally, the back cover is always adorned by a watercolor illustration of one of the numerous church buildings of Shanghai, an illustration realized by Jiang Huangji 將煌紀 in a style strongly reminiscent of the art school of Tushanwan that was manned by Xujiahui Jesuits from 1864 until their expulsion.

This is obviously a highly qualified team, and its composition testifies to an active networking among Catholic intellectuals. Although the leadership remains in the hands of priests, often trained abroad, lay persons, and especially laywomen, are an integral part of the endeavor. Additionally, the stability of the team certainly constitutes an asset, though some of its members are starting to

---

4 A position equivalent to Associate Professor in the Chinese system.

wonder whether it might not also limit its diversity and development, and if some new blood might not be soon needed.

Crafting a Style

Printed on glossy A4 paper, the magazine has progressively increased from forty-four to fifty-two pages. This allows for the main contributions to reach around 4,000 characters (a few longer ones reaching 8,000), and for some full-page illustrations to be inserted. The art editing is careful and abundant, with a majority of illustrations coming from the Western Canon, and others from Chinese Christian art or Shanghai-related iconography.

The cover topics of the first thirty issues run as follows:

January 2018:	Christ's Gospel is the Gospel of Peace (International Peace Day, 1968–2018).
February 2018:	The Readers that the Gospel of John Is Waiting For.
March 2018:	Celso Costantini.[5]
April 2018:	Community San Egidio, Angel of God's Peace.
May 2018:	The Holy Mother of Lourdes.
June 2018:	The Sacred Heart of Jesus
July 2018:	The Liturgical Year, Road of Catholic Spirituality.
August 2018:	World Synod on the Family.[6]
September 2018:	Pope Paul the Sixth.
October 2018:	World Synod ["Young People, Faith, and Vocational Discernment"].[7]
November 2018:	Padre Pio.[8]
December 2018:	Candida Xu.[9]

---

5 As a Nuncio in China, Cardinal Celso Benigno Luigi Costantini (1876–1958) is known for his advocacy of the agency and inculturation of the local Church. His cause for sainthood commenced on 2016.

6 This took place on October 2015 and was followed in April 2016 by Pope Francis's apostolic exhortation, *Amoris Laetitia*.

7 The issue appeared at the time of the opening of the Synod. The issue focuses on the synodal institution, including an introduction to the Acts of the Apostles.

8 The mystic friar Padre Pio (1887–1968) was a controversial figure during his life and afterwards but was declared a Saint by the Church in 2002.

9 Candida Xu (1607–80) was the granddaughter of Xu Guangqi and acted decisively as the "Mother" of the nascent Shanghai church. She is known mainly through a biography written by the Jesuit Philippe Couplet.

January 2019:	The Vatican. (The lead article introduces its readers to the status, organization and mission of the Vatican.)
February 2019:	Lu Zhengxiang.[10]
March 2019:	The Season of Lent: Its Historical Transformations and Its Spiritual Reality.
April 2019:	Easter, Summit and Basis of Christian Life.
May 2019:	The Sheshan Pilgrimage.
June 2019:	Luo Wenzao 羅文藻, the first Chinese bishop.
July 2019:	Great Shangri-La, the Church in the Depth of the Mountains. (On the small Catholic Tibetan Community at the frontier of Yunnan and Tibet)
August 2019:	The Consecrated Virgins of the Chinese Catholic Church.
September 2019:	The Baroque Master: Rubens.
October 2019:	*Maximum Illud* at One Hundred: Past and Future of the Chinese Catholic Church.[11]
November 2019:	Catholic Funerals in Late Ming and Early Qing.
December 2019:	The Liturgical Meaning of Christmas.
January 2020:	The Week of Prayer for Christian Unity.
February 2020:	The Spiritual Road of Wu Jingxiong 吳經熊.[12]
March 2020:	Patron Saints for Times of Plague.
April 2020:	Vincent Lebbe, a Chinese.[13]
May 2020:	Saint Damien.[14]
June 2020:	A Cathedral that Memorializes the Faith: The Xujiahui Church.[15]

---

10 Lou Tseng-Tsiang or Lu Zhengxiang (Lù Zhēngxiáng) (陸徵祥 1871–1949), a Chinese diplomat who was twice Premier of the Republic of China, eventually became a Benedictine monk in Belgium.

11 *Maximum Illud*, Benoit XV's Apostolic Letter of November 1919, stresses the need to separate missionary work from political alliances and to develop an indigenous clergy and Church leadership.

12 John C. H. Wu (Wu Jingxiong, 1899–1986), a famous lawyer and constitutionalist, who converted from Methodism to Catholicism.

13 The title of this issue highlights the degree of assimilation with the Chinese people reached by the missionary Vincent Lebbe (1877–1940), famous for his struggle in favor of the indigenization of the Chinese Church.

14 Saint Damien (Jozef De Veuster, 1840–1889) lived and died in a leper colony in Hawai'i.

15 The title refers to the St. Ignatius Cathedral (the term "cathedral" remains controversial as the transfer of the bishops' seat from St. Xavier to St. Ignatius has never been canonically sanctioned, but it is implicitly acknowledged by most Catholics in Shanghai).

There are several ways of appreciating and classifying these cover topics.[16] Roughly speaking, thirteen covers have been dedicated to subjects linked to inculturation and the Chinese Church, ten to spirituality, Scriptures, and devotional topics, and seven to Global Church concerns and history. The resources that are offered certainly help readers to assert their local identity. At the same time, inserting readers into a world community of worshippers as well as fostering a personal faith journey are imperatives that receive at least as much attention in the magazine. Over time, the statistical growth in cover topics dedicated to inculturation may be read as a kind of lip service paid to the state requirement to work toward "Sinicizing" the Church.[17] Still, the figures, places, and topics selected as exemplars of inculturation are traditional and consensual ones among Shanghai Catholics.

Crafting a "Catholic Style"

For the purposes of analysis we will look at the whole content of a specific issue. In January 2020, *Divine Love* opens with a presentation of the historical sequence that led to the Week of Prayer for Christian Unity, recalling the Oxford Movement, the role played by Taizé or the Groupe des Dombes and joint declarations between the Catholic Church and the Lutheran World Federation. The article ends with the visit made by Pope Francis to Sweden on October 31, 2016 for the opening of the 500th anniversary of the Reformation.

The issue continues with a detailed exegetical analysis of Mark 6: 30–44, which does not spare the reader excerpts of the Greek original and references to Mark's rhetorical techniques. This is followed by shorter doctrinal contributions, first on "faith" and then on the liturgical uses of the tabernacle and their theological background. The contribution by Fr. Chen Kaihua presents Tatian the Syrian (ca. 120 to ca. 180 AD) and his works (*Oratio ad Graecos* and *Diatessaron*), mildly rebuking some of the moralistic views of Tatian while noting how his intellectual itinerary between East and West opens up space for imagination. This is followed by a contribution, by Xie Hua, on the controversies around "pure love" (*querelle du pur amour*) in seventeenth-century France. Offering a sympathetic, albeit moderate interpretation of Fénelon's *Maximes des Saints*, Xie Hua ultimately relates "pure love" to the Sermon on the Mount's guiding inspiration:

---

16 Let us note that the cover symbolically underlines a topic covered in the issue, but that, as a general rule, only eight pages are dedicated to the subject matter.

17 See Benoît Vermander, "Sinicizing Religions, Sinicizing Religious Studies," *Religions* 2019, 10 (137): 1–23.

the decision to separate love from any satisfaction that may be drawn from it ("Love your enemies"). The ecclesiastical and political sanctions taken against Fénelon, notes Xie, eventually compelled the beleaguered French prelate to give an incarnated expression of his theological quest for love fully devoid of self-interest. Whether its ultimate objective be reachable or not, abandoning such a quest would constitute an irreparable loss. The Pure Love Controversy is still relevant in today's context.

Other articles in the same issue expound the architectural and theological project behind the Basilica of St. Denis as conceived by Suger (1080–1151); muse about Chinese translations of C. S. Lewis's *Surprised by Joy: The Shape of My Early Life* (which notably relates the author's conversion to Christianity) and of Martin Buber's *I and Thou*; detail the vision behind the "Death Gate" of St. Peter's Basilica completed in 1964 by the sculptor Giacomo Manzù; relate a pilgrimage to Rome at Christmas time; and finally introduce the reader to the toponomy of some Shanghai churches.

While a glance at other issues may reframe the picture slightly, some conclusions may be drawn from this review: it is primarily a *Catholic culture* that the magazine tends to instill, which has to do with historical consciousness, inner life, appreciation of beauty and the exercise of the senses, as well as with the correct use of reason when the latter meets matters of faith. Such culture is solidly rooted in Western tradition as it developed through the centuries, but it is enriched and interpreted by local contributions and by the insights naturally brought to them by the use of modern Chinese as mastered by authors able to navigate from one tradition to another. In many ways, the outlook of *Divine Love* is not very different from the style and model that Fr. Xu Zongze 徐宗澤 (1886–1947) developed in his writing and editorship of the then-preeminent Roman Catholic magazine in the 1930s, as Xu wrote and thought in specific forms, where "those forms shape the theology that emerges" and "Xu's Christianity is deeply entwined with his textuality."[18]

However, let us note that this emphasis on culture contrasts with comparatively weak social concerns and the avoidance of thorny ethical issues (which were a central part of Xu Zongze's stance and interests). *Divine Love*'s worldview seems to be more oriented toward the past than toward current challenges, such as the ones brought in by technological or socio-economic transformations. At the same time, it is clear enough that—things being what they are in today's

---

18 Chloë Starr, *Chinese Theology: Text and Context* (Yale University Press, 2016), 126–27.

China—articles around contemporary concerns and issues would be submitted to strict censorship, threatening the continuation of the magazine. There seems also to be an implicit agreement between the authors that social and political subjects should be avoided, because of differences of opinions among them: the journal is meant to express a kind of "Catholic consensus," which leads its editors to avoid a certain number of topics.[19]

On the whole, it is hard to escape the impression that the editorial team has made the magazine something of an island in which to perpetuate humanistic values and references anchored in Catholic culture and history, in contrast to the larger environment that tends to restrict such references to the minimum. When it comes to the Global Church, privileged attention is given to Papal documents as well as to European expressions of the faith as can be found in arts and writings. No mention will be found of Africa, Latin America, or of other Asian Churches. Catholic tradition is thus partly "idealized" according to deeply rooted cultural standards.

Discourses and Contrasts

The Republican Period and the Birth of a Theological Style

Notwithstanding these (important) reservations, the editorial team certainly operates a "discernment of the times." At least some of its members clearly find in the Republican period models for thinking through its own positioning. As Hu Xuewei writes in the issue dedicated to Wu Jingxiong (John C. H. Wu):

Famous people in the modern history of Chinese Catholicism—Li Wenyu, Ma Xiangbo, Ying Lianzhi, Lu Zhengxiang, Su Xuelin, etc. . . . had a background in traditional Chinese culture and religion, [while] some had grown up in Church schools. In an era characterized by the meeting between East and West, their foundations made them naturally accept both Eastern and Western thought. Most of them access Christian faith through self-reflection. At that time, social conditions, national dilemmas, changes in international politics and other factors affected cultural choices and the way people were evaluating Eastern and Western

---

19 In private conversations, some editors even utilize the terms "left-wing" and "right-wing" to characterize these contrasts, though what these terms refer to in Chinese context remains complex.

cultures. These Chinese scholars, represented by Wu Jingxiong, could basically maintain an attitude that transcended East and West, the Old and the New. . . . Every era has its own basic problems, which entangle its very soul. These converted Christian intellectuals of the first half of the twentieth century found their spiritual value throughout a process of conflict and reconciliation between the Eastern and the Western spirits. All knowledge—Eastern and Western, scientific and religious, rational and intuitive, practical and mystical, human and divine, secular and sacred—is nothing more than the pursuit of God, nothing more than a continuous struggle to return to our true home, i.e. the warm embrace of God.[20]

Little wonder that one of Hu Xuewei's columns is dedicated to the *Revue Catholique* (*Shengjiao zazhi* 聖教雜誌) and its most well-known editor, Xu Zongze, referred to above.[21] During its twenty-seven years of existence, insists Hu, *Shengjiao Zazhi* influenced the Chinese Church well beyond the limits of Shanghai, with subscriptions coming from twenty-four Chinese dioceses as well as from overseas communities. It bore enlightened witness to all of the important changes that affected the Chinese Church during the Republican period. Behind the diversity of the topics treated by Xu Zongze, Hu Xuewei discerns a desire to progressively systematize a Catholic Chinese approach to both social and scientific issues, as well as a resolve to make theology a field open to all faithful, and not only to professional theologians.

This desire is obviously shared by the book editor: in another issue, Hu Xuewei, introducing her readers to a collection of theological readings edited by the Catholic Seminary of Hong Kong, asks herself how to read theology today. While insisting on the importance of the exercise of reason in the development of one's faith, she also stresses that theological reading must take place from within a communal and liturgical setting. This is the way, she asserts, to develop a "taste" that testifies to the fact that one's quest for things divine is not based on our own efforts alone but is inspired by God himself.[22]

---

20 Hu Xeiwei, "Following the Spiritual Path of Wu Jingxiong," *Divine Love* (February 2020): 2–9.

21 Hu Xuewei, "A Bridge between Catholic Faith and Social Life," *Divine Love* (July 2019): 38–41. Among other examples, Hu Xeiwei also offers oral accounts of life in the Jesuit-led Xuhui High School from 1938 until 1951 ("Thirteen Years at Xuhui High School," *Divine Love*, (October 2018): 44–46.

22 Hu Xuewei, "Encountering Theology: To Understand is to Improve One's Faith," *Divine Love* (October 2019): 41–43.

Orthodoxy and Tradition

The Covid-19 pandemic provides the magazine with an opportunity to take stock of another aspect of the Catholic tradition. In an article that introduces the reader to a number of saints identified with their struggle against an epidemic, Li Teng writes:

> Since ancient times, human history has been accompanied by various infectious diseases. These diseases have brought tremendous suffering to humankind, not only causing physical and mental trauma to individuals, but having also a huge impact on entire nations and countries, sometimes even becoming a catalyst reversing the development of human history. . . . Today, humans are once again confronting the invisible enemy, the new coronavirus. . . . We want to pray for those who live in the affected areas, the ones who suffer and the ones who have died. At the same time, we must also reflect on our faith through this period where everything has stopped. . . . The history of the Church is an abridged edition of human history. The Church has experienced several major plagues in its history. In the Old Testament, records of the plague appear from time to time; in the New Testament, the apostles were no strangers to the plague; in the early days of the Church, plagues in the Roman Empire following repeated persecutions allowed the Church to rely on love for its neighbor, so as to make Christians build an extended social assistance system; in the Middle Ages, the Black Death that swept Europe brought a near-fatal blow to the Churches of the continent. . . . Many saints have been revered by the Church for "bringing immunity," this being due to different experiences but similar saintly virtues. Through their intercession, we pray together so that this plague that affects the whole of China and is spreading to the whole world may disappear as soon as possible. To this day, humans are still unable to overcome diseases, especially sudden infectious diseases, which always bring unrest and even panic to society at large. We pray to these saints who during the history of the Church showed their charity in periods of epidemics and who prayed with fiery faith for the extinction of the plagues, so that they inspire us to similarly practice charity and pray towards the elimination of the disease; [we

also pray to them] so that—even more importantly—we may, in this test, be filled with hope and faith in God.[23]

Li Teng develops an approach of the Church based on the observance of Tradition, especially in its ascetic dimension. Among other topics, he writes on St. Bernard of Menthon (April 2018), Thomas Moore (May 2018), Belgium's Benedictine monasteries (August 2018), the Carthusian Order (May 2019), Rupert of Deutz (June 2019), Hugh of Cluny (July 2019), Bernard of Clairvaux (April 2020), and on the eleventh-century, Milan-based Pataria movement, which aimed at ecclesiastical reform, and notably at enforcing papal prohibitions against clerical marriage (December 2019). One may find in Li's editorial choices a vision of the Church as a counter-society anchored in monastic ideals, purity of conduct, and strict preservation of dogmatic orthodoxy. The subject selection may also sound a criticism of several aspects of the present state of the Chinese Church. Such positioning (which, in this present case, benefits from an impressive knowledge of Church history, especially the medieval period) is far from being marginal among Chinese faithful today, though its expression varies according to educational levels. For those who promote such a path, fully complying with orthodoxy and Tradition opens up the only way to ensure the eventual survival of the Church in today's China. For them, the Chinese Church of today needs to operate on the model of the monastery.

Reviving Spiritual Theology

The editor of the Spirituality column, Xie Hua, appeals to a different brand of Tradition; although the range of spiritual figures and issues she discusses is broad, her favorite topics center around the *devotio moderna*, Ignatian tradition, the Spanish sixteenth-century mysticism and the French seventeenth-century spiritual school. At the same time, Xie aims at unfolding the mystical dimension of some devotions that are at least as popular among Chinese faithful as they are in countries of longer Catholic tradition:

> The veneration of the Sacred Heart crystallizes in history the faith lived
> in the heart, is the source of actual love, and calls us to hope in the future.
> The wounds in the Sacred Heart opened the spacetime of salvation; the

---

23 Li Teng, "The Lord is Our Stronghold. Patron Saints for Time of Epidemic," *Divine Love* (March 2020): 3–10.

hearts of the people of the past and of the present, the hearts in the East and in the West, all have—through this same eternal heart—crossed the centuries so as to meet, and flown across the oceans so as to connect. The gift of the Sacred Heart also endows us with a mission: *with my heart, you must live my life; through my life, travel my path; and, following my path, continue my work.* As Meister Eckhart (1260–1328) said: "Everything [that belongs to] him became ours, everything [that belongs to] us became his, our hearts and his heart became one heart." Same heart, same faith; same faith, same path. All those who wish to become the servants of God nurture the same desire in their heart."[24]

Xie Hua's article on the *devotio moderna* movement contrasts in interesting ways with the style of Li Teng: while the latter puts the stress on memorable figures and deeds, Xie Hua insists on the fact that the initiators and members of the movement have remained largely anonymous, even more so with the Protestant Reform soon intervening in the very places where the movement had flourished and breaking down all institutional expressions of it. It is this anonymous character, she remarks, that makes these discreet mystics a collective image of Christ. While Li Teng details monastic rules and institutional reforms, Xie Hua summarizes the message of *devotio moderna* by quoting Matthew 11:30: "my yoke is easy, and my burden is light." What ultimately remains of *devotio moderna*, she insists, is a text, the authorship of which remains controversial—but a text that has been enormously influential: *The Imitation of Christ.*[25] In the same light, Xie Hua introduces the Christian tradition of fasting not as the holding to a rule but rather as an education in inner freedom.[26]

Complementary accents can be found in Xie Hua's contribution on the visions of Hildegard von Bingen. Reading the Saint's narrative today reminds us that below the calm water of Reason we need to learn to deal with deeper waves: "spiritual theology" connects seen and unseen realities, senses and faith, in a way that leads to the invention of a new language.[27] Here, it is the primary reliance on

---

24 Xie Hua, "The Spiritual History of the Devotion to the Sacred Heart of Jesus," *Divine Love* (June 2018): 10.

25 Xie Hua, "'My Burden Is Light.' Contempt for the World and Anonymity in the *Devotio Moderna* Movement," *Divine Love* (September 2019): 28–32.

26 Xie Hua, "The Freedom of Keeping a Fast", *Divine Love* (March 2018): 19–21.

27 Xie Hua, "The Eyes Directed towards God Only and the Heart Embracing the World: The Visions of Hildegard of Bingen," *Divine Love* (August 2019): 27–30.

well-rehearsed dogmatic expression that is questioned, even challenged, though in an indirect and cautious way.

It would be erroneous to overemphasize the differences in accent that can be perceived from one contributor to another. Here, I have chosen to privilege a cursory reading of three lay authors whose particular personality and training transpire through their contributions. Without doubt, they follow lines that are mutually distinct. At the same time, they share in the same mission, and very probably consider that these contrasts make for a richer publication. *Divine Love* intends to build up a Catholic culture that is both Chinese and global, but such culture cannot be unanimous in character; it necessarily reflects at least part of the variety in positions and sensitivities that can be found in present-day Catholicism.

Theological and Pastoral Perspectives

The *Divine Love* editorial team unites around a design that comprises an array of dimensions: (a) building up a Shanghai Church that shares and articulates strong common references; (b) making sure that these references nurture at the same time her faith, universal in scope, and her local identity; (c) making the style and riches of the Shanghai Church a resource for the Chinese Church in its entirety (including, at least implicitly, for Chinese Christians of other denominations); (d) bringing in a faith-based perspective on culture, arts, and (to some extent) personal development.

Fulfilling this mission proceeds in four different ways:

Some contributors (priests, chiefly) provide readers with dogmatic, scriptural and, at times, liturgical resources in a manner that may be called "catechetical."

Authors like Hu Xuewei and others (notably those working on the Arts column) make cultural appreciation the core of their approach; they do so by unearthing the Christian origins and inspiration of a number of artistic and literary references that have become commonplace in secular China; highlighting the specific contribution of modern or contemporary Catholic artists and writers, and developing a hermeneutic of the resources approached that nourishes life and faith.

A third current, exemplified by Li Teng's contributions, finds in historical and dogmatic explorations material that fosters a vision of the Church as a counter-culture. The reference to monastic institutions is important in the sense that it models a way of life in a society perceived as fundamentally secular and hostile to the faith. If ordinary Christians cannot live a monk or nun's life, they can find inspiration and guidance in the example of the Church giants of the past.

Finally, an approach inspired by what can be called modern spirituality (prepared by spiritual theology, Eckhart and *devotio moderna*, and expressed through variants of Ignatian spirituality) puts much less emphasis on institutional reinforcement than the previous approach, inciting readers to nurture a contemplative approach within the secular society in which they are fully immersed.

The difference in focus and options is considerably softened by the necessity to ensure editorial consistency, as well as by political and institutional constraints, making the writing strategy indirect. Exchanges among Catholics on WeChat and other media are much more vigorous than anything that can be found in *Divine Love*. These exchanges can often be polemical, especially when it comes to assessing the teachings and actions of Pope Francis. The influence exercised on some currents of the Chinese Church by American conservatives has made a number of the faithful very vocal in that respect, for example, to the extent that a priest-led WeChat group entitled "The Shield of St. Ignatius" (*Najue zhi dun* 納爵之盾) now aims to foster better appreciation of Francis's vision among Chinese Catholics (the group was granted a WeChat public account in June 2020). The editorial team remains anonymous, although it advertises the fact that it counts thirty people holding a doctorate and twenty Masters in their ranks, the majority of them being priests (and a few religious sisters) who have frequently studied abroad. The mission statement of the group notes that Internet voices developing positions critical of Vatican II and papal teachings "impact on the image of the Church, mislead the faithful . . . and hinder evangelization." Working as a kind of Internet journal, the group provides articles and analyses aimed at correcting these misperceptions.

In contrast to "The Shield of St. Ignatius," the editorial team of *Divine Love* is not actively engaged in one ecclesiological direction or another (some of its editors incline toward pro-Francis positions, while others decidedly do not), although, as a matter of principle, papal teachings are put in a favorable light. Priests active in the "Shield of St. Ignatius" network are generally Northerners (often considered in China to be more direct and confrontational in their way of expressing themselves), while the team of *Divine Love* reflects a Southerners' tendency toward the avoidance of open conflict.

Under the mainstream, truly "Catholic" approach sponsored by *Divine Love*, the challenges (if not the aporias) encountered by the Chinese Catholic Church appear in the negative space of the text. Which corpus should be favored to nourish the life and beliefs of the faithful today? Should one first build a Catholic counter-culture, which structures its references and ways of proceeding exclusively as the ones of an autonomous community, or should we privilege a spiritual education inspired by the parable of the leaven in the dough? How to articulate the references to the Chinese and Shanghai Christian past with regard to those common to the universal Church? And how can one better appreciate the extent and diversity of the latter? Or again: how to react to the paradigmatic changes driven by Pope Francis, when Chinese Catholics have long defined their identity through a fierce defense of a Tradition threatened to its foundations by a secular state and society?

As we have seen, most of the time these questions are articulated only indirectly by the authors of the monthly. Sometimes issues arise spontaneously in the mind of the reader, without her being able to ascertain whether they are problematic for the authors themselves. However, taking into account the present context, as well as informal exchanges with some of the authors, confirms that: (1) the central questions can only be expressed indirectly, and it is indeed by design that some authors interpolate "silences" in their writing; (2) these silences cannot be accounted for only by external pressures but by a shared editorial design: that of creating a "common base" on which more differentiated expressions of Catholic identity may eventually flourish. Part of a dual tradition, local and global, *Divine Love* has not given up sowing the seeds of the future, even on ground that is now experiencing major, threatening shifts.

INDEX